Bob's Legacy

I can see clearly now.

A user's guide to God, Man, & the Universe

Understanding life, it's purpose and meaning – and learning to accept death with grace and dignity.

HAVE YOU EVER...

Felt that this whole world and system you find yourself in is somehow *not real?*

Felt like a stranger in this world? You are aware of your own conscious intelligence and that you have a body, but it is just that, *a body that is **not** "you".* **You** are not the entity of flesh and blood that is using the body, but that *you* are the stranger within that body and merely looking out through the windows called "eyes", observing this world.

Have you ever wondered, "is it all a dream, or is this all real? What if *none of this is real?"*

Felt that the sky could "crack open" at some time and reveal an *underlying reality* that you are sure is just below the visible threshold of all you see?

Have you ever vaguely felt that there is more going on than you may have full understanding or knowledge of? Have you ever felt or suspected that a lot of what has been happening, reported on, or claimed as fact in this world may all be a con? Have you ever really wondered why or marveled about the sheer amount of disharmony, conflict, confusion, and abuses of all sorts so prevalent in the world? Are you a little concerned about the seeming progressive impoverishment and enslavement of the world's populations?

THERE IS AN ANSWER TO ANY QUESTION YOU CAN POSSIBLY ASK. MOST ANSWERS ARE IN HERE. THEY REALLY ARE, THE REST YOU CAN VERY SOON ANSWER FOR YOURSELF. THIS IS MY LEGACY, SOLUTIONS FOR THE IMPONDERABLES.

Bob Maddison Upper Hutt, New Zealand

Name: Bob Maddison Location: Wellington, NZ I was born in Queensland in 1945 and have lived in New Zealand since 1973. My life has been enriched by many children and now grandchildren. I have always sought answers to life's questions, and finding answers generate more questions. I would like to share some of these experiences and answers, trusting they may educate, entertain, or at least amuse or cause one to think, and in thinking, ask questions. Join the journey of Life, living, and the richness freely offered. Contact is available at maddison.nz@gmail.com

Whereas the last book was written for my benefit,

this one is for you.

It would be almost criminal to take the entire

contents of my mind with me when I go.

So here is a small part of it for you.

First published November 2009.

Second edition. Revised, edited, and additional
materials completed 20 May 2010,

Third Edition, Re-format, corrections made to text,
Articles edited where stated, 1 new section
September 2013

"Now the guy in the bed next to me is really not well – lung problems and out of surgery. Restless, rattley etc, moans and groans. After near a day of it, it is decided it's back to surgery for him. He admitted in a trembling voice how scared he was, and anyone could see that. There was no way he was anywhere near ready to peacefully depart this world. I got to thinking how sad it is that we have been failed by Christianity or its sectarian religions. We have not been taught our place in eternity, time, or space. We have not been given a full nor true understanding of our nature or make up. The ritualized garbage and hollow prayers, words, and creeds of millennia have failed to prepare this single man to face death with peace or dignity." (Bob 4 September 2004)

****

More than ever I now question myself. In view of the risks inherent with open-heart surgery (the valve replacement) and by-pass, how exactly am I ready if such a thing happens, to "meet my maker"? How can I accept that the last mortal face I see may be those in the operating theatre, and the last words heard be: "I am going to give you the anesthetic now."

****

"Then I woke up or was fully aware – with full awareness of all the levels referred to. It was SO QUIET. SO peaceful. Then I knew "this is dead" – but I was fully awake/aware/alive; but I knew I was dead. Hastily I 'submerged' back into the previous level so as to re-emerge to mortality – DEAD AGAIN. A third time lucky, if you call access to only 3 – 4 levels lucky. But if association with fellow mortals is lucky, then I am lucky." (Bob 4 September 2004)

****

With thoughts and experiences such as these, I launched into a quest to find the answers to all the questions. I wanted to know **everything**. This is a record of the quest, and the discoveries made along the way. It is not completed yet.

ARTICLES (not chapters)

"Mortality, life on earth is a deceptive thing.
We think it is "all there is" and absolutely real.
Alas it is not so. It is no more than a dream we have
when we call and deem ourselves "awake".

It is as real as our other experiences in the dream
world of our sleep.

We are "switched off" (click) from our reception and
perception of this world and dimension when we
go to sleep, and "switched on" (click) into
perceiving and receiving that dream dimension.

We are as though dead to mortality (the "little death"
of sleep) but alive in dreams.

When we awaken, it is merely a change of "stations",
channels, or programmes, and returned to another
dimension of your same self.

Death is another "click" and a new reality, another
Dimension emerges

It is the one same self that we see is operating across
several, perhaps many dimensions, and only
our "tuning" is adjusted."

(Bob Maddison 28.3.2008)

PART ONE – PREAMBLE, BEGINNING
ASKING QUESTIONS.

"Sometimes it is difficult to say for certain if we are merely animals playing at being gods, or whether we are gods playing at being animals." (Bob, January 2009)

At this time it is not necessary to decide that issue, but it illustrates that generally we do indeed find ourselves in a very confused, sad, and miserable state. Frankly there are just so many things going wrong or that could be a lot better, and in so many areas that directly effect human life on earth that one could be forgiven for thinking such chaos surely must be intentional or planned.

Prior to 2003, like a lot of people, I had a vague idea that all was not right with our species on this earth. There was nothing I could specifically identify as a universal cause of so many human problems, troubles, worries, and woes in so many diverse areas. Many things are not good or could be better. However like most people (or so it seems) I kept playing the game of being a compliant little citizen, not thinking to try to look behind the curtains to identify who was our puppet master and certainly just accepting of "our lot". I was accepting of our life of "bread and circuses". I was thankful to be born when and where I was born. Historically speaking they are peaceful and civilized, enlightened days. Or so it seems at times if one is not in the hostile zones. Countless others constantly suffer miserably.

Although I had suffered several "small" heart attacks, my life continued relatively unchanged from day to day. Until one particular day….

A BAD DAY FOR BOB

14 May 2003, I was getting ready to get a bus to work as usual but as I was feeling somewhat different from normal, I decided to remain home. Things were not "right".

100 -DAD IN HOSPITAL…..(Colleen, 14/5/2004)(from her manuscript)

Dad was feeling pain at the level of about 2/10, around quarter to seven in the morning, so I convinced him to call an ambulance which arrived 15 minutes later.

He was put into the assesment room at A and E, they ran (word not readable) a scan everything seemed well it looked as though dad would be out by mid afternoon after the blood test was returned. I told dad I would go out for a smoke and bring him back a cup of tea.

While I was away dad felt intense pain, 9/10 so a nurse went to get him some morphine.

When I walked into the room with dad's tea he was having a cardiac arrest, he was seizuring, frothing at the mouth making horrible gargling (gagging?) sounds, his heart line was flat and his face was dark purple blue as though he was dead. Immediately I began to panic while the doctors cut off his singlet and began CPR. They shoved a tube down his throat to open his airway and pump oxygen into him as a last resort they used one shock on dad to start his heart. Dad made a terrible gurgling sound and he was sweating profusely and while I held his hand trying not to cry, it was all clammy. When dad came to he was scared and disoriented not knowing where he was or how he got there and his primary worry was contacting work. Immediately dad was given numerous injections and put on an IV. As they went to wheel dad to coronary care his last words were "don't leave me". I rang mum and told her to come to the hospital. The doctors told me to wait in the heart cares living room till all dads machinery was connected. I waited 30 minutes when I saw mum, the reason why doctors havent got me yet was because dad had another cardiac arrest this time it took 15 minutes and 8 electric shocks to resussatate (sic) him.

When I came in to see him he was sweaty, clammy, unable to speak as that tube was in his throat in case his airway blocked again. Although doctors said he could hear us speaking to him. The doctors said they would move him to ICU because he was so unstable. In the waiting room I broke down hysterically concerned dad was going to die especially after the heart specialist told us it didn't look good and that dad could have brain damage/personality change/die to lack of oxygen to the brain. They sedated dad with the tube down his throat and only after a medical team from Wellington had arrived to assist dad to the hospital could dad be moved.

While this happened mum and I went home and worried.

Later on we all went to Wellington Hospital to see you in ICU and mum said you were too groggy to really see but I went in anyway, you were asleep and looked so vulnerable breathing heavily with all the tubes in you.

As soon as I touched your hand you opened your eyes and looked at me slowly you began to wake up more and asked frantic questions "where am I? Am I dying? Am I going to die?" with tears I told you, you were getting better and you were the healthiest looking patient there. You were going to be sick so I removed your oxygen mask and held a container for you to spew into (it was blood and phlegm). When I tried to tell you what happened you fell asleep you were so exhausted, I came in two hours later at 11pm that night and as I kissed you on the forehead goodbye for the night you opened your eyes and seemed really alert. I told you they were taking you out of ICU the next day and you'd be alright and you went back to sleep. Then you were transferred back to the Hutt where you seemed much better but weak and tired. (end of manuscript)

(addition to above: the next day an angiogram and angioplasty was done and a stent placed in one coronary artery, another artery left untreated. The mitral valve condition was untreated. Cardiac nurse Aline Wilson at Lower Hutt coronary care unit who was involved in the CPR tells me the CPR lasted more than 45 minutes in total nearly an hour. She confessed it was hard work indeed, but smiling said it was worth it. Future heart surgery is needed, a double by-pass and mitral valve replacement is scheduled, but no date given as yet.)

SEPTEMBER 2004

Time went by and recovery was slow and very painful. I had discovered that one does NOT know what is happening as one is dying in this manner, and it is not painful beyond the brief initial "stab of pain". The real pain is experienced as one crawls back to life and resumes existence in a traumatized body. That body hurts badly, many ribs and sternum broken in resuscitation processes.

Some 16 months later it was time for the surgery and the repairs. During this time I became aware that I was indeed lucky to be alive at all, and was in effect having a second chance at life. My entire way of life and thinking was changed. Being aware that there was no assurance that I would return from surgery I decided to make notes wherever possible about the experience, mainly for my own presumed future reference. Those notes follow:

003 -ARE YOU READY?

As recently as this morning again I went through a mental checklist of my current status as I see it. On 21 June 2004 I went to the Wellington Hospital for what they call 'pre-assessment', the blood tests, x-rays, ECG, and interviews etc prior to the cardiac surgery. Among other things, it is clearly told to you what exactly will happen to you on a day-by-day basis following admission. We will not go into it in any detail, I started to stop listening after I had mentally counted 8 tubes, pipes, drains, wires, catheters etc being inserted. I presumed surgery would follow within days. Not so. Seeing as how a valve was to be replaced it was needful for me to get a dental clearance prior to surgery to ensure there is no risk of any infection from dental problems. Sure enough dental work was needed, 2 fillings, one extraction, and a de-scaling and this meant a delay of weeks to both allow it and ensure healing. The work is done, I am healed and now wait the 'call up'.

More than ever I now question myself. In view of the risks inherent with open-heart surgery (the valve replacement) and by-pass, how exactly am I ready if such a thing happens, to "meet my maker"? How can I accept that the last mortal face I see may be those in the operating theatre, and the last words heard be: "I am going to give you the anesthetic now."

One is being asked to entrust totally one's life to the hands of those he does not know. To total strangers he hopes are having and going to continue having a good day, and who are at a peak of alertness and mental fitness. Also to machinery and computer driven systems that are totally adequate for any contingency, are thoroughly serviced, free from defect, that will sustain life in that mortal body of mine for about 8 hours non stop. (Hopefully not running on "Windows") Hmmm. A big ask to accept all this, and one that not only demands a great exercise of faith, but demonstrates it and puts it to the supreme test.

These are some of the reasons one goes into mental hibernation at times to search more fully one's understanding and reasoning as to "what it is all about", or maybe, "what it **was** all about". To find peace with the thought that those faces and words in the theatre may be the last of mortality.

••

I recall reading maybe decades ago of an 'Eastern' sage who thought it strange of our western society that it did not teach people how to die (in peace, or at peace with the world) nor to be ready for it. Certainly the bulk of western religion offers no practical help nor philosophy that give deep comfort in the face of death. Even the western funerals tend to be ritualized beyond reason, although there emerges a trend to now celebrate the life of the deceased, but these are seen to be shallow meaningless obituary style presentations with no "meat" for those attending to take away and mentally chew on and come to terms with. **Where oh where is the meat??**

I had the opportunity to speak at my mother's funeral on 17 July 2003 and as I was preparing (mostly mentally) for this task I realized the need to serve 'meat' to those attending, so that later in their lives, there would be something to recall and perchance supply comfort to them in their hour of need when facing death.

However I do not think the poor mental or spiritual diet we suffer is only the result of the ritualization of western religion. We are living under and with a total collapse of society values and virtue. Almost everything that could be, or could go wrong has done so. Collectively, as a human species, we have almost without exception lost the plot. Our species is as a colony – a huge global colony – of ants running around doing whatsoever we will, totally immersed and preoccupied with whatsoever it is that currently occupies our priority. And like that vast ant colony, totally oblivious to the fact that 'someone' or 'something' exists outside of their little world and is observing their hurried existence, and marveling at its lack of awareness.

Society from Government to media exhort us follow the common path they decree as the ideal. They point us to the way to achieve status, wealth, possessions, and the subsequent presumed and often portrayed happiness. We are presented with a host of supposed celebrities, wealthy and beautiful beyond reason, to idolize and be our role models. Houses, wealth, abundance of cars and possessions, jewelry, designer label clothing, holidays and trips to places deemed exotic, status to be envied by those who possess less are shown to us. Consumerism gone mad, I see a trend now called "multi buy" by our retailers and supermarkets, you know the jive, buy 4 at a special price etc. One is probably enough. I see even cell phones at buy 2 for $x. Yet half the world's population live in shacks or worse, barely have food enough to sustain themselves, and suffer high mortality as a result. We can see millions spent on saving an animal, extravagant projects that are purely wasteful, and marvel at the imposed sense of values, maybe. But what can one person do to change things? Let's try telling others of our disapproval of the status of things.

Humanity is not united. Now I do not say if that is good or not. A vision of utopia often presumes a united world, and for thousands of years we have been presented with visions of a utopia. The ancient Greeks presented the vision, and if they had that vision one is assured that thousand of years before that it also existed. Seems we will never have a utopia on earth, and for good reason. As was well pointed out by philosophers hundreds of years ago, man as an individual of the species is selfish and self centered by nature, he will fight (war) lie, cheat and steal if it is to his advantage. He is not afraid to kill to get his way. He will form alliances, treaties, pacts and governments if it is to his advantage, but will break them when that is more advantageous. Such is the portrait of man presented by philosophers who have devoted the pre-requisite thought and analysis to such a conclusion before publishing. History would certainly tend to confirm this conclusion. The same mistakes of judgment and fact are made with monotonous regularity. The same human weaknesses and ambitions (eg: to rule the world) emerge again and again. A similar cycle of saviours, prophets, and reformers emerges. To what avail? Perhaps you have already wondered at this endlessly repeating cycle. Later we will explain why this is so.

It seems that invariably within a few centuries at most, the warnings, admonitions, and teachings of all those saviours, prophets etc (call them what you will) have been turned into a 'religion' or 'sect', ritualized, become compromised, buried, lost or turned into esoteric mysteries. Whereas unity was taught, the end result in many cases result in originally unintended divisiveness. This emphasizes the nature of man, if he can turn anything into a personal advantage, gain power, status and prestige, he will do so, even if it compromises the purity of the original message.

Logically and surely there is but one ultimate and "top" GOD. Yet from the state of man, one could be excused for thinking that there are many. Worse than that, the followers of one perceived god make war with and kill those that follow a different perceived god. It's seen as a case of 'our god is the only one, and anyone who dares think differently must be killed'. Now although that may seem and sound a totally stupid thought, that is precisely what has been happening on this planet for millennia, perhaps from the start of man.

But do we know for sure there is a god/GOD?

To find out, I say search your own heart and mind. You probably will not find the answer to this in conventional religions. Bear in mind the body is dust of the earth, it is born of dust, it is sustained by dust or elements of the earth, and there comes a time when it will return to those same elements, to dust of the earth. Yet it lives, loves, laughs, begets the next generation, and thinks. All mankind of all races colours etc are of the same dust of the earth. The dust of Africa is as it is in New Zealand, Asia, or Africa. There can be **neither doubt nor dispute** that we are, in the flesh, all of one common substance and heritage. (It is a strange thing that the things we presume to own or possess, houses, lands, cars etc etc, outlast us, perchance indicating that those 'possessions' actually possessed us)

I believe it is logically a small step to conclude that if we are all of one substance in the flesh, and are all equally sustained by the same substances of the earth (food, water, air, etc) then we are all following the same course or path. This has been the message of the reformers. Jesus told us that there is neither Jew nor Gentile, bond nor free in the kingdom of heaven. Race or status on earth is an obstacle or stumbling block for us in mortality on earth only. It is not a reality. It matters not ultimately if we have brown hair or black hair, or no hair in mortality. We are the same. We are of the same substance and of equal status and importance. This is why and how one such as Jesus (again) states that if we have done something to the least (esteemed) of men, then we have in fact done it to him, and equally to yourself.

Something sustains us, turning dust into carrots, cattle and fish, as well as mortal humans, using solar energy to fuel a self-sustaining, recycling system. Mortals that pass on are returned to dust and, yes, the dust recycled. Some 6 billion current inhabitants of earth created from the few inches of global topsoil, which provides the sustenance and food source for that many, generation after generation. Yes I see a hand that I cannot identify, and I call that 'GOD'. That GOD sustains all of us freely and equally. It is man alone that has made any inequality that has deemed the status of one as more than that of another. It is man alone that has for selfish greed taken more than an equitable share, called that inequitable share 'wealth' and demanded the adoration of those from whom it was taken. It is man alone that despises others who dare think differently, or who look differently to his image of ideal, or control less than he, thus deemed of supposed lower standing and importance.

But some call this GOD by one name, and others use a different name. As a child I was subtly taught to mistrust (even secretly despise) those of another Christian group or sect. It still happens, regardless of all the talk of Christian unity etc. "We worship GOD this way, and HE accepts only that manner of worship." "But you at least are better than 'those' who worship that god of a different name in a different (and most absurd) manner." It goes on and on doesn't it? Man made divisions, all in error.

Yes, I see the hand of GOD in all things. Yes, I see the error of mankind and of his ways and of his institutions, governments, religions, his society and values. Yes I understand the vision of unfulfilled and unfulfilable utopia.

But most importantly, I see what is required of me as an individual. I must separate myself spiritually from the deception and error in the earth. I should not fall victim to the false values esteemed by mankind and blind myself in the pursuit of the offered values, status, wealth and warmongering. I should hold fast to the values of the equality of mankind and of his relationship to his GOD and his species on earth and in eternity. I put my trust in that GOD, more than I obviously put my faith and trust in those who will replace my mortal heart valve.

I have seen through it and have seen truth. I do not fear, yes, I am ready.

NOTES FROM HOSPITAL. (notes made in hospital)

"Death" is a primitive concept. We still have little real knowledge of what lies on the other side of the line of existence we call life. It is like different states of matter. Nothing is destroyed, only changed. You end up facing the universe in a different guise. Myself, I am somewhat of a romantic. They were good souls all, your fellow fighters. If they hadn't been they wouldn't have been starfighters. I rather like to think of them as battling evil in another dimension." (Grig, from "The Last Starfighter" p152.)

Captains log- Wednesday 1 Sept.2004, 1830 hours N.Z. time though I am a little confused about the day and date. Today ends day 2 in cardio thoracic ward at Wellington hospital.

I have had an evening meal and am now eating a monstrous chicken sandwich on whole grain bread, & having a cup of tea. I will eat a row of salad sandwiches later. I am doing this for several reasons:

1. All food and fluids become forbidden at midnight and I am certain to get no foods tomorrow. I am also a pig, and meals here though marvelously tasty (no kidding – or I really am humble on diet.) they are small.

2. I am assured by a nurse who shaved my chest, forearms, inside legs, groins, that I will lose weight over the next several days. (prophesy sure fulfilled)

3. I am aware of a possibility that it could be, like the condemned man, the last meal – ever.

Being the day before surgery it has been a day of meetings with lots of participants in the event and its consequences.

A surgeon, not 'the' man, but a surgeon who will obviously be there, tells me "matter of factly", and in the interests and pursuit of full and total disclosure, that there is a 1% chance of worst case scenario- that the heart just cannot be re-started once the work is done. In this case one simply just does not 'wake up' – not in the mortal life anyway. (my observation: & if reincarnation is a reality then rebirth as an infant or other life form will not do much for individuality, memory, nor ego.)

Then there is a 1 to 5% chance of stroke (he continues), or further heart attack during or immediate post surgery which increases to up to 15% if one has had past strokes. (I am not aware of any and I claim that is a natural 'rugged' look of mine) Now I am not clear if this is combined stroke/heart attack figures – or per event/item.

Then there is a small risk, about 1% (they love the single digit don't they?) of an allergic or bad reaction/shock to the anesthetic. (it gets hard to remember it all, that's why I'm writing it now, but cannot post this writing for weeks yet – if I survive)

A further risk of almost nil to certain death exists as a result of blood transfusions, which can be a virtual certainty. 'Almost nil' if I get the right stuff. 'Sure death' equals a cock up and getting the wrong stuff incorrectly labeled for me. (YES surgeon is laying all this on me) Add a very small possibility of rejection or reaction adversely to the artificial mitral valve.

Complicate this with about once a month (no numbers given) someone has to come back to check why they do not stop bleeding – no further information on this.

Now I haven't done the math's yet. Nor will I soon, as I don't want to get alarmed, nervous or concerned by it, plus, I'm not sure if stats are per event or together/either %. (But I figure if you're a 1% no re-start individual, none else matters.)

But I know this: I have been lucky to survive about 16 months since the double arrests/resuscitations of May 2003, and at the rate I am declining I will not survive more than a few years at most unless some internal alterations or 'fixes' are put in place.

The surgeon (THE man) who also I met today with my wife and last son at home, fully explained the above also, and gave added value/info on the only alternative, which is 'no surgery'. Here is summary: The mitral valve regulates (my simplified explanation) flow of blood from the lungs into the heart. If damaged, it allows blood to flow back into lungs – this creates breathing difficulty, breathlessness etc, and causes it to enlarge. As it enlarges the valve 'flaps' become less of a seal and allow less blood to effectively pass. The heart has to work harder for even less effectiveness. (currently my last assessment was about 52% cardiac efficiency.) It continues to get worse and worse till death is assured from 'heart failure'. The condition of my mitral valve now warrants surgery in itself.

Added to this are the bypasses. (This is the surgeon explaining) Now I had been told 2, but hey, I can read charts and figures and do math's. I saw 3 on his chart, the stent on one, another to the side which I recognized from angiograms past, and yet another to the rear of the heart. Then he is also looking to source veins/arteries to graft. First he will take arteries from inside the chest cavity, 2nd will be legs, 3rd will be arms, this is also why I now look like a plucked chicken.

As an aside, I actually do notice the cold against my body now. So that body, leg, arms chest etc hair that in my case I consider far from simian, modest even, is sure warming. You gotta lose if to find out.

*But to answer Dirty Harry's question, "yes I feel lucky." God I have seen some sick looking people in this ward that make me look and feel like an athlete. The guy who was in the bed next to me had his similar surgery today (By-passes only though) now he is 6 years older, also has diabetes, is not as robust, and looks like a vampire's victim. He survived well. Another older still guy same room went home today, successful result (later I failed to recall this) God I would have thought dental work would have been his undoing. Adrienne's (my wife) friend has cancer, diabetes, weighs 60kg, had 2 heart attacks 10 days apart, discovered an enurism in the heart, had about 5 by-pass jobbies and survives well. (*she later died within 18 months)

Yes I feel lucky, lucky enough anyhow. The surgeon also apologized – he has never seen anyone who has had or endured as many surgery postponements as I had.

I mentioned the visit from the razor wielding nurse, a physiotherapist came to show and demo post operative stuff- and an anesthetist also came to burden me.these 5 are all I recall at the moment and now I am tired.

Some others did their stuff yesterday. An ECG, blood tests. X-ray, dental check, at least 4 yesterday and I know others are yet to show up and make my day.

I gotta get medications started tonight, about 9pm. I'm told and I hear a urine test still to be done. There are a lot of people involved. I've only mentioned the 'specialists', not the support staff at all.

Now to use the words of my early childhood. I believe the next time I am conscious it will be over….

"Now I lay me down to sleep, I pray the Lord my soul to keep. If I should die before I wake, I pray the Lord my soul to take" and don't tell me if the latter is the case when I wake up or the shock of the bad news may kill me. (Stop groaning please)
Brief final notes 9.45pm Just had final antiseptic scrub down, supplied urine, and night medications, with '3 little pills' – it begins.

Oh yes, it was explained why one has difficulty breathing on bending down- the mitral valve is compressed and if already operates poorly, then it gets more poorly until it just about doesn't work – blood is held in the lungs – no more oxygen absorbed etc etc. No wonder people drop dead bending down to pick up the 'pegs'.

Did I mention clicking? The new valve will have an audible click of which I will be aware, though I hear it from the 'inside' the outside or both cannot be said, but it is said others will also be able to hear its clicking operation- people will hear me coming.

Over and Out.   Bob.

NOTES FROM THE EDGE…meet "IT"..

(I am typing this on 21/9/04 for records and posting, and will try to avoid adding in later or current comments, but re-produce notes as they are. However some later notes may appear in brackets.)

Captains Log Friday 3 September 2120 hours.
Well of course it just did not happen. (no surgery done despite preps and medications)

Saturday 4 September 2004 7.29am:
I have just woken up alive (to this earth) this time. That may sound strange – but previously I have "woken up" twice and been dead to this world. I will go clean teeth and get my head around this thing.

The "other world" incorporates this world, totally entwines it – but from this side of it (mortality) one cannot full access/express or explain the full relationship or its reality.

At 1.29am I woke up in severe pain – like a cramp on my left side chest and arm – severe and nasty. I rang for a nurse and found my nitro spray – used it and pain subsided totally in a few minutes. I dozed and dreamed often. Got up at 2.30 for toast and honey.

In dream to waking state I was having difficulty as in 'dream' I was aware of 'levels' up to at least 10, but as I got closer to and more fully awake, these levels evaporated, no longer available, and in waking I could only access or know to 4 levels. Somehow I knew – in waking – I was not "right", so submerged into "sleep", and sure enough – awareness/knowledge of 10-11 levels again. Faded into waking, same evaporation or non access even full awareness of these levels.
It was exhaustingly frustrating and I did realize that in 'waking' those levels were simply not available, but names and things of the lowest 4 levels only could be had.

Then I woke up or was fully aware – with full awareness of all the levels referred to. It was SO QUIET. SO peaceful. Then I knew "this is dead" – but I was fully awake/aware/alive; but I knew I was dead. Hastily I 'submerged' back into the previous level so as to re-emerge to mortality – DEAD AGAIN. A third time lucky, if you call access to only 3 – 4 levels lucky. But if association with fellow mortals is lucky, then I am lucky.

I have memory of things that are going to be near impossible to share or explain. I am at peace, a little physically uncomfortable, but at peace.

Now the guy in the bed next to me is really not well – lung problems and out of surgery. Restless, rattley etc, moans and groans. After near a day of it, it is decided It's back to surgery for him. **He admitted in a trembling voice how scared he was, and anyone could see that. There was no way he was anywhere near ready to peacefully depart this world. I got to thinking how sad it is that we have been failed by Christianity or its sectarian religions. We have not been taught our place in eternity, time, or space. We have not been given a full nor true understanding of our nature or make up.** *The ritualized garbage and hollow prayers, words, and creeds of millennia have failed to prepare this single man to face death with peace or dignity.* (We lack understanding of life and death.)

I am sorry, but that criticism of the supposed official state religion is factual. **And if it failed that one man, then it failed millions over the centuries.** (Countless billions actually.)

Nor has it instilled generally the ethic that underlies the principle. Society has been failed, families and communities have been failed and we have been reduced to a society that is as Godless as it is without any true concepts of morality or justice. Even the so called "do-gooders" have been diverted down endless, mindless, side-tracking, involving trivial rubbish of no major import what-so-ever, except inasmuch as some of those tracks may further undermine the integrity and stability of our crumbled society.

Waiting, waiting, waiting.

Sunday 5 September 2004 7.20am:
Been up for hours now. Yesterday was not a really good day for me. It started with a waking to severe pain. Temperature rose to 38 degrees, pulse to 106, blood pressure lower than I have ever seen mine, 110/76. The day was mostly drifting into and out of consciousness. I could not eat much. (I suspect much of this was due to anesthetic procedures that had been commenced in anticipation of surgery that was postponed)

By 9pm I was fairly much recovered, but all 'slept out'. A restless night followed. I tried to ring home but got no answer as the phone cut immediately to answer phone – I hate that. Spent a lot of time thinking about man's condition or state in this world – about the churches rather than religion. The concept and theory may be fine, but the implementation is in the hands of the mighty corporate type bodies with a fierce grip on a "good thing". Its run like a huge money sucking racket. Thought about our relationship and unity with our planet – how we are part of it. Doubtless if I live longer some of these thoughts shall emerge in future writings and challenges.

SATURDAY 11 SEPTEMBER 2004
I figure I should write a few things before I forget all things – as last night my world ended suddenly.
Let's start 'back there' and work forward as, or if, I can.

Surgery was Monday (6 September) know nothing. I A & have had some interesting difficulties.(??) The family came to see me, but that was just as I was told. There is only one vague memory, vague, waking up and being spoken to: "Do you know where you are?"...later, "Do you know what happened?" Yes to both. Wellington Hospital and had surgery – it seemed to satisfy as the insistence went away. Something in my throat, holding it open – I cannot close it, nor can I really try. Later I am aware of a plastic throat tube being pulled out from my throat – sore. Then blessed unconsciousness takes me away.

TUESDAY, day after surgery.I think it – I know something – now I know nothing No memories except swirling embracing all devouring evil. I was devoured. I was hopelessly and forever trapped in a recycling evil dream of vast unpleasantness.

WEDNESDAY (8th) Again may be one I know something. I listened to a nightmare of noise and voices – people being asked if they knew where they were, or what had happened. Some got it right, Wellington hospital and surgery. Others didn't have a clue.
Hallucinations started I think on Wednesday. Blobs. Blots, intricate spots and such. The mind wandered endlessly as one insane, and it hurt. I HAD to stay awake or "it" would surely "get me" – don't ask – I don't know. But "it" got me – and hurt me – messed my whole mind.

THURSDAY (9TH) can't have been much better (than the day before) Little to no memories (of events or things of this day) I was out of intensive care ward and even the step down ward. I walked to ward 31. Bad dreams – horrible.

FRIDAY (10th) Adrienne and Daniel came – boy was I glad to see them. (They say my eyes were 'different' - like beads) Going to bed I HAD to keep saying endlessly- and again, 'this is Saturday AM – I am here and I am OK. Focus only on those things I know.

It was while I was tooling around focusing on what is real (presumed real) that "IT" got me. I was real, Adrienne was real, but I also could plainly see that she is and was of the same substance as me. Daniel is real. But we are also the same, and while I was thus cataloguing people etc that "IT" bit.

IT WAS SUDDENLY ANNOUNCED THAT I WAS WRONG. AND ALL MY WORLD WAS TO BE 'UNDONE'

With a rapidity that would spin heads my world was undone, unraveled – ended. I fled the room to a light source. I had to see it did not end and it did not. Now all over again, "I am here and OK – focus". Finally with some residue of terror I got to sleep about 5am.
I know a few days ago I had reality problems, but Friday nite was kind in comparison. I know in a few days without notes, I'd probably benefit with no memories of any of this either.
Spots, dots, patterns, everywhere – now I gotta rest some. God, I listen to what some people got told – there's some really not well people in here. Scary.

Oh yes its SATURDAY (11th) and I am losing control of some things – my memory comes and goes – I don't think it is really working at all, or if I am functioning at all. I think I could be dead and not know it. If I think about it, I should worry, but I don't know who to worry to, or even if that is an appropriate response. I feel my mind is slipping away more and more, but don't know why. I have a wife and children somewhere. I am having serious problems with whats real and not, and don't know what to do about it. Does anyone know I am here? I'm sad. But a nurse just told me its normal.

Did I just have (big curse) heart surgery? I wish someone would come for me. Why did I have surgery? What happened? Suddenly I have no idea at all. I just remembered I have no idea where I am. I see it's a hospital, but I may as well have had my brain removed. I don't think I know where I lived anymore. I know I had a mother. She died.

A chap came and rested in my allocated bed this afternoon. I thought he was just being friendly as I was sitting in the day chair. Then a lady turns up after an hour or so, claims him and takes him away. He thanked me for my time speaking to him. Later I found out he was more lost than I – thought it was his room and bed & I was the visitor. I thought I had problems

Tea is shit, jelly was shit and the mince pure muck. Mash spuds like muck. I'll go for a walk now and hope my confusion ends.

Now as I'm about to go to bed everything is as though covered by a few feet of swirling clear water. Goodnite at 10.26pm. Its now extremely grotesque – gone 12.30 (night time) and EVERYWHERE I focus or look there are zillions of fluorescent tube like worms, only smaller than cotton, all writhing in a mist, like little thread worms – all waving into the air. They are not there of course, and this I can demonstrate (and do so) by careful close study of a surface. But it gets scary what this effect can do to one's face, or clothes, in a mirror. Everything is alive with colourful waving, flowing worms.

SUNDAY (12ᵗʰ) 7.46am. Now I have it all figured out – we are all gonna die here. See people only check in and never check out. Well I've been here since 30/8/04 and I have never seen people, anyone, go home. (yet earlier I note someone gone home!!) They come in and those left sane, disappear in the night. Now I gotta be careful who sees this, and I gotta get out this morning. I waked finally only to find a cold and bleak day with the laws of physics no longer working. I'm dead or in hell, so are the others obviously. Last nite I spoke with an Indian Doctor, one of the surgeons. He knows that some of us see the walls, floors, etc as moving. Last nite an older lady in the ward "cracked up" and was wheeled off to an isolated room. We go insane in here some of us.

SUNDAY (12ᵗʰ) 7.11pm I have learned that some times it is necessary to not only ignore things but to "not see them" at all. It is beyond any powers of denial – it is for survival.
Thus today I determined not to see nor dwell on floors, walls, clothes or sundry other things as have in the past been 'alive'. In consequence my sanity is preserved, *but the poor lady patient wheeled out last nite may have had experience none would enjoy – not the vilest horror movie sadist even. That lady did look calmer today, and is wearing an oxygen mask.*

MONDAY (13ᵗʰ) 7.57am. Awake- I am getting to be no longer 'sure', if ever one was such, of what was or is "real" and happened and what is not or did not happen. Sore but well. I cannot believe I made so many notes. Slept well but it seems in about 2 sessions. I am losing weight again since the surgery and find myself amazed I've been here OVER two weeks and that surgery is done.

I believe I had valve repairs, not replaced, as bits were missing and seems the surgeon was describing a hole in the heart itself, a leak from one chamber to another. This defect hole between chambers he repaired and then repaired the 'flappy valve thing' also. I feel well and got lots of sleep. Now I am not sure what was real and what was not – **I wonder does it even matter.**

TUESDAY (14TH)Slept poorly 2 sessions of about 2 hours each on Monday nite I went home on Monday 13th. Today went by bus about 10am to Lower Hutt with Adrienne, exchanged a 'phone at Dick Smiths store and went to a clinic for blood test. Went to a supermarket for a few items and got a bus back home. At home I sorted out a lot of computer gear. Whereas weeks ago Adrienne said she would get rid of my excess 'stuff' while I was in hospital and I ranted about 'no way', today I determined to get rid of all excess. (about 12 monitors, 6 keyboards, 6 system boxes, loads of mother boards and components, 5 printers – all just 'collecting dust') I had a nap and a first shave in weeks, and yes, I used a razor against advice, with no 'life threatening' endlessing bleeding cuts. (I am now on daily anticoagulant medications) I have periods when my hand/hands go totally numb and lose all sense of feeling and also lose all strength. It only lasts a brief time. Nurse from Lower Hutt Hospital made a home visit.

WEDNESDAY NITE THURSDAY AM. 15th. Woke 1.50 am. Noted that sequential dreams in 'normal' colour mode and style have returned and resumed. 1st time noted since surgery. I will get my chest 'drain hole' stitches removed today…

End of notes.

PART TWO

001-THE FABRIC OF THE UNIVERSE

The evidence is conclusive that a "reality" commonly known as "the fabric of the universe" exists. In my earlier writings I came to the conclusion that underlying all things is the ultimate source of all things, a universal energy field. I named it the "quantum soup".

The truth is that mankind has known such a thing for thousands of years. However any claims for such have been studiously ignored by science etc. for all this time on the basis that it could not be proven. Whereas one culture may have given the name "prana" to the phenomena, other cultures and tongues gave it other names. No matter the name, the claims and principle remained the same.

What is remarkably evident is that when one comes to describing the nature and attributes of this recently proclaimed and acceptable "fabric of the universe" one cannot help but see the parallels to what the western world define as the attributes and nature of the god of their orthodox religions. Some have simply named this universal force "spirit", and that of course is their prerogative. However I avoid using that word as it has too many narrow connotations in the western world, too many correlations with over-use of the word in often contradictory ways by religions. In other words mere use of the word "spirit" invites confusion, introduces a reader's preconceived ideas, and is therefore best avoided. "Fabric of the Universe" or "quantum soup or sea" isn't so subject so to immediate mis-understanding.

If one wishes to come to an understanding of time and space, matter and mass, of the "laws" or principles that govern all that is or can be, one must come to a basic understanding of this underlying fabric of the universe, my quantum soup, or "prana" by whatever name. Once its basics are understood, then one will be able to progress intelligently to the subsequent steps, namely understanding the nature and characteristics of what we call "god", and then of our own nature.

ENERGY AND INFORMATION

One may ask or wonder, "how is it, or can it be, that a probable infinite number of dimensions (or realities etc., call them as you will) can exist simultaneously, in the same "place" or space?" I am not yet going to ask or address the issue of "where" all of this is taking place, of "how big" it all is, nor how much space it actually occupies. (E.g. Does it indeed occupy the entire cosmos, and then some.) Indeed I still have a sneaking suspicion that perhaps none of it is actually "real". It may be "just" information existing within the quantum sea and "vibrating" at a level we can perceive or it may all be simply a mental construct. Although "who's mental construct?" would be a most challenging of questions when I come to consider that one, and be assured the question is on the agenda when the time is right. However I understand the very fabric of the universe itself, that quantum sea, is intelligent. Or is intelligence. I read an article recently wherein the author likened our reality to a mere hologram and thought that somewhat appropriate. Other issues and questions need to be dealt with first.

I recall a comment I heard decades ago to the effect that maybe all that exists including us, are just thoughts in the mind of "god". Interesting thought, and as one learns, one begins to understand the line of thought which views the entire cosmos as actually alive, and that it is also one all encompassing single intelligent entity. Omnipresent, omniscient, and omnific. This is where one sees the nature of the fabric of the universe confused with and into our various descriptions of the attributes of a "god". The underlying "power" is universally seen.

Oh, the confusing and varied explanations or understanding of the elusive nature of reality. Consider our 3D reality, this world, and all our mortal perceptions. We "see" them because we have been designed, or are designed so that we are "tuned" to perceive only a very small faction of all that there is, of the whole. We perceive only those vibrations or signal levels to which our organism or mentality is adjusted. (Light, sound, heat etc.) All else is lost to us, or to most of us, as there are those who demonstrably have perceptions not common to all our species. It is also well known that our animal kingdom is tuned somewhat differently, being able to perceive that which is lost to man. ("Man" being the species of course) I read that elephants can discern sound from great distances through the earth via the medium of their feet. And whereas Elephants can detect sound from some 10 miles or more away, sea mammals have a range in the 1000s of kilometers in their watery element, or so I read. These issues are just to demonstrate the difference in the way the species are tuned and adjusted. Birds can discern the "voice" of an individual mate amid the simultaneous confusing noise of thousands of their species. Simply because we fail to see, hear, or otherwise detect some event or phenomena does not remotely imply its non-existence.

Adrienne sat watching t.v. engrossed by a seeming reality, and reacted as though what was being portrayed was reality. Hey, it's a TV show, it has a script. But consider: the environment all around us is filled with innumerable signals from probably hundreds of thousands of broadcasting stations, radio and t.v. of all frequency levels. Add to this the signals to and from probably of billions of cell phones, all at a slightly different signal or "vibration" level. Add to these the natural cosmic radiations and others I have missed. The electromagnetic signals, vibrations, call them as you will, effectively make our atmosphere, indeed, space itself, an endless and "solid block" of vibrating signals. And these signals are carrying information. If we could actually see all there is, we would find ourselves swimming effortlessly in a solid sea of electromagnetic waves, signals and energy. The entire electromagnetic spectra from the finest of cosmic radiation, through light, radio, sound, heat etc. are continuously encasing us. They are always there, completely filling the space/time within which we believe we live. We are oblivious to most of them. We are also a component part of them, vibrating at our own unique "wavelength".

However nearly all of us in mortality are tuned into just the same one single channel, perceive it with different degrees of clarity, and accept it as a reality, probably as the only and sole reality. Generally most will not even question the reality of our picture generated by so few of the existing and available signals, yet alone question what the other existent information is channeled into. Just like when watching the one t.v. station, generally we become oblivious to all the other signals and information simultaneously existing out there. With a simple adjustment to the tuning of the receiver set to an alternative frequency, a new signal, a different new reality emerges from the chaos of the "atmosphere" with the flick of a switch or the push of a button. I believe it is really from the "chaos" of information carried in the fabric of the universe.

Here is a marvel. None of this is linear. Go anywhere, and the signals can be received. We bathe in a sea of information and are truly surrounded by it, in fact more than surrounded, for in reality the signals find us transparent and actually pass through us as though we do not exist. Certainly we are no barrier to the signals. We would be hard pressed to determine any source for it. Every spatial dimension we could name is so filled, and that simultaneously.

Likewise we bathe in the fabric of the universe, my "quantum soup" as I called it earlier. That makes the vastness, potential, and content of the sea of information beyond our imagining, incorporating the entirety of all that "can" be. This fabric even fills what we once thought of as "space" within the atoms, and as space even within the nucleus. We are now told this fabric exists at those levels, and it vibrates with information.

Blessed ignorance. We neither perceive or know anything of it. Perchance we are a congealed lump of energy, imbued with intelligence, manifest but localized for a short time wherever we perceive ourselves to be within this entire sea of energy that obviously functions at many levels. Of potentially billions of possibilities, our individual energy/intelligence package is tuned into planet earth, 3D (4D) world, here and now. Or what we identify as "here and now". Why? Because our physical mortal body is of the same frequency and vibration as this mainifest temporal dimension. Frankly I doubt those words ultimately will have much meaning. Decades ago I read of the "eastern" principles of "prana", and of the western mystic's "vibration levels". No one was really listening to them then, and most are probably not listening now. But those thoughts are increasingly validated, and given new names that disassociate the concepts from the earlier proponents. Gosh, you mean "ectoplasm" may be a reality? We'd best give it a new name so people won't bundle us in with those we all called fruitcakes.

So here we all find ourselves. In this big bowl of quantum soup wherein there is no such thing as empty space at all. No, not even squeezed hard against the nucleons. Information and "signals" are everywhere, omnipresent. Again a confused claim of an attribute for "god".

This solid database of universal information of which we are a small part is ultimately omnific, and as such certainly is the indisputable ultimate source of all things. Being itself pure energy, it thus has ability, power and potential to literally organize or create, then arrange all and any "elemental matter" into what ever universes, galaxies etc. as it may see fit. If such language use or implications of "as it may see fit" is appropriate, for it could be just a mindless engine. N'est ce pas? Could it all really be purposeless and unguided? (Einstein $E=mc2$ matter and energy interchangeable) All the information and the fabric or "soup" exist in an eternal "now" state, all dimensions equally co-exist "now" and it is only their existence that gives the illusion of time and space. Within that illusion of time and space, we find our little patch of intelligence congealed into "matter", tuned into just this one "station" for the time being. Be assured, the other "stations" are right here with us "now" and its just a matter of tuning frequency that keeps us locked into this channel, just as our t.v. set may be tuned to channel 3.

Is there a source? Where is it all sited? Do those questions have any meaning? Do we have the capacity to understand the nature of the questions and locate or understand answers? The trick will be, or so I believe, to find precisely the right question to ask in the correct sequence, then understanding will come.

TIME AND SPACE, SIMPLIFIED

This segment will be as simple as I can make it. If you want more depth for any of the matters touched upon, then you will have to satisfy that wish elsewhere, as this book is not designed as a resource or textbook on subject matters that are mentioned.

Energy (e) exists and is manifest throughout all that we can perceive. It even exists within the space that we once commonly thought of as empty space, or even as a possible void within the atom or even perhaps between the component parts of a nucleus. Simply put, there is no "place" where it does not exist or is manifest.

This then is the "fabric of the universe" and it exists in an everlasting or eternal "now" state. In no sense does our concept of time or space have any application in relation to this universal energy field.

Einstein revealed to us the mathematics of the phenomena of matter (m) being converted back into energy, and simple reasoning allows a formula for energy being converted into matter. The atomic bomb adequately demonstrates the validity of the theory and maths. It is further established that the energy field, the fabric of the universe can seemingly spontaneously create matter (and anti-matter) where none previously existed. This is apparent and true "creation", but unlike the claimed "creation" that is so often the subject of ridicule by the wilfully ignorant, it is not creation of matter "out of nothing". Matter is created from energy by conversion of existing energy using a now understood formula.

Does any of this mean or prove "god" exists?

Interesting question with no simple answer as "god" is not adequately defined. Therein is the nub of all the problems associated with trying to validate "religion" using "science". The languages are different. Whereas science generally uses a precise language of mathematics that is unambiguous, religion uses subjective words and terms that are subject to a myriad of often opposing translations. However if you define "god" as an omnific, omnipresent, and omniscient intelligence, the only omnific source of all things, and that encompasses all things, then "yes" it establishes such exists and may well be called "god". But the very use of the word "god" immediately introduces confusion and a host of would be exclusive claimants. Let us not therefore put a single name to such, nor try to identify such on an individual or even group basis. On the other hand, if you use the above to establish that the god of the bible or Christendom is real and exists, then it is "no".

When a conversion of energy into mass occurs the creation of this new matter or mass creates a seemingly finite "bubble" of "space" within which to exist within the field of the underlying fabric of the universe. Note that it does not displace any part of the underlying fabric/field but truly becomes another dimension within the same location. In effect we now have two "things" (2 at least, one of which is "new") co-existing at the same location. In point of fact there may well be an infinite number of realities or dimensions already existing at any given point but all having been created in their own time/space dimension. Any occupants in such "dimensions" would be ignorant or unaware of the other dimensions at the same "location".

The appearance of this new "bubble" of matter or mass **now defines a space** where no such definable space previously existed. In reality a "space" has been created at the same time as the organisation or creation of matter. (I think it of no small co-incidence that this process of a field of "chaos" giving rise to the creation of matter finds a remarkable parallel in those early chapters of Genesis that are so often reviled and ridiculed.)

The appearance of this new "bubble" of matter or mass also **marks the commencement of time** (as we commonly understand it) for this newly created and finite matter or mass. It matters not whether the matter or mass is of subatomic particle, human body, planet, star, or galaxy size. Time is the period for which energy in the form or guise of matter or mass will be manifest before it rejoins the underlying fabric of the universe. The matter or mass is finite, and it will have a beginning and an end. This then is space/time. Ultimately the measurement and division of such time is purely subjective and largely irrelevant unless one's intelligent individual self is participating in the particular sphere.

By deduction then we see that space is created for the newly created matter or mass, and this will quite probably be established as the underlying cause of why we perceive our known universe as "expanding". It will also help explain the universal distribution of matter and galaxies within the universe. I also believe that this creation of new mass and subsequently of time/space will correctly replace the "Big Bang" theory as the cause of the creation and ongoing expansion of the universe.

When the matter or mass (m) is destroyed or reverts to its form of energy, time and space such as we perceive it in this temporal state cease to exist. The energy which cannot be destroyed must return to the fabric of the universe. In biblical terms, it returns to the god that gave it. It follows that all that exists does so because it is a part of the very fabric of the universe, and that includes every one of us. It also follows that once our time here ceases and life energy is extinguished or lost, then by doing so it necessarily returns to the very fabric of the universe. Again all of this has been known for millennia.

BIRTH AND DEATH

The "event" of birth marks our individual creation and entry into this space and time of our temporal world and universe. At this point it is not an issue of if there was any former or prior state or existence, and that will not be discussed at this time.

The "event" of death marks our individual cessation of life and extinguishment of existence from this dimension and its time and space.

Thus we enter this dimension and we leave this dimension.

By reason and logic we may conclude that in entering this dimension that the underlying "energy" which manifests as us, or intelligence or call it what you will, came from or "left" another dimension, certainly it originated from the fabric of the universe. In like manner we may conclude that in leaving this mortal dimension we must revert, return, or pass to another dimension, or at least to the underlying fabric of the universe. Also let us not forget that for the duration of existence in this material (made of matter or mass) world and sphere, the very fabric of the universe still completely fills the very same "space" we perceive as the domain of our mortal body. In other words at all times, even the eternal "now", we are always a part of the very fabric of the universe. Things only change.

QUESTIONS

- Is what we do here of any importance?
- Is how long we are here of any importance?

- Is when we are here of any importance?
- Are we in fact of any importance?

002- ACCIDENTAL OR INTENTIONAL - ORIGINS

I believe it is most reasonable to say that if we are to ask, then subsequently pursue to discover if there is any meaning or purpose to life, that we must **first** establish with some reasonable degree of conviction and irrefutability the basic facts regarding the nature of our actual very existence.

Put simply, we need to firmly and convincingly establish whether we are in fact creatures of chance evolution on this earth, or are we "manufactured" bio-mechanical devices organised countless millennia ago in circumstances and events now unknown, presumably to fulfil some long forgotten purpose? After all, any question about the meaning or purpose of life seems to presume some such forgotten purpose. In short, the alternatives seem to be very few, was it intervention or was it all chance?

IMPORTANT BASIC FACT TO REMEMBER IN READING ALL THIS.

Materials presented or quoted, such as the following by Lloyd Pye, and other materials of Watson or Kaku, are by no means isolated cases or the sum total of information available on any subject under discussion. They are merely illustrative examples on any such given subject generally from a vast amount of writings from many sources, often freely available on the internet. My purpose is not to give exhaustive volumes of evidences (inclusive of all the finest details and known materials) nor reasons for my conclusions. It is to nudge one in a specific direction, to give a clue as it were, for establishing vital evidential materials on specific matters that will directly effect the outcome of our stated quest. Be assured that for all cases and illustrations given there will be a vast library of similar resources for you to find and check up. There is in fact no bias in my writings.

Indeed a reader may well know of a better illustration or example to establish many issues. (If that is so, please feel free to e-mail me details – e-mail details are in the "my profile" at the front of the book.)

BACK TO THE MATTER BEING CONSIDERED,

Evolution or intervention? This is a case where the resource materials are mind numbingly vast and confusing. Evolution is taught by state institutions such as schools as though firmly established fact. (Later we will cover why this is so.) To contradict or dispute it will result in severe censure and incur the actual wrath and indignation of so called authorities. You will frankly be mocked and ridiculed as though a complete idiot. Lucky, as centuries ago you would have been burned at the stake in the town square as a warning to all others that the authorities are not to be questioned, but blindly followed. Today one is not burned with fire, but one is burned nonetheless.

Evolution theory is severely flawed, and its proponents actually know that, but still they stick to the "story". I think there is a covert reason for this, and even its vociferous proponents may not be aware of that. The standard "Creation by God" theory is also severely flawed, frankly not the least bit credible, and indeed both of the standard model theories can be quickly demonstrated as quite inadequate and wrong.

Unfortunately the majority of people simply do not think for themselves, and just accept on face value that which the majority unquestioningly accept as the established facts on most matters. "After all," they may reason, "the teachers, authorities, and government or even religious leaders would not tell us lies or lead us astray would they?" A simple review of recent or long term history will show that "Yes they will, and for a whole bunch of reasons, mostly bad reasons." But your neighbourhood government wants and needs you blindly and unquestioningly to follow the standard models. They want it so badly they **need** it, and this is why laws and censure are imposed, to ensure compliance. Reasons for the need for compliance will be covered later in this series.

Back to the issue of intervention or chance evolution. I have selected the following copyright material to include, as it is both well written and full of very relevant and fascinating elements that probably irreparably shatter evolution theory. Certainly it is sufficient at this time, and if you want additional material, as I would expect, then go to the Internet to research to your heart and mind's content.

By Lloyd Pye © 2002
E-mail: lloyd@lloydpye.com
Website: 15/08/2008

THE ABSURDITIES OF DOGMA

In 1905, a 25-year-old patent clerk named Albert Einstein demolished the 200-year-old certainty that Isaac Newton knew all there was to know about basic physics. In a technical paper only a few pages long, Einstein sent a huge part of his current "reality" to history's dustbin, where it found good company with thousands of other discards large and small. In 1905, though, Newton's discard was about as large as the bin would hold.

Now another grand old "certainty" hovers over history's dustbin, and it seems only a matter of time before some new Einstein writes the few (or many) pages that will bring it down and relegate it to history. And, as was the case in 1905, every "expert" in the world laughs heartily at any suggestion that their certainty could be struck down. Yet if facts are any yardstick--which should always be the case, but frequently isn't--Charles Darwin's theory of evolution by natural selection is moving towards extinction.

Please note this: not everyone who challenges evolution is automatically a Creationist. Darwinists love to tar all opponents with that brush because so much of Creationist dogma is absurd. Creationists mulishly exclude themselves from serious consideration by refusing to give up fatally flawed parts of their argument, such as the literal interpretation of "six days of creation". Of course, some have tried to take a more reasonable stance, but those few can't be heard over the ranting of the many who refuse.

Recently a new group has entered the fray, much better educated than typical Creationists. This group has devised a theory called "Intelligent Design", which has a wealth of scientifically established facts on its side. The ID-ers, though, give away their Creationist roots by insisting that because life at its most basic level is so incredibly and irreducibly complex, it could never have simply "come into being" as Darwinists insist.

Actually, the "life somehow assembled itself out of organic molecules" dogma is every bit as absurd as the "everything was created in six days" dogma, which the ID-ers understand and exploit. But they also suggest that everything came into existence at the hands of God (by whatever name) or "by means of outside intervention", which makes clear how they're betting. "Outside intervention" is a transparent euphemism for "You Know What" (with apologies to J. K. Rowling). [In Rowling's "Harry Potter" books, the arch villain is so despicable and dreadful, his name should not even be uttered; thus he is referred to as "You Know Who". Similarly, the very idea that humans might have been created by extraterrestrials is so despicable and dreadful to mainstream science and religion that no mention of it should be uttered; thus the author refers to it as "You Know What". Ed.] To Darwinists, Creationists and ID-ers alike, creation at the hands of You Know What is the most absurd suggestion of all. Yet it can be shown that You Know What has the widest array of facts on its side and has the best chance of being proved correct in the end.

Virtually every scientist worth their doctorate will insist that somehow, some way, a form of evolution is at the heart of all life forms and processes on Earth. By "evolution", they mean the entire panoply of possible interpretations that might explain how, over vast stretches of time, simple organisms can and do transform themselves into more complex organisms. That broad definition gives science as a whole a great deal of room to bob and weave its way towards the truth about evolution, which ostensibly is its goal. However, among individual scientists that same broadness of coverage means nobody has a "lock" on the truth, which opens them up to a withering array of internecine squabbles.

In Darwin's case, those squabbles were initially muted. Rightly or wrongly, his theory served a much higher purpose than merely challenging the way science thought about life's processes. It provided something every scientist desperately needed: a strong counter to the intellectual nonsense pouring from pulpits in every church, synagogue and mosque in the world.

Since well before Charles Darwin was born, men of science knew full well that God did not create the Earth or anything else in the universe in six literal days. But to assert that publicly invited the same kind of censure that erupts today onto anyone who dares to challenge evolution openly. Dogma is dogma in any generation.

Darwin's honeymoon with his scientific peers was relatively brief. It lasted only as long as they needed to understand that all he had really provided was the outline of a forest of an idea, one that only in broad terms seemed to account for life's stunningly wide array. His forest lacked enough verifiable trees. Even so, once the overarching concept was crystallised as "natural selection", the term "survival of the fittest" was coined to explain it to laymen. When the majority of the public became convinced that evolution was a legitimate alternative to Creationism, the scientific gloves came off. In-fighting became widespread regarding the trees that made up Darwin's forest.

Over time, scientists parsed Darwin's original forest into more different trees than he could ever have imagined. That parsing has been wide and deep, and it has taken down countless trees at the hands of scientists themselves. But despite such thinning, the forest remains upright and intact. Somehow, some way, there is a completely natural force at work governing all aspects of the flow and change of life on Earth. That is the scientific mantra, which is chanted religiously to counter every Creationist--and now Intelligent Design--challenge to one or more of the rotten trees that frequently become obvious.

Even Darwin realised the data of his era did not provide clear-cut evidence that his theory was correct. Especially troubling was the absence of "transitional species" in the fossil record. Those were needed to prove that, over vast amounts of time, species did in fact gradually transform into other, "higher" species.

So right out of the chute, the theory of evolution was on the defensive regarding one of its cornerstones, and more than 140 years later there are still no clear-cut transitional species apparent in the fossil record.

Because this is the most vulnerable part of Darwin's theory, Creationists attack it relentlessly, which has forced scientists periodically to put forth a series of candidates to try to take the heat off. Unfortunately for them, in every case those "missing links" have been shown to be outright fakes and frauds. An excellent account is found in Icons of Evolution by Jonathan Wells (Regnery, 2000). But scientists are not deterred by such exposure of their shenanigans. They feel justified because, they insist, not enough time has passed for them to find what they need in a grossly incomplete fossil record.

The truth is that some lengthy fossil timelines are missing, but many more are well accounted for. Those have been thoroughly examined in the past 140-plus years, to no avail. In any other occupation, a 140-year-long trek up a blind alley would indicate a wrong approach has been taken. But not to scientists. They blithely continue forward, convinced of the absolute rightness of their mission and confident their fabled missing link will be found beneath the next overturned rock. Sooner or later, they believe, one of their members will uncover it, so they all work in harmonious concert towards that common goal. Individually, though, it's every man and woman for themselves.

TWEEDLEDUM AND TWEEDLEDEE

Plants and animals evolve, eh? Alright, how do they evolve?

By gradual but constant changes, influenced by adaptive pressures in their environment that cause physical modifications to persist if they are advantageous.

Can you specify the kind of gradual change you're referring to?

In any population of plants or animals, over time, random genetic mutations will occur. Most will be detrimental, some will have a neutral effect and some will confer a selective advantage, however small or seemingly inconsequential it might appear.

Really? But wouldn't the overall population have a gene pool deep enough to absorb and dilute even a large change? Wouldn't a small change rapidly disappear?

Well, yes, it probably would. But not in an isolated segment of the overall population. An isolated group would have a much shallower gene pool, so positive mutations would stand a much better chance of establishing a permanent place in it.

Really? What if that positive mutation gets established in the isolated group, then somehow the isolated group gets back together with the main population? Poof! The mutation will be absorbed and disappear.

Well, maybe. So let's make sure the isolated population can't get back with the main group until crossbreeding is no longer possible.

How would you do that?

Put a mountain range between them, something impossible to cross.

If it's impossible to cross, how did the isolated group get there in the first place?

If you're asking me just how isolated is isolated, let me ask you one. What kind of mutations were you talking about being absorbed?

Small, absolutely random changes in base pairs at the gene level.

Really? Why not at the chromosome level? Wouldn't change at the base pair level be entirely too small to create any significant change? Wouldn't a mutation almost have to be at the chromosome level to be noticeable?

Who says? Change at that level would probably be too much, something the organism couldn't tolerate.

Maybe we're putting too much emphasis on mutations.

Right! What about environmental pressures? What if a species suddenly found itself having to survive in a significantly changed environment?

One where its members must adapt to the new circumstances or die out?

Exactly! How would they adapt? Could they just will themselves to grow thicker fur or stronger muscles or larger size?

That sounds like mutations have to play a part.

Mutations, eh? All right, how do they play a part?

This game of intellectual thrust and parry goes on constantly at levels of minutiae that boggle an average mind. Traditional Darwinists are one-upped by neo-Darwinists at every turn. Quantum evolutionists refashion the work of those who support the theory of peripheral isolates. Mathematicians model mutation rates and selective forces, which biologists do not trust. Geneticists have little use for palaeontologists, who return the favour in spades (pun intended). Cytogenetics labours to find a niche alongside genetics proper. Population geneticists utilise mathematical models that challenge palaeontologists and systematists. Sociobiologists and evolutionary psychologists struggle to make room for their ideas. All perform a cerebral dance of elegant form and exquisite symmetry.

Their dance is, ironically, evolution writ large throughout science as a process. New bits of data are put forth to a peer group. The new data are discussed, written about, criticised, written about again, criticised some more. This is gradualism at work, shaping, reshaping and reshaping again if necessary until the new data can comfortably fit into the current paradigm in any field, whatever it is. This is necessary to make it conform as closely as possible to every concerned scientist's current way of thinking. To do it any other way is to invite prompt rejection under a fusillade of withering criticism.

This system of excruciating "peer review" is how independent thinkers among scientists have always been kept in line. Darwin was an outsider until he barged into the club by sheer, overpowering brilliance. Patent clerk Einstein did the same. On the other hand, Alfred Wegener was the German meteorologist who figured out plate tectonics in 1915. Because he dared to bruise the egos of "authorities" outside his own field, he saw his brilliant discovery buried under spiteful criticism that held it down for 50 years. Every scientist in the game knows how it is played and very few dare to challenge its rules.

The restrictions on scientists are severe, but for a very good reason. They work at the leading edges of knowledge, from where the view can be anything from confusing to downright terrifying. Among those who study the processes of life on Earth, they must cope with the knowledge that a surprising number of species have no business being here. In some cases, they can't even be here. Yet they are, for better or worse, and those worst-case examples must be hidden or at least obscured from the general public. But no matter how often facts are twisted, data are concealed or reality is denied, the truth is out there.

THE EMERGENCE OF DOMESTICATED PLANTS

There are two basic forms of plants and animals: wild and domesticated. The wild ones far outnumber the domesticated ones, which may explain why vastly more research is done on the wild forms. But it could just as easily be that scientists shy away from the domesticated ones because the things they find when examining them are so far outside the accepted evolutionary paradigm.

Nearly all domesticated plants are believed to have appeared between 10,000 and 5,000 years ago, with different groups coming to different parts of the world at different times. Initially, in the so-called Fertile Crescent of modern Iraq, Syria and Lebanon, came wheat, barley and legumes, among other varieties. Later on, in the Far East, came wheat, millet, rice and yams. Later still, in the New World, came maize (corn), peppers, beans, squash, tomatoes and potatoes.

Many have "wild" predecessors that were apparently a starting point for the domesticated variety, but others--like many common vegetables--have no obvious precursors. But for those that do, such as wild grasses, grains and cereals, how they turned into wheat, barley, millet, rice, etc. is a profound mystery.

No botanist can conclusively explain how wild plants gave rise to domesticated ones. The emphasis here is on "conclusively". Botanists have no trouble hypothesising elaborate scenarios in which Neolithic (New Stone Age) farmers somehow figured out how to hybridise wild grasses, grains and cereals, not unlike Gregor Mendel when he cross-bred pea plants to figure out the mechanics of genetic inheritance. It all sounds so simple and so logical, almost no one outside scientific circles ever examines it closely.

Gregor Mendel never bred his pea plants to be anything other than pea plants. He created short ones, tall ones and different- coloured ones, but they were always pea plants that produced peas. (Pea plants are a domesticated species, too, but that is irrelevant to the point to be made here.) On the other hand, those New Stone Age farmers who were fresh out of their caves and only just beginning to turn soil for the first time (as the "official" scenario goes), somehow managed to transform the wild grasses, grains and cereals growing around them into their domesticated "cousins". Is that possible? Only through a course in miracles!

Actually, it requires countless miracles within two large categories of miracles. The first was that the wild grasses and grains and cereals were useless to humans. The seeds and grains were maddeningly small, like pepper flakes or salt crystals, which put them beyond the grasping and handling capacity of human fingers. They were also hard, like tiny nutshells, making it impossible to convert them to anything edible. Lastly, their chemistry was suited to nourishing animals, not humans.

So wild varieties were entirely too small, entirely too tough and nutritionally inappropriate for humans. They needed to be greatly expanded in size, greatly softened in texture and overhauled at the molecular level--which would be an imposing challenge for modern botanists, much less Neolithic farmers.

Despite the seeming impossibility of meeting those daunting objectives, modern botanists are confident the first sodbusters had all they needed to do it: time and patience. Over hundreds of generations of selective crossbreeding, they consciously directed the genetic transformation of the few dozen that would turn out to be most useful to humans. And how did they do it? By the astounding feat of doubling, tripling and quadrupling the number of chromosomes in the wild varieties! In a few cases, they did better than that. Domestic wheat and oats were elevated from an ancestor with seven chromosomes to their current 42--an expansion by a factor of six. Sugar cane was expanded from a 10-chromosome ancestor to the 80-chromosome monster it is today--a factor of eight. The chromosomes of others, like bananas and apples, were only multiplied by factors of two or three, while peanuts, potatoes, tobacco and cotton, among others, were expanded by factors of four. This is not as astounding as it sounds, because many wild flowering plants and trees have multiple chromosome sets.

But that brings up what Charles Darwin himself called the "abominable mystery" of flowering plants. The first ones appear in the fossil record between 150 and 130 million years ago, primed to multiply into over 200,000 known species. But no one can explain their presence because there is no connective link to any form of plants that preceded them. It is as if dare I say it? they were brought to Earth by something akin to You Know What. If so, then it could well be that they were delivered with a built-in capacity to develop multiple chromosome sets, and somehow our Neolithic forebears cracked the codes for the ones most advantageous to humans.

However the codes were cracked, the great expansion of genetic material in each cell of the domestic varieties caused them to grow much larger than their wild ancestors. As they grew, their seeds and grains became large enough to be easily seen and picked up and manipulated by human fingers. Simultaneously, the seeds and grains softened to a degree where they could be milled, cooked and consumed. And at the same time, their cellular chemistry was altered enough to begin providing nourishment to humans who ate them. The only word that remotely equates with that achievement is: miracle.

Of course, "miracle" implies that there was actually a chance that such complex manipulations of nature could be carried out by primitive yeomen in eight geographical areas over 5,000 years. This strains credulity because, in each case, in each area, someone actually had to look at a wild progenitor and imagine what it could become, or should become, or would become. Then they somehow had to ensure that their vision would be carried forward through countless generations that had to remain committed to planting, harvesting, culling and crossbreeding wild plants that put no food on their tables during their lifetimes, but which might feed their descendants in some remotely distant future.

It is difficult to try to concoct a more unlikely, more absurd, scenario, yet to modern-day botanists it is a gospel they believe with a fervour that puts many "six day" Creationists to shame. Why? Because to confront its towering absurdity would force them to turn to You Know What for a more logical and plausible explanation.

To domesticate a wild plant without using artificial (i.e., genetic) manipulation, it must be modified by directed crossbreeding, which is only possible through the efforts of humans. So the equation is simple. Firstly, wild ancestors for many (but not all) domestic plants do seem apparent. Secondly, most domesticated versions did appear from 10,000 to 5,000 years ago. Thirdly, the humans alive at that time were primitive barbarians. Fourthly, in the past 5,000 years, no plants have been domesticated that are nearly as valuable as the dozens that were "created" by the earliest farmers all around the world. Put an equal sign after those four factors and it definitely does not add up to any kind of Darwinian model.

Botanists know they have a serious problem here, but all they can suggest is that it simply had to have occurred by natural means because no other intervention--by God or You Know What--can be considered under any circumstances. That unwavering stance is maintained by all scientists, not just botanists, to exclude overwhelming evidence such as the fact that in 1837 the Botanical Garden in St Petersburg, Russia, began concerted attempts to cultivate wild rye into a new form of domestication. They are still trying, because their rye has lost none of its wild traits, especially the fragility of its stalk and its small grain. Therein lies the most embarrassing conundrum botanists face.

To domesticate a wild grass like rye or any wild grain or cereal (which was done time and again by our Neolithic forebears), two imposing hurdles must be cleared. These are the problems of "rachises" and "glumes", which I discuss in my book, Everything You Know Is Wrong - Book One: Human Origins (pp. 283-285) (Adamu Press, 1998). Glumes are botany's name for husks, the thin covers of seeds and grains that must be removed before humans can digest them. Rachises are the tiny stems that attach seeds and grains to their stalks.

While growing, glumes and rachises are strong and durable, so rain won't knock the seeds and grains off their stalks. At maturity, they become so brittle that a breeze will shatter them and release their cargo to propagate. Such a high degree of brittleness makes it impossible to harvest wild plants because every grain or seed would be knocked loose during the harvesting process.

So, in addition to enlarging, softening and nutritionally altering the seeds and grains of dozens of wild plants, the earliest farmers also had to figure out how to finely adjust the brittleness of every plant's glumes and rachises.

That adjustment was of extremely daunting complexity, perhaps more complex than the transformational process itself. The rachises had to be toughened enough to hold seeds and grains to their stalks during harvesting, yet remain brittle enough to be collected easily by human effort during what has come to be known as "threshing". Likewise, the glumes had to be made tough enough to withstand harvesting after full ripeness was achieved, yet still be brittle enough to shatter during the threshing process. And--here's the kicker--each wild plant's glumes and rachises required completely different degrees of adjustment, and the final amount of each adjustment had to be perfectly precise! In short, there is not a snowball's chance that this happened as botanists claim it did.

THE EMERGENCE OF DOMESTICATED ANIMALS

As with plants, animal domestication followed a pattern of development that extended 10,000 to 5,000 years ago. It also started in the Fertile Crescent, with the "big four" of cattle, sheep, goats and pigs, among other animals. Later, in the Far East, came ducks, chickens and water buffalo, among others. Later still, in the New World, came llamas and vicuna. This process was not simplified by expanding the number of chromosomes. All animals--wild and domesticated--are diploid, which means they have two sets of chromosomes, one from each parent. The number of chromosomes varies as widely as in plants (humans have 46), but there are always only two sets (humans have 23 in each).

The only "tools" available to Neolithic herdsmen were those available to farming kinsmen: time and patience. By the same crossbreeding techniques apparently utilised by farmers, wild animals were selectively bred for generation after generation until enough gradual modifications accumulated to create domesticated versions of wild ancestors. As with plants, this process required anywhere from hundreds to thousands of years in each case, and was also accomplished dozens of times in widely separated areas around the globe.

Once again, we face the problem of trying to imagine those first herdsmen with enough vision to imagine a "final model", to start the breeding process during their own lifetimes and to have it carried out over centuries until the final model was achieved. This was much trickier than simply figuring out which animals had a strong pack or herding instinct that would eventually allow humans to take over as "leaders" of the herd or pack. For example, it took unbridled courage to decide to bring a wolf cub into a campsite with the intention of teaching it to kill and eat selectively and to earn its keep by barking at intruders (adult wolves rarely bark). And who could look at the massive, fearsome, ill-tempered aurochs and visualise a much smaller, much more amiable cow? Even if somebody could have visualised it, how could they have hoped to accomplish it? An aurochs calf (or a wolf cub, for that matter), carefully and lovingly raised by human "parents", would still grow up to be a full-bodied adult with hardwired adult instincts.

However it was done, it wasn't by crossbreeding. Entire suites of genes must be modified to change the physical characteristics of animals. (In an interesting counterpoint to wild and domesticated plants, domesticated animals are usually smaller than their wild progenitors.) But with animals, something more something ineffable must be changed to alter their basic natures from wild to docile. To accomplish it remains beyond modern abilities, so attributing such capacity to Neolithic humans is an insult to our intelligence.

All examples of plant and animal "domestication" are incredible in their own right, but perhaps the most incredible is the cheetah. There is no question it was one of the first tamed animals, with a history stretching back to early Egypt, India and China. As with all such examples, it could only have been created through selective breeding by Neolithic hunters, gatherers or early farmers. One of those three must get the credit.

The cheetah is the most easily tamed and trained of all the big cats. No reports are on record of a cheetah killing a human. It seems specifically created for high speeds, with an aerodynamically designed head and body. Its skeleton is lighter than other big cats; its legs are long and slim, like the legs of a greyhound. Its heart, lungs, kidneys and nasal passages are enlarged, allowing its breathing rate to jump from 60 per minute at rest to 150 bpm during a chase. Its top speed is 70 miles per hour, while a thoroughbred tops out at around 38 mph. Nothing on a savanna can outrun it. It can be outlasted, but not outrun.

Cheetahs are unique because they combine physical traits of two distinctly different animal families: dogs and cats. They belong to the family of cats, but they look like long-legged dogs. They sit and hunt like dogs. They can only partially retract their claws, like dogs instead of cats. Their paw pads are thick and hard like a dog's, but to climb trees they use the first claw on their front paws in the same way a cat does. The light-coloured fur on their body is like the fur of a short-haired dog, but the black spots on their bodies are inexplicably the texture of cat's fur. They contract diseases that only dogs suffer from, but they also get "cat only" diseases.

There is something even more inexplicable about cheetahs. Genetic tests have been done on them, and the surprising result was that in the 50 specimens tested they were all, every one, genetically identical with each other! This means the skin or internal organs of any of the thousands of cheetahs in the world could be switched with the organs of any other cheetah and not be rejected. The only other place such physical homogeneity is seen is in rats and other animals that have been genetically altered in laboratories.
(Cue the music from The Twilight Zone)
Cheetahs stand apart, of course, but all domesticated animals have traits that are not explainable in terms that stand up to rigorous scientific scrutiny. Rather than deal with the embarrassment of confronting such issues, scientists studiously ignore them and, as with the mysteries of domesticated plants, explain them away as best they can. For the cheetah, they insist it simply cannot be some kind of weird genetic hybrid between cats and dogs, even though the evidence points squarely in that direction. And why? Because that, too, would move cheetahs into the forbidden zone occupied by You Know What.

The problem of the cheetahs' genetic uniformity is explained by something now known as the "bottleneck effect". What it presumes is that the wild cheetah population--which must have been as genetically diverse as its long history indicates--at some recent point in time went into a very steep population decline that left only a few breeding pairs alive. From that decimation until now, they have all shared the same restricted gene pool.

Unfortunately, there is no record of any extinction events that would selectively remove cheetahs and leave every other big cat to develop its expected genetic variation. So, as unlikely as it seems, the "bottleneck" theory is accepted as another scientific gospel.

Here it is appropriate to remind scientists of Carl Sagan's famous riposte when dealing with their reviled pseudoscience: "Extraordinary claims require extraordinary evidence." It seems apparent that Sagan learned that process in-house.

It also leads us, finally, to a discussion of humans, who are so genetically recent that we, too, have been forced into one of those "bottleneck effects"

48

that attempt to explain away the cheetah.

THE ARRIVAL OF HUMANS

Like all plants and animals whether wild or domesticated, humans are supposed to be the products of slight, gradual improvements to countless generations spawned by vastly more primitive forebears. This was firmly believed by most scientists in the 1980s, when a group of geneticists decided to try to establish a more accurate date for when humans and chimpanzees split from their presumed common ancestor.

Palaeontologists used fossilised bones to establish a timeline that indicated the split came between five and eight million years ago. That wide bracket could be narrowed, geneticists believed, by charting mutations in human mitochondrial DNA--small bits of DNA floating outside the nuclei of our cells. So they went to work collecting samples from all over the world.

When the results were in, none of the geneticists could believe it. They had to run their samples through again and again to be certain. Even then, there was hesitancy about announcing it. Everyone knew there would be a firestorm of controversy, starting with the palaeontologists-- who would be given the intellectual equivalent of a black eye and a bloody nose and their heads dunked into a toilet for good measure! This would publicly embarrass them in a way that had not happened since the Piltdown hoax was exposed.

Despite the usual scientific practice of keeping a lid on data that radically differs from a current paradigm, the importance of this new evidence finally outweighed concern for the image and feelings of palaeontologists. The geneticists gathered their courage and stepped into the line of fire, announcing that humans were not anywhere near the official age range of eight to five million years old. Humans were only about 200,000 years old. As expected, the howls of protest were deafening.

Time and much more testing of mitochondrial DNA and male Y-chromosomes now make it beyond doubt that the geneticists were correct. And the palaeontologists have come to accept it because geneticists were able to squeeze humans through the same kind of "bottleneck effect" they used to try to ameliorate the mystery of cheetahs.

By doing so, they left palaeontologists still able to insist that humans evolved from primitive forebears walking upright on the savannas of

Africa as long ago as five million years, but that between 100,000 and 200,000 years ago "something" happened to destroy nearly all humans alive at the time, forcing them to reproduce from a small population of survivors.

That this "something" remains wholly unknown is a given, although Creationists wildly wave their hands like know-it-alls at the back of a classroom, desperate to suggest it was the Great Flood. But because they refuse to move away from the biblical timeline of the event (in the range of 6,000 years ago), nobody can take them seriously. Still, it seems the two sides might work together productively on this crucial issue. If only.

Apart from disputes about the date and circumstances of our origin as a species, there are plenty of other problems with humans. Like domesticated plants and animals, humans stand well outside the classic Darwinian paradigm. Darwin himself made the observation that humans were surprisingly like domesticated animals. In fact, we are so unusual relative to other primates that it can be solidly argued that we do not belong on Earth at all that we are not even from Earth, because we do not seem to have developed here.

We are taught that, by every scientific measure, humans are primates very closely related to all other primates, especially chimpanzees and gorillas. This is so ingrained in our psyches that it seems futile even to examine it, much less to challenge it. But we will.

***Bones**. Human bones are much lighter than comparable primate bones. For that matter, our bones are much lighter than the bones of every "pre-human" ancestor through to Neanderthal. The ancestor bones look like primate bones; modern human bones do not.*

***Muscle**. Human muscles are significantly weaker than comparable muscles in primates. Pound for pound, we are five to ten times weaker than any other primate. Any pet monkey is evidence of that. Somehow, getting "better" made us much, much weaker.*

***Skin**. Human skin is not well adapted to the amount of sunlight striking Earth. It can be modified to survive extended exposure by greatly increasing melanin (its dark pigment) at its surface, which only the black race has achieved. All others must cover themselves with clothing or frequent shade or both, or sicken from radiation poisoning.*

***Body Hair**. Primates need not worry about direct exposure to sunlight* because they are covered from head to toe in a distinctive pattern of long body-hair. Because they are quadrupeds (move on all fours), the thickest hair is on their back, the thinnest on the chest and abdomen. Humans have lost the all-over pelt, and we have completely switched our area of thickness to the chest and abdomen while wearing the thin part on our back.

Fat. Humans have ten times as many fat cells attached to the underside of their skin as primates. If a primate is wounded by a gash or tear in the skin, when the bleeding stops the wound's edges lie flat near each other and can quickly close the wound by a process called "contracture". In humans, the fat layer is so thick that it pushes up through wounds and makes contracture difficult if not impossible. Also, contrary to the propaganda to try to explain this oddity, the fat under human skin does not compensate for the body hair we have lost. Only in water is its insulating capacity useful; in air, it is minimal at best.

Head Hair. All primates have head hair that grows to a certain length and then stops. Human head hair grows to such lengths that it could be dangerous in a primitive situation. Thus, we have been forced to cut our head hair since we became a species, which may account for some of the sharp flakes of stones that are considered primitive hominid "tools".

Fingernails and Toenails. All primates have fingernails and toenails that grow to a certain length and then stop, never needing paring. Human fingernails and toenails have always needed paring. Again, maybe those stone "tools" were not only for butchering animals.

Skulls. The human skull is nothing like the primate skull. There is hardly any fair morphological comparison to be made, apart from the general parts being the same. Their design and assembly are so radically different as to make attempts at comparison useless.

Brains. The comparison here is even more radical because human brains are so vastly different. (To say "improved" or "superior" is unfair and not germane, because primate brains work perfectly well for what primates have to do to live and reproduce.)

Locomotion. The comparison here is easily as wide as the comparison of brains and skulls. Humans are bipedal; primates are quadrupeds. That says more than enough.

Speech. Human throats are completely redesigned relative to primate *throats. The larynx has dropped to a much lower position, so humans can break typical primate sounds into the tiny pieces of sound (by modulation) that have come to be human speech.*

Sex*. Primate females have oestrous cycles and are sexually receptive only at special times. Human females have no oestrous cycle in the primate sense. They are continually receptive to sex. (Unless, of course, they have the proverbial headache!)*

Chromosomes*. This is the most inexplicable difference of all. Primates have 48 chromosomes. Humans are considered vastly superior to them in a wide array of areas, yet somehow we have only 46 chromosomes! This begs the question of how we could lose two full chromosomes--which represents a lot of DNA--in the first place, and in the process become so much better. Nothing about it makes logical sense.*

Genetic Disorders*. As with all wild animals (plants, too), primates have relatively few genetic disorders spread throughout their gene pools. Albinism is one that is common to many animal groups as well as humans. But albinism does not stop an animal with it from growing up and passing the gene for it into the gene pool. Mostly, though, serious defects are quickly weeded out in the wild. Often, parents or others in a group will do the job swiftly and surely, so wild gene pools stay relatively clear. In contrast, humans have over 4,000 genetic disorders, and several of those will absolutely kill every victim before reproduction is possible. This begs the question of how such defects could possibly get into the human gene pool in the first place, much less how they remain so widespread.*

Genetic Relatedness*. A favourite Darwinist statistic is that the total genome (all the DNA) of humans differs from chimpanzees by only 1% and from gorillas by 2%. This makes it seem as if evolution is indeed correct and that humans and primates are virtually kissing cousins. However, what they don't stress is that 1% of the human genome's three billion base pairs is 30 million base pairs--and to any You Know What that can adroitly manipulate genes, 30 million base pairs can easily add up to a tremendous amount of difference.*

Everything Else*. The above are the larger categories at issue in the discrepancies between primates and humans. There are dozens more listed as sub-categories below one or more of these.*

To delve deeper into these fascinating mysteries, check The Scars of

Evolution by Elaine Morgan (Oxford University Press, 1990). Her work is remarkable. And for a more in-depth discussion of the mysteries within our genes and those of domesticated plants and animals, see Everything You Know Is Wrong.

BREAKING RANKS
When all of the above is taken together--the inexplicable puzzles presented by domesticated plants, domesticated animals and humans--it is clear that Darwin cannot explain it, modern scientists cannot explain it, not Creationists nor Intelligent Design proponents. None of them can explain it, because it is not explainable in only Earthbound terms.

We will not answer these questions with any degree of satisfaction until our scientists open their minds and squelch their egos enough to acknowledge that they do not, in fact, know much about their own backyard. Until that happens, the truth will remain obscured.

My personal opinion, which is based on a great deal of independent research in a wide range of disciplines relating to human origins, is that ultimately Charles Darwin will be best known for his observation that humans are essentially like domesticated animals.

I believe that what Darwin observed with his own eyes and research is the truth, and that modern scientists would see it as clearly as he did if only they had the motivation or the courage to seek it out. But for now, they don't so, until then, we can only poke and prod at them in the hope of some day getting them to notice our complaints and address them. In order to poke and prod successfully, more people have to be alerted to the fact that another scientific fraud is being perpetrated.

Future editions of Icons of Evolution will discuss the current era when scientists ridiculed, ignored or simply refused to deal with a small mountain of direct, compelling evidence that outside intervention has clearly been at work in the genes of domesticated plants, animals and humans. You Know What has left traces of their handiwork all over our bodies, all through our gene pools. All that will be required for the truth to come out is for a few "insiders" to break ranks with their brainwashed peers.

Look to the younger generation. Without mortgages to pay, families to raise and retirements to prepare for, they can find the courage to act on strong convictions. Don't expect it of anyone over forty, possibly even thirty. But somewhere in the world, the men and women have been born who will take Darwinism down and replace it with the truth.

The fat lady is nowhere in sight, but that doesn't mean she's not suiting up.

About the Author:

Lloyd Pye, born in 1946 in Louisiana, USA, is a researcher, author, novelist and scriptwriter. His independent studies over more than three decades into all aspects of evolution have convinced him that humans did not evolve on Earth, or at least are the product of extraterrestrial intervention. His book, Everything You Know Is Wrong - Book One: Human Origins, is available by ordering through http://www.iUniverse.com or Barnes & Noble at http://www.bn.com. Visit Lloyd Pye's website at 15/08/2008.

INTERLUDE

Have you ever looked out of a window on a stormy night, or day, and been awed, perhaps frightened or even terrified by the tempestuous and raging world out there, and been somewhat comforted by the thought that you are somewhat safe within the confines of your current condition/location? Your world is violently shaking, the sounds can be terrible, others may be suffering, but in your "cocoon" you feel safe. In so observing, have you ever been thankful for your safety from exposure to such terrible experiences that so obviously are presented to "those" out there who are not so safe or protected? You are not vulnerable nor susceptible to the horrors or discomforts that are obviously there for others, less prepared or less protected "others". You know people can perish in such conditions, yet you know you are "safe".

Question is: will you go out to help, rescue, or gather others?

Let me share some fascinating real facts about this earth. You will now know where to find these things when next you want to refer to them.

1: **ANKOR WAT** is a site in south east Asia covering about 1,000 km area so far discovered. It is said to be larger in area than New York, and was once home to over a million people. It is now an ancient ruin. It seems the cause of its fall and destruction was that the forests surrounding it were felled and destroyed. (possibly as a source of fuel, as seems the case of other ancient sites.) This resulted in a catastrophic change of the environment (ecology) that resulted in drought and famine. After that there were (of course) the floods. Seems that the inhabitants, not understanding the delicate relationship of the environment to them and their actions caused a disaster.

Lacking trees and forests, the local waterways, after initial following rains, silted up because of erosion. Forests attract or even help cause rains, preserve and maintain top soil; top soil provides forests: rainfall failed. When the rains finally came then floods were the result of no forests, silted up waterways.... The civilization failed and now is a ruin. This is not a unique "one off" scenario.

2: **SECROVIA TREE** is the name of a tree that is a world of environmental relationships. It allows ants to live within it. (I use the word "allows", but you make your own judgment after reading all these writings.)

Locusts in their season attack the trees, and of course everything else that grows. When this happens, the ants go out there and attack the locusts, biting them on the leg joints. (In human terms, "knees", but we have only one "knee" per "leg". Isn't life so varied and interesting?) The locusts will lose and leave the protected tree because of the unrelenting attacks of endless and painful ants. However, as a departing gesture, the locusts deposit and spew out a "glue" intended to trap ants that come into contact with it. This is obviously designed to kill off the ants. However, the ants are observed to go on rescue missions and pull out and save trapped fellow ants.

Sloths also invade this tree, and as annoying as that may be to the ants, the sloth is impervious to the ants, as is the tree to any sloth damage.

Seems like each "unintelligent" element of the events has a full understanding and measure of the others.

And the absolute winner is this.

3. **THE BRAZIL NUT.**
This nut will not survive without forests. Like most plants it needs bees to pollinate its flowers. This is the beginning of an amazing story. Be glad human survival is not so precarious.

To be an ongoing species bees need to procreate, and here the strangeness (to humans) begins. The male bee will only mate with a female bee that has a "certain" smell. That "certain" smell is only obtained by a female bee that visits and obtains it from one specific orchid. She must "steal" the orchid's smell to get a mate. (to make the next generation of bees, etc.) No forest = no orchids. No orchid = no smell = no mating. No mate = no new bees. No bees = no pollinated flowers = no nuts etc etc.

It gets infinitely more complex.

There exists only one type of rodent that can open the nut pods produced by the brazil nut tree. These pods are formidable. It took a test human with a saw half an hour to open the nut pod. The nuts are within the pod, kind of like the segments of a mandarin within the outer skin of that fruit. Now the rodent probably can not eat all of the nuts in one or two sessions, so like rodents (squirrels etc) they know to bury those left over as a stash for "later". It seems only those nuts so buried, and forgotten, by the rodent, end up sprouting and becoming potential brazil nut trees. (who will be looking for orchid smelling female bees to promote mating with obsessive male bees, and as an aside, trusting the local rodents have flourished.)

Now that is a complex relationship. If the forest is disturbed it can mean end of species.

Ah well, such is life.

003 -WHICH BODY....

"I can't do what god does either – but I am learning." Bob Maddison
22/5/09

There must be thousands of ways to introduce a subject, and probably there is no best way. It is difficult to know just how to lead most effectively into this subject, so let's start with an event that my memory recalls as a recent happening.

> *I was exploring an area to which I had never previously been, very lush and green with vegetation. It was as though on a plateau on top of a mountain, like a mesa. Odd and old ruins of some strange former inhabitants were seen, but not entered. I reached the edge of the plateau, and my progress forward came to an end. For some reason I did not think to go back in the direction from whence I came, but was compelled to go only forward, however looking over the precipitous edge, I felt that might not be possible. Maybe I could find the way and it occurred to me to check some safety first. I jumped into the air, knowing or at least trusting that if I could successfully float above the ground, then I could surely be safe to step out over the edge and drift down to the valley below. That worked, and feeling thus reassured, I did step over the edge, and yes, I was able to successfully and gently float down gracefully to the valley below.*

Now that was an interesting train of thought and decision to make, and a bold experiment to try, but in retrospect I admire the intelligence and caution involved in testing an idea before literally jumping in. At the time of course I had no idea that it was not "me" involved in that experience or decision, it was a different manifestation of 'me' that appears to come into existence in my so-called dreams. I wonder if it is all that simple and tidy though. You see "me" was surely asleep on a bed, switched off, and dreaming, so thus that other manifestation cannot surely be "me" at all, merely a phantom in a dream. Yet it showed purpose, intelligence, thinking skills, decision making skills, ability to analyze, observe, and on numerous other occasions, all the skills, pleasures, joys, tears and fears I would have thought the exclusive rights and domains of my conscious waking self. Apparently I was and am mistaken in that assumption. Not only that but check out this fact: That 'me' experiencing a rich life in what I in the waking state consider was a dream, was seemingly oblivious to what is surely the real me's existence. It acted as though it was the sole me in existence. Perhaps it was, for intelligence and awareness seemed to have been transferred to it, if not natural to it.

So, as is usual, but perhaps not mandatory – nor a universal absolute, I woke up, and the phantom me simply vanished and conscious experience returned to a more physical me of this earth. Question: if one did not wake up, but died in sleep, what happens to either manifestation of "me"? I am not going to address that issue, but raise it here as a matter of interest and to broaden our thoughts and the implications of them.

SUPER POWERS AND FLYING

A main point in the above is that when one sleeps, a dream body is experienced, and that **dream body** can act with intelligence and function much like one would if one was awake – though it seems possessed by attributes lacking in the waking state that remove many limitations of the earthly body. It is innately possessed of what we may consider 'super powers'. Different laws of nature and physics come into operation and apply. It is not encumbered by a physical body of "gross" elements, and free from laws connected with such "gross" mortal elements. Keep in mind the fact that many laws of physics as apply in this temporal world do not apply in that dream world. Thus in that dream word into which we enter, certainly we are able to "fly" at will. It is simply a matter that different laws of physics operate when in a dimension free of "mortal or physical" elements of which this world, this mortal body is a part. In that dimension it seems that simple will power, or thought, enables what to us in mortality would be "super powers".

Does that dream body ever question its existence? Does it ever ask the classical questions: "who am I", "what's it all about?', "where did I come from", "why am I here", or "where am I going". Probably not. In many respects it seems like a 'dumbed down' version of our perceived intelligence and ourselves. Certainly from the waking state some of its acts etc appear rather strange if not outrightly stupid. Is that dream body aware of its true nature? I doubt it because generally we are not possessed of that knowledge even in a waking state. Is it aware of its temporary nature, or even its fleshless existence? It does not need flesh, and functions perfectly in its environment. Perhaps it would find the concept of 'flesh' or the need for such an encumbrance rather pointless or unintelligible, were it given to philosophical thoughts. Yet this body came from somewhere and has its origins. Likewise it will 'go back' somewhere, and yet having gone back, will return again. Probably such thoughts are quite invalid, as the dream body quite simply is really "us" operating in a different dimension or manner, without the physical body.

Our dreams are as factual and eventful as our lives in mortality. Perhaps more eventful. In mortality, we can form the questions above: 'why am I here', 'where did I come from', 'who am I', 'where am I going'. We may confess total ignorance, maybe have some concepts that are valid, perhaps follow some creed blindly, kidding ourselves that we fully understand. Perhaps we just don't go there, or don't care.

The situation is that the '**dream body**' is as a duplicate of the waking body. Both suffer similar limitations, ignorance, and diversions. If we rarely, or if ever, consider the nature of the dream body, and it never seems to consider the nature of a waking body, then can we expect that we would naturally understand the nature of the mortal man, encompassing that dream body?

BODY OF EARTH

Let's have a lightning tour of life as we know or experience it. You may then at your leisure flesh it out and consider its component elements. You may be surprised how rewarding this may be.

For all of us it appears to begin with the birth of the individual. We emerge into this world from the womb naked and helpless. We are given (freely) a body, a tiny (relatively speaking) helpless little body, and emerge generally in a state of trauma. The body is literally of this earth, and can be chemically analyzed and shown as consisting of the same elements of the same atomic structure – with the same sub-atomic particles – as those of which the very earth is composed. Many will be familiar with some of the facts: the body is about 60% water, It contains x% of stated chemicals, which I do not propose to list here, and that if all the 'space' were eliminated between between atoms, and the atomic components the resultant solid matter would be about the size of a full stop on a printed page.

It follows almost without saying that this mortal earthly body is thus **illusion** itself, and about as substantial as the dream body which functions quite well with a fleshless body. I have heard it described as a hologram, and that is perhaps appropriate.

This chemical package of a body now begins its existence in a time and space we call mortality on earth. It breathes elements of the earth and assimilates some of them. It suckles, later eats, elements of the earth and likewise assimilates some of them. It is a separate miracle how elements of the earth are transformed into, say, a carrot, or an apple, and one that will not be ventured into at this time. However feel free to take time out to meditate and ponder on this most marvelous of things. The point here and now is this: From its very beginnings the individual is solely nourished by the elements of the earth. There is nothing I know of that is assimilated into the body at any time that is not of the earth. (That is a great and diversified "evolution" to explain isn't it?)

We are totally enclosed and in a 'closed' and isolated environment and condition. Everything is of the earth, our parents being exactly the same. Eventually, as we know 100%, this body will return to the earth to be buried, burned, eaten, slowly disintegrate – however you call it, re-cycled. Perhaps it's one of those 'conservation of energy' points rarely considered. But die, re-cycle, is an assured future for the physical body.

Now I cannot say that when we emerge in birth that we have any thoughts, memories, regrets, etc or not. So total is the isolation of this 'mortality', that when we are born we have no power of speech, possibly little to no sight, and no means of communication except that which we learn –discovering early that screaming quite often will get attention. There is obviously intelligence present, because we learn behavioral patterns from our environment and speech from listening and observation. In short time we find ourselves endowed with the ability to recall past events, a memory. Level of intelligence is perhaps dictated by the amount of stimulation involved, motivation to remember, communicate, etc. Point is we started out this life in a blackout, and started to learn things about this world, this life, this existence, for it is all we have and know. We accept it and think of it as our reality, the only reality. But perhaps the reality is about as substantial as the body of flesh, mostly illusion and as solid as a full stop.

Lets stop for a moment and look at the human body, or for that matter almost any other body that shares the experience of life, and see if we can come to some interesting thoughts.

The body design and its parts seem dedicated to specific mortal requirements and functions, but bear in mind that it will not function without the sum total being present, functioning, and accounted for. There is however a generous redundancy built into the system. We find that the 'body' is an ultimate **gestalt**. The sum total certainly being more than the total of its components. Now no matter how I address this, nor in what order or method, some will scream with disagreement, so in reading the following bear in mind: Yes, I know there are many ways to present this, I could go according to systems: endocrine, circulatory etc etc. But, hey, it's my writing and I will do this my way, as it is ample for the illustration. If you want it another way it's OK, just take time out now and spend the time contemplating it your way, it doesn't matter, it's another road to Rome. Probably just as good, just as valid, just as interesting, perhaps more educational. But like the opening lines state, there must be thousands of ways to present....

So this is for the non-medically or non-specialist trained among us, and I presume that is the bulk of humanity.

A digestive system, the bulk of the torso, to take elements of the earth, to absorb 'earth' into the body enabling growth and development, one of the key requirements to get from 'newborn' to 'ready to die'.

A circulatory system, the bulk of the chest, to enable one to suck in more elements in the form of the atmosphere, and absorb it into the body to ensure it stays healthy and alive. Blood to nourish and feed the elements of the body.

Skeletal frame and structure, to carry the whole thing around – including the nerves muscle and bone.

A brain and nervous system, I guess the head comes mostly to mind for simplicity, gives us control of input and output, hearing, sight, control of the body. Seems to be demonstrably connected with a lot of 'intelligence' functions. Mental activity stimulates brain areas. Interesting that. It is the mental activity that stimulates the brain, not brain activity stimulating mental activity, as in intelligence. I realize 'purists' will scream and point to clinical events that 'prove' that when x part of brain is stimulated, then a certain mental reaction will follow. (A smell, a sound, a memory etc) I know this and the average reader will know it. My point is that it is intelligence that is capable of creating the chain of events that cause brain activity, that cause reactions that release 'chemicals' that cause an effect. Let's make a simple example that is idiot proof and understandable to all. A male thinks of sex. It causes his brain to act, chemicals are created, released, and he gets physically excited, the chain of thought to brain activity thence physical action is clear. I think you see the point. Or on another level, we think of a sad thing, we cry.

It seems all things about the body are for, and specific to the physical dimension, this earth, which is as one would expect, for it is 100% of the earth. This is why, like a beautiful rose, it starts as a bud, blossoms beautifully, is attractive, develops beautifully to maturity then wilts and withers. Finally it will fall off and return to the earth of the ground below. We are as roses, flowers, and like them we thrive on fertilizer, water, and sun, also are subject to fungus, disease, and wilful people who go about cutting roses. And life in society reflects the rose garden. People see and admire the buds, love and adore the blooming flower and the mature blossom, and ignore or even fail to see the wilting rose. I am sure you see the analogy here. I for one am now largely invisible in this world.

This "mortal" flesh body **is** created of and **for this earth.** Thus it is "gross" elements of the earth and will and does die to this earth. The dream body dies to its realm as we awaken. But learn a lesson. Having died, it still lives on to experience endless new dreams. It "always" exists, surviving countless "deaths". The dream body does not need flesh, it is **not** of the physical material earth. It is a manifestation of "us" that evidences our ability to leave this temporal earth and function in what is essentially a different dimension, a dimension without the physical elements of this earth. It begs the question; "does it also permanently die?"

The baby, all and everywhere, died to its former existence, else it would not have arrived here. Only mortal flesh is made here. Earth is a "body" factory.

LIFE GIVEN

The flesh body is made of elements of the earth, "dust of the earth", to be populated or inhabited by some manifestation of intelligence, an individual, that is **not** a natural component or property of the materials of the physical earth. Mere meat, flesh, does not have the property of intelligence nor consciousness. That **intelligence** is **"cosmic" stuff**, not "star stuff" which is the lifeless chemical elements of the universe, the byproducts of known material fusion and ejected by stars. The elemental earth body is a work unit, purpose built specifically to accommodate the new arrival, the "new to this earth" individual. If that expected "new arrival" does not arrive or stay remained encased in the flesh, that body of earth is re-cycled as dead, or dying matter. Back to the earth that gave it. There just seems to be no reasonable or logical way one can consider the "new arrival", the inhabitant, to be a natural component, element, by-product or whatever, of the newly made and readied earth body. Flesh, blood and bone, are lifeless and totally devoid of intelligence as manifest by "individuals".

I read once that sleep/dreaming has been known as or called 'the little death' – does this surprise us at all if it is so named? For surely we lie ourselves down, and shut down, surrendering our consciousness to whatsoever shall follow, oblivious to the consequences, occasionally waking with memories of an existence and experience outside of our mortal experience.

So we have us 'dying' to mortality or more correctly mortal consciousness, but awaking elsewhere. (In a dream world as 'real' as this one) A dream body dying to its sphere, but our consciousness re-awaking in 'this' earthly sphere. A newborn baby arriving into this earthly sphere. A newly dying person leaving this world and leaving behind the mortal shell….

Oh yes. The mortal shell. I guarantee many a reader thought "he lost the plot", raced ahead of this writing and made their own similar correlation when I discussed the body just before. It begs the question: Where in this mortal shell is the intelligence, the essence of individual identity housed? We can name where it is not, but we cannot place it. I read, as you may have, that when taken together every part of a human body removed has failed to reveal a seat of intelligence unless the body is rendered dead. It reaches a non-functional state that is death. The body needs the whole to function and house 'us', which I said at the time. Short pay it and it won't function.

Seems like we have somewhat of a history and experience of changing bodies or dimensions or what ever you may choose to call this phenomena, but mostly we are oblivious to it.

DEATH EXPERIENCES

Some may have additional experiences probably common to mankind, but not often remembered, for strangely it is in our nature to forget such events and their significance. A death or near death experience. I have related how on a bad day of 2 cardiac arrests, culminating in almost an hour of CPR/resuscitation efforts, I was fully restored to mortal functioning. (previous book, Bob's Legacy) I also related how hospital staff could not directly answer my lovely wife when she asked if I was alive or dead. Later she was told I could be brain dead, or if not, perhaps severely changed, possibly have no memory of past events at all. Yet here I am - for a short time longer. I think it is me. I have the memories of me. I act and speak like me. Therefore it must be me. The interesting issue is this: Where is "me" located? Where was it for nearly an hour as my body shut down and heartbeats stopped? Where was it as ribs broke in CPR and staff labored for near an hour? Where was it, that it could resume habitation so comfortably, and be complete in (so far) all respects?

I awoke, but I was still in this place.

An individual awoke, but was in a different place, in the body of a newborn baby.

The baby awoke to find a prison of earthly mortal life – no escape from its isolation.

The body went to sleep, and awoke in a dream body with unlimited powers. It was no longer confined to this earth.

The dream body died, as the body woke to find itself still in mortality.

The mortal individual died, and where did he find himself..?

Where is God in all of this? Is there a god at all? This brings us back to 'those' questions.

Well before one can hope to find or understand God, by whatever name or concept, one should first discover the self. If you become able or care to understand and discover yourself, then you will be able to find and discover god/GOD. The man Jesus is recorded as saying in effect 'the truth shall make you free', and thousands of cults and goodness knows what use those words as a door opener to their weird or wonderful ways. I do not. I just say that the words are a stand alone self-evident truth, and not subject to one construing 'truth' in a unique way. Truth is reality. Reality is self-evident, elegant, simple, and requires no doctorate or theological degree to determine, explain, or understand. To be exposed to truth means we need no longer be subject to ignorance, doubts, uncertainties, worries, fears, limiting thoughts, feelings of inferiority, the dictates and control of others, flagrant demands of priestcraft, the lists are endless.

An interesting thing I have noticed is that when one is "awake" and fully in this world, one has knowledge and awareness of one's independent existence in the "dream world". In contrast, this awareness of duality is rarely if ever felt or recognized when in the dreamworld – why is this? I think this is because when we are awake in the flesh, the self/spirit (or whatever name one uses) being burdened with a "gross" flesh earther body, knows it, and recognizing this, can clearly recall and have awareness of experiences unshackled from this flesh. The duality of self is known. Thus in the waking conjoined state, one knows about the fleshless existence and experiences, of and in that other manifest reality. (Perchance some times we may be envious of "its" freedom, its powers and ability perhaps as revealed in the 2nd paragraph of this section.) However, when "asleep and dreaming", the self (etc) is **not** so burdened, it is "fleshless". Why should it mentally dwell on a seemingly inferior state of being?

Truth generates growth and development. Truth has no hidden mysteries. Truth appeals to no 'secrets' of an all-concealing god, and instead of hidden mysteries or secret initiations, it has a natural progression of understanding, rather like mathematics. No secrets, just a progression of understanding, free to all – at your pace. I love truth, for it makes me free. As a bonus it gives me understanding in an elegant mentally digestible manner.

I am sure you will love it too.

And its free, all you have to do is ask questions, discover the answers - then question the answers. When you find yourself answering most of the questions yourself and those answers raise more questions, chances are you're onto the right thing.

004 -MIND..

"Whatever the mind can conceive and believe, it can achieve" – so I learned in the late 1960's in early sales training. (Napoleon Hill or W. Clement Stone.)

That plus a thousand other such motivational phrases can be dragged out of my memory.

Not only do we as humans live, but we experience self-awareness. We have a memory of our past, and we can speculate upon our future. We can contemplate "cause and effect", but I can see my cats can also do that. Generally we deny that others, not of our species, have these inherent rights of life. Generally we choose to believe that we, the human species on earth, are unique in the universe. So unique, we alone are presumed even to have a god that favors us with his divine providence and 'blessings'. Alas, generally we fail to see that all species seem equally to enjoy such divine providence. Although I do not accept that we as humans are so unique or "special" (generally I hate the use of that word) it would seem certain that something beyond our normal mortal perceptions is going on. That qualifies as something special. Then also perhaps, all life in all forms share that "something special".

Let's see if we can formulate a precise and relevant question.

Once I asked the question: "If the universe really is untold billions of years old and of an incomprehensible size, why then would a truly cosmic god of all choose to favour this time and place to become manifest to such an insignificant life form and group on a "nowhere" planet for such a (cosmically speaking) staggeringly brief time?" A fair question I submit, but it is one that also is bound to raise other questions.

If we as mortals on this earth are indeed "star stuff" as previously defined, and also "God stuff", partakers of the essence of the "cosmic god" or the very fabric of the universe, then equally is should be asked: "why should we manifest ourselves here and now on this puny planet – when there is the immensity of limitless space and time available?" And having become manifest on this nowhere planet, why remain for a lifespan of incomprehensibly brief and short duration, when measured against the claims made about our true nature, and of the size and age of the cosmos?

If one understands the equation and question, then I think that question is a reasonable one to ask. If the concepts of mankind as a combination of "star stuff" and "god stuff are correct, then there is some explaining or understanding to be done.

Let's get to specifics and define the questioning.

1: Is there anything uniquely important about this "here and now", or the assumed reality we perceive? No, I doubt it.

2: Is there anything unique or important about the participants, about each and every one of us? MAYBE, YES. Each of us is a unique consciousness, and indeed could make a valid claim that yes, "it is all about me, I am the centre of the entire cosmos, or at least the cosmos as I uniquely see it."

Each person is really so much the centre of all that exists, it could be said that indeed when that person shuffles off from mortality, then this entire perceivable cosmos would cease to exist. (This is limited to "this" cosmos as one perceives during the mortality of that person) That person also blinks out of our, the survivors, conscious perception and our cosmos.

As a brief aside here, let me add some information. Although each person may indeed be a unique consciousness, it can be demonstrated that all of us are mentally "wired" very much the same as others. Decades ago I watched someone trying to solve a multiple maze puzzle with almost unlimited alternatives. It seemed odd at the time, but each failure was followed by a different assault on the problem in almost exactly the same order that I as a spectator was mentally using. Definitely people tend to think very much the same and along similar lines of thought.

REAL OR IMAGINERY EVENTS?

I should also add a warning here. IT IS ALSO A KEY ISSUE IN THE UNDERSTANDING OF LITERALLY ALL THINGS. The mind of man is not able to distinguish real from imaginary events. The mind will respond to "unreal" or "imaginary" events as though they were all "real" events and equally valid.

Read that again, it is vital for the understanding of ourselves and others. Then read it a third time and think what that means and could mean. The potential inherent in that FACT is totally mind blowing. The potential exists to enable Individuals to unleash "powers" normally associated only with the gods. Probably there may be a fair length of road to be traveled before that will happen. (Jesus told us that all have the ability to manifest greater "miracles" than those recorded as being made manifest by him. You doubt that? Then check your bible. It is there, and it is unqualified and totally clear.) Thing is that in this mortality we generally have, relatively speaking, minds and mental powers such as infants manifest. Generally we just do not have the understanding, the vision, and certainly not the wisdom to cope with the potentials. Perhaps most don't have the desire to learn or understand, being so engrossed and tied down with a "grab bag of mortal goodies". Many remain willingly ignorant.

In truth it means, and can be evidenced, that real and imaginary events are all the same as far as our reactions and dealing with them go. To the mind there is no such thing as "real" or "unreal", they are simply just ONE reality, regardless of how we may try to break it down. I once demonstrated this to a group I was training. It goes thus: Close your eyes and relax. Imagine you are at a tennis court with a major game in play. You are sitting alongside the net in the middle, you have a player to your right and one to the left. (I am observant, and saw the knowing looks on many faces as they resolved 'you won't catch me out on this obvious demonstration'. I didn't have to catch them out, their own mind did it, let me explain.)

I did the now obvious verbal description of watching a tennis game, player on left hits to player on right, player on right returns ball over the net in front of you to player on left. Back and forth, rapidly describing a long volley hit by hit. Needless to say, not a single head moved, and later they all sat smugly looking at me, till I asked one question: "OK, no heads moved, but hands up if your eyeballs moved back and forth in their sockets." Every hand went up. The mind, hearing and perceiving an imaginary event caused and causes a totally unnecessary physical reaction, as though it was a "real" event. You can cause this effect and demonstrate its truth in millions of ways. It was proven even with dogs, with the aid of a bell I believe.

It is so powerful a principal that it underlies almost all miracles of healing, both by faith or by the giving of medical placebos. Because of this principal people die because of a curse or voodoo, and in like manner we laugh or cry because of a story of movie. Yes an obvious fiction can cause reaction as though real.

How many of us are able to recall a dream? Maybe one dream stands out and is remembered long term. Imaginary events stored long term as though, and no different from so called real events. In those "imaginary" dreams do we not manifest some rather unusual abilities?

FALSE MEMORY.

I once saw a documentary about "false memory". Sadly it related how some have been imprisoned or lost family, friends, jobs, status etc. because of false memories induced by and at the hands of "**psychologists**" and their genre. Their counseled "victims" provide memories of abuse etc. at their questioning, and those "victims" believe in their reality to such an extent that testimony has convicted and imprisoned innocent people. Doubtless many have suffered death as a result of equally false memories. (As opposed to actual false evidence as normally understood.)

Further it is demonstrated that an individual when made vulnerable can acquire false memories about the self, and in consequence can be made to really believe they have done some things or accept some things that are just not true or real. What is commonly known as "**brain washing**" falls within this category. But the category is far more extensive and its results far more insidious.

Consider the following quote relating to false memory.

The game we play is let's pretend
and pretend we're not pretending.
We choose to forget who we are
and then forget that we have forgotten.
Who are we really?
(we are) the centre that watches
and runs the show
that chooses which way it will go
the "I AM" consciousness -
that powerful loving perfect reflection
of the cosmos.
But in our attempt to cope with early
situations we chose or were hypnotized
into a passive situation to avoid
punishment - or the loss of love.
We chose to deny our response/ability
pretending that things just happened
or that we were being controlled -
taken over.

We put ourselves down, and have become
used to this masochistic posture, this
weakness, this indecisiveness...
but we are in reality free,
a centre of cosmic energy.
Your will is your power - don't pretend
you don't have it - or you wont.
(Bernard Gunther)

We should begin to awaken, and begin to see how such things as "faith healing", miracles, and much unusual phenomena are now within the reach of understanding and can and do have a valid and actual existence. However these things are generally unmeasurable. No "proof" as credential waving "experts" demand, is forthcoming, just actual experienced reality. Yes, I have witnessed so much for which such proof would be asked in vain.

A final part of the warning: FEAR itself has been defined as 'False Evidence Appearing Real'. However to continue.

WHY HERE AND NOW?

Why here and now? Is it random? Is it planned or part of some grand plan?

By way of introducing a concept let me say that so called "eastern sages" etc. have been saying for as long as our history itself, that this world and life is all illusion.

If so, then time and space as we understand them in mortality simply must also be illusion, and not really exist. Wouldn't that be a tidy way to dispose of the part of the question that asks "why here and now?" Do I hear or perceive a veil of ignorance and misunderstanding beginning to tear wide open?

Just possibly there is no "here and now" as we see or imagine it, but just that cosmic universal "**NOW**" that the cosmic GOD/entity alone was presumed to experience, not bound by time and space as it seems to us "mortals". It has long been suggested that in fact there only exists a state called "now". Perhaps that state of "now" only appears to change and move to create an illusion of passage of time. Certainly we can only ever really exist in, and experience a condition of "now". Are all other experiences in the mind? Remember science now understands that in physics, at sub-atomic levels there does exist a universal "now" that transcends time and space as we know them. (Hence "omnipresence" & particles aware instantly with no regard of "distance".)

It is also certain that a "past" or a "future" do not actually exist, these being constructs of the mind, and one is totally unable to go to or visit either to dabble with changing things. The classical "time travel" of fiction and Doctor Who seems impossible for the want of an actual or real venue. It seems we stay "here and now".

I for one have had difficulty coming to grips with "linear time" and its consequences and paradoxes. One is forced to conclude and accept that there must of necessity be untold and unlimited local "now" states. Individuals being separated/distanced by space, each individual as the centre of his own sphere, have a unique "now" not experienced by anyone else exactly as he experiences his "now". The distances, no matter how small, mean that all events conveyed by sight or sound experience a delay in transmission from person to person, caused by the limiting speeds of light and sound. End result – each person's "now" varies. Not a very practical situation it would seem. Or is there something wrong with that picture and logical conclusion, or our understanding of things?

SLEEP AND DREAMS.

Previously we looked at the body we experienced and from which we operated when asleep, the "dream body". To us, on the waking side of the dream, all of that and the experiences are illusion. Illusion that evaporates into nothing but perhaps a memory once we have "passed on" from the sleeping dream state and entered back into our conscious waking state. Equally, I am sure, when we are in the sleep/dream state, that side is deemed the reality, and perhaps our waking state is not even known about, acknowledged as existent, nor considered as any form of recognizable reality. It begins to appear that **generally** each state is largely unaware and ignorant of the other state. They are as strangers each to the other. How absolutely fascinating that is, and what potentials could exist when the two states meet and merge each with the powers and abilities of the other. Each state is of course a manifestation of the **same Individual**. A fractured and fragmented Individual.

Sitting here firmly rooted into the waking conscious mortal state with its perceptions of reality and linear time, there is something unsettling about this evident lack of cohesive consistency of experiences and yet of us having a body form and experiences that are demonstrably illusion when awake or conscious. At the same time also being able to know that we have in reality a second form or manifestation (the dream body and experiences) seemingly independent of the other. Yet such certainly seems to be the reality of the situation. Are we beginning to see much strangeness in this situation? Do we begin to see some flaws appearing in our understanding of what we generally and unhesitatingly accept as ourselves? **Are time and space as "we" understand it, a reality?   In fact, are even "we" a reality?**

All matter is mostly space between its sub-atomic parts. An atom is like a galaxy, SEEMINGLY mostly unoccupied empty space. The actual solid matter in an atom is as a grain of sand in a house. The actual "matter" in a human body is about the size of a typewritten full stop, relatively speaking. Recent writings suggest basic particles (electrons) actually have NO substance.

So here we sit. Uncomfortably close to the brink of provable (? Prove that) non-existence, yet we actually exist. WE EXIST.

Science would have me submit "proof" that we exist. It would further require "proof" that I have intelligence. It would require untold "proofs" that I can have a language and speak – enough. When will one submit "proof" that science is as religion, and all bound in eternally self-replicating mental and intelligence constipation.

There are infinitely more significant questions to address. Here come some of them.

If we accept/consider mortality is, as claimed, on a level equal to 'what we experience as dreams' then what are we? I, for one, of mortals, scream for help and understanding, because all of this implies that nothing much about me, or my world, is in fact REAL. Have I seen it all in the movie, "The Matrix", and if so, missed something?

So here is what we need to come to grips with: when awake we believe the dream body and state is all "unreal" and "illusion". Our mind tells us that.   When we are asleep and in the dream world, we are generally oblivious to any other form of "reality" or existence.   In waking conscious state we can by use of logic, reason, and with understanding of science/physics, give ample evidence that in fact we have no real form or substance and that all is "empty space and energy", therefore we should not even exist.

It brings one to an awful reality. Time and space as we have been led to understand them most likely do not have actual existence or meaning. Everything seems to be illusion perceived by "our" mind and ultimately of no real substance. Even "our" own minds are really much the same as almost all others. We are as bits of **shattered glass** all originating from the one original sheet of glass, just separated by an "event". That "event" is our arrival into this state and place we call "life on earth, mortality here and now". Just as each fragment or chip of glass has no memory or concept of its origin in the larger pane, so we have no memory or concept of our true source or origin.

YOU ARE THE CENTRE OF THE COSMOS.

One cold sobering thought seems certain, without each individual's continued existence within this state, then probably all of this state is lost and would cease to exist in **his** cosmos. Thus each individual is indeed the centre of "his" entire cosmos, and yes, it IS all about that individual. Each of the rest of us are merely bit players with a minor or even no role in his cosmos. Thus as each leaves this cosmos by mortal death, so ends the entire illusion, including all the bit players, yes even us. Each Individual's perceptions and experiences are the only valid reality for that person. But then I have experienced dreams wherein other known mortals appear, and if I have experienced such, then so surely must everyone. Indeed in dreams even those known to be dead in mortality appear and take an active role. But all these appearances are surely illusions, mere phantoms. I hope.

Now that raises yet another question that needs to be asked and hopefully understood. I think that is a sure sign that logic has not failed, when progress is still able to be made without coming to an impassable "brick wall", or sinking to religion's trick of dismissing issues as a "mystery of god", or science's trick of dismissal as a "missing link" or a not yet found/discovered secret.

The question is: Why does it all seemingly continue as **linear time**, with the illusion being carried over from generation to generation? Surely illusion should come to an end. Surely it should not perpetuate, outlasting those who create or participate in it. What of accountability? What of purpose? The dream ends as does the movie or the novel, and we are able to see the distinction between those and what we consider to be the "real". Where is the distinguishing line between what I suspect is illusion and that which passes as reality? Is it really seamless?

The dream goes on. The illusion continues. I live and exist within my own purpose created life and cosmos. All else are "props". Everyone is the same. Thus billions of cosmic individual's bubbles exist, some overlapping, often enclosing complete bubbles that are not our own individual ones. As one bubble is extinguished others come into existence, sometimes at the same time, sometimes sharing only a piece of time, sometimes one never experiencing the other.

Each bubble inhabitant has his own "illusion" life, world, and cosmos. Each shares his illusion, his individual reality with others that co-exist. Each shares his experiences, his beliefs, values, perceptions with others. We share our perceived universe and we accept the thoughts and perceptions of others, from numerous sources, even ancient records. We accept these as valid and thus perceive all that is so presented to us as actual and factual reality – we imprint it into our "mind" and it becomes our ongoing reality. Thus we participate in shared "communal" illusions. But are "facts" (perceptions, interpretations mostly) presented to us necessarily actual or factual? "It aint necessarily so." For example, there exist numerous alternative perceptions as to who built the ancient pyramids of Egypt, of why and when. In short there are different realities to different people for the same data. We have all heard of, and probably experienced "differences of opinion" from other people. This is a simple case of the same information or data being interpreted differently with the result that their "facts" are somewhat different from our acceptable "facts".

But perhaps there really is only an eternal "now", and changes in our perceptions and "now" state, being interpreted as, or seeming as linear time, confuse us. The illusion does not "continue"- it just "is".

Having accepted some of our perceptions and those obtained from outside ourselves as the only acceptable reality, we then share it and even bequeath it to others, deemed as "the next generation", too carry on and continue the illusions we held. We accord it historical importance to ensure the legend continues for presumed millennia of this earth. But was it reality? We have heard that only the victors have the privilege of writing the history. But if we have not had the "history" presented or shared with us – then we do not perceive it at all, and thus it has NO reality to us. Kind of like the noise of the tree falling in the forest if no one is there to hear it. Does it make a noise? Is this becoming slowly more clear? Or does it simply confuse and hurt the head?

In this manner we were taught by parents, or at the laps and later the schools, classrooms etc. of others. The illusion passes from one to the others. The common illusion becomes firmly established and accepted as true and valid. Yes, we all "know" that Vlad was a really evil and terrible person; but was it really so?

None of this necessarily requires or actually really proves "linear time" – it CAN all occur in an eternal universal "now" state. It is perception or experiences that change, and change only infers or implies time elapsed. This plus the reality of other entities or Individuals entering (as new beings or otherwise) or leaving our allowable, perceivable and personal/Individual "now" reality, give us an impression of past and future. In other words we give a special name to thoughts of events that are obviously not actually taking place in our current "now" state.

Back to where we began this section. The mind cannot distinguish real (by whatever definition) from imaginary (again by whatever definition) events. The mind treats even the most obvious illusion as a reality. (Do we not cry etc. in movies?) We adopt the perceived reality of others and demonstrably allow such to become our own reality.

In this sphere we see things made that rust, rot, fall apart, get lost and ultimately recycle into the recycling cosmos. Is anything new in a cosmos seen as unknown billions of years old that has given life experience to undreamed of numbers? Could well be that untold thousands of years ago in perceived linear time man on earth made planes and bombs also, and dreamed he was the ultimate purpose of "it all". It cannot be doubted that undreamed of numbers of life cycles must have passed and that it is increasingly obvious that this tiny span of existence here and now is not the reason for the existence of an entire cosmos. (What a waste of resources if that were the case) It is an indisputable reality that other Individuals enter and leave our personally experienced cosmos.

LEARNING AND EXPERIENCE

We may ask, why is nothing new (to us) being dreamed up? Why are we not now at the stars? Why do we still use petrol in cars using rubber tyres on road surfaces? I think it has to do with capacity and overload. Or that we do share a common illusion. Each participant in this existence has to start at the very beginning and learn, for example, that 1 plus 1 does equal 2. Further, that math does have meaning, not just as a combination of words or as an abstract thought. By the time one has become the rocket scientist or physicist, their time is about all gone. He "blinks" into and out of the "now" state. Transmitted and shared knowledge has become so vast people are forced to specialize in ever narrowing fields of study.

So much for the learning. People do not gain wisdom or experience from learning, but from the participation in and doing of things, and in the doing of things all people, as pointed out, being somewhat all mentally wired up the same, make the same choices and judgments, and thus make the same mistakes. So yes, Napoleon and Adolf both thought the Russian plains invasion was a good idea. Both made the same mistake as no doubt countless un-named others in antiquity have, and yet future others will also. We cannot and will not learn from books or history, because our mentality and perceptions are that we alone are "special". Thus some blunder on, oblivious to the fact that the hordes facing them are each unto themselves equally "special" and not sharing our plans or dreams. Endlessly repeating history.

OUR POTENTIAL

Perhaps its time to move on from this and turn thoughts to such things as "what then is our individual potential?" Perhaps we should gently prod at that which was previously held or believed to be the impenetrable, imponderable mysteries. I think there is a ray of light and understanding shining from behind the doors closed on knowledge. Maybe we CAN gain that knowledge and in the words of Genesis, "become as one of" the gods. I believe that in asking the right questions in the right sequence we can build upon understanding until a perfect knowledge is attained.

Above all, there surely is a sequence to be followed to get there, just as surely as there is a sequence that needs to be followed in the understanding of, say, mathematics. If you do not learn basic mathematics, the simple counting, add, subtract, multiply and divide, then you may never understand what lies beyond that stage, say of geometry, economics, or of quantum physics etc. Even then, if one does not master that higher or advanced stage, how shall we proceed to where we can design then later with yet more ability, build pyramids, bridges, cars, or rockets, and perchance ultimately even build worlds, planets, galaxies, or new universes.

Now, about our future potentials once we unite our fragmented Individual selves....
(Or is that the state some visualize as or call a "resurrected body"?)

It could be that what we call "death" is just really "walking" out of this "now" room, and opening a door and going into another "now" room. My memory certainly plays back the actual experience that the death, no matter how painful and slow it may have appeared to onlookers, was really quite painless and instant. Onlooking witnesses to my deaths in May 2003 reported and recorded the most horrible of convulsions, gurgling, and such things. It was only in the coming back to this side of mortality that the pain was experienced with almost unbearable "reality", such as all my ribs broken, sternum broken, tongue chewed to an ugly blacked useless mass, and other not nice things.

(I recommend you mentally play around with that universal eternal "now" concept – but do take a break once your mind or head starts to hurt because of its stretching and bending looking for comprehension.)

005 – "WHY" ARE WE?

Men occasionally stumble on the truth, but most of them pick themselves up and hurry off as if nothing had happened.
Winston Churchill

The whole key to understanding each seemingly isolated fact is to ask "why", or "how" or other appropriately phrased question that will lead to the full understanding of the issue and give ability to correlate it with other information or facts. Only then can a full, clear, and cohesive explanation or understanding be achieved. It's kind of like a **jigsaw** puzzle. You see the piece, and get some vague idea of where it goes, but until you have built up the pieces around it, you cannot be totally sure if your thinking was right. Perhaps it is a talent, but it surprises me that so few else seem to come up with the same big picture that once understood, is capable of fully explaining *everything* quite satisfactorily and without the dogma and trappings of science or religion. Perhaps one has to look for things in a specific manner to get a "big picture".

SOME THINGS THAT YOU REALLY MUST LEARN AND NEVER FORGET:

If you haven't done so already that is. These are generally not understood, and will have a profound effect on how your life will unfold henceforth.

1: You are *not* your body. That body, a bag of flesh and bones etc., elements of this temporal earth is really "just" a bio-mechanical device that the *true you* uses solely while operating in this temporal, earther, mortal, or call it what you will, dimension. When a body is "dead" and being buried or otherwise disposed of, it is **not** that person that is being buried or whatever, but literally just the mortal star stuff remains. If you have trouble understanding this, then go back to *bobslegacy* and have a read or re-read of the appropriate sections. "You" get around in it, and view only a limited amount of what is available (because the mortal eyes and senses are effectively limited or dumbed down to see or perceive a mere fraction of what really exists) through those windows we call eyes. (Some have senses that are less restricted, and are able to effectively "see" more. These are they who we call seers, sensitives, psychics, etc. or generally refer to as nutters.) Understand "You" are not just mere *star stuff.* The body of flesh is **just one of the bodies** available and on call for our use.

Remember that dream body? When used, we and our intelligence are located within that dream body, and "out there" interacting with other entities, doing things, having adventures, doing heaps, all without the flesh body we often mistake as "us". Start to take note of and remember dreams. You will find that your true intelligence operates effectively with all the senses, emotions, and feelings we assume to be available only to awake states. You will taste the dust in your mouth, feel the full range of emotions. It's every bit as complete as the awake state, but with **additional abilities.** Enough on this now, but start really thinking about it all.

Then there is also the whole subject of "**astral projection**" or the same phenomena by whatever name you may call it. **Paul** in the bible had an interesting way of saying it: "*I knew a man in Christ above 14 years ago, (whether in the body, I cannot tell; or whether out of the body, I cannot tell: God knoweth) such an one caught up to the third heaven. And I knew such a man, (whether in the body, or out of the body, I cannot tell: God knoweth:) How he was caught up into paradise, and heard unspeakable words, which it is not lawful for a man to utter." 2 Corinthians Ch 12. (King James Version)* Some may call it spirit separation, some may call it hallucination or a bad "best forgotten" experience, even drugs. However once you have done the journey, you will have no doubt that here is yet another body one can experience without taking the star stuff mortal body in tow. Intelligence is exteriorized from the mortal body, and finds itself operating within a fully functional alternative body.

Additionally there is a body that is manifest when the mortal body is in a dead or dying state. For the entire personality, memory, and contents of the mind of an individual is preserved in full, with all those memories, personal traits, etc. able to resume normal life should it later restore itself to within the star stuff body. This is how a brain dead flatlining body may be successfully **resuscitated** and the individual fully restored to functional life. The true "self" was effectively "parked up" and external to the body of flesh and bones for a while to allow time before an irreversible decision to fully and permanently vacate the body of flesh.

Bottom line: get to know, understand, and accept your true nature and who or what exactly you are. You are not a mortal body, and demonstrably able to survive without that body.

2: Your brain is not the seat or center of your intelligence etc. The brain is an element and part of the mortal body, composed of star stuff, and "just" part of the hardware package that comes with life and a body suitable for this mortal dimension. "Just" is so inadequate however, for it is an extremely fine **quantum interface** that connects the true you to the controls of the mortal body. (To continue the analogy, "you" are the software without which the hardware is useless, inactive, and literally mere dead elements) Remember you can stop using the physical brain, as in coma or brain dead, and find later that if or when the mortal body and brain is taken up for use again, the same true you is restored to the driver's seat. Again, this is why some resuscitations are successful, and the person "returns" to function within the body again, while in other unsuccessful cases, though life may be preserved, and the body alive, it remains brain dead. Too much damage and it becomes useless for its true purpose, that of quantum interface. Such a damaged body is rejected by the individual and left for recycling.

Oh dear, numerous case histories exist of near death experiences wherein people have said they were "told" to return to the body, or pushed back into it. They are only called "near death experiences" simply because permanent death did not occur, but rest assured, in most cases they were really "dead". Or as Lyall Watson may have it, at least a little bit dead. Yes, there are such things as "a little bit dead" and **"temporary death"**. At times death is reversible.

I leave it to you to do the research and get the details, but personally I have experienced a "little bit dead" and "quite considerably dead" and come back to reclaim the body and the brain for further use. All the memories, personality, the entire package that manifests as "me", that was "parked up" somewhere while the body was flatlining and shutting down, dead (resulting in a totally inactive brain) restored to the body, reactivated the brain and body, reclaiming it for further use. Though doctors expected a brain dead drooler to result at best, the resuscitations proved effective simply because the true self returned from wherever it went for the time it took to make the star stuff body suitably habitable and useful again. The death was reversed, and life re-instated.

3: Don't blindly believe the so-called experts or authorities. Their track record is not too good. People were killed once for disagreeing with their assertions that the earth was no only flat, but the center of all that there is or can be. Men like **Galileo** often had to hide their discoveries. Do the research; doctors and the medical profession actually cause the death of more people than from any other cause. Dentists still cram teeth with proven deleterious **amalgam** fillings containing some 40% mercury, one of the most dangerous of heavy metals. Then of course the health experts of the various ministries, the governments etc., all under guidance of the "experts", dump the most toxic of chemicals into our water supplies, I speak mainly of **fluoride**. Do some research on fluoride, for instance, do a google on "fluoride and Nazis". The issue of fluoride will be taken up in more detail later when we come to consider its true purpose in being force-fed to populations. The list of experts in error is almost endless.

So if the dentist says you need a root canal, or a doctor says you need **chemotherapy** or radiotherapy, you may probably be much better off not taking that advice. Learn to think for yourself and to doubt or at least reserve decision on all things till you have done a full job of researching for the truth.

Learn to ask an appropriate question, then seek the answer yourself.

4: Your personal guru or mentor will not show up, they don't exist. Many decades ago, when this body was much younger (see how "that" thinking should work?) and the world's population was about half of what it is now, I read that "when you are ready, your guide, guru or mentor will turn up" and I kind of believed that or hoped it would be the case. Wow what a nice quick fix that would be for the void in understanding, knowledge and wisdom.

Some 40 years later, the guru has not showed up. What did show up were a lot of teachers of falsehoods and errors. If you look for the quick fix, it is almost guaranteed you will be shunted down a sidetrack to become anchored and stunted in some total dead end and erroneous path. I know of many good people blindly believing they have achieved ultimate heaven on earth, truth or wisdom, singing their hymns, or chanting the mantras while anchored with a teacher at a "dead end going nowhere" or "no further than here" state. Although things may feel good at first, however like eating tasty but bad oysters, ultimately it'll do you no good. So be wary of the feel good **proselyters**, the select groups that may promise heaven either now on earth or later as some vague unearned reward. You must learn all things for yourself, and you must *prove all things* for yourself. You will need to question all things and accept absolutely nothing on **faith**, or simply because "someone" makes claims or assertions *expecting* them to be accepted , believed or followed on their say so.

I know of one religious group which teaches that once the leader has spoken or made a proclamation, then it is not the prerogative of members to even think about the issue, but to accept it as the word of god himself.

(Yes "himself") Now that's a guaranteed recipe for disasters at all sorts of levels.

....

You cannot idly ask about the meaning or purpose of life, expecting to find enlightenment, without first knowing about and understanding your true, full and precise nature correctly. If you want answer to those questions then it will only make any sense if you know "yourself". However do you really want to know the purpose or meaning of life?

Have you ever vaguely felt that there is more going on than you may have full understanding or knowledge of? Have you ever felt or suspected that a lot of what has been happening, reported on, or claimed as fact in this world may all be a con? Have you ever really wondered why or marveled about the sheer amount of disharmony, conflict, confusion, and abuses of all sorts so prevalent in the world? Are you a little concerned about the seeming progressive impoverishment and enslavement of the world's populations?

All this and more, lots more, will be dealt with as we progress. We will make every effort to present all things without the trappings of awe, mystery, and all of the pompous pretentiousness common to those expounding matters that touch on religion and science. I make no claims for the accuracy of anything, and certainly do not present anything as one with authority or a mandate from undisclosed "higher sources". These will be the reasonings, correlations, and thinking of Bob alone. Please do not be offended if somethings so presented go against your personal bias or accepted beliefs, but understand that most commonly accepted dogma are contrary to other dogma, and thus at best, highly suspect of not being really totally correct.

A word of warning: Be prepared to become very uncomfortable, and very, very afraid. Some of the content will certainly be very disturbing for many.

006 – OTHER'S WISDOM, new conclusions

"The great tragedy of science - a beautiful hypothesis slain by an ugly fact." - Thomas Huxley

Paul Davies, SUPERFORCE, 1984 Simon & Schuster hardcover.

*"The weird effects of quantum physics and relativity on our traditional ideas of space and time imbue the world with a vagueness and subjectivity the belies its everyday normality. Normality is a consequence of the exceeding limited range of experience with which we are familiar. In our daily lives we never travel at speeds great enough for timewarps and spacewwarps to become noticeable, and most of us do not delve into the fuzzy and nebulous realm of the atom. **Yet the rational, orderly, commonsense world of experience is a sham.** Behind it lies a murky and paradoxical world of shadowy existence and shifting perspectives.*

*The nebulous surrealism exposed by the new physics is particularly acute when it comes to matter. The solid dependability of, say, a rock, reassures us of the concrete existence of objects in the external world. **Yet here again closer scrutiny undermines commonsense impressions.** Under a microscope the material of the rock is revealed to be a tangle of interlocking crystals. An electron microscope can uncover the individual atoms, spaced out in a regular array **with large gaps in between. Probing the atoms themselves, we find that they are almost entirely empty space.** The tiny nucleus occupies a mere trillionth (10 to –12) of the atoms's volume. **The rest is populated by a cloud of neither-here-nor-there ephemeral electrons, pinpricks of solidity whirling about in oceans of void. Even the nucleus, on closer inspection, turns out to be a pulsating package of evanescent particles. The apparently concrete matter of experience dissolves away into vibrating patterns of quantum energy."* ------*"Especially attractive is the strong holistic flavour of the new physics."* (*pages 37/38*)

"….we shall see how two particles, even when apparently isolated by great separation, are nevertheless linked into a coherent pattern of behavior…..In some mysterious way the electron encodes information about a comparatively vast structure in its neighbourhood, and responds accordingly…..evidently the macroscopic and microscopic worlds are intimately interwoven." (sounds like the ancient "as it is above so it is below, as it is below, so it is above." Philosophy. Also reminds me of the principle of "super position" where something can be in two locations at the same time. Also smells like the old claims of clairvoyants, that

everything has its own vibration and aura. Spooky? Yes we will get to "spooky" later in the natural sequence once thought altering concepts have been presented.)

"...*The best known lepton is the electron. Like all leptons it appears to be an elementry point like object. As far as we can tell, an electron has no internal structure, i.e. it is not 'built out of' anything......another well known lepton, ...of the chargeless variety is the neutrino.... In spite of their intangibility, neutrinos enjoy a status unmatched by any other known particle, for they are actually the most common objects in the universe, outnumbering electrons or protons by a thousand million to one.* In fact the universe is really a sea of neutrinos, punctuated only rarely by such impurities such as atoms.* It is even possible that neutrinos collectively outweigh the stars, and therefore dominate the gravity of the cosmos.*" (pages 83/84)*

"*It is a curious fact that the ordinary matter in the universe is made from just the two lightest leptons (the electron and its neutrino) and the two lightest quarks (up and down). If the other leptons and quarks suddenly ceased to exist it is probable that very little would change in the world.*" (page 90)*

"*...The German physicist Otto Frisch, the discoverer of nuclear fission, describes the classical picture as follows: 'It takes the line that there is definitely an outside world consisting of particles which have location, size, hardness and so on. It is a little more doubtful whether they have colour and smell; still, they are bona fide particles which exist there whether or not we observe them.'*

"*We might call this classic philosophy 'naïve realism'.*

"*In quantum physics this simplistic classical relationship between the whole and its parts is inadequate. The quantum factor forces us to perceive particles only in relation to the whole. In this respect it is wrong to regard the elementary particles as things that collectively assemble to form bigger things. Instead the world is more accurately described as a network of relations.*

"To the naïve realist the universe is a collection of objects. To the quantum physicist it is an inseparable web of vibrating energy patterns in which no one component has reality independently of the entirety; and included in the entirety is the observer." (pages 48/49)

*"The source of the trickery can be traced to Heisenberg's uncertainty principle as it relates to the behaviour of energy. In Chapter 2 it was explained how the law of energy conservation can be suspended by quantum effects for a very short interval of time. **During this brief duration energy can be 'borrowed' for all manner of purposes, one of which is to create particles.** Any particles produced in this way will be pretty short lived, because the energy tied up in them has to be repaid after a minute fraction of a second. **Nevertheless, the particles are permitted to pop out of nowhere, enjoy a fleeting existence, before fading once again into oblivion.** This evanescent activity cannot be prevented. Though space can be made as empty as it can possibly be, there will always be a host of these temporary particles whose visit is financed by the Heisenberg loan. **The temporary 'ghost' particles cannot be seen, even though they may leave physical traces of their existence. ...***

"What might appear to be empty space is, therefore, a seething ferment of virtual particles. A vacuum is not inert and featureless, but alive with throbbing energy and vitality. A 'real' particle such as an electron must always be viewed against this background frenetic activity. When an electron moves through space, it is actually swimming in a sea of ghost particles of all varieties – virtual leptons, quarks, and messengers, entangled in a complex melee..." (pages 104/105)

One could go on and on, quoting the words. But just the few words above give us some unbelievable information. Factual information based on physics.

My, what a wonderful world and time we live in. We can understand laws and principles. We can understand some mechanics of the universe. We can begin to understand life, how it may have originated. We have insights into creation, and just possibly we can in truth begin to intelligently (without need for "faith") perceive what we call GOD. And we can get an insight into how 'little old us' fits in to all 'this'. Or do we? Do we even have the capacity to mentally correlate and digest it all and its meaning? Some will, some may in part, some will not, most will not care. Ask yourself why this is, why such a variety of interest/response? Now, let us try to make some *understanding out of all the "data"*.

I am going to try to write this as intelligently and sequentially relevant as possible. This will take countless revisions before the result you are reading will be released. Even then, it may not be coherent enough. I pray to be able to write in language that all may understand, for in the understanding of this writing, one will have access to all that there is. To all that our capacity will allow understanding and access.

Here Goes.

We have before us two seemingly opposing views on and of reality. Each will seem to deny not only the existence of the other, but even of it's possible existence. The well proven knowledge of quantum physics and of the ultimate 'construction' of matter as we know it, will prove it an illusion. The above quotes seem to me to be adequate evidence of that. Simply put, we do not exist, nothing exists, there is only a seething 'quantum sea', a 'solid' universe of particles that creates and uncreates and is, yes "alien" to our understanding. There is not even the tiniest area within one trillionth of the area within the space of the components of a subatomic particle that this force is not present. It is this force which denies and 'proves' we do not exist and are not real.

That "force" exists. Call it what you will. Background radiation, Prana, Aether, Spirit, It simply does not matter what you call it, it exists. It is in fact the fabric of the universe. Once we can mentally digest that this exists, then and only then can we proceed with our quest. If you cannot or do not have the capacity to understand this, then stop reading this section now. Have a nice life.

If you do understand this, then one can go further. Heck, can one go further with a 'quantum sea' of unlimited power? And we are part of it? The "God stuff" and not the "star stuff" I wrote about earlier? Buckle up and go for a ride.

■■■

The quantum sea is the fabric upon which all things seem to be painted, the origin of all we can see, understand, that can exist ever in any dimension. It IS THE CANVAS. THIS IS WHERE "GOD" BEGINS TO ENTER MORTAL THINKING. What is interesting is that for millennia we have heard of it through the "mystics", as prana, the spirit world etc etc. By logic it evidences nothing can be real or exist beyond its own self-existence.

"Mortal life" is our current actual experience and awareness. It is all we know, and the sum total of awareness and existence. It is where "ME" is located, and "me" really experiences a here and now that seems denied by quantum physics. Try as one may to

understand Quantum physics, and its ramifications, "I" still do exist, have life, and see a universe whose existence is repudiated by quantum physics. To me time and space actually exist and have tangible reality. Matter is solid, time passes, I have a past, present, and future. I can even bleed. My reality cannot be denied as it is experienced.

■■■

And thus far we have just two seemingly contradictory conditions. There may well be more dimensions. There is a well-reported and recorded so-called "**astral world**". Please do not sigh and mentally turn off. Read on and understand. It is a dimension wherein one is located when one's intelligence is separated from the physical body and ventures off "ex parte". Not talking about dreams etc, but when one leaves the physical body and "drifts" or "flys" off with awareness of the event as it is actually happening. This is not "dead" nor a near death experience etc. It is a temporary separation of mind and body, well documented which I do not intend to go into here, do the research if you doubt,

More than these, shall we say three levels, there are lots more.

Most familiar with mortals is the **dream world**. A dimension of mind and experience that "seems" to have no actual or tangible reality. In this state we experience events almost exactly like we do in mortality, including memory of the "events" experienced during the dream.. Only careful observation and recording will reveal that a lot of "memories" that we have do not originate in normal waking state mortal life but to this dream state. (actual experience: walking through supermarket in waking life and seeing glue sticks at $2.95, I recalled how I knew they were at 80 cents at the $2 shop, but was once charged $4.95 for the same item and objected. This "knowing they were 80 cents etc" part was in reality memory of a dream event where I objected to being asked for $4.95) Such are the specifics of memories made or caused by dreams. Hell, I can accurately recall **KNOWN DREAM EVENTS FROM OVER 40 YEARS AGO,** and if I have such recall, then others must also have that ability.

Recall that the mind of man cannot distinguish real from imaginary events. Do not try to tell me this dimension of reality does not exist. Even our imaginings can create long-term reality type memory, later possibly confused with actual real events. Where else is the source of so many great novels, movies etc. Events from those can find their way into our personal memories, and confused as 'ours'.

Figure me this: If my dreams that seem uniquely centered on me, and are and become my reality that can be remembered **for life,** just as my first marriage, then what is real? NOW answer this: HOW MANY REALITIES EXIST? 6 billion to match the worlds inhabitants? Each has his own reality. And covered earlier, each has his own cosmos and universe.

Does reality become a little clouded yet? But wait there's more.

. . . .

All of these pale into insignificance when we consider the realm of "MIND".

The dimension of the mind seems to be the bridge between the Quantum Sea of the first reality and the "earth" existence of the other. Thought is intangible, but the results of its actions to the mind are as real as any event experienced by the 'physical' body in mortality. **Dream events can become totally absorbed into the mind's memory of events and indiscernible from any other memories. There becomes no difference or distinction.** This ability underlines and causes one of the dangers of **"hypnotism".**

The dimension of mind transcends time and space. Its operating ability speed exceeds that of light.

The mortal body is anchored in star stuff. Made of star stuff. The "mind" possesses it, animates, and uses it, for a short time only. The mind expresses itself via the mortal body although it is not a natural component of star stuff flesh.

The mind can only experience "**NOW**", for the mind can only exist in "NOW". Accept that this "NOW" as known by the mind can recall. It can 'recall', 're-live', 'project' etc, but observe when doing so it must momentarily release the possession of it's current concept or observations of "now". In reality, it is only changing its patterns and concepts of a current or "now" reality to visualize the memory or thought, and that is still happening "NOW". This is the mind that earlier I proposed was the actual author of all we experience. I suspect that is true, as the mind also experiences our dreams which in memory terms have equal validity to claim as factual events. This "NOW" is seemingly given substance by our ever-changing experiences on earth. But as the "NOW" changes, that which was mentally viewed or reviewed before, is gone and **only available as memory, just as are dreams.** And these dream memories we must admit are as acceptable and real as, if not at times better than, reality on earth. Oh dear, what is real, what is better??

Now where was I again?

■ ■

So we have quantum sea, earth life, maybe astral worlds, certain dream worlds, and worlds of mind and imagination. That's not all, you have only 4 dimensions so far. My Hospital experience told me that we have access to only "4 or so" out of some "11". I had no idea what that was about at the time. Stay with the thought.

■ ■

There are other dimensions.

Like it or not. Accept it or not. Deny it or not.

I wrote from my hospital bed to the world in 2004 of the reality of all these (other) dimensions. I Wrote how I would not remember them, how I "died" etc. and regained life and awareness seemingly in a different place, not of this mortal world. Whatever, here it comes, we are not alone either in this world or in the universe.

Now you have always already known or been prepared for that..

We were told or taught of angels, demons, elves, spirits, by whatever names, not us "non worldly" entities. For millennia we have been told there exist beings called such names as Imps, devils, fairies, goblins, little people, and innumerable other names. The legends and stories are too global to glibly dismiss all as fanciful, but perhaps they do exist in another dimension we do not all normally perceive.

■ ■

Then of course there is the **realm of the dead**. Or is there, or is that one of the above, or one of pure fanciful imagination? However there are those who claim to be, or are capable of communicating with the dead. This opens many doors for many associated phenomena often attributed to the dead, whether rightly so or not. It could very well be that an extremely large percentage of such phenomena are the result of the **"PK" effect**, or ESP, etc. Recordings on tapes, film, etc. hauntings etc. all are probably phenomena that are reality events, but not necessarily "belonging" to this everyday mortal dimension in which we seem to live.

Dare we create another category for Aliens/UFOs? It has been well illustrated by others that the UFO and alien phenomena have all the same hallmarks of the ghosts and demons "industry". Again there could well be that PK effect link at the root of a lot of events on record.

We could add a lot of other phenomena. Let's call the list 'ULTIMATE PHENOMENA" AND ADD EVERY THING WE DO NOT UNDERSTAND OR ACCEPT, whether it be faith healing, levitation, "mind over matter", mere spoon bending, dowsing, telepathy, seeing the future, revealing the past, psychometry, spells, materialization's, visions, "seeing", and countless other attested manifestations of psychic or occult events.

Everything that can exist, happen, or occur must have its roots in the quantum sea because that quantum sea, the very fabric of the universe, permeates and contains the entire cosmos. That obviously **includes our minds**, our mortal bodies of this dimension, and all the various phenomena to which we have alluded. The interesting question is: "At what level or depth within the Quantum Sea does each have its origin or roots, and across how many levels or realities does each extend, to be discernible from our level?"

In our mortality we discern only a dim view of a seemingly material universe where time and space, including "empty" space are seen as reality. Anything outside of this observable universe of our mortality state, is seen as "unreal", "alien" or just dismissed as not possible. Thus those who claim to have experienced or are able to actually practice or use, even implement some of the "phenomena" are often equally dismissed as devoid of reality, deluded, deranged, or plain charlatans, On rare occasions however, there has been ample unimpeachable testimony to establish the actuality of some individuals claims or ability, and some are accepted by the community at large and the giftee called a "saint" or similar.

Given that we operate in a strictly limited and restricted sphere or range in mortality, and that the phenomena referred to probably lie embedded perhaps much deeper within the Quantum sea, it becomes obvious why there is always lacking the much demanded element of proof or repeatability. There is always the element of uncertainty inherent in quantum events, and the uncertainty is magnified or multiplied when events or phenomena must need cross or operate at several levels, spheres, or dimensions within the sea, more so when the connection at the mortality end is just one individual. It is remarkable there are any "hits" at all in such a "hit or miss" situation, and more so if witnesses are available to observe the rare "hits". Note that it also recorded in quantum physics that the mere presence of an **observer** and the very act of observation also cause a variable effect on any quantum event.

It is tempting to venture into the question of the point of origin of any given phenomena. However that would require the reality of space and time. It could even be just possible that the origin of all and any events and phenomena lie within each individuals own mind. After all the mind can create within and of itself entire universes of imagined reality. (Hence the novels and movie scripts etc.) But I do not intend to venture into that area of speculation, as my purpose in this writing is only to analyze "what is" or "what can be" and to present it logically to one's understanding. Each individual then may speculate as one will, and indeed create their own universe and learn how to "become good gods".

In this mortal world we are as a mere "point" on a **two dimensional surface.** As all seeing and knowing as a dot on a sheet of paper. We would see only very limited amounts in extremely restricted directions and know of nothing other that what lies on our two-dimensional surface, so far as no line or other device blocks and limits our line of vision. In no way could we begin to comprehend that there is an unfathomable dimension called "above", or that there is an alien creature that is vastly more than a "point" but has "mass" and exists in (to us) unknowably more dimensions than we comprehend, and that he is observing us. A 2 dimensional world does not allow for such and its inhabitants live in ignorant bliss perhaps.

Perchance if an individual on that two dimensional surface claimed knowledge of the Observer, or that he had learned to elevate himself above the level of the surface at times, (whatever that would be supposed to mean) who would believe him if he could not perform the "miracle" on demand? I am sure the analogy is understandable. Whether a fellow "point" person believes his story of "other dimensions", or "other beings not like us" but living outside of their known universe is of course of absolutely no consequence other than to confirm their blindness and ignorance, perhaps arrogance also. Denial does not repudiate another's real ability to discern or know what is generally unknown.

I believe most of the phenomena and manifestations one hears about are likely to be factual, but that our understanding or interpretations of what exactly they are leaves a lot to be desired. I suspect a large percentage of phenomena have origin within the operating ranges of individual mental ability, and that individuals really can dip into the quantum soup bowl at times and extract such as is necessary to create or cause that which is desired, be it an healing, a curse, or a levitation, in short, for whatever purpose is one's will.

The "trick" is to be able to develop the ability to so dip into the quantum sea at all, then to learn to manipulate the "force", then to be able to do so at will. That could be interesting couldn't it? That ability must approach the privileges and powers we assign almost exclusively to "god". Thus perhaps a "god" is exclusively a multidimensional being who can operate at many levels and dimensions to cause his will to become manifest. However I really think that if it were generally so "permitted", then it would spell disaster for this entire mortal cosmos. Imagine an Adolf Hitler dipping endlessly into the "soup bowl", and the potential abuse becomes frightening.

In this manner, I believe that many claimed apparitions or manifestations may also have a very real element to them, but because of the nature of their Quantum Sea origin in other depths or dimensions, and that the vast majority of mortals are too conditioned to this sphere to have ability to discern them, they are not more generally or widely observed. In short, some are gifted with discernment and observational ability that most lack, and they get to witness the "intrusions" into our dimension. (Just as some animals have greater discernment of sight or sound ranges to the human species.)

So here we are imprisoned within our "x" dimensional universe, generally blissfully unaware of what reality is all about. We bumble about in what we believe is the only time and space that exist, and yes, believe that matter is "solid" and space is "empty". Few will want to know anything beyond Newton's physics. Most believe that we are the sole occupants of the cosmos, the highest level of all that is, unless a god is considered as a possible reality. Perhaps we concede a god to cover the contingency that just maybe we don't have all the answers or understand it all, and need to invoke an "all powerful" to intervene and save us in our ignorance.

007 – WAKING UP.

"The genius of men like Newton and Einstein lies in that: they ask transparent, innocent questions which turn out to have catastrophic answers. Einstein was a man who could ask immensely simple questions." (The Ascent of Man – Jacob Bronowski)

HAVE YOU EVER…?

Felt like a stranger in this world? You are aware of your own conscious intelligence and that you have a body, but it is just that, *a body that is **not** "you"*. ***You*** are not the entity of flesh and blood that is using the body, but that *you* are the stranger within that body and merely looking out through the windows called "eyes", observing this world.

Felt that this whole world and system you find yourself in is somehow *not real?* Although it all seems and appears solid and tangible, you suspect that somehow "things" are just not *right.* It is as though it's all unreal, a stage as the great bard once said, and we are mere actors on some cosmic stage.

Felt that the sky could "crack open" at any time and reveal an *underlying reality* that you are sure is just below the visible threshold of all you see? Reality is there but it's hidden from us.

Wondered why it is that in a dream you can do anything you determine to do, and you have seemingly no limits? Yes you can fly; easy. Have you ever marveled at the similar (but not as obvious) state in mortality, the conscious waking state, where it is truly said, "You can become what you think about", and a whole host of similar sayings?

Have you ever wondered, "is this life and world all a dream, or is any of all this real? What if *none of this is real?"*

Ever wondered why and how our mind, or presumably the mind, for that is what we are "told", creates or *enables* things and events, and just how and why do or can we become what we think about? ("The Secret" etc. etc. Success Through a Positive Mental Attitude. 1000's of books deal with the transmutation of desire, thoughts etc. into (terrestrial) reality.) Is there a "power" or "force" that causes or enables all things and that we are generally and in most people's cases, unaware of it?

How come some people seem to have unbelievable "luck" when I have none?

Hopefully this section will help us to understand all of those things, and a lot of other questions and issues. There should be no mystery about anything, no, not about anything. **All things should be able to be revealed and understood, and that is the purpose of this section. As Einstein once said, "I'd like to know the mind of God, then all the rest are just details."**

WATSON'S CONCLUSIONS: (Lyall Watson "The Romeo Error")

(From the chapter, "Conclusion")
*"........I am confronted with something rather alarming. There is a barrier in action. Not just a limit to understanding brought about by our lack of knowledge, but **an absolute embargo on certain kinds of information.** ....it appears that some things cannot or will not be known. Or at least not by our present approach.*

*So we try to find new and less direct approaches, but it seems that **there is a line beyond which we cannot move** at any one time. ....It is possible that we are doing battle on these frontiers with our own unco-operative unconscious minds; or, as some suggest, that **we are kept in check in our planetary kindergarten by a cautious cosmic nanny.***

*I do not know the answer, but I am beginning to learn that **the builder of this barrier** is not necessarily always benign. I will go on with the search for a new way to gain the understanding we need, but I must admit that right now on the edge of this **unexpected chasm, I am a little afraid."***

With those words Lyall Watson ended his remarkable book "The Romeo Error", in 1974. I recommend it as vital reading.

A UNIFIED THEORY:

I am currently re-reading a book, "Hyperspace", by Michio Kaku, a well-qualified physicist who reveals an interesting parallel from the science of physics. (More recently he produced a 4-part documentary called "Time".) Not only does his book deal with the problems Watson (above) attempts to resolve, but also provides valuable additional data and methodology that quite probably are the key to **fully resolve a truck load of seemingly unrelated issues**. We will list some of those issues soon, and that list will not by any means be an all-inclusive or complete list of such seemingly unrelated, unresolved, or contentious issues.

The problem facing physicists, including Einstein, was that there is a lot of known data and established facts that just simply "don't add up". Each phenomena has its own set of formula, math's, and equations. Each has its own devotees, for want of a better description of the followers in its area. The areas are Strong nuclear force, weak nuclear force, electro-magnetism, and gravity. 4 forces. Each force is undeniable, but they do not seem to fit in together so as to provide an understandable working "whole" that is simple, elegant, and understandable. Logically they should all fit into one harmonious whole with one set of rules; not 4 seemingly separate "disciplines". In the section immediately following this one it will be shown that in the 1800's Reimann and Maxwell both came to some astounding conclusions that would fully resolve the seeming incompatibility issues. Unfortunately both died prematurely before completion and publication, and in the case of Maxwell, his works were "edited" after his death to leave us with the electromagnetic equations alone in tact.

The search for a unified theory has since baffled the best minds for decades. Proof as always is elusive. Trouble is the scientific community and such like always seek some sort of repeatable at will demonstrable physical evidence. I believe this is a completely invalid criteria or approach, and at best has limited value to settling disputed or dubious matters solely limited to this "mortal and temporal world". Such an attitude prohibits those demanding it from acceptance of obvious facts. Such as: where is the evidence that faith healing works, when there are people produced that say they have been so healed; there is no proof that aliens, UFO's etc. exist when thousands give testimony of them; etc. etc. In any case, why should one even bother with such attitudes as to vainly attempt to convince such that proof exists? We shall see that many things are in fact incapable of being proven.

As these issues in Physics are not the subject under discussion, regardless that it is very intimately related to all issues, I will be brief here. By introducing the mathematics of **added dimensions** all the unresolvable clear up and a clear unified theory emerges. It is still, alas, not accepted as fact for the want of "proof". But the elegance and logic is just too good not to be right.

THE PROBLEM.

For many decades I have been vaguely uneasy and troubled by the seeming lack of logical correlation of all the many claimed "phenomena". No acceptable "proof" existed for almost all of them, yet the circumstantial evidence and testimonies of many made for a most compelling case for the reality and actuality of many different and varied phenomena.

But not only was I troubled by the lack of correlation of causes and types of "phenomena", but of other matters relating to mortality, religion, and more, that should have some logical explanation and all form part of what should surely be one intelligible, understandable harmonious whole. Things should not be, nor remain shrouded in mystery. This is why I have always asked questions, and actively mentally pursued the question until a beautifully simple underlying fact emerged. (For example in the 1970's I was asked to give a discourse/lesson to a group of priesthood on the "fact" that there was only two sources of "power", that of God and that of the Devil. It was thus believed that if a healing for instance, occurred that was not under the hands of god's acceptable servants, then it must be of the devil. I studied the matter and formed lots of questions. Questions that asked: shall I conclude all claimed miracles except for a small number at the hands of a select group of Christians, be of the devil? It rapidly led me to a search for other "sources of power" and of course very soon I found there were other sources of "power" readily identifiable. The lesson was given, but not fully what was expected at all.)

So the "problem" was and is to find the common source, cause, correlation, and explanation of *all phenomena,* so that none stand-alone, are isolated or left out from what must be a ***grand unified theory of phenomena***.

The interesting thing is that parts of it were "given" to me years ago, but at the time I did not even realize that I was looking for any such thing. Re-reading "901 Notes from the hospital" and "902 notes from the edge" (Printed in "Bob's Legacy") I find some of the answers given then, but not fully understood nor correlated correctly. I also re-discover that it was given to me in part as recorded in 016, "reality goodbye". Well I guess **now** is the time to deal with that issue, as I proposed one day to do.

Personally:

I have experienced many things. I have found myself dead a few times, and been dead a few times, and returned to tell about it. I have been fully awake, alert, and conscious, but separated from my physical body, of which I had full awareness in its place and position as I found myself in a different world. I have full awareness of the vitality of the dream body with its ability to have memory of former experiences, and to be fully pro-active in the dream. Also at rare times *to be aware that it is a dream body and that a physical body exists* elsewhere, even where it exists. And of course I function in the temporal mortal world. Further I have participated in levitation, numerous healings, and ouija boards that gave uncanny information, among many other "phenomena" experienced. These things are not said to boast, but to elaborate on the diversity of *phenomena* that commonly exist and the need some rationalization and correlation to reveal *one common cause or origin,*

Without further ado here is a non-exclusive list of phenomena or situations that needed correlation and understanding under an *harmonious whole.*

SOME OF THE THINGS THAT NEED SORTING, CORRELATING, AND EXPLAINING:

These are not in any special sequence or considered order of importance or merit.

The seeming **pointlessness of life:**

In a cosmos of incomprehensible age and size, of what value is a mortal life of a few decades in such an insignificant world as this temporal earth?

The **injustice and inequity** of mortal states:

One is born into wealth, luxury, and abundant opportunity. Another is born into poverty or slavery. One was born a primitive 'savage', another into a world of wondrous technology and plenty. Without resort to 'karma' or whatever is offered of a similar ilk, what can one say about equal opportunity? Fair?

The very **briefness** of mortal life:

70 or 80 earth years if one is lucky, now is that meaningful in any way when one considers the endless eternity of space/time, or of that promised

by various religions? Are we to be eternally judged as is claimed for what is as "one day in the life of John Doe"?

Death itself should have some logical place and **purpose:**

Our body is **programmed** to die. Once that hayflick (?) limit is reached, then its goodbye from all of us to all that we know or experience in mortality. Why are our bodies designed to self-terminate? Is this a huge cosmic waste of time, resources, energy and resources? Is it "mindless" or is there a purpose?

What is death and what is recycled:

Is it just a body, flesh and bones etc. which is dust of this earth, star stuff, returning to that which gave it, or is it the total end to the intelligent entity that 'used' the body? Are we laying to rest just an empty shell, or is it what was once the total person? Something that logically fits in to a "big picture" would be helpful in understanding so many different ideas put out about death and survival of death, or perhaps understanding the *real* situation that is involved with death.

Why do we, and how can we have **dealings with those "known" to be dead:**

There seems to be a body of evidence to support this statement. No "proof" of course. But I suspect most people have encountered and had dealings with those deemed as "known" to be departed, dead to mortality. I know this as such have frequent interaction with me, and therefore with others, in the *dream world.* Is this just a mental construct or is there some reality basis for such experiences?

Why do or can some deal with known dead in their everyday mortal awareness state:

Then there is a body of evidence indicating some "*sensitives*" have such interaction when awake and their conscious state of mortality. Is this a genuine experience limited to those tuned in to more "frequencies" than is common to man, or are they deluded by themselves, or dare I say it, by "demons"?

What is claimed **reincarnation** really all about?

So many variations on this subject exist as to cause total confusion. What *flavor* of reincarnation is one talking about at any given instance? The "case" looks really like solid evidence in many cases, too solid to simply dismiss out of hand, but how seriously should one take it? Is it important, even if it can be established as an irrefutable reality? Like, should we lose sleep over it even if it's a genuine event? What can it possibly mean, and what does this do to various religious creeds?

What exactly is **"Astral Projection"** and is it real:

I've been there and experienced that several times, or so it seems to me. My mental jury has been "out" on that subject and the experiences for decades mainly because I was unable to correlate the claimed (and experienced) phenomena with anything else. It would not "fit" into my perceived or accepted reality. I read lots of materials and case histories but had been left confused, totally puzzled as to what it "means". Let's face it, it's a reasonably common event for those in mortality, but *is it a real phenomena or is it a mental creation?* If it is only a mental construct, then it creates real and valid life like memories. If it's physically real, its earth shattering in its importance. So what is it really? Or where is it really? It would be nice to place it in an acceptable and understandable niche so there is neither confusion nor misunderstanding.

Multitude of **seemingly unrelated phenomena manifest:**

There are just so many different phenomena manifest that it becomes difficult to even attempt to list them. The following is again a *non-exclusive* list of some of some more commonly reported types, and forgive me if you can name many more that I have failed to list. They all have a few elements in common: there is no "proof" for any of them, there are many accounts that seem unimpeachable, and all are difficult to understand or fit within a framework to our satisfactory understanding. One would hope there is *one single underlying cause for all such phenomena.*

Why do some people see and or deal with a multitude of seemingly unrelated phenomena when others do not, or can not, should they even try or believe in them. One sees a ghost; the one next to him does not. Not everyone present at Fatima saw the manifestations.

UFOs sightings and contacts. Real or imagined? From near or far far away?
Ghosts and/or haunting, poltergeist activity.

Contact with or by spirits of known or presumed dead (no known identity)
Ability to manifest PK phenomena of various types (such as the Geller type)
Foretell future events or see past events.
Why are some seeming effective mediums and others not?
Foretell future events accurately.
Have an ability to "read" or get information from objects. (psychometry)
Some can cause healing, or perform *psychic surgery* etc.
Some can be healed others not, even if they "believe"
Some have visions of various types.
For some the ouija board gives new unknown information.
Some claim past life memory and produce convincing evidence.
Some have "dreams" then wake up with new knowledge or discoveries.
"Seeing at a distance" seems valid, but impossible.
People or things can "disappear", and things can be made to appear, literally out of "thin air".
And what exactly is this "channeling" all about?

All such events if "real" should have some *understandable place and cause in a* **unified reality.**

But what if **all such phenomena and events** were the by-products or minor manifestations of a single cause, of one single reality, a reality before us, but just unseen and unrecognized?

Why do we experience a **lack of capacity to understand?**

Let's be real here. Some things really hurt the head to try to understand or figure out, and I'm not just talking about physics in all its disciplines. And lets also ask, why do some have greater capacity than others? Could it be that some are *more awake* than others, speaking of *capacity* only, and not opportunity.

Why does **"proof" evade** us or not exist:

Proof is almost always missing for the really interesting things. Could it be simply that the paradigm used is all wrong. The fact that one has experienced, seen, or heard constitutes proof to that individual and perhaps should be acceptable as proof to us also so far as that individual, and perhaps phenomena is concerned. Although "proof" can be used to identify fraudsters and liars, generally a requirement of "proof" is simply a method of denial used by people wanting to claim "authority" for whatever personal reasons, and to establish that they "know better, are better, and should be recognized and treated or favored as such. How dare we question or claim otherwise."

Just **who am "I"** in the center of "my cosmos" and experience:

I have dealt with the uniqueness of each individual's personal cosmos elsewhere in these writings. It is remarkable that each *is different.* It would be nice to be able to understand why so many different individuals exist, what is the purpose, and why in fact so many and so diverse. Then there is the individuality of all partakers of all forms of life to be considered.

Why is it said most of "us" are **"asleep in mortality"?**

Why is it suggested in mortality that we **use only about 10%** of our capacity?

If this is in fact so, then what is the potential or capacity of our mind and indeed of ourselves? Can or will we ever use a larger percentage of our individual potential or capacity?

Can anyone ever fully understand **sleep and dreaming?**

I continue to read that "science" is still baffled by the whole thing.

What is meant by all is "illusion" **what is the "illusion":**

We have all heard it said or read it. The claims of the sages, the mystics etc. that this entire world is *illusion.* Now what does or can that possibly mean? Seems solid and real to me, so should I attempt to understand this claim? I mean, so many for so long have given this as the sum total of their wisdom. Ravings or real? How important?

Does **quantum physics** have any relationship to, or reveal these matters:

Now this gets decidedly uncomfortable because now the **physicists**, not only the religious **mystics**, also claim that *all is illusion,* that ultimately it's all energy that creates matter, that creates space and time. How does this sit with what we have been led to understand and believe since infancy? I for one would love to understand where "I" fit into all this illusion, after all its *really only all about me!!* And of course 'you' are another 'me' – the difference is: you are not me and you have your own cosmos of which you are the centre.

I have a copy of a recent **documentary called "The Day I Died"**, and I am going to seriously recommend that all get a copy and watch it carefully. It is a really solid in-depth study of life itself, and more so of consciousness and intelligence. The absolute earth shattering information starts at 37 minutes into the show, when one eminent physician categorically states the evidence is that **information** (personal memory etc.) is retained *outside of the brain*, and later fixed in the memory circuits when successful resuscitation occurs. In other words, the brain of the individual has ceased to function, is literally inactive or brain dead. Yet later after a "good" resuscitation, that person has a restoral of personal memory. However the brain was not functioning and thus could not have nor retain any form of memory under conventional understanding of human physiology.

Now this is exactly the case and what happens to a "good" resuscitation. I know, for I have been there twice. Flat lining, and that for a period of time that forced the doctors and emergency staff to pronounce that, although later resuscitated and functionally restored physically, I may well be permanently brain dead, or at best, probably a "human vegetable". However "I" came back into the body. My **memories** seem to be all there. (How would I know if some were not?) Yet in some resuscitations, the "bad" ones, the result is a human "shell", physically alive, but as it is said, "no one is home". Why is this? What makes the difference? Does one's exteriorized intelligence decide "yes the body is now OK, I can go back? It will continue to serve me." Or perhaps conversely decide "No it's too far gone to be used by me, I'm out of here now." While the medical staff continue to keep a body (empty of the intelligent consciousness) merely physically functioning.

At 38 minutes into the show, a **Professor Stuart Hamarov** who is working in conjunction with Penrose, discusses his discovery and work with microtubules that are deep within the brain. He refers to them as quantum computers, and states that **everything is interconnected with everything else, that particles can be in two or more places at the same time**, called "**superposition**" in space/time geometry. This reveals the very fabric of the universe. When one goes into the space within the structure of an atom, between the subatomic or quantum particles, there is a "wave" manifest, **and that "wave" carries information**. It is that wave and information he says, that gives rise to our individual and very own consciousness. The **microtubules** are the "receptors" that bring the information into individual intelligent consciousness within what we call the human body. (And thus you become "you" in this world.)

From this starting point surely everything else becomes just "details". We have now exposed the very fabric of *our* universe, as that which carries information, energy. This is what I have referred to previously and will still call it so, *the quantum soup. Thus we are indeed creatures of the quantum soup* now clothed in "star stuff" and taking on the appearance of a mortal body *for this particular universe.*

Who were the once so active "Gods" and where are they now, 1000s of years later?

I deal with the gods and my mental indigestion in another section. But still there is a case to answer. There are gods of countless cultures that are recorded as actively dealing with men, and then we have millennia of silence. Why is that? Are the records mere fiction, over-imagination or is there a factual background? Why are so many religions jumping on the bandwagon and teaching confusingly different things? And let's ask the question that should be basic here: "What exactly constitutes a god? How can we define the requirements to enable identification or qualification for being deemed a god?"

If there is a truth out there, it should be identifiable, found, and revealed. More, it should make obvious sense without resort to "imponderables" or "mysteries".

Do "gods" exist?

The ultimate *aliens, or at least "not humans"*. Are all those accounts pure fiction or are there some intelligent beings not of "our" species active now or in the past in this world? Are they from a different reality and more powerful than us in mortality? Are we in fact gods ourselves, or will be ever reach such a level or status? Some religions think so and teach such.

And what about this "heaven" by whatever name, claimed as the abode of any of the various gods? Real, myth, fable, or true?

What are angels, guardian angels, devils and demons all about?

Here again we have no "proof" of existence such as the scientific community would demand, but the sheer weight of testimony must confirm to any jury that a case is established. Men have been hanged on less evidence than we find supporting claims for these subjects.

So if such as these exist and are not only in the minds of man, what are they, where are they and why is there a seeming interaction between them and us? Genesis (bible) seems to indicate at one time some of such came and lived and bred with mortal humanity. Now that's one huge claim not to be ignored surely.

A coherent true *unified theory* should be able to fully explain, identify and show the origin of such unworldly *aliens.* "Aliens" in as much as they are not of our mortal species nor world.

What of the **"others"**, elves, fairies and mythical peoples:

So much myth, legend, folk lore from all over the world, from so many cultures and different ages exist that one is almost compelled to accept that there just may be some actual and factual basis for perhaps some such claims. Even if of the same origin and realm as the angels, devils and demons, they demand some intelligent understanding and placement in the *order of things.*

Is there **life after death** or is death just a part of the cycle life:

This type of question has been posed for the entire history of man. Obviously it is of vital importance and interest to all. Alas it is also the cause of so much confusion and so many conflicting claims, not to mention the cause of so much contention and abuse.

 I think perhaps a better question may well be "do we in fact exist concurrently in many other dimensions"? Is it possible that this mortality is just one of many lives being experienced and shared by the individuals intelligent consciousness? We can establish that even in this mortal life we have full awareness of a duality, two states of existence, sharing with a "dream world". If this were so then saying farewell to mortality on this earth is merely closing one chapter of a larger than we imagine life. Is this why we only access a small percentage of our capacity in this world and life?

Is there really an eternal battle of **"good" versus "evil"?**

This is of course a fascinating question, but too vast to deal exhaustively with in this series of writings. However if we can come to a basic understanding of *ultimate reality,* then we can formulate the question more meaningfully. We shall touch upon it later in this book.

How or why is it that we can **become or achieve** whatever we really want?

Why is it said we **become what we think about** most of the time?

Is **"the secret"**, so called, for real:

What power or potential is really available for us? In fact, who or what are "us" even? One cannot understand what is at stake or what potential exists unless one understands the nature of "self". So long as an individual intelligence remains asleep in mortality, which mortality itself perhaps is a form of sleep, then that individual intelligence cannot achieve or realize, nor even understand the potential.

Can we become whatever we want to become? Really? That sure needs some deep explaining and understanding. Surely mere flesh and blood, star stuff of this earth, cannot be empowered with such ability, or can it?

Why do our thoughts and **minds vastly exceed our physical potential/ability?**

Physically we cannot deny we are *star stuff.* Elements of the earth that will return to the earth. But without question there is something about the animated mortal body that is truly an amazing gestalt. Intelligence inhabits those mortal elements and it is far above and beyond the nature of the mortal elements. What is it, and what are its source, potential, objectives, and destination? Why is it housed in an unsuitably inferior body that is incapable of remotely fulfilling our imaginings?

Why and how can **our minds create** a sustained illusion that becomes our reality?

Perhaps you are familiar with the phenomena of *false memory.* It's a memory that is simply not based on actual physical events as we know them. It became notorious and recognized as the cause of a lot of persons imprisoned for offences not committed by them. They were (falsely) accused as a result of (false) statements taken from the supposed memory of children in the USA and elsewhere. Children produced *memories* of abuse and worse at the interrogation and suggestion of "counselors" and psychologists etc. Those memories were simply not true.

So often I read in claimed *alien abduction* cases, that the information came to light only after the alleged abduction victim has been subjected to *hypnosis.* Strangely I am no longer surprised to find so much claimed phenomena is only uncovered and revealed *after hypnosis.*

One often reads of the same underlying origin in the case histories of *claimed reincarnation* with monotonous regularity. The claimant was the subject of *hypnotic regression,* and once regressed so far, having nowhere else to go, presents a previous life memory for the hypnotist who is in all probability willing such an event to manifest. There is abundant evidence that shows that an observer, the **therapist**, can dramatically effect the result, and in fact **cause or implant** the suggestions to the other party. If the "PK" effect is real, and it seems this may be the case, then the thoughts or suggestions do not even have or need to be vocalized. We discover that most *false memories* are literally made to order for the precise requirements of the so-called therapist involved. They want such a memory or statement for whatever reason, and the subdued "patient" or other participating party obliges as a result of the implanted expectation.

The interesting thing is that the *mind cannot distinguish the difference between real and imaginary events, and acts on all thoughts as though they are real* actual events. I had this actually demonstrated to me once, and was subsequently able to prove the reality of this to a group of about 30 participants at one time. It is a simple demonstration involving mere suggestion, and can be done without any prior preparations or conditions required. It's a nice simple demonstrable undeniable fact.

WARNING: To submit to hypnosis may effectively be giving someone the ability effectively to re-write your memories of your life, together with your attitudes, habits, beliefs etc. In fact, they can re-write your entire being.

Brain washing is a term which probably almost everyone has heard. Same type of process involved. Subdue the subject's will by hypnosis, drugs, fatigue, or whatever, as it all leads down the same path. Once adequately submissive and receptive, the desired new mental programs can be installed and become operative, reality, without question.

Now a conclusion from Watson:

"It seems that we each have within us all the necessary mechanisms for producing elaborate, coherent and sustained images without any of the external stimuli that form the basis of normal waking perception. ...."
("The Romeo Error" page 105)

Why is the human gifted with such ability? Flesh and blood, the products of this temporal world surely would or should not be so advanced "mentally".

<u>We read of physical manifestations of things, flowers, etc. etc. How and what gives?</u>

In the late 1800s and early 1900s the mediums materialized **ectoplasm**, so called. Recently one Baba of India manifests flowers, gifts, and ash, fairly much you name it and he can literally produce it out of "nothing" and in front of witnesses. How can this possibly be? We are talking about the ability to "create" matter. The phenomena are reasonably common and often reported or claimed.

Lyall Watson records in "The Romeo Error" of witnessing, within a few feet of the events taking place, the actual and real physical creation and manifestation of organs, tissue, blood etc. by "**psychic surgeons**" in the Philippines. Sure, we all know there is much fakery and fraud in some cases, but the testimony is in and is valid. Strange and actual manifestations of material "things" **are** actually occurring.

Now how can this be? How does one get to satisfactorily explain this type of phenomena?

<u>Are we really just **animals** of a temporal world?</u>

<u>How does **Psychic Surgery** work? Do hands enter into the patient's body?</u>

Quite apart from the manifesting of physical things mentioned above, there are these recorded witnessed account of (some) psychic surgeons actually inserting their *hands into the body of another mortal.* It gets better and stranger, there are no scars, incisions or any subsequent evidence of any form of intrusion. Healings can be validly effected. How can one possibly occupy the same space/time used by another? How can two parties be within the same place at the same time? Not environs, but the *same temporal space or position.*

Do we dismiss these claims because we find no ability or capacity to understand or explain what has happened? Do we put it down to illusion, suggestion, faith healing that we would deny as a stand-alone claim, or is it just possible there is a way for it to actually happen as claimed and witnessed? It sure needs a good explanation, and deserves one. Well, the news is that there is a good explanation.

SHARING:

Let me start off here with a bold statement. I no longer think that my individual intelligence, personality, memories, all those things that make the whole mortal "me" as one conceives the body housing me, is at all unique and exclusive to this terrestrial or mortal star stuff world or universe. I am forced to conclude that I am not a "one off" entity unique to and in this world alone. This waking mortal world conscious body is not the sole or only manifestation of "me".

I seriously started to wonder when after two resuscitations, I was still able to be "me". Brain ceased functioning, all supposed contents erased, all life signs ceased. The head nurse in emergency department told me, that the first time resuscitation took 18 minutes. Yes 18 minutes, surely that is irreversibly dead. So I thought. So we all are told and believe. I am told the 2nd time that it took 45 minutes, which frankly I find staggeringly unbelievable. Certainly I would not accept it if someone made such a claim to me. Surely they must have some misunderstanding of something. It becomes an inescapable fact then, that **if** these statements by those actually doing the hands on resuscitations are true, then my memories, personality, and goodness knows what else, had to either have been "backed up" somewhere to enable a later "restoral", or else I had vacated the body and somehow returned later to take it up again. Smells mighty like "superposition".

Most of us will readily agree, know, and have personal experience with their own dream world and of their participation and activities within it. We bring back memories of some events that transpired in that "universe" and carry the memory over to be accepted as a valid and real memory of such events into the star stuff body of this world. Later those memories originating in dreams will be indistinguishable from "mortal life" memories. There seems so little doubt that it is the same "us" that is experiencing the dreams that we know as "us" in waking mortality that it barely is worth pursuing. Thus "Us", "me", by whatever name, participates in this manner in – so far - two separate or distinctly different realities or "universes".

Some people have or do get to experience what is commonly called **"astral projection"**. I do not intend to go deeply into either the subject or techniques that may or may not be involved here. Sufficient to say, that for those who have experienced it, it is a very real occurrence. The body and conscious intelligence do find themselves in two separate places, but still "somehow" connected perhaps. (Superposition of the mind/body) My point here is this: The realm into which that exteriorized conscious intelligence ventures is not exactly the same one as that to which the star stuff mortal body finds itself restricted. It is in fact a different reality or universe, another dimension if you will, into which we either stumble by accident, or as claimed by many, venture intentionally. Be that as it may, the fact is that it is the same "me" or "us" that finds itself functioning in another reality with "another changed or different" body. We note the structure and laws of nature and physics are different in that realm. Here then is a third reality or universe that our conscious intelligence can access and participate. Interestingly one can easily bring back and retain memories of events within that "astral" universe.

Now lets cut this short and look at just one more inescapable conclusion. A conclusion that reveals yet another (the 4th so far in this limited count) realm into which our conscious intelligence has access. The documentary "The Day I Died" reveals many people whom have literally had a very real "death" experience. It is salted with validating commentary from physicists, researchers etc., and the evidence would be acceptable in a court of law, but not to "proof seekers". There is no doubt these people went "somewhere" and had various experiences, and yes, brought back memories of events that transpired at the time. Many more must have experienced that realm, including myself, because there seems no other explanation as to how or where their individual conscious intelligence survived when the body and brain had ceased their functioning. They came back to a repaired and restored body as themselves, complete with all attributes and memories, and at times even slightly improved or "changed" a little. (My personal "changed a little" included the immediate ability to change my entire lifestyle without any difficulty. Then there are the "mental" and "value" changes…..)

It would seem that, and be reasonable to accept that these various realities or universes are not all subject to the same *"laws of nature" or physics* as we know and experience them on this temporal mortal world. Certainly it could be said that we know this is the case with the universes of the dream and astral worlds, and I am sure that it equally is true of the "world" of those dead to, or removed from this temporal and mortal world, regardless of how permanent or temporary that departure may be.

In short we are beings that inhabit and exist within multiple dimensions simultaneously. Certainly it is the same "us" or individual conscious intelligence that manifests and experiences these realms. The above information only counts *four such dimensions, and I see no reason whatsoever why that is the final count.*

The implications of this are staggering to imagine. It may well be that there are an infinite number of dimensions, alternative universes, call them what you will, that all exist simultaneously in space/time wherein we manifest ourselves and participate in life or existence.

Let me quote **Michio Kaku**, that great physicist who for decades has worked on string theory and quantum physics.

*"The problem, we see, is that there are also millions upon millions of other solutions describing universes that do not appear anything like our universe. In some of these solutions, the universe has no quarks or too many quarks. In most of them, **life as we know it** cannot exist. Our universe may be lost somewhere among the millions of possible universes that have been found in string theory."* ("Hyperspace" page 170)

It seems to me that there are an infinite number of intelligent individual entities or consciousnesses, of which we each are (most likely) but one, these existing within and over an infinite number of dimensions, universes, or realities. It seems such can travel via the wave information and form that is stated as the very fabric of our universe and is identified within and below subatomic structure levels. The name we give them is not the important issue, but the understanding of what I am saying is important. Further it seems that we as such an individual intelligence or consciousness, have the ability to exist simultaneously within some, if not all, of those dimensions. We are after all, bathing within and **are a component part** of the fabric of the universe. Perchance we are merely just not consciously aware of such existence by that small percentage of our capacity accessible to us in this mortal life and world. Our individual conscious intelligence manifest here (while merely inhabiting temporal *star stuff* elements of this universe) is not unique or restricted to this temporal state in which we now find ourselves. We are in fact, sharing ourselves around. This life it seems may be only one small facet of our real selves, the true "us" if you will.

Now obviously temporal space and the availability of suitable *star stuff* on this temporal and mortal world that we daily experience is somewhat finite and limited. It cannot simultaneously contain the infinite numbers of entities that evidently exist; thus we see a ***real reason why physical death is not only inevitable, but also required.*** Hence our *star stuff* temporal bodies are programmed to destruct after a given maximum span of time on this world or dimension, and no escape from it is allowed. (The "hayflick limit") After our turn on this temporal world in this dimension, (and our collecting our brownie points or badge) for a span of life, existence, experience, etc. it becomes a requirement that the *star stuff* be broken down to be recycled. Recycled to allow organizing into more new bodies, more new carrots to be consumed by those new bodies, and more new trees to consume and help recycle those bodies. The **cycle of life** finds a coherent explanation.

UNIFIED THEORY OF ALL THINGS:

The reality of **hyperspace**, of multiple dimensions, and our being conscious entities within them, all part of the *quantum soup,* now presents us with the working space and the ability to be able to find the reasons, the mechanics, and the reality of almost any phenomena that seems to exist or can be claimed to exist. Aliens, so called, that pop in and out of **perception**, along with ghosts, angels, demons and a whole host of unworldly entities now become understandable and explainable. So also the ability to effectively "create" or produce matter or artifacts seemingly out of nothing has its explanation. With a little thought, it can now be a simple matter of mental exercise to establish the probable cause of most, if not all, phenomena. It is now only individual details that need to be considered and understood with regard to any of the many things listed above.

Simply put, we are multiple dimensional entities existing in more than this one temporal dimension, and the many puzzling phenomena have their origin and cause within another "part" or dimension of this multidimensional hyperspace that is simply just not perceived by the *ordinary* (normal or usual, common) abilities of the temporal mortal body. We err if we look for the cause or origin of many such things as being "on this earth", and contained solely within our knowable time/space. For this reason we are unable to understand so much phenomena. For this reason any "proof" eludes us, cannot be found, nor phenomena repeatable "on demand" as science would require. That scientific paradigm is just not valid in such a far-reaching operational realm as is hyperspace. Our earth is contained in merely one dimension of the probably infinite number of dimensions literally surrounding us.

The majority of us are tuned, and finely so, to perceive and interact solely within the temporal *star stuff* earth and its limited dimension. Some it seems are not so limited in their range of perceptions or interactions, and it is this that enables them to witness or perform a host of events and manifestations that are incomprehensible, alien, or just unacceptable, not to mention unbelievable, to most of humanity. Now we can understand why not all see the same UFO or manifestation or the claimed visions and manifestations at Fatima etc.

Just as the acceptance of hyperspace allows quantum physics and mechanics the "space and room" to successfully incorporate all of the 4 forces, and thus understand them each in relationship to the others, so the same hyperspace puts everything into its place with regard to all phenomena that can exist.

WAKING UP:

This so far is a bare bones overview and summary of what "it is all about" and the underlying cause of so many puzzling effects and phenomena. That is the sole purpose of this writing. It behooves each individual to mentally digest and understand the basic principles outlined here, then by asking the right questions in a logical sequence, (I doubt there is a preferred or "right" sequence.) one is capable to coming to a full and total understanding of all things. Yes, of all things. Sure some of the details may be brushed over and not bothered with. For instance, who would want to do the math's involved in quantum, hyperspace or string theory? Indeed that is not necessary, as that is just *details.*

It is hoped the contents of this section will come as a wake up call. That it will stir the sleeping giant within each of us, to realize and recognize that in truth each of us is truly a grand and cosmic individual intelligence with unlimited potential.

APPLICATION, OR WHERE TO FROM HERE:

Once one understands the situation we are currently in, then one will become able to more fully understand the self, its place and potential in the grand scheme of things. Then when one so understands and appreciates the **greater reality** situation, one will be able to see past the dream of mundane mortality and (hopefully) gravitate naturally towards higher ideals than most mortals ever see or realize.

With mental exercise and this working model you will now be able to answer those questions posed above. You will understand that we swim in a sea of cosmic quantum realities, and that we are, in the mortal state, generally tuned to perceive just one reality, and that reality is just an illusion. You will soon be able to figure out for yourself who the gods are and from whence they come. Likewise you will figure out the logical cause of any and all phenomena. You will no longer be subject to blind faith or ignorance.

RELUCTANCE TO MAKE PUBLIC:

I had been reluctant to publish this sort of information for some time because I see potential for misuse or outright abuse of such information. I can visualize untold scams resulting, as mortals tend to find a way to gather personal gain or power and authority from almost anything.

Some of the facets of this information would be capable of supporting sectarian type of groups making almost all sorts of claims and/or promises. All for money or domination over others of course. And of course the larger percentage of mortals would just be too nieve or lazy to bother to understand or to "wake up" and thus be unwitting victims of the scammers.

Some will claim to reveal your true self. Some will claim to be "**jedi** knights" in other dimensions and thus attempt to gain your wealth and adoration. Some will seek to gain followers based on such claims and to gain great personal dominion. No doubt a false Christ or so will arise with marvelous claims. Given time, competition and persecutions could follow. Eventually even wars could result.

Any reformer or revealer of information would look back and wonder if it was all worth while. However I believe all this information is already "out there", and even if that is not so, then few if any will even bother with this knowledge or information. Nonetheless I do hold reservations about the wisdom of publishing all of this information in this order and form in the one place. I do believe however it will do more good for more individuals than any harm that could result. Pray I am right.

(29/2/12, I find it hard to believe I actually wrote all this. Glad I did, because already I "have lost the memory of it", and therefore learning it again as I read it. Bob)

008-HYPERDIMENSIONAL PHYSICS

"When you once see something as false which you have accepted as true, as natural, as human, then you can never go back to it" - J. Krishnamurti

(The following article is not written by me, but off the internet and of interest.)

Undoubtedly, the premier website with respect to Hyperdimensional Physics is Richard Hoagland's <http://www.enterprisemission.com/hyper1.html>. The only disadvantage of this particular website is that it has a lot of information, and thus takes some time in consuming. (Which is why portions of it are condensed here.) However, Hoagland's work is well written, has lots of intriguing graphics -- many of a geometrical nature -- and is scientifically plausible. Highly recommended as some intriguing, speculative material.

A briefer, Hoagland-style version is <http://www.enterprisemission.com/physics.html>, where the introductory portion discusses the field of hyperdimensional physics as one based on geometry and mathematics, and which involve other spatial dimensions. According to Hoagland (with due regard to Tom Bearden, et al), hyperdimensional physics goes back to the 19th Century, where mathematicians and physicists began delving into "theoretical 'non-Euclidian' geometries (geometries involving spatial dimensions in addition to 'length, breadth and height'), and a set of specifically predicted physical interactions of energy and matter determined by those 'non-Euclidian geometries.'"

This introductory site also includes "the results of continuing, world-wide, contemporary physics and 'free energy' experiments... which are now confirming increasingly specific predictions of the 'hyperdimensional' model." This includes: Zero-Point Energy, and the basis of Connective Physics, although the latter is not referenced in the website.

Nevertheless, <http://www.enterprisemission.com/hyper1.html> is worth reviewing in detail (including its some five or six detailed, elaborate webpages). Hoagland notes, among many other things, that the anomalous energy being radiated by the giant planets of Jupiter, Saturn, Uranus, and Neptune can be explained by Hyperdimensional Physics. In essence, these planets' energy output is "over unity", i.e. they are giving off more energy than is being absorbed from the Sun energy impinging upon them. Furthermore, when Uranus and Neptune are "normalized" (i.e. their different distances from the Sun are taken into account), these two planets are roughly equal in their output. Hoagland then explains that all of this can be accounted for if we assume:

"The existence of unseen hyperspatial realities... that, through information transfer between dimensions, are the literal 'foundation substrate' maintaining the reality of everything in this dimension."

That statement says quite a bit. Reread it and think about it. Hmmmmmm...

Via <http://www.enterprisemission.com/hyper1.html> -- and the continuation of the narrative on subsequent webpages -- Hoagland goes on to discuss the following:

z **"Vortex atoms" -- tiny, self-sustaining "whirlpools" in the so-called ether -- one envisioned by William Thompson (1867), which he and his 19th Century contemporaries "increasingly believed extended throughout the Universe as an all-pervasive, incompressible fluid."** The latter included James Clerk Maxwell -- undoubtedly the patron saint of modern electromagnetic theory -- who developed a mechanical vortex model of an incompressible ether in which Thompson's vortex atom could exist.

z The use by Maxwell of quaternions (ordered pairs of complex numbers), who made it clear in his writings that his choice of quaternions as mathematical operators was predicated on his belief that three-dimensional physical phenomena -- including quite possibly human Consciousness -- was dependent upon higher dimensional realities! Some of these writings are included herein as Hyperdimensional Poetry. A brief diversion.

z The disastrous "streamlining" after Maxwell's death of his quaternion equations by two 19th Century so-called mathematical physicists, Oliver Heaviside and William Gibbs, who simplified to extinction the original equations and left four simple (if woefully incomplete!) expressions. This was done by Heaviside's drastic editing of Maxwell's original work after the latter's untimely death from cancer. The four surviving, "classic" Maxwell's Equations -- which appear in every electrical and physics text the world over, became the underpinnings of all 20th Century electrical and electromagnetic engineering -- from radio to radar, television to computer science, and were inclusive of every hard science from physics to chemistry to astrophysics that deals with electromagnetic radiative processes. The classic equations never appeared in any of Maxwell's papers or treatises!

z **The introduction in 1854 by Georg Bernard Riemann the idea of hyperspace,** i.e. the description and possibility of "higher, unseen dimensions", a fundamental assault on the 2000-year old assumptions of Euclid's The Elements -- the ordered, rectilinear laws of ordinary three dimensional reality. "In its place, Riemann proposed a four-dimensional reality (of which our 3-D reality was merely a 'subset'), in which the geometric rules were radically different, but also internally self-consistent. Even more radical: Riemann proposed that the basic laws of nature in 3-space, the three mysterious forces then known to physics -- electrostatics, magnetism and gravity -- were all fundamentally united in 4-space, and merely 'looked different' because of the resulting 'crumpled geometry' of our three-dimensional reality..." In lieu of Newton's "action-at-a-distance theories, Riemann was proposing that all such apparent forces were the result of objects moving through three dimensions, but distorted by an intruding geometry of 4-space.

z The fundamental problem of an alleged lack of experimental or experiential evidence of a fourth spacial dimension. This was addressed in part in 1919 by Theodr Kaluza, who suggested a solution to the mathematical unification of Einstein's theory of gravity with Maxwell's theory of electromagnetic radiation, via the introduction of an additional spatial dimension. Kaluza also proposed that the additional spacial dimension had somehow collapsed down to a tiny circle -- an idea now prevalent in Superstrings! This idea was expanded in 1926 by Oskar Klein, who applied the idea to Quantum Physics and came up with the idea that Kaluza's new dimension had somehow collapsed down to the "Planck length" itself -- supposedly the smallest possible size allowed by quantum interactions -- thereby tying in with Heisenberg's Uncertainty Principle.

z A rebirth of hyperdimensional physics in the guise of Superstrings (beginning in 1968), in which fundamental particles and fields are viewed as hyperspace vibrations of infinitesimally small, multi-dimensional strings -- with updated versions of the old Kaluza-Klein theory; discussions of a modern supergravity hyperspace unification model; and the exotic "String Theory" itself. The enormous increase in interest represents a fundamental revolution within a major segment of the worldwide scientific community. A significant factor is the number of dimensions: 10 (or 26, depending on strings rotation). And still, all additional dimensions are still within the Planck length!

z Discussions by Thomas E. Bearden, including, "Maxwell's original theory is, in fact, the true, so-called 'Holy Grail' of physics... the first successful unified field theory in the history of Science... a fact apparently completely unknown to the current proponents of 'Kaluza-Klein,' 'Supergravity,' and 'Superstring' ideas...." "...In discarding the scalar component of the quaternion, Heaviside and Gibbs unwittingly discarded the unified electromagnetic/gravitational portion of Maxwell's theory." "The simple vector equations produced by Heaviside and Gibbs captured only that subset of Maxwell's theory where EM and gravitation are mutually exclusive. In that subset, electromagnetic circuits and equipment will not ever, and cannot ever, produce gravitational or inertial effects in materials and equipment."

z The unwarranted restriction of Maxwell's theory, also impacted Einstein who restricted his theory of general relativity, and thus by fiat prevented the unification of electromagnetics and relativity -- as well as experimental evidence of the general theory due to any local spacetime curvature being excluded.

z The exclusion by quantum physicists of Bohm's hidden variable theory, "which conceivably could have offered the potential of engineering quantum change -- engineering physical reality itself." "Each of these major scientific disciplines missed and excluded a subset of their disciplinary area..."

z The loss to science by the limiting of Maxwell's equations of: The electrogravitic control of gravity itself, in effect, the ability to curve local and/or distant spacetime with electromagnetic radiation. "Whittaker accomplished this by demonstrating mathematically that 'the field of force due to a gravitating body can be analyzed, by a spectrum analysis' into an infinite number of constituent fields; and although the whole field of force does not vary with time, yet each of the constituent fields is an undulatory character, consisting of a simple-disturbance propagated with uniform velocity." [emphasis added] Significantly, the waves would be longitudinal and require gravity to be propagated with a finite velocity, which however did not have to be the same as that of light, and in fact may be enormously greater.

z The measurement of the hidden potential of free space by Yakir Aharonov and David Bohm in 1959, the resulting "Aharonov-Bohm Effect" providing compelling proof of a "deeper spatial strain -- a scalar potential -- underlying the existence of a so-called magnetic force-field itself. This potential is equivalent to the unseen, vorticular stress in space first envisioned by Thompson." "And stresses, when they are relieved, must release energy into their surroundings!"

z Quantum Electrodynamics Zero Point Energy of space -- vacuum energy -- in which is created, then relieved stresses in Maxwell's voticular ether (a process equivalent to tapping the energy of the vacuum -- a vacuum which, according to quantum physics, possesses a staggering amount of such energy per cubic inch of space.

z **"Given the prodigious amount of 'vacuum energy' calculated by modern physicists (trillions of atomic bomb equivalents per cubic centimeter...),** even a relatively minor but sudden release of such vast vacuum (ether) stress potential inside a planet... could literally destroy it." Or alternatively, in a far more controlled fashion, provide the anomalous infrared energy output of the planets Uranus, Neptune, Saturn, and Jupiter; or even the same source of energy for stars, including the Sun.

z A model of hyperdimensional physics based upon angular momentum -- the mass of an object and the rate at which it spins -- but an orbital momentum connected to four-space, and simultaneously affected by the planets' satellites (or in the case of the Sun, the planets, or even companion stars where applicable). A plot of total angular momentum of a planet or solar system against the total amount of internal energy being radiated into space, results in a "striking linear dependence which seems to hold across a range of luminosity and momentum totaling almost three orders of magnitude." The resulting math, equivalent to $E = mc2$, is that a celestial object's total internal luminosity seems dependent upon only one physical parameter, it's total system angular momentum (the celestial body, plus all orbiting satellites), and given by $L = mr2$. [L is the total system angular momentum, m each of the individual masses at a distance, r, from the center of the rotation.]

z The Earth-Moon system constituting yet another example of over-unity radiating of energy (as opposed to the Earth's internal energy being derived from "radioactive sources"). Implications involve major effects on past and future geological and climatological events, which may be driven, not by rising solar interactions or by-products of terrestrial civilization (e.g., accumulating greenhouse gases from burning fossil fuels), but by hyperdimensional physics!

z An explanation of the missing neutrinos from the Sun, where the assumed thermonuclear reaction model to account for the Sun's output should be resulting in over twice the number of neutrinos actually observed. But when the Sun's primary energy source is hyperdimensional (i.e. its angular momentum -- including the planetary masses orbiting it), the problem can be addressed. [The Sun has 98% of the solar system mass, but only 2% of its total angular momentum -- the latter due to the variable r, the distance of the mass from the center of rotation!] But in the hyperdimensional solution, another big planet (or a couple of smaller ones) far beyond Pluto are needed! (In this theory, about 30% of internal energy is still expected from thermonuclear reactions.)

z Hyperdimensional physics requires that energy generation in planets and stars be variable -- in effect, a mechanism resulting from an ever changing hyperspatial geometry. In effect, the changing pattern (gravitationally and dimensionally) of interacting satellites in orbit around a planet or star must change the stress pattern, in something of a geometrically twisted ether. [This tends to explain Astrology, but Astrology does not directly incorporate the ellipsoidal motion of the planets, which has a dramatic effect on r, the orbiting distance parameter. I.e., the time-variability of the hyperdimensional geometry -- yet more Cycles! -- is a central hallmark of the theory.]

z Application of hyperdimensional physics to technologies based on the same ideas -- and **which may explain free energy machines, electrochemical Cold Fusion,** and the reduction of radioactivity in nuclear isotopes (or the acceleration of the process such that half-lifes are dramatically reduced). "The implications for an entire 'rapid, radioactive nuclear waste reduction technology' -- accomplishing in hours what would normally require aeons -- is merely one immediate, desperately needed world-wide application of such 'Hyperdimensional Technologies.'"

z A hyperdimensional explanation of the anomalous motion of the **Giant Red Spot** on the planet Jupiter with variations in longitude and latitude -- not the result of gravity or tidal actions by the moons of Jupiter, but due to the lever (the "r") of angular momentum.

z **Hyperdimensional astrology,** where variations in energy output from planets would be due to the constantly changing hyperdimensional stress due to their relative interactions, and variability in orbits. The "changing interactive stresses in the 'boundary between hyperspace and real space' (in the Hyperdimensional Model) now also seem to be the answer to the mysterious 'storms' that, from time to time, have suddenly appeared in the atmospheres of several of the outer planets. The virtual 'disappearance,' in the late 80's, of Jupiter's Great Red Spot is one remarkable example; Saturn's abrupt production of a major planetary 'event,' photographed by the Hubble Space Telescope in **1994 as a brilliant cloud erupting at 19.5 degrees N. (where else?!),** is yet another."

z Variability of solar phenomena -- such as solar flares, coronal disturbances, mass ejections -- in terms of the **sunspot cycle -- 11 years (or closer to 20 for the complete solar cycle)**. The observation of short-wave radio communications and their connection to the sunspot cycle, and to the motions of the major planets of the solar system, the latter an astrological correlation between the orbits of all the planets (but especially, Jupiter, Saturn, Uranus and Neptune), and major radio-disturbing eruptions on the Sun! What had been "rediscovered was nothing short of a **'Hyperdimensional Astrology'** -- the ultimate, very ancient, now highly demonstrable angular momentum foundations behind the real influences of the Sun and planets on our lives." The research also noted that when Jupiter and Saturn were spaced by 120 degrees [an astrological trine -- interpreted as an excellent aspect] -- and solar activity was at a maximum! -- radio signals averaged of far higher quality for the year than when Jupiter and Saturn were at 180 degrees [an astrological opposition -- interpreted as challenging], and there had been a considerable decline in solar activity! In other words, the average quality of radio signals followed the cycle between Jupiter and Saturn, rather than the sunspot cycle!!

z Recognition that hyperdimensional physics allows for a disproportionate effect on the solar system by the planets due to the lever arm ("r") of the angular momentum equation, a physical mechanism -- Maxwell's changing quaternion scalar potentials -- to account for anomalous planetary energy emissions, and the reason for **sunspots at the predominant solar latitude of 19.5 degrees.**

z Noting and explaining the observed (by Voyager) **polar hexagon around the north pole of Saturn,** and with five radii extending from the center!

z The **implication of extremely distant undiscovered planets of this solar system, which theoretically (via Kepler's Third Law) could involve orbital periods of thousands (if not tens of thousands) of**

years -- and which because of their disproportionately large effect on the leveraged angular momentum could account for long-term cycles in the Sun's total luminosity. **Given that Jupiter and Saturn return to their same geometrical positions roughly every 20 years (i.e. the complete solar sunspot cycle), then it is equally plausible that unknown planets in our solar system could have a much longer term effect, and may be causing a cyclical increase and decrease of the misnamed solar constant, with the result of the already observed increase in solar energy, which may trigger profound, millennia-long climatic changes on Earth -- "Including, melting ice caps; rising ocean levels; dramatic changes in jet stream altitudes and activity; increased tornado intensities; increased hurricane wind velocities... and a permanent "El Nino"** (whose warmest waters, satellites report, are at ... ~**19.5 degrees**)." Hyperdimensional physics then might explain the very long term Cycles observed by Browning.

z Conclusion by Thomas Van Flandern "that **Mars' uniquely elliptical path around the Sun (of all the inner planets) is highly consistent with its 'escape' from... a 'missing', former member of the solar system."** Hyperdimensional physics could then be utilized to consider whether or not **entire worlds within our solar system might have been destroyed.** Alternatively, to consider "the demonstrable, historically-unprecedented changes currently occurring in our own environment -- from mysteriously-rising geophysical and volcanic activity (some of the most significant now occurring at that suspicious **"19.5 degrees!"**), to increasingly anomalous climatological and meteorological activity (does anyone notice that hurricanes have always been born at an average latitude of... **19.5 degrees**?) -- verifying the effects of a changing 'hyperdimensional physics' in our own neighborhood."

z An accelerating slow-down of the Earth's spin on its own axis over the last 20 years -- a progressive phase-shift now occurring between the rotation of the Earth and the quantum standards of an atomic clock. Additionally, the experimental observation of a change in the Gravitational Constant by as much as 0.06%, such that the suggestion that gravity during the era of the dinosaurs was less (to allow the dinosaurs to be able to stand) and that simultaneously, the Moon was precisely at a distance of 60 times the radius of the Earth... suddenly, these ideas are no longer far-fetched. In fact, hyperdimensional physics predicts such variations. [See also, Hyper-D Physics Connection and/or Planet X.]

z And finally, Hoagland suggests an intrinsically changing physics, "affecting every known system of astronomical, physical, chemical and biological interaction differently over time -- because it affects the underlying, dynamical **hyperspace foundation of 'physical reality' itself**." "And now, according to all accumulating evidence and this centuries-old physics... we are simply entering once again (after 'only' 13,000 years...) a phase of this recurring, grand solar system cycle 'of renewed hyperdimensional restructuring of that reality .'" [emphasis added]

Hoagland <http://www.enterprisemission.com/hyper1.html> thus makes an excellent argument that Hyperdimensional Physics is not only good science, but is highly relevant to our modern world.

The mathematics of Hyperdimensional Physics -- including quaternions -- are not trivial, but some simplified mathematics can be instructional.

For example, in connection with the **Golden Mean**, it is instructive to consider the ratios of various tangents of angles which predominate in any 5-fold geometry. These angles are 18°, 36°, 54°, and 72°. The Table shows these angles and others which have the common property of **reducing to 9**. (In Numerology, reducing a number is simply adding each of the digits (and adding again if necessary) until a single digit is the sum. For example, the number, 314.8884 reduces to 3+1+4+8+8+8+4 = 36 = 3+6 = 9.)

Table

tan 18° / tan 36° = tan 54° / tan 72° = 0.447213595... = 1 / Ö5

tan 18° / tan 54° = tan 36° / tan 72° = 0.236067977... = Ö5 - 2

tan 36° / tan 54° = 0.527864045... = 3 - 4 f

tan 18° / tan 72° = 0.105572809... = (3 - 4 f) / 5

A summary of the Table would suggest the ratios of tangents which involve the **Golden Mean** are intimately associated with 5-fold geometries. This ties in the trigonometric angles associated with 5-fold geometries, and the relationship Ö5 = F + f. Tangents are also important in ancient and modern of monuments, on and off Earth! See, for example, the connections between Southwest England and the Cydonia region of Mars.

Another interesting revelation involving the trigonometric tangents derives from the relationship defining a particular angle, q, i.e. $Ö5 = f + F = 2p \tan q$, from which we can calculate q to be equal to 19.5897...°. To within an accuracy of 99.39%, this angle is related to the tangent squared of 30° by the identities: $\tan2\ 30° = 1/3 = \sin j$, where j = **19.4712...°.** This latter angle turns out to be of critical importance in Hyperdimensional Physics (the latter which may be thought of as a modern day child of Sacred Geometry).

For example, if one inscribes **within a sphere, a tetrahedron with one point of the tetrahedron at the pole of the sphere, then the other three points of the tetrahedron will lie at 120° intervals along a latitude of 19.4712...°.**

This latitude corresponds, on a planetary scale, to possible sources of immense energy from the internal regions of a planet. For example: 1) Mauna Loa volcano in Hawaii, 2) Iztaccihuatl and Popocatepetl volcanoes near Mexico City, 3) the absolutely huge Mare Orientale on the Moon's far side (but near the edge of the Earth-side/far-side interface), 4) Olympus Mons on the planet Mars, (the solar system's largest volcano), 5) the Great Red Spot on Jupiter, 6) the Great Blue Spot on Neptune, and so forth, are all located at or very near to 19.5° latitude. In addition, The Great Pyramids of the Sun and Moon at Teotihuacan, Mexico are also located near this latitude, suggesting the ancient architects may have had an inkling of this "energy source".

The significance of this hypothetical, inscribed tetrahedron is due to the somewhat esoteric belief that this geometrical anomaly may be connecting with other dimensions (outside of the four dimensional space-time continuum), and therefore represent the stuff of "tapping into the Zero-Point Energy" as envisioned by such researchers as Moray King [1] and others. **Additionally, Chris Tinsley [2] has recently reported on an anti-gravitational effect (which may be tapping into the ZPE) by rotating a disc composed of superconducting material. This suggests that perhaps the more ideal experiment would be to rotate a tetrahedron shaped object -- or better yet a Merkaba (two tetrahedrons interlocked within an inscribed sphere). In either case, if the tetrahedrons were composed of superconducting material, the results could be stunning.**

One might also wish to incorporate in any new energy system design the slight difference between q and 19.4712...° -- which was on the same scale as the relationships connecting the planetary orbits. One can show, for example, the following approximate equalities:

p = 3.14159... @ (6/5) F2 = 3.14164...   (within 99.85% accuracy)

p = 3.14159... @ 4/ÖF   = 3.144606...   (within 90.41 accuracy)

e = 2.71828... @10 x (ÖF - 1) = 2.720196...   (within 92.96% accuracy)

Similarly, if Ö5 = f + F = 2p tan q, where q = 19.5897...° @ j = 19.4712...°, and 1/3 = sin j, then Ö5 = f + F @ 2p tan (19.4712...°) = p / Ö2, or

f + F @ p / Ö2

Ö5 @ p / Ö2   or   Ö10 @ p

(both within an accuracy of 99.35%)

The slight inexactitudes of these three Transcendental Numbers (and which may be thought of as one of the properties of the transcendental numbers) is extremely note-worthy. Just as the universe would rapidly collapse were it not due to angular momentum (and/or spin), it may be that the nature of transcendental numbers have similar properties with respect to the design and construction of effective energy systems based on Zero-Point Energy, and/or The Fifth Element of Connective Physics.

Nevertheless, **there is clearly a connection here between hyperdimensional physics and Sacred Geometry, or the Golden Mean!**

Another website, possibly worth investigating (and which has considerably more hard science) is <http://www.rialian.com/rnboyd/physics.htm>.

Finally, <http://www.enterprisemission.com/corbett.htm> asked the question of how long have the powers-that-be been aware of hyperdimensional physics? [Strangely of all the enterprise mission

125

webpages, this one is now missing. Hmmmm...] In any case, the argument may evolve down to much of the information about everything being already known to some, but not being given to the world at large, except in measured, carefully selected parcels. There may also be the supposition that 94% of the people will never get it, but that portions of the other 6% - those slated to be capable of joining the Education elite -- will. And that, perhaps is enough. [The above website also used to include an excellent picture of the Apollo 13, "Orion" patch -- where you could just scroll about 40% of the way down. Is that why it's now missing?]
References:

[1] King, Moray, Tapping the Zero-Point Energy, Paraclete Publishing, Provo, Utah, 1989.
[2] Tinsley, Chris, "Table-Top Antigravity?", Infinite Energy Magazine, Concord, 1997.

The Library

of ialexandriah

2003© Copyright Dan Sewell Ward, All Rights Reserved

INTERLUDE and OVERVIEW

THE UNCHANGED HUMAN CONDITION

It also gives us a very special, secret pleasure to see how unaware the people around us are of what is really happening to them." ~Adolf Hitler

Is it that we humans as a species just do not learn from past obvious mistakes, or is it that we have been designed with a defect in our mental ability? It may be because a little of each element is involved that we find ourselves in our condition. In one section of these writings we look into the "who or what" is responsible for our very being and make up as well as the "purpose" for our being on this planet. If that is an accurate proposition then it would validate the claim that the human species has all the hallmarks of a domesticated species.

Regardless of the nature of our origin or purpose (if any) for being on this planet, it would appear to me that there is in place a cunning, carefully designed and implemented plan (or plot) to direct our path and mould or shape our collective races in a specific manner. Call it the mother of all conspiracy theories if you will. If all of this is totally wrong, it makes an interesting interpretation out of a lot of given facts and established data, and should be entertaining reading. When one looks at the evidence that will unfold in the next several sections one may not only agree with that premise, but one may also start to feel rather insecure and afraid. It is not the purpose of this book to frighten or alarm, but to open our eyes, make us aware of possibilities, forewarn us, and show that regardless of our worst nightmare becoming manifest, there is truly light at the end of the "tunnel".

For a long time now, in some cases for many decades, various voices have been raised in protest and to enable public awareness of various real dangers being foisted upon humanity. They have largely been ignored, and the small percentages that have not ignored the warnings but joined the aware group of protesters have been unable to cause any change to the adverse situations. Frankly we have been "attacked" on too many fronts simultaneously and the defending ranks are too thin to enable effective defence in so many diverse directions as to ensure safety for our species. Warnings about most obvious and in many cases self-evident dangers are blatantly ignored by the "powers that be", those who could make changes. Over the course of these writings we will identify the "powers that be".

The absolute dangers to mankind in the use of **fluoride** in water supplies, **amalgam** fillings (loads of toxic mercury) in dental work, **vaccines**, **chemotherapy**, radiotherapy, electroshock treatments, **microwaves** (not only in stoves), and a host of similarly dangerous issues have been not only ignored, but actively and willfully suppressed. (If you doubt this, then do some Internet research to establish all issues and concerns.) These and other issues are loudly and vehemently declared as quite safe for use or implementation by the "authorities". The **media** carries that biased one-sided opinion, the dictates of "authority" without question and gives little to no coverage of the nature and issues of concern. This has been going on for decades, it has not changed and probably will never change. Protest is virtually useless. Why is this?

It is as though there really is an orchestrated assault against mankind on as many fronts as can be found.

Authority goes unquestioned in or by the media, allowing the most ludicrous of claims to become established as indisputable facts in the minds of the populations. It is well known that if someone shouts the most obvious of lies loud and long enough it will come to be accepted by most.

Therein is a key to a lot of problems. A lot of people simply do not **think** for themselves, and are accepting of what "**authorities**" dictate. Think about this. What is an expert or authority in most cases? Most are merely people who have gone through some educational institutions and learned what to accept, what to think, what to say, and having proven by examination that they can effectively recite the dogma of their branch of study, they are awarded some certification to that effect. These then become new peers to the closed group that monitor all aspirants and venturers into their field of "expertise".

Thus such a self-perpetuating closed group of "experts", custodians of the sacred dogma, forever control any given branch of learning or endeavour. Thus they can ignore protest with impunity, for they and their gospel will outlive any given protesters. A good example of this in action is the age of the **Sphinx** issue. The evidence of geologists presented decades ago is still totally ignored by "**Egyptologists**", who shifted the discussion to how "insensitive" the protesters were. The real issues have never been addressed or answered, as ignoring them has proven the most effective of manner in which to deal with such embarrassing (for them) questions or issues. This same tried and proven effective method is used with regular monotony whenever experts or authority (political leaders are skilled in its use) are faced with indisputable valid evidence of error in their thinking and dogma.

We see questions and error ignored in many fields. Theory of evolution is one dealt with in this book. "Big Bang" theory is quite nonsense and impossible to reasonably understand or accept. There are numerous cloudy issues we are asked to blindly accept because we are told to and quite simply that is the way things are. If "they" speak, we are expected to remain silent and accepting for the thinking has been done on our behalf. Religion is rife with "don't think about it" issues.

Why don't most people think?

We will look into that very basic question in a section that deals with the **education** system imposed upon us by our diligent and vigilant government authority. We are carefully brought up and educated so as not to think independently. Our common **religions** train us in acceptance and not to think for ourselves. And should you join any **military** force, then in most cases and issues you become forbidden to think.

The populations at large are mostly **compliant** and subservient to the authority and experts that they enable and allow to rule and preside over them. We will look into this issue as well. We will see that there may indeed be "something in the water" that should give us all cause for major concern. Yes collectively we drink the **reticulated water**, eat the **processed foods**, have our **vaccine** shots, take the **medications** of corporates, then wonder why there is an epidemic of early deaths or the populations are obese and unhealthy. We are addicted to and enslaved by an epidemic of alcohol, tobacco, and addictive drugs. Organized crime is almost in control in some areas.

Most **religions** are far from user-friendly. We will look at this claim in more detail later and see that untold human misery and death result because of this insidious control method. Now understand that there is a huge difference between "religion" and "**spirituality**". I am not against the latter, but assuredly have no more time for the former. Essentially "spirituality" is what one has or feels from "within", it is an expression of self. "Religion" is from "without", extraneous to the self and is a set of proscribed scripture, doctrine, dogma, beliefs, creeds, etc. It is control and regulation. It is rarely conducive to peace and harmony. Also understand that I am not against "GOD", but that I have no time for and am against those named entities proclaimed as gods by the many "religions" or sects. "GOD", or the intelligent field of the universe has absolutely nothing whatsoever to do with religion. Yes I know we have all been brought up and trained quite differently than to even think that kind of thought.

A huge troublesome issue with most religions it that they are frequently used as a vehicle by some to impose their will and way (often narrow, self-promoting, sometimes nefarious) upon others. Such will generally find within their acceptable scriptures some text or quote, interpret it (generally out of context) to validate or justify the imposition of their will to establish their ends. They loudly proclaim that it's from the very words of god, and thus must not be questioned but obeyed and implemented. Thus holy crusades were launched and entire cities and populations perished. Too many people let the religions and its leaders do the thinking for them.

Additional to all the above controls over mankind we are also subject to others, and one of the more far-reaching and devastating is the use of almost total control of "**finance**" to dominate and control the bulk of humanity. This method of control is used against us in such forms as taxation's, prices of essential energy sources and commodities, price gouging monopolies, price-fixing, dependency on banking and interest rates, finance availability and qualification for, property values, wage levels, profit margins allowed, employment conditions, etc. The "etc." is simply too vast to elaborate further here. I see it as a real economic warfare against the bulk of populations, a form of literal enslavement and ever increasing impoverishment.

Nothing succeeds like a "good" **financial crisis** and market crash to put the average worker in fear or actual loss of employment and in his "rightful" subservient and dependent place. In this way the "**working class**" can be easily manipulated to work for minimum wage or even less, and even made thankful for being "lucky enough" to have even the most menial of jobs. Meanwhile the rich actually do get richer and more established in their control and ownership of whatsoever is their will. I suspect such crises may generally have their origin in power plays and struggles to capture even more wealth and power by the "elite" highest in the social order.

So there we have a simplified overview of some of the many issues and problems assaulting mankind. Not only have we been seriously cheated, but also we have been misled and blatantly told great lies.

Generally individuals do not even know their true nature, their actual and real identity. This has been withheld from them. They believe they **are** a mortal body and being. They are vaguely told they "have" or will have a spirit and even its fate is determined by their degree of obedience and subservience. They are governed property. They are compliant, obedient and blindly accepting of whatever is told or given them. They don't know what they want or what to do with this life, yet look forward to another life that will be "eternal". They are taught that they must pray to some god, that they are "sinners", need forgiveness always and need his mercy and grace. They have no clear understanding of what the whole "god" thing is all about, and thus know almost nothing of reality. They trust the religions and its leaders for their vague future salvation and pleasure in an ill-defined heaven, if they've paid their "dues". They view this "hologram" of a world as a reality and look for a god as "the man behind the curtain", one who will make it right and see to justice in the next world or life.

Generally fearing death, they do not know how to die with grace or dignity, and often do not know how to live with grace and dignity. Worst of all, few will ever question the "status quo" and seek to understand anything that is not available at the mall.

PART THREE

MAN AND GOD

WHAT OF GOD? WHICH, WHO, AND WHERE?

"A truth's initial commotion is directly proportional to how deeply the lie was believed...When a well-packaged web of lies has been sold gradually to the masses over generations, the truth will seem utterly preposterous and its speaker, a raving lunatic." --Dresden James

This essay comes with a caution. I cannot guarantee it or any section or segment of it is correct in any way or at all. It is to be read purely as a mind opening exercise to guide you along many avenues of thought. Neither is it intended in any way to be a definitive statement of fact or in fact my final opinion in any area at all. Perhaps it will be an ongoing essay and updated from time to time, for such is the nature of human understanding, wisdom, unknown prejudices etc etc.

The initial iteration was dated 16 October 2006. Bob is still alive years after the dark clouds gathered over him. Do not therefore consider this the final words on any thing contained herein. But I'd be reasonably sure the general concept would remain virtually unchanged.

I asked myself seriously just once, for one serious asking is enough on this vital matter, if it is indeed serious in intent, "What am I to make of this Jehovah thing?" Call him Jehovah, Lord, or 100 other names, it is the traditional god of Israel to which I refer. We all know that to which I refer. The god of "Genesis", of Abraham, Isaac and Jacob. I finally dared to address and form my unasked questions that I secretly harboured but denied expression for too long.

Let's get some perspective.

Our earth has existed, we are told, some 4-5 billion years, and the known or perceived universe some 15 or more billion years. At the edges of our perceived (bubble shaped?) universe galaxies are receding from us at near the speed of light, and galactic expansion ultimately means that some will forever be lost to our perceived "universe" ("universe" being used herein to describe the collection of galaxies that can be detected by or know to us) As the distances and expansion factors grow they will retreat logically, faster than the speed of light surely (the red shift thing), or get real close. And what of a creature on those distant galaxies seeing us depart at near light speed? Now he is the centre of his "universe" (or bubble) and surely, looking the about face from our direction he is privy to and sees galaxies lost to our view. In essence, by extension of the same factors and logic, surely his universe overlaps our known universe, and includes another of which we have no knowledge, for parts of his known universe having receded long ago from us. Those parts must lie beyond our perception range. And if our perceptible range is the 15 odd billion years old, what age is attributed to that which logically lies beyond? Infinite time and space takes us to a new level of understanding if we can perceive a chain of "observable universes" from the viewpoint of a being on the "edge" of the prior universe in the chain. By the same extension, this must occur in every direction possible from any given starting point.

Or has 'science' got it all wrong? Are we just marbles in a super alien's marble bag? Remember our atoms are mostly space, almost no "solid" – just like out there in the vast reaches of "space". A distant galaxy looks as though solid yet we are told 2 galaxies could pass one through the other with barely two component stars colliding. "Solid" is an illusion it seems.

How many universes are there then? The question almost has no meaning. It's too vast to really come to grips with, as is its age. Tens or possibly hundreds of billions of years according to our time measure may be a painfully inadequate guess. This principle of overlapping universes endlessly reaching out in every direction from any starting point, consuming and creating unimaginable space/time would severely damage the commonly accepted **"Big Bang Theory"**. Perhaps it is time for us all to have a rethink about many things. Of what importance then is "our" temporal earth time measure except for us to measure our meagre life span or planetary cycles?

Yet for some reason we are asked to accept – and generally blindly do so – that given this above overlooked scenario, He who is the supposed creator of it all, who is omnipresent, omniscient, omni "everything", decides to slum it down to this "nothing" of a planet, in this equally nothing special a galaxy. He does this at this one unique time out of untold zillions of years to fraternise with just one or two selected mortals out of millions of such planetary mortals. He then identifies himself and demands to be acknowledged for his 'godship'. This select few are then entrusted, so we are asked to believe, to be responsible for the saving (whatever that means) of all humanity. That's it. A one time shot at it. Is it too bad, bad luck indeed, for the countless generations existent before the event? Or what of those in really remote non-local places? (Mormons profess to address this seeming grotesque unjustness to those not privy to this god's timing or grace. Another story there.)

What gives? Does not sound right or equitable to me. Is he not supposed to be always present? Or is his presence like a McDonald's special, for a limited time only? Have these gods not got enough time to get around to all? Has he been busy elsewhere for the countless years before his revealing of himself to the most fortunate lucky few? As a Hebrew prophet once mocked at other gods, "perchance he was in his 'chamber'". What was wrong with say the Chinese, Indian, Negro, Celt or whoever that they were not privy to this favour? If this is a manifestation of a true god then it is frankly not good enough.

It seems and smells like the Jehovah thing is a very local and probably unreal event indeed. Looking at it coldly in the light of ancient literature discovered over the past 100 years or so, it seems to be an adopted and adapted tribal thing. After all, other groups, tribes and nations around the earth had equally valid and equally realistic claims to the sole revelation of (a) god. Strangely and tellingly all these (local) gods have a prejudiced favour for the 'locals'. There is an almost uncomfortable localness of each such claimed god. For decades I had unformed questions as to why god would seem to be so local, prejudiced, and secretive, not to mention so limited in the allocation of his "dealing with us" time. Seems like one just passing through. Sure all religions can seem to justify all those issues, but that is all it is: justifying those things by apologists in action. I submit they are all false and in error because of the inconsistency and patent unjustness of the premiss. "The" ultimate god could not be so inconsistent in dealing with his claimed creations that he could only be judged as downright nasty as times. A god who is recorded to be loving, jealous, vengeful, destructive and gives obvious preference is surely not to be trusted, especially when he operates for a limited time only in a limited area with a select group. Generally of course he is totally unknown and unrevealed to any others not of the favoured group or generation. Also the god of Genesis is obviously not omniscient.

I suggest and respectfully submit that any group who claim to know or reveal a god that has a non-universal specific given name, has a seeming limited sphere of control, authority or influence who does not reveal himself freely and equally to all, is under the influence of wishful thinking. Or contriving a stratagem to control or entrap our species. Such claimants tend to resort to persecution sooner or later. Generally they will kill in 'his' name if they can get away with it. Jehovah has a following with a most foul bloodstained history.

Blindness and ignorance of such adherents is symptomatic. For instance by way of illustration, a Roman Catholic school principal, who is surely presumed to be a reasonable authority or agent of the god, claims that "animals have no spirit". Think deeply about that a moment. It just has to scream total ignorance or a totally deceiving limited authority god. Yet such are sectarian leaders. My daughter protested this very issue to me and rightly so for she could see and recognise unjustness, limitations and error. The educator could not.

By definition, any god who is worth consideration has to be a god that encompasses all that is, all that was, all that will ever be, across endless universes at all times. (And that defines the omnific fabric of the universe.) He does not hide on a mountain or in a burning bush nor reveal himself as such to a select few or many. (I use the He, him etc as a convenience, and as such in no way presume to infer gender, race, shape, form, localisation or any such things.) Indeed other articles point to my thoughts and conclusions. Just as we are "star stuff" elements of the earth, equally we are also "god stuff", part of the life giving intelligence given by the omnific fabric of the universe, the quantum sea etc.

A true GOD must be an intelligence that fills and encompasses the vastness of untold and limitless universes, overlapping universes if you will, that is literally all present everywhere at the same time, that has immediate knowledge of all events as they happen, unhindered by limitations of time and space as we see them. An intelligence and energy that is in fact the entire sum total of all universes, that endlessly creates, re-cycles within and of itself would indeed be GOD. Such a one needs no name, nor preachers to reveal a hidden name or doctrine. Such a one is GOD of all and to all, for all are not only his creation, but in very fact **part** of GOD. Thus the true GOD must be discernible and knowable to and by all without assistance or the need for others, chosen or not, to reveal him to us. The real GOD by nature of his very reality must become **self evident and self revealing.** Otherwise such fail to qualify to be acceptable or considered for the role. This accessibility of necessity includes all life including non-humans such as we call animals, (I wonder what they call us, each in their own tongue. Most likely dangerous savage killers.) and any other thing or species not of our 'kind'. All life, of whatever form, indeed all matter of whatever form, is a creation of and part of the fabric of the universe and constantly bathes within it.

So Jehovah, Enki, Enlil, Isis and all others, I do not question whether or not you exist or existed in reality. I do challenge the idea that such as you are GOD, for surely you like us, are also star stuff enlivened by GOD stuff, and like us, will recycle. Is that why such as you are not around today?

202-MOULDING HUMANITY

*"People do not like to think. If one thinks, one must reach conclusions.
Conclusions are not always pleasant."
-Helen Keller*

This section presents ideas and materials that lead to a conclusion that came as a surprise to me. While researching and correlating materials, I gathered enough to be able to formulate a plausible theory that encompasses data seemingly from quite unrelated and different sources. Data that when thought about for some time, correlates into one big picture that really makes a lot of sense. It also is able to incorporate a lot of things that when standing alone, do not seem to make any sense at all. Additionally, almost all so called (current) "conspiracy theories" fit very comfortably into the framework of the theory. There emerges a possibly terrifying story that may well be able to explain "it all". Above all, it enables understanding and answers to those big questions: "what is the meaning and purpose of life?" and "is there an ongoing battle between good and evil?" The whole "who is god and what is the relationship?" falls well within the framework of this theory.

So far as I am aware, and please correct me if I am wrong, the Bible seems silent as to the actual or any real reasons as to why "God, GOD, or Lord GOD" created us at all. Certainly no purpose is stated in Genesis. If you doubt this, take the time to fully read it.

Let's briefly discuss the bible and its source. The Old Testament is a record of the race/nation of which the Jews and Arabs seem the sole survivors. Others are only there because of interactions. They trace and claim ancestry back to one Abraham. (Abram) Abraham's father, Terah, left Ur of the Chaldees and is thus Sumerian of origin. Note that this Abraham is also stated as commanding what amounts to a small army.

There is a wealth of information in the records from both sources, that of Israel and that of the Sumerians, and although seeming unrelated, they are both in fact relating the same elements of the early story or history. The Sumerian records would seem to be the source materials for the initial chapters of the book of Genesis, and those chapters contain the most contentious issues and elements. These are the chapters relating to the ante-deluvian period, the "pre-history" as it could be said. Similar elements are found in, and come from Egyptian records, more particularly relating to Isis, Horus, Set et al. It is when researching the Sumerian records where names are given that one finds the "purpose and reasons" for the creation of our species.

Now I do not intend to document every or even many references in this writing, but you can certainly locate them easily enough, more so with the Internet search engines. Some of the interesting and difficult to understand rationally (without a "big picture" framework with which to work) are as follows.

Genesis gives two accounts of the creation, and they differ considerably. Different entities seem implied as chapter one recounts "God" as the creator, while chapter 2 introduces us to "LORD God". Chapter 2 appears to specifically relate to a physical organization of man using elements of the earth. It also more than strongly suggests that more than one entity is involved in this organization of the human species. ("Aha", some Christians will shout, "but that is Jehovah and the Father God." Be that so, then we still have a situation of more than one god in genesis, discussing and deciding issues as equals.) Possible cloning using anesthetic or "deep sleep" is mentioned in 2:21. In chapter 3:8 we find the creator/s seemingly walking in some "gardens" talking audibly and overheard by the "man", and at 3:22 we have a group decision made and stated by them, with a sentence pronounced. Fear of the "man's" ability to "live forever" is clearly expressed, and a decision is announced to essentially terminate the species so recently organized. At some times the god seems quite nasty and destructive to man, and at other times very helpful. This nastier and destructive nature of the god/gods of Genesis is largely glossed over and certainly not brought up by various "clergy" of Christendom who attempt to convince us that god is always a god of love who would never hurt or harm any of his "children". What utter rubbish that is and how easy to demonstrate gods genocidal and human hating characteristics.

These things betray Genesis' source materials, the Sumerian records. In those records the gods are less mysterious, they are simply beings who came to earth, have names, have family groups, and have "issues" similar to us today. They argue and disagree among themselves. They may live a hugely long life span, have untold and unimaginable powers and abilities, incredible technology, but they also appear to age and be mortal, Now whereas Genesis is silent as to the reasons for the organization of our species, the materials from Sumer give the information. We were created to become laborers for them. Manual labour on planet Earth did not suit them. Genesis 3:23 gives indication of the labour requirement, and chapter 4 introduces the fact that humans seem required to give "tribute" to the creators. Seems like a straight up situation to me.

Now the interesting bits to correlate into the picture. From Genesis we see the "gods" and the "sons of god" had free rein on the earth, doing whatsoever pleased them. We read that in time, they considered the human females as "fair" and took them as "wives" fathering children with them. Those children are specifically mentioned in Genesis. Some of the "gods" treated man well, and interacted pleasantly with selected humans. Enoch was removed from humans and taken into their fold. Noah was warned of the impending destruction to befall the planet. Later, much later, Abraham entertained a couple of such beings as they visited him while he sat at his tent door. Abraham gave them a meal; they organized for his wife Sara to have a child, and then departed en route to destroy Sodom and Gomorrah. Abraham even reasoned with them, making an agreement designed to save the cities. Presumably the same beings then turned up at those cities, met Lot and his family and saved them from the following destruction. They appeared as humans among humans, and even the citizens of the doomed city could not identify them as non-human, they wanted "their way" with them.

An interesting aside here as it becomes relevant. The deluge/flood/destruction recorded as in the days of Noah and of which he was forewarned seems to have been a real event. I will not address the implied biblical dating for it, but only within the human context.

It seems that about some 12,000 years ago new cultures and civilizations spontaneously seemed to spring up all over the globe. We see various sciences saying that about then animals were domesticated, crops and plants also developed (supposedly by primitive man from wild varieties, but that is dealt with elsewhere) and homo sapiens sapiens were established in the world. Before this period there is almost no indications of substantial culture to be had.

There is a remarkable amount of evidence indicating that the great pyramid and sphinx of Egypt in fact date from about this time, some 12,000 years ago, and that the Sphinx actually has damage indicating water erosion is the real cause of most damage to it. In the precession of the equinox, Leo was the sign then, just as Aquarius is the up and coming one now. Leo and the Sphinx makes a fascinating combination that I recommend one follows up. All the materials are out there to validate all of this regardless of the denials or more correctly, of the lack of evidence to the contrary by the "expert Egyptologists". It would seem that Egypt was indeed a center of civilization some 12k years ago, and that deluge was the cause of its destruction about then. There are ancient Egyptian writings that would confirm this, and also claim that its early pre-dynastic rulers individually lived for thousands of years, gods or demigods in fact. Of course the modern men of science will have none of this, despite the records. Could it be that the long lost original face from the sphinx was that of one of these "gods", the non-human residents on the planet, those that organized our species?

Some writers state that there is no evidence that the Anunnaki ever actually left this planet. I clearly recall reading that they did so, perhaps only temporarily, at the time of the deluge. Genesis says it was Noah warned, the Sumer records give a different name for such a one warned by Enki, one of the Anunnaki. The destruction was to be so vast, complete and total, that they abandoned this planet, leaving their "created" humans to their own fate and end. Genesis says it "repented" god that he had made man, and that man was to be wiped out as a species. It was to flee this pending destruction itself that they left the planet to preserve themselves.

In the final segment of these writings there is an amount of additional materials to read relating to the above issues. That material is merely a small representation of what is freely available on the Internet should one choose to search for additional materials or verification of matters mentioned above. I have reproduced the articles in full as they appear and were extracted off the Internet as perhaps most people would not do such a search or simply find it inconvenient to attempt or access materials off the Internet.

SEEKING PURPOSE OR MEANING OF LIFE

I think it imperative that if one seeks to establish or find any purpose or **meaning for life** that one must understand the true nature of the human species, or at the least be aware of what possible origins could be involved. Additionally one should have a reasonably accurate knowledge of their own true nature and self. It is prudent to go into the search divested of any rose coloured glasses through which they may have viewed the world as the creation of a loving devoted individual deity that knows and cares for each person individually. The reality and the evidence even from the bible simply do not support that sort of thinking or claim.

There are in fact those who fearlessly claim that the god of Christendom is in fact quite an evil human hating "individual", and let's face it, there is sufficient evidence and historical record to give some credibility to that line of thinking. More on that and associated issues as we progress. I am not presenting any particular line of thought as absolute fact, but exploring and analysing existing materials in an effort to make sense of so many subjects that if considered alone simply make no sense, have no seemingly valid cause, and appear totally unrelated to anything else whatsoever.

Let's now proceed to a review and analysis of some confusing and worrying materials, and see if any sense can be made of the "man" and "god" thing, and probe at those most vexing issues of good and evil, and the ongoing conflict of good and evil. Once again understand that my attitude is simply that all things should and must be capable of being understood. I think it is merely a matter of putting things in a more logical sequence and then asking the "right" or appropriate question at the appropriate time when one has as much relevant information as possible before them. A good analogy is putting together a jig saw puzzle. Individual pieces standing alone are impossible to understand or place within the "big picture". However when picked up at an appropriate time, analysed together with other pieces that are beginning to construct an intelligible picture, then questioned about what it means and where it goes, those mysterious pieces add to the picture until the entire scene is perceived.

MOULDING HUMANITY

At some time in our pre-historical past humans realized that it is difficult or even impossible to control or use a herd of wild beasts. Before beasts that are now cattle could be made useful for mankind they had to be tamed and domesticated. The same holds true for all the beasts for which mankind has a regular use.

Once the herd is tamed and compliant it can be handled and dealt with relatively easily. We are taught that all that it took was some selective breeding, a little manipulation, and time. That all seems straight forward and seemingly unquestionable, and there probably is a large amount of truth in it. But it is not entirely satisfactory and possibly a little flawed. We really should address the question of just what it was that gave our human species such a sudden surge of development that resulted in culture, civilization, domestication of plants and animals, technology. It seems unlikely at least to me that suddenly primitive savages collectively gathered simultaneously around the globe, and came to a united decision to become something different from what they had been for the past supposed millions or hundreds of thousands of years. I think that would need and indicate some sort of organization.

However we have dealt with this issue in more depth earlier, and I raise the issue again only as an introduction to discussion of the likelihood that the entire human race is currently being manipulated, domesticated, and made entirely compliant. I suspect that the non-compliant will be among the first to be eliminated if I am right, and that in due course, possibly quite soon, a culling of the species may begin. Quite possibly the killings such as are recorded in "**203b**-They're Coming to Take Me Away" may be merely a "practice run" to see just what can be done with impunity. Pol Pot determined that his country's population would be reduced from some 7 million to just 1 million. No one stood in his way, and the killings continued unabated with the "world's Policeman", the USA as it likes to think of itself, and others, doing nothing about it. It took neighbouring Vietnam, a communist country, to step in, invade and end the slaughter, in about 1 month. That would evidence to any reasonable person that if a country or amalgamation with arms at their disposal such as the USA has, the madness could have ended much faster and far earlier. It need not have lasted 4 years. Why was this allowed to happen? Yes, "allowed to happen". Now it gets weird, really weird and uncomfortable. The United Nations has supported the ideal that the world's population would be reduced from near its current 7 billion to around 1 to 2 billion.

If what I fear is correct then we should be able to identify specific indicators which warn us that all is indeed not well for our human race globally.

Human compliance is assured by the implementation of specific programs, often seemingly unrelated, but when put together paint a sinister pattern that has the hallmarks of deliberate organization. Viewed together we see a pattern of deliberate erosion of liberty, a dumbing down of the entire population, a definitely debilitating interference with the health of the community at large, and chemicals imposed through the absolute essentials of life that erode human health and will. These items could be considered as recent (historically) innovations to already tight control kept and maintained over populations at large by direct impositions of governments and religion and of what could now be called complete financial control over all but the exclusively elite.

203-THE WAR AGAINST HUMANITY.

*"And there was war in heaven: Michael and his angels fought
against the dragon; and the dragon fought and his angels,
And prevailed not; neither was their place found any more in heaven.
And the great dragon was cast out, that old serpent, called the Devil,
and Satan, which deceiveth the whole world: he was cast out
into the earth, and his angels were cast out with him.
(Revelations 12:7-9 KJV)*

*"Now there was a day when the sons of God came to present
themselves before the LORD, and Satan came among them.
And the LORD said unto Satan, Whence cometh thou?
And Satan answered the LORD, and said, From going to and fro
in the earth, and from walking up and down in it."
(Job 1:6-7 KJV)*

Those are just two quotes from the bible that are representative of a vast amount of information from that book that should alert us to the fact that there is indeed more going on, and more agendas afoot than most people either know or care to know about. Short verses that relate a story to the effect that in what most people think of as a peaceful "heaven", often presumed the sole habitation of an enthroned God being constantly worshipped and adored by hosts of (harp playing) devoted angels, there is or has been serious disharmony that at some time in an obviously past time resulted in war. The losers were exiled to planet earth and literally walk among mankind.

It would be easy to dismiss this totally if it were the only such source of such a seeming fanciful tale. However it is not the only source of such tales, and its not only the ancient Hebrew, Jewish (call it what you will) records that give us tales of wars among the gods. Those from "India" give far more details of the wars and methods, weapons, and destruction caused upon this very earth as a consequence of the disharmony among the gods. However I will not linger on this ancient aspect of the wars that are so recorded, nor dwell on the sources of information that have survived to be available today. What I would like to establish is that these stories are almost certainly not fanciful imaginings written for amusement or teachings of morals, but represent very real events that involved both planet earth and venues not on planet earth.

By "venues not on planet earth" I mean precisely that. I do not care to say if this is in some hyperdimensional space, in some mythical heaven, or whether it is and was in our perceivable and known universe. The establishable fact seems to be that the wars as recorded spilled over and physically took place on our planet, that human lives were lost, and civilizations destroyed in consequence. If you determine to establish the facts from our pre-history, a simple internet research will reveal a vast amount of information regarding areas of ancient devastation scattered around our globe.

Question is, were or are these "gods" spiritual beings, or are they a little more physically substantial in our dimension or world? Either way it probably makes little or no difference, for the end result of the disharmony is evidenced by physical scars on the planet.

A vastly more important question would be: Where are these beings called "gods", "angels", and "devils" now? Then perhaps we could seek to identify just who is being spoken of in say the bible records, as God, LORD, Michael, Satan, devil, dragon, etc.

Let's paint a picture and see what that picture solves and eliminates from our dusty "mysteries" folder.

EARTH & BEGINNINGS

An unknown long time ago (in the 100,000s of years ago bracket) a super intelligent species or race that existed on this planet (and possibly still exist here) came to a decision to genetically modify another species found on the earth, for the purpose of using the so modified species as workers and thus remove from them the burdens of tedious manual work. It could be likened to a decision being made today to genetically modify and change say the gorilla or chimpanzee, give them more intelligence, enhance their physical appearance and ability, then train them for certain tasks. At this point of this proposal it does not matter how long each species had been on earth, nor does it matter at present if in both species were in fact native to this earth.

Let us call the intelligent beings **"species A"**. And let us call the lesser intelligent and inferior being or race **"species Z"**. It is recorded (Sumerian) that the original modified humans (as we now know them) were borne by selected females of **"species A"**, and presumably thus born into the world in the normal way. It is also recorded that the embryo of combined **"species Z"** and **"species A"** was transplanted into the females of the latter species. Thus the resultant new species, lets call them **"species X"**, for in effect they are a crossbreed, were truly "in the image" of their "creators". In short, the genes of species "A" were spliced in to those of species "Z". Whereas even less than 100 years ago such a proposition would have been preposterous, not to mention heresy, today in a world of cloned sheep, genetically engineering of life forms including plants, perhaps even this is not too far away from us, the descendants of species X.

It may well be that the "species A" were also of many different races, as we understand the word, as ancient art certainly indicates some of the "gods" as black. This together with the information that many birthing mothers were used could well explain the many different races now existent with us, "species X". Those of "species A" are thus the creators of modern man, it was their earth, and they made all the rules. They are the ones that had the fabulous flying machines that are recorded, the weapons so well described in ancient writings, the incomprehensible advanced civilisation of legends, and the ability to use science and technology that is even still beyond our understanding. These are they who built the vast structures around the globe incorporating mathematics and techniques that still amaze or puzzle us today. Many of their personal names are in fact recorded and known to us, as is the fact that they apparently lived for what is to us an astounding, even unbelievable, life span. Tens of thousands of earth years, perhaps even hundreds of thousands of our years seem to be in evidence. Some of them are named in the lists of ancient kings for some of the ancient civilisations.

These are they who in council decreed "let us make man in our image, male and female..." (Genesis) Bear in mind the title "man" applies only to us, the "species X". They are not and were never "man". (Man being Adam or earther) Some of them played the part and role of "gods" to us, and remarkably this exact scenario is central to the storyline of the movie **"Zardoz"**. There an earth-based group of immortals lived isolated from beastial mortals, but maintained communications through certain of their ranks, some of whom played the role of being gods to the lesser mortals. Quite a revealing movie to see, as it reveals the god of the movie, (who calls himself Zardoz) as a clever immortal playing at being the Wi**zard** of **oz**, and manipulating events, even to the hero's breeding and birth, from "behind the curtains".

"Species Z", the source of humans, seems to have either died out, or been absorbed or incorporated into the current crop of "species X". Some write that the species to which I refer as "species Z" was what is known as homo erectus, and that the current earthly breed of humans did in fact really replace that species with no evidence of ever cross breeding with them. I suspect they may have been represented by the Neanderthal, and have read excellent articles that go a long way to evidencing the Neanderthals have in fact been absorbed into human stock with the genetic code from them identifiable among us. Again this contributes to explaining some of the vast differences in the human species.

In a nutshell, that was the start of the plot, and as they say, all the rest is mere detail. However in splicing the genes together the (genetic) engineer, called a "god", made the new species a little too smart for their proposed basic purposes and specifications, and made them so that the final edition was actually able to breed and self produce. Seems this was not in the original production plans, and whether intentional or not, became the source of huge problems. At least one of the chief executive expressed horror with words along the lines of "who told you that you are naked...." (Genesis again) And all of the stuff that goes along with knowing about nakedness, sex, and so forth.

Procreation, the ability to self produce and breed, was indeed the "fruit" of the **"tree of life"** thing that it seems was expressly forbidden and not allowed to this newly created species. Think about it. The creating "gods" would have little control over a species that had the ability and propensity to get out of control. Worse still is the simple fact of mathematics involved in any breeding, even if a single breeding pair is all that exists. Two becomes four (or more) four becomes eight, eight becomes sixteen etc. Recall the story of the horse shoes. The noble was reluctant to pay a farrier's price, so the farrier suggested 1cent the first nail, and double it for each succeeding nail. The ignorant noble agreed and the farrier laughed away to himself as he placed the 16 nails. After 16 nails or generations, 65,536. Worse, if the humans had long life spans as Genesis indicates, we may have close to the sum total of the entire "breed" alive simultaneously. That's in excess of 130,000 per breeding pair in a relatively short time. Words like "rabbits" and "small city" come to mind. Control could get very difficult if not impossible. No wonder an elimination decree was made later. More on human numbers later.

After that revelation, he didn't want to have anything to do with the new species, they were not the requested specifications or stock. So he rejected them, told them to get lost, threw them out of **"the garden"** (the residential compound of the superior beings if you will) to fend for themselves in the big bad outside world. He sent them out to die. "for from dust of the earth you were taken, and to dust you will return". This is us then, species X, earthers, made of earth, eat, breathe, drink of the earth, live and die, then recycle body back to the earth. Obviously the evicting god was not omniscient, for indeed we did not perish nor die out as a species.   No, I don't accept that his words accompanying the eviction refer to a mere imposition of a mortal death to mankind. That contention just does not fit into the whole or "big" picture.

The good news is that the entire executive was not "anti" the new species X mankind. It is recorded that some who are named, including the engineer who "created" us, actually protected and preserved us. But for mankind, a new species trying to survive in a hostile world, our troubles were only beginning. It is recorded that some of our species were so favoured as to be able to live with and among some of them, and they thus lived in **"paradise"**, ate the food of the gods, food that gave them greater life span than those on the "outside" living in **"hell"**. A real problem arose as it is recorded, when some of those of species "A" decided that our human females were really cute and desirable little creatures. They wanted them for more than one wants mere brute labour or domestic pets. It is recorded that some of these "sons of god" saw the human daughters of men as fair and took of them wives…. (Genesis yet again)

Introducing yet **another new species, "species XA"**. This introduced another crossbreed to the human gene pool. It added an immediate 50% boost for the offspring of such unions, to their levels of "creator gods" species "A" genetic code. It goes without saying that this welcome boost of presumably beneficial and superior genetic code would be almost universally distributed among the entire human species after even a few millennia, but in the earlier days immediately after the events, it is recorded that it made a huge difference. It is recorded that the offspring of those unions were **mighty men of renown**, perhaps even giants. (I guess there are many definitions of "giants", not necessarily referring only to stature) It is not recorded if females of species "A" took males of species "X" as partners, and is probably of no consequence really, apart from the fact that it would seem quite probable given what we already have in the records. Almost universal legends exist often naming some who are claimed to be fathered by the "gods" in union with mortal women. **Achilles, Hercules** immediately spring to mind. Oh yes, the Greek pantheon elaborates on the residence of the gods on the mount and of their special food. (**Ambrosia**, food and drink of the gods that gave everlasting youth and beauty.)

The scenario to just this level now indicates four humanoid species contemporaneously upon the earth.

The "not us" creator engineers and their "species A"
The root stock of "us", no longer extent, "species Z"
The newly organised work force, rejected "species X"
A crossbreed of human female and "them", "species XA"

The latter crossbreeds, species XA in all probability enjoyed vastly superior qualities than all but pure species "A". Assuming any of this is factual, then it gives us the clear reasons why the keeping of who begat whom was so important. No doubt about it all, selective breeding among humans and pedigree records were all started countless millennia ago. Also assuming any of this is factual, then I have little doubt that the "species A" have not departed, died out, or totally disregard us. If it happened once it will happen again, and they could take and crossbreed with humans as they see fit. After all, it is their planet and they make all the rules. They also probably have all of the gold.

A strange and interesting aside here is that a high percentage of **"abduction"** claims and reports involve the victim thereof claiming they were subjected to the experience of "medical" and associated examination of the reproduction systems.

Lets take a break from the scenario, and figure out some of what this means.

I can barely begin to present the full significance of these newly developed (for me) ideas.

Several immediate issues need raising. Can a race or species superior to earther humans secretly co-exist with us on this planet, and if so, then how?

I was once asked why I spent so much time watching movies and made the immediate reply that one could learn much from movies of almost any type. Certainly one learns a lot about human nature and attitudes, values, ethics etc. However a few movies stand out because of the nature of what was presented. One was **"Zardoz"**, which showed how easily an advanced group of immortals can conceal themselves on earth among mortals. Also, in **"Beneath the Planet of the Apes"** we saw another movie wherein an advanced species secretly shared the world with a more primitive species, wherein the lesser species, the apes, were totally oblivious to the others' presence till the "crunch" day. Another was **"Highlander"**, wherein Connor McLeod reveals how he lived undetected for centuries, preserving his individual wealth using the anonymous structure of **corporate bodies**. In fact the mysteries of the accumulating wealth and power of corporations can clearly fall into place now and find a purpose. That purpose could be very sinister indeed. Yes, it is a very simple matter for such a thing to be happening right now with the bulk of humanity not having the vaguest idea of what is really going on.

Also recall that it is recorded that they walk among us and are not identifiable as "**not us**". These are they who met physically with Abraham at his tent door, who then went to Sodom and were taken as and assumed to be regular humans, homo sapien sapien. These are they who saw the daughters of men were fair, and took wives of them, interbred successfully and had "half-breed" children who were described as mighty. Remember that I said to be ready to be a little bit afraid? An increase of knowledge and understanding may now give us cause to become very much afraid. Genesis indicates permanent residence on earth for those "cast down". Oh yes, I guess it's a reasonable assumption and it is recorded that they also breed or procreate, and not only with mortal women. Purebreed "species A", the descendants of the original "gods", the next generations, must surely be a reality.

A reasonable review of all the "imponderables" and "mysteries" long held in abeyance seems to allow most, if not all, to be now fully and reasonably resolved. Perhaps the best way to present this is to overview briefly some of the different areas involved in the great file of "unexplained".

Ancient and pre-history

The probable fact that we are not the prime species on earth but were preceded by a vastly superior race that in fact were responsible for our existence, the then newly developed "homo sapiens sapiens", resolves the following issues from a huge portfolio of ancient mysteries:

The lack of that transition species, commonly called the missing link; The whole "what happened to Neanderthal?" issue. The seeming tracability of human ancestry to a common individual or source. This latter is now well documented "out there".

Who were responsible for the construction of the megalithic structures that still amaze and puzzle us in the 21st century? Contradictory claims exist for the ages assigned to various structures to fit into a preconceived "text book" of human history that is loudly declared by the "experts" as the only possibility and truth. (The old "if these structures exist, and they do, then they have to be built by us, -because there is no one else- and that means they cannot be more than "x" years old." way of thinking.) At least we have advanced from the older school of belief still held by some fundamentalists that nothing can pre-date 4004 BC because that was when god created the earth.

Why there was a sudden and almost global flourishing of civilisation for the new homo sapiens sapiens with newly manifested civilisations, agriculture, writing, religions, domestication of animals, abandonment of cannibalism, use of metals, engineering, etc. Why was there a universal quest for gold?

The unbelievable ages assigned to the names of some of the ancient kings of the ancient kingdoms; Strangely the authorities accept those named on such lists that have what are now considered acceptable "normal" mortal ages that appear after the anomalous names and years. Also the great ages claimed for Genesis' patriarchs finds resolution.

Numerous archaeological anomalies that have failed to be suppressed; The consistent and global legends of super civilisations preceding the "flood", and that had global influence; Why some ancient writings contain information far beyond the assumed knowledge held at the time. Flying machines, weapons that have to be nuclear, astronomy, knowledge of the earth, of dilated time and space. (That constant and nagging statement that "**1000 years** is as a single day". Also the ancient spacefaring human who when asking if he could return home, was told his peers were then long dead.)

Religion

All of the seeming inconsistencies of the Christian Bible now find resolution as Jehovah becomes just one of the super race and his obvious localised sphere of influence becomes fully understandable. The reason why there has never been revealed to man a universal, global, or cosmic creator god is now obvious. All our earth records are manmade and deal with localised powerful super beings and not true gods. It now becomes evident that the records of the "gods" of many cultures and races now prove every bit as valid as those of Judaism, Moslem, and Christianity, all of which are Jehovah (by whatever name or spelling) based. It would seem that all these are at least kinfolk of Enlil who is almost certainly the same one known as Jehovah and clearly identifies as him.

Once this is mentally digested and understood, then we will see that the time has fully come to put aside all animosity and division based on what are spurious claims foisted upon us as or in the name of religion. If one claim is false, then it is possible all claims are false, and in view of the self-evident contradictions that exist even within just one religion, there is unimpeachable evidence of false claims or statements.

I say beware of religion. This has nothing whatsoever to do with **spirituality**, which is what we should really be seeking and desire as our true wealth and treasure. Those that are religious are not necessarily spiritually inclined in any way whatsoever. Indeed quite the opposite, "religious" are often closed minded, bigoted, prejudiced, and foster persecution and **pogroms**.

The occult stuff

I cannot think of anything, real or claimed, that does not now "fit in" and find acceptable explanation and understanding within the framework of these theories. Let me just go into the **"UFO"** situation briefly.

There are just so many theories and so much evidence scattered among probably millions of publications that are believable. Only a few things are certain. One is that they are probably not "ours". "Our" being mortal earther humans. Whether they are multi and interdimensional or single universe space vehicles is mere detail, probably if real they are both. Perchance they may be restricted to just our observable 4 dimensional time/space, and manned by unbelievably long living super beings. Whether they are physical to this dimension and used for real space travel across vast distances or merely within our solar system again is irrelevant and mere detail. (Unless of course we are individually invited to go along for the ride in one of them.)

The issue here is that they now become understandable, have a logical origin or at least base, and become acceptable. It has long been suspected by some that any such vehicles must be of this earth. No proof even of existence is required, and **no proof will be forthcoming**. Proof would shatter the illusion that we are alone and masters of our planet if not the galaxy. "They" would be revealed to all, but obviously would wish to remain hidden from a species that can now "do whatsoever they imagine to do". (The Genesis concern of "god") It is recorded that this was the foundation of their fear of us. I have little doubt that the pitchforks would be taken up and torches would be lit across the globe to eradicate them should they be made manifest or exposed as real. Doubtless "they" would know this, and just how nasty the humans are. If legends are right, they have manipulated and used us for wars and use us to self destroy. Now how many movies have shown you the autopsy room prepared for the visiting alien? It was an unsettling element of the movie "**Starman**".

The ghosts, demons, aliens, healings, psychic abilities etc. have been dealt with elsewhere in these writings, so I'll just re-state that they now no longer need be mysteries. Again no proof is forthcoming, and can only be had by participation or understanding. In other words, it becomes something that is your individual responsibility to find, and not something given to you from outside of yourself.

Remember that just because you have not seen or experienced something does not mean it is not real or does not exist. That is an arrogance of the scientific method, and effectively stunts individual learning and development. I doubt you will find anything that will not fit in with the two grand theories outlined herein.

Current world issues

I have long puzzled over the issue of **corporate bodies.** (see next section: Corporate Rule) They are indeed artificial individual entities, with individual and legal status, and have unlimited if not true immortal life status. They are now the front line for ownership of the world in a very real sense with many well acknowledged as richer and more powerful than individual nations. Additionally, being transnational, they need respect no national boundaries, and can control world wealth along with virtually any commodity that can be named. Unimaginable wealth, endless existence, being free from any form of government, censure, or punishment coupled with total unaccountability within any named country and control of the world's resources makes them truly powerful world owners. They control all the media, the governments, the banks, medicine, and I guess about everything you could name that touches our life every day. The Highlander's hiding place perhaps.

We can now also begin to appreciate why the **sciences** are so rigidly controlled and even from within and including the field of **education**. Further we can now see reasons why state education is vigorously enforced with home and private education absolutely forbidden in many countries. People are going to prison in some places for teaching their own children. New ideas, insights, even ways of thinking and values etc., that are contrary to the accepted dogma of the professed "authorities" simply do not get a hearing or publicity, and no chance of promotion, funding for research or anything else. The ruling authorities are as the blinded "flat earthers" of old and preach an unchanging dogma. I read of a German, Alfred **Wegener**, who near a century ago claimed what we now know as "plate technology" as fact, but was laughed and mocked into oblivion. It simply was not what the authorities had learned and therefore was scientific heresy. (The implication is that if "they" do not know of a thing, then that "thing" cannot be a reality.) Same sort of thing happened to **Velikovsky** and his claims, many of which are stunningly accurate and acceptable some 50 and more years later today.

Big bang theory and evolution are rigidly taught as fact, not theory, and to contradict or question them is to run the reality of ridicule and personal attack. It would be self-evident that any super race upon the earth with control of its wealth and governments in its hands would surely demand these be taught. This way dumbed down humans would not question their own origin, but accept it as a mere accident of nature, an evolution of matter. Creation or intervention need to be excluded simply because it could lead to their discovery by us. Sure, the current and accepted "scientific" way tells we are alone and supreme in a galaxy devoid of intelligence apart from our own. It would be difficult to imagine a more effective censorship and embargo on information than the enforced teaching, acceptance and adherence to these flawed theories. As one great writer once said: Theory = best guess. There is none so ignorant as one who thinks he already knows all there is that is knowable.

This is another reason why **scientific authority** is so vigorously stressed as final and unquestionable. (Other reasons being given elsewhere in these writings.) The largely unlearned and ignorant public must never be allowed to believe any alternatives even exist or are possible other than those that they dictate to us. After all "everybody knows" that only "ignorant fools" dare to claim otherwise, or contrary to the dictates of "authority". This after all is precisely what the equally controlled corporate **mass media** proclaim, and any who dare venture to voice alternative views, or provide evidence or information contrary to accepted and official dogma, are simply ignored, ridiculed, slandered, or otherwise sent to oblivion.

We're no threat so long as we just don't know anything other than what the controlled education systems are instructed to give us. And yes, they do know that some of us "know", but that just does not matter. You see the knowing among us will die, hopefully of old age and not at a heretic's pyre. The Wegener's and Velikovsky's have passed on. But the spurious dogma along with those immortal corporates and institutes will out-live us individually. So we as individuals, no matter how loudly we shout or how many hear or even believe us, simply do not matter. Also so long as the vast majority either don't know or don't care, our voices are simply drowned out, and that is very easy when "they" control the sideshows of all mass media. Thus we have an endless as it is mindless procession of trite rubbish dished up, even on the 6 o'clock news. "Gee, what are Ange and Brad doing now? And what about that Jen? Get a life of your own now Jen!" I'm sure you see how futile it gets.

It is of course well known by those who control things, that when times get rough and tough for the populace that all they want and need in the end are **bread and circuses**. They also know the principle that predicts that if you beat people up long and hard enough, that when you stop or ease it up they will be grateful for the relief and thank you for it. Of course they will then willingly accept a situation far worse for them than that which existed before the times of trouble.

I am just 63 now, and I have noticed a massive dumbing down of the entire education system since I finished formal education in the 1960s. I have often wondered why this is so, and why such spurious and inconsistent theories are pushed so vehemently upon us. We become prevented from achieving self-actualisation, but then, if any of this be true, that would be among the last things "they" would want or allow.

Perhaps these theories' possible realities create the main reasons why so many suspected hidden agendas and so-called "conspiracy theories" are rampant now. Theories that if true are not theories but are conspiracy facts. I mean things like **fluoridation** of water, **vaccinations**, "**war on terrorism**", toxic **food additives**, control over media, the emerging fascist governments, proliferation of war and arms, the absolute infiltration of **drugs** into society at all levels, the handing over and virtual control of health to "**big pharma**" drug companies etc.

So many things, almost too numerous to mention here, all work against the human species, and effectively lead to our individual and collective destruction or at least to our debilitation. Why? The "alternative media" is flooded with reports and information from vast numbers of people who clearly see that there is "something" really wrong with the way mankind is being destructively manipulated. Unfortunately the list of topics is as huge as it is dismal. If my proposed theories have any validity then we can also see why the world is now also in financial chaos. A chaos and control that began implementation probably well before world war one with **bankers** funding both sides. There is absolute evidence "banks" have continually supported and financed all sides in wars and armed conflicts. It is said, "in confusion there is profit", let it be said, "in war banks make big billions". A burning question is: for whose benefit or for what purpose is the profit and misery generated?

The movie "Zardoz" shows that if the immortals pretending to be gods give the mortal beasts enough guns and weapons, plus teach them intolerance and hatred, they will kill themselves off, saving the real masters the task of the culling. **Genocide** is rampant in our history. Further, we can see why in implementing genocide the more intelligent and influential are selected first for the kill. For these reasons wars, logically seemingly avoidable and undesirable, are generated, started, and kept going regardless of the human toll or cost to the human species. It defies what would be normal human logic or reason.

Good versus evil.

Is there really an ongoing battle between "**good and evil**"? I don't think so as such. Apart from being largely subjective principles, it is obvious that what is "good" for one may not obviously be good to another. For instance, it was "good" for the Nazis to take and occupy Russia in WW2, but certainly "evil" in the eyes of the Russians who were victims of cruel and merciless genocide.

However there is certainly much evidence of a conflict of a most serious nature involving the human race on the one side, and a very difficult to identify protagonist. Even the bible tells us we face an ongoing conflict. Certainly it does involve us individually and as a species, the human race. Equally obvious to all who will see is the absolute fact that it involves "forces" that are beyond the range of mortal's normal perception. At times the unseen forces are clearly working against the human inhabitants on the earth, and death and destruction rain mercilessly and unceasingly upon us. Our gods fail to hear us and fail to render aid. We are obviously individually and collectively totally abandoned, regardless of how apologists may try to disguise that painful fact. You cannot expect a reasonable person to accept that a Jehovah allowed millions of Jews to perish wretchedly and miserably in death camps so either their persecutors may be justly "punished", or that they become martyrs and thus "saved". On rare occasions however a benign influence is discerned.

My contention is that the unseen "forces" that are so often assumed to be, or called, demons and angels (by whatever actually used names or titles) with leaders called God and Satan, (the devil, or some equivalent names however called) can now be revealed. They are all inhabitants of this very earth, existent before our human race was fashioned, and that we are unwitting participants in their conflicts. I see none as exclusively on "our" side. I do not see the "angels" as totally benign white clad winged and halo wearing entities endlessly singing the praises of god while seeking good works to perform among mankind. Sorry about that, in plain language they are "**not us**" and have their own agenda and concerns, and we represent one of those concerns. I also believe they are now dealing with those concerns.

It is recorded that even "the gods" had wars among themselves upon our planet in our ancient past, and that is not just from one source. (Sumer, Egypt, India, Jewish, specifically) It is recorded that in those wars among themselves the human species were effectively used, taught the arts of death and war, then used to fight in their wars and that on all sides of such wars. Soon ensuing wars between one group of humans and another were fostered. Our gods decreed wars upon us. We still oblige them, and the most effective method of culling our species, the humans, is to get us to do the killing ourselves.

World Populations

We have another issue to face and it is probably a major cause of the critical situation we face right now. That is the sheer numbers of us and (to "them") our terrifying rate of increase. The following figures come from Readers Digest "Book of Facts" (1987, 3rd reprint) world population.

About 14ad estimated 256 million
About 350ad estimated 254 million
About 600ad estimated 237 million
About 1000ad estimated 280 million
About 1340ad estimated 378 million
About 1600ad estimated 498 million
About 1750ad estimated 731 million
About 1900ad estimated 1668 million
About 1950ad estimated 2525 million
About 1980ad estimated 4432 million
About 2008 we near 7000 million human people on earth.

Now that phenomenal rate of increase is certainly going to cause massive unrest and a big "re-think" of their tolerance of us on "their" earth.

(assuming these theories are right) That is an additional 5 billion humans in about 100 years. Assuming "they" who are "not us" exist, then we begin to see the thinking behind some events of the 20th century. Small wonder wars on a global scale, genocide, death factories were manipulated into existence. Yes, manipulated. Read the history and think about how these things happened. Small wonder we see programmes implemented by ruling powers and huge multinational corporations that only work towards the death and destruction or our race. Small wonder we see bodies like the United Nations etc. clearly stating world population control is a vital and urgent target. Small wonder we read of involuntary sterilisation in targeted ethnic groups, nations, and social groups. It will get worse. The concentration camps will re-emerge.

Perhaps (again) all the movies picturing the massive death and destruction of the human race and the pathetic state of the post-apocalyptic survivors are being produced to prepare us for what is probably ahead of us. I doubt "they" want "us" totally destroyed, but the figures above show that once we are and were below the 1 billion figure there were no global problems or large scale culling of our species. Population control targets see the bulk of humanity done away with. Famine, plague, and wars will ensure that once unleashed upon us.

Human future?

I recall seeing yet another movie wherein an alien intercepting with earth concluded that the earth was the subject of infestation of carbon based life forms that were polluting the planet. A decision was made by the alien form to save the earth by removing all the offending scum, namely the human species. I believe it was an earlier Startrek movie. Interesting observation I thought.

When I was a primary school child I suspected that all was not well or right with the Christian God as taught and presented. I figured and thought that if indeed I focused and concentrated upon the image of a small golden elephant that I had as a pencil sharpener, it could probably be just as effective as the worship and prayers to a false god. Heck of a thought for a young man not in his teens. And now I have in my own mind dismissed and terminated not only the Christian deity, but also those of all mortal's religions. Where would that leave us? What shall fill the void?

Now is indeed the time to unite as a single and common species and recognize that we are certainly cosmic stuff given life by and through the omnific "quantum soup", the fabric of the universe itself. We are all creations of the intelligence and fabric of this universe, and as such partakers of that supreme, yes even Divine, single source and force. In reality the Real Divine essence is actually already within us, and it has always been thus. This is the power inherent in man that I realized existed when I was in my early 30s. We should be celebrating the human species and cosmic soul stuff as already filled with and having divine potential. We need to be focusing on our collective and individual nature, then reaching out to develop and fill its potential.

As for our "star stuff" mortal body, we need to be aware that physically we appear to be a created species, and that spliced into the genetic structure of each and every mortal individual there is an abundance of the genetic materials of our designers. We therefore share and have a possibly undreamed of and unrealised potential and inheritance. Michio Kaku's "Time" series would indicate that there is nothing identifiable in our DNA or structure that determines we are programmed to die when we generally do. The "designers" are the long-lived super beings who, as it is recorded, later resented having designed and created us with almost no limits, and set us free upon this earth. They set us free with an early death in effort to prevent us reaching out and doing whatsoever we set our minds to do. Scriptures, not only Christian, hint at our divine potential and also the ability to create even greater miracles than were recorded of Jesus. The evidence is that some mortals are able to reach into the fabric of the universe and literally perform what are commonly called miracles. Yes, it happens.

However in all of this, and notwithstanding that which I have written and concluded by logic alone, I see no fault in allowing ourselves to be willfully deluded a little while longer. A lifetime of belief and religious training cannot be shed or replaced easily. I have little doubt that given enough contemplative time, then at the hour of my own final death or passing from this world into that which by logic and reason I know to be but a mere awakening (elsewhere) I shall probably invoke the company and solace of my imagined god. In so doing perhaps and possibly I may in reality be invoking my own inherent divine spark that is generally hidden or hiding from me but which is within me. Our comfort will be to know it is there within us, but more correctly and in correct perspective, that it is in fact really the true nature of "us".

I think we have been so long accepting of the concept of a watchful all seeing and caring "god", one who knows each of us personally, that probably we may be incapable of coping with life itself without invoking such a one. More so when one's individual stress is just too much to accept and deal with in one "dose". In principle perhaps there is nothing wrong with this, and it has proven over the millennia an extremely valid and useful method of focusing one's thoughts and spiritual energy that are key elements in each individual. This is verified by the fact that it is probably the most common method of invoking faith healing and numerous other events claimed as miracles.

We need to know, understand, and accept that a divine entity that we identify as "us" exists as "us" within the mortal body that houses "us". We are not mere bodies of flesh and blood, we are spiritual beings temporarily housed in and using a body of flesh and blood while on this earth in this dimension. We need to know, understand, and accept that as such all of us are equally important and are of the same substance, literally "one with each other". We need to learn how to live our mortal span of existence in the best possible manner to effectively afford self-realization and become all that we are capable of being – given mortal limitations. Perhaps and just possibly we are part of the hosts of "heaven" and cast down to the earth and mortality to continue that "war" and to test our individual integrity. I know of one religion that teaches such as doctrine.

Death comes to all. Perchance we could think of it as an awakening from sleep. Some sleep for a very short time and awaken very soon after settling down. Some leave mortality after only a very short time. Some sleep for a very long and satisfying time. Some spend a very long and satisfying time in mortality before the parting. Bottom line is that all of us will one day be parting company with earth and all its elements. When we so part company, we leave our body of flesh and bones behind for recycling, and we go back to that other dimension.

And when the time comes, we need to be able to leave this mortal life with dignity, trusting we are about to awaken from this sleep and dream that is mortality.

****

The following picture illustrates even our ability to now successfully perform gene splicing.

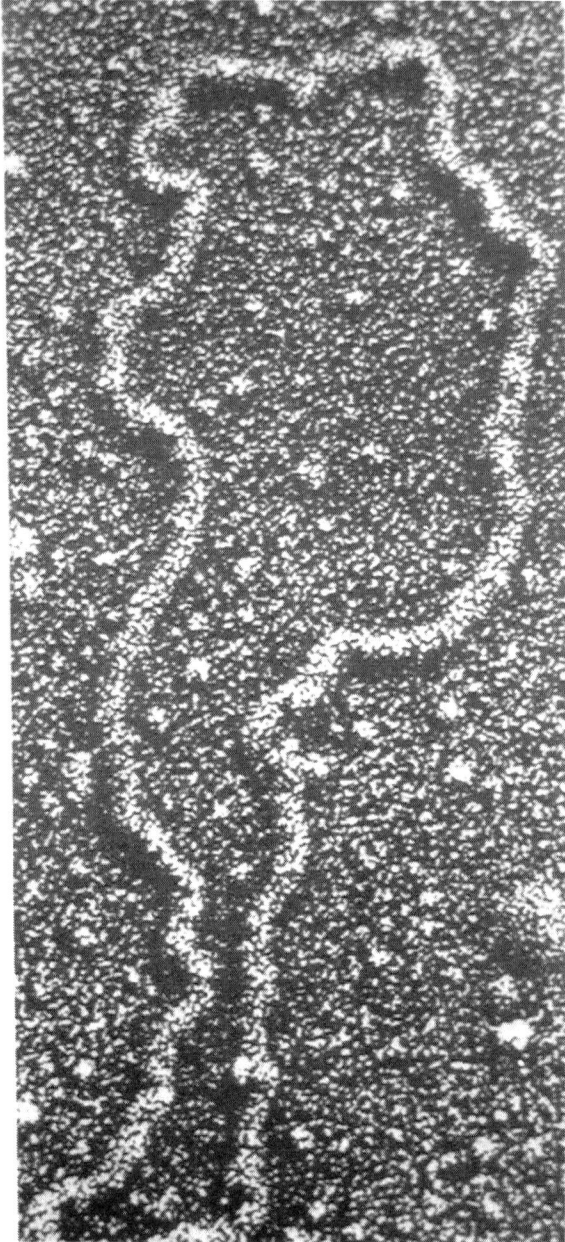

PIONEER GENES *This rope-like molecule of DNA, here magnified more than 170,000 times, was the subject in 1973 of the first successful attempt at genetic engineering. The rope consists of two spiral strands twisted together and joined like the rungs of a ladder – a double helix. Scientists from Stanford University in the USA severed the loop (taken from Escherichia coli bacteria found in the human gut) and spliced it to another piece of DNA from the same species. They introduced the new genetic combination into a living cell, and encouraged the cell to multiply. The new cells had properties derived from both the original pieces of DNA – proving that the splice had worked.*

203-1   SOMETHING IN THE WATER

If you think that something is right just because everyone believes it, then you are not thinking" - Vivienne Westwood

The following article (in italics) is copied from off the Internet and is freely available. I have reproduced it in full as I doubt that many readers would bother or have the ability or time to search out information for themselves. It of vital concern and relative to the issues being presented as it is indicative of something far more nefarious than mere lunacy. "Something" is afoot and a vast amount of resources, time and energy is being expended to implement just this one universal component action that seems designed solely to debilitate, dumb down, and enslave the entire human species. This one component when added to other similar seemingly unrelated components spell out in very large letters that all the suspicions behind numerous so called conspiracy theories (really conspiracy facts) are almost certainly well founded. The entire human race and species is being wilfully targeted and marked for destruction, or decimation at the least.

Yes, it is time to become very afraid, and to be very alert as to what is really going on, then try to make some preparations as one may see as adequate. Those preparations may at this late stage of the "game" to merely be able to face death with dignity.

Read on, the article is not modified or corrected in any way, except for the making of some text bold as a highlight. Almost needless to say this article is not unique in its revealing the effects of sodium fluoride, but it was selected because of its brief and comprehensive nature. The truth really is out there.

FLUORIDE and STUPIDITY

SICKNESS CONTROL 101: FLUORIDE, THE LUNATIC DRUG

"TELL A LIE LOUD ENOUGH AND LONG ENOUGH AND PEOPLE WILL BELIEVE IT." (Adolph Hitler)
"EARTH IS AN INSANE ASYLUM, TO WHICH THE OTHER PLANETS DEPORT THEIR LUNATICS." --Voltaire (Memnon the Philosopher).

Controversial fluoride is one of the basic ingredients in both PROZAC (FLUoxetene Hydrochloride) and Sarin nerve gas (Isopropyl-Methyl-Phosphoryl FLUoride).

Sodium fluoride, a hazardous-waste by-product from the manufacture of aluminum, is a common ingredient in rat and cockroach poisons, anesthetics, hypnotics, psychiatric drugs, and military nerve gas. It's historically been quite expensive to properly dispose of, until some aluminum industries with an overabundance of the stuff sold the public on the terrifically insane but highly profitable idea of buying it at a 20,000% markup, injecting it into our water supplies, and then DRINKING it. Yes, a 20,000% markup: Fluoride-- intended only for human consumption by people under 14 years of age--is injected into our drinking water supply at approx. 1 part-per-million (ppm), but since we only drink 1/2 of one percent of the total water supply, the rest literally goes down the drain as a free hazardous-waste disposal for the chemical industry, where we PAY them so that we can flush their expensive hazardous waste down our toilets. How many salesmen dream of such a deal? (Follow the money.)

Independent scientific evidence repeatedly showing up over the past 50 years reveals that fluoride allegedly shortens our life span, promotes cancer and various mental disturbances, accelerates osteoporosis and broken hips in old folks, and makes us stupid, docile, and subservient, all in one package. There are reports of aluminum in the brain possibly being a causative factor in Alzheimer's Disease, and evidence points towards fluoride's strong affinity for aluminum and also its ability to "trick" the blood-brain barrier by looking like the hydrogen ion, and thus allowing chemical access to brain tissue.

Scientists who have attempted to blow the whistle on this mega-bucks PR ploy have consistently been given a very unscientific Black-PR treatment, and thus their valid points disputing the current vested interests never arrive in the press. Follow the money to find the control. In 1952 the slick PR campaign which ramrodded the concept of fluoridation through via our Public Health departments and various dental organizations was likened to a highly-emotional "beer-salesman's convention" instead of the objective scientific experiment which it should properly have been. It's continued in that vein right up to present time. To illustrate the emotional vs. the scientific nature of this issue, just look at the response given by people (perhaps yourself included?) when the subject of fluoridation comes up. Ask yourself, "Is this response EMOTIONAL BLUSTER, or is it UNBIASED AND OPENLY- INTERESTED OBJECTIVITY?" There is a tremendous amount of emotional, highly unscientific know-it-all attached to fluoridation. Many truly independent (unattached to any vested-interest) scientists who've spent a large portion of their lives studying and working with this subject have been subjected to a surprising amount of uncalled-for and unfair character assassination from strong vested-interest groups who profit from the public's ignorance as well as from their illnesses. (Follow the money.)

Do you have diabetes or kidney disease? There are reportedly more than 11 million Americans with diabetes. Since many diabetics drink more liquids than other people, then according to the Physicians Desk Reference these 11 million Americans probably shouldn't drink fluoridated water, because in doing so, they'll receive an excessive dose of fluoride.

Kidney disease, by definition, lowers the efficiency of the kidneys, which is your main route of fluoride elimination. --So those people with kidney disease also shouldn't drink fluoridated water. Cases are on record (Annapolis, Maryland, 1979) where kidney patients on dialysis machines died, due to a fluoride overdose in the city water supply. Let's begin at the beginning:

The first occurrence of fluoridated drinking water on Earth was found in Germany's Nazi prison camps. The Gestapo had little concern about fluoride's supposed effect on children's teeth; their alleged reason for mass-medicating water with sodium fluoride was to sterilize humans and force the people in their concentration camps into calm submission. (Ref. book: "The Crime and Punishment of I.G. Farben" by Joseph Borkin.)

The following letter was received by the Lee Foundation for Nutritional Research, Milwaukee Wisconsin, on 2 October 1954, from Mr. Charles Perkins, a chemist:

"I have your letter of September 29 asking for further documentation regarding a statement made in my book, The Truth About Water Fluoridation, to the effect that the idea of water fluoridation was brought to England from Russia by the Russian Communist Kreminoff. "In the 1930's, Hitler and the German Nazi's envisioned a world to be dominated and controlled by a Nazi philosophy of pan-Germanism. The German chemists worked out a very ingenious and far-reaching plan of mass-control which was submitted to and adopted by the German General Staff. This plan was to control the population in any given area through mass medication of drinking water supplies. By this method they could

control the population in whole areas, reduce population by water medication that would produce sterility in women, and so on. In this scheme of mass-control, sodium fluoride occupied a prominent place. ...

"Repeated doses of infinitesimal amounts of fluoride will in time reduce an individual's power to resist domination, by slowly poisoning and narcotizing a certain area of the brain, thus making him submissive to the will of those who wish to govern him. [A convenient light lobotomy]

"The real reason behind water fluoridation is not to benefit children's teeth. If this were the real reason there are many ways in which it could be done that are much easier, cheaper, and far more effective. The real purpose behind water fluoridation is to reduce the resistance of the masses to domination and control and loss of liberty.

"When the Nazis under Hitler decided to go into Poland, both the German General Staff and the Russian General Staff exchanged scientific and military ideas, plans, and personnel, and the scheme of mass control through water medication was seized upon by the Russian Communists because it fitted ideally into their plan to communize the world. ...

"I was told of this entire scheme by a German chemist who was an official of the great IG Farben chemical industries and was also prominent in the Nazi movement at the time. I say this with all the earnestness and sincerity of a scientist who has spent nearly 20 years' research into the chemistry, biochemistry, physiology and pathology of fluorine--any person who drinks artificially fluorinated water for a period of one year or more will never again be the same person mentally or physically." CHARLES E. PERKINS, Chemist, 2 October 1954.

Quoting Einstein's nephew, Dr. E.H. Bronner (a chemist who had also been a prisoner of war during WWII) in a letter printed in The Catholic Mirror, Springfield, MA, January 1952:

"It appears that the citizens of Massachusetts are among the 'next' on the agenda of the water poisoners.

"There is a sinister network of subversive agents, Godless 'intellectual' parasites, working in our country today whose ramifications grow more extensive, more successful and more alarming each new year and whose true objective is to demoralize, paralyze and destroy our great Republic-- from within if they can, according to their plan--for their own possession. "The tragic success they have already attained in their long siege to destroy the moral fiber of American life is now one of their most potent footholds towards their own ultimate victory over us.

"Fluoridation of our community water systems can well become their most subtle weapon for our sure physical and mental deterioration. ...

"As a research chemist of established standing, I built within the past 22 years, 3 American chemical plants and licensed 6 of my 53 patents. Based on my years of practical experience in the health-food and chemical field, let me warn: fluoridation of drinking water is criminal insanity, sure national suicide. Don't do it.

"Even in small quantities, sodium fluoride is a deadly poison to which no effective antidote has been found. Every exterminator knows that it is the most efficient rat-killer. ... Sodium fluoride is entirely different from organic calcium-fluoro-phosphate needed by our bodies and provided by nature, in God's great providence and love, to build and strengthen our bones and our teeth. This organic calcium-fluoro-phosphate, derived from proper foods, is an edible organic salt, insoluble in water and assimilable by the human body, whereas the non-organic sodium fluoride used in fluoridating water is instant poison to the body and fully water soluble. The body refuses to assimilate it. "Careful, bonafide laboratory experimentation by conscientious, patriotic research chemists, and actual medical experience, have both revealed that instead of preserving or promoting 'dental health,' fluoridated drinking water destroys teeth, before adulthood and after, by the destructive mottling and other pathological conditions it actually causes in them, and also creates many other very grave pathological conditions in the internal organisms of bodies consuming it. How can it be called a "health" plan? What's behind it?

"That any so-called "doctors" would persuade a civilized nation to add voluntarily a deadly poison to its drinking water systems is unbelievable. It is the height of criminal insanity. "No wonder Hitler and Stalin fully believed and agreed from 1939 to 1941 that, quoting from both Lenin's Last Will and Hitler's Mein Kampf:

"America we shall demoralize, divide, and destroy from within."

"Are our Civil Defense organizations and agencies awake to the perils of water poisoning by fluoridation? Its use has been recorded in other countries. Sodium fluoride water solutions are the cheapest and most effective rat killers known to chemists: colorless, odorless, tasteless; no

antidote, no remedy, no hope: Instant and complete extermination of rats.
...

"Fluoridation of water systems can be slow national suicide, or quick national liquidation. It is criminal insanity--treason!" Dr. E.H. Bronner, Mfg. Research Chemist, Los Angeles.

-------------------------------- Earliest available Russian fluoride evidence:

"I, Oliver Kenneth Goff, was a member of the Communist Party and the Young Communist League, from May 2, 1936, to October 9, 1939. During this period of time, I operated under the alias of John Keats with number 18-B-2. My testimony before the Government is in Volume 9 of the Un-American Activities Report for 1939.

"While a member of the Communist Party, I attended Communist training schools in New York and Wisconsin ... and we were trained in the revolutionary overthrow of the U.S. Government. "... We discussed quite thoroughly the fluoridation of water supplies and how we were using it in Russia as a tranquilizer in the prison camps. The leaders of our school felt that if it could be induced into the American water supply, it would bring about a spirit of lethargy in the nation, where it could keep the general public docile during a steady encroachment of Communism. We also discussed the fact that keeping a store of deadly fluoride near the water reservoir would be advantageous during the time of the revolution, as it would give us opportunity to dump this poison into the water supply and either kill off the populace or threaten them with liquidation, so that they would surrender to obtain fresh water.

Related Research:
The Crime and Punishment of I. G. Farben
by Joseph Borkin (out of print book search)

Health Effects of Ingested Fluoride
by Bernard Meyer Wagner

Fluoridation : the Great Dilemma
by George L. Waldbott

Fluoride the Aging Factor :
How to Recognize and Avoid the Devastating Effects of Fluoride
by John, Dr. Yiamouyiannis

Scientific Knowledge in Controversy :
The Social Dynamics of the Fluoridation Debate
by Brian Martin

Medical Mafia by Guylaine Lanctot

Racketeering in Medicine by James P. Carter

The Cure for All Diseases by Dr. Hulda Regehr Clark

Censured for Curing Cancer :
The American Experience of Dr. Max Gerson
by S.J. Haught

In a letter abstracted from Fluoridation and Lawlessness, published by the Committee for Mental Health and National Security (with obvious implications) from the aforementioned Charles Perkins, U.S. appointed post-war head of I.G. Farben, to the Lee Foundation for Nutritional Research, Milwaukee, Wisconsin, October 2, 1954, we read the following:

"We are told by the fanatical ideologists who are advocating the fluoridation of the water supplies in this country that their purpose is to reduce the incidence of tooth decay in children, and it is the plausibility of this excuse, plus the gullibility of the public and the cupidity of public officials that is responsible for the present spread of artificial water fluoridation in this country. However - and I want to make this very definite and positive - the real reason behind water fluoridation is not to benefit children's teeth. If this were the real reason, there are many ways in which it could be done which are much easier, cheaper and far more effective. The real purpose behind water fluoridation is to reduce the resistance of the masses to domination, control and loss of liberty."

●●

1944. When a severe pollution incident occurred downwind of the E.I. DuPont de Nemours Company chemical factory in Deepwater, New Jersey. The factory was then producing millions of pounds of fluoride for the Manhattan Project whose scientists were racing to produce the world's first atomic bomb. The farms downwind in Gloucester and Salem counties were famous for their high-quality produce. Their peaches went directly to the Waldorf Astoria Hotel in New York City; their tomatoes were bought up by Campbell's Soup. But in the summer of 1944 the farmers began reporting that their crops were blighted: "Something is burning up the peach crops around here." They said that poultry died after an all-night thunderstorm, and that farm workers who ate produce they'd picked would sometimes vomit all night and into the next day. "I remember our horses looked sick and were too stiff to work," Mildred Giordano, a teenager at the time, told these reporters. Some cows were so crippled that they could not stand up; they could only graze by crawling on their bellies. The account was confirmed in taped interviews with Philip Sadtler (shortly before he died), of Sadtler Laboratories of Philadelphia, one of the nation's oldest chemical consulting firms. Sadtler had personally conducted the initial investigation of the damage. The farmers were stonewalled in their search for information about fluoride's effects on their health, and their complaints have long since been forgotten. But they unknowingly left their imprint on history: their complaints of injury to their health reverberated through the corridors of power in Washington and triggered intensive, secret, bomb program research on the health effects of fluoride.

1945. May. Newburgh's water was fluoridated, and over the next 10 years its residents were studied by the New York State Health Department.

1945-1955. Much of the original proof that fluoride is safe for humans in low doses was generated by A-bomb program scientists who had been secretly ordered to provide "evidence useful in litigation" against defense contractors for fluoride injury to citizens. The first lawsuits against the American A-bomb program were not over radiation, but over fluoride damage, the documents show. Human studies were required. Bomb program researchers played a leading role in the design and implementation of the most extensive US study of the health effects of fluoridating public drinking water, conducted in Newburgh, New York, from 1945 to 1955. Then, in a classified operation code-named "Program F", they secretly gathered and analyzed blood and tissue samples from Newburgh citizens with the cooperation of New York State Health Department personnel. The original, secret version (obtained by these reporters) of a study published by Program F scientists in the August 1948 Journal of the American Dental Association1 shows that evidence of adverse health effects from fluoride was censored by the US Atomic Energy Commission (AEC)-considered the most powerful of Cold War agencies-for reasons of "national security". The bomb program's fluoride safety studies were conducted at the University of Rochester-site of one of the most notorious human radiation experiments of the Cold War, in which unsuspecting hospital patients were injected with toxic doses of radioactive plutonium. The fluoride studies were conducted with the same ethical mindset, in which "national security" was paramount.

1995.Dr Phyllis Mullenix, former head of toxicology at Forsyth Dental Center in Boston and now a critic of fluoridation. Animal studies which Mullenix and co-workers conducted at Forsyth in the early 1990s indicated that fluoride was a powerful central nervous system (CNS) toxin and might adversely affect human brain functioning even at low doses. (New epidemiological evidence from China adds support, **showing a correlation between low-dose fluoride exposure and diminished IQ in children.**) Mullenix's results were published in 1995 in a reputable peer-reviewed scientific journal.

1995. The University of Rochester's classified fluoride studies, code-named "Program F", were started during the war and continued up until the early 1950s. They were conducted at its Atomic Energy Project (AEP), a top-secret facility funded by the AEC and housed at Strong Memorial Hospital. It was there that one of the most notorious human radiation experiments of the Cold War took place, in which unsuspecting hospital patients were injected with toxic doses of radioactive plutonium. Revelation of this experiment-in a Pulitzer Prize winning account by Eileen Welsome-led to a 1995 US presidential investigation and a multimillion-dollar cash settlement for victims.

There can no longer be any doubt that fluoride is an extremely dangerous toxic chemical that has almost immediate and long-term deleterious effects on humans. It can no longer be considered that it is ignorance alone that allows or causes the continuance of its use as an additive to water supplies, toothpastes etc. and enforced upon human populations. It also stinks of something far more nefarious than mere greed and the associated corruption. Nor can it be considered "cost effective". I read that somewhere near only half of one percent of such reticulated town water supplies is drunk by the populations, the rest going down the toilets, drains, car washes, etc. I wonder if our pets and gold fish enjoy sharing our madness?

BUT WAIT, THERE'S MORE

Here is a little information about more modern madness and the killing and poisoning of populations.

It is not possible in this book to expose or deal with every assault upon humanity, nor to deal with those mentioned at any great length, but only to point an accusing finger in the direction of some of them. Again any quotes or information supplied is only the "tip of the iceberg", enough merely to establish that there is a prima face case against the matter raised. Each reader will then be able to research more details until the whole filthy business lay exposed. In the meantime however know that all indeed is not well with humanity, nor what is foisted upon us as safe for our use, and this by those we have been conditioned to believe we can trust with our lives and health.

1965. Aspartame is the technical name for the brand names, NutraSweet, Equal, Spoonful, and Equal-Measure. Aspartame was discovered by accident in 1965, when James Schlatter, a chemist of G.D. Searle Company was testing an anti-ulcer drug. Aspartame was approved for dry goods in 1981 and for carbonated beverages in 1983.

1981. Aspartame was invented by the G D Searle Co. (1965) acquired by Monsanto in 1985. For 16 years FDA refused to approve it until 1981 when Commissioner Arthur Hayes overruled the objections of a Public Board of Inquiry and the protests of the American Soft Drink Association and blessed it. The tests submitted by Searle were so bad the Department of Justice, initiated prosecution of Searle for fraud. Then the defence lawyers hired the prosecutors, Sam Skinner and Wm. Conlon, and the case expired when the statute of limitations ran out. **Aspartame/Nutrasweet, a toxin that blinds, drops intelligence, eradicates memory, grows brain tumors and other cancers, brings fatigue. Depression, ADD, panic, rage, paranoia, diabetes, seizures, suicide and death**. This toxin is supported by unlimited advertising and the manufacturers pay off the American Dietetics Association, the American Diabetics Association, the AMA, and whomever else, to convince us its safe as rain. These lies are backed by a Federal Bureaucracy knowing it may kill your child, but the bureaucrat who approved the poison got a fat job as have many of his successors. Suppose this government watchdog, ignoring thousands of consumer complaints, has become an Attack Dog protecting corporate corruption. This is the bitter reality of Aspartame/Nutrasweet, Monsanto, the FDA, Coca Cola, Pepsi, and the hundreds of food, drink and drug makers who add to their products a known poison Conceived in Fraud and Dedicated to the Proposition that Profit is all that Matters! (They're Poisoning Our Kids - Aspartame Warning The Facts From Betty Martin <mailto:Mission-Possible-USA@altavista.netMission-Possible-USA@altavista.net< /FONT>

1987. Dr Louis Elsas, Professor of Paediatrics & Genetics at Emory University, testified before Congress; "Aspartame is in fact a well known neurotoxin and teratogen [triggers birth defects] which in some undefined dose will irreversibly in the developing child or foetal brain, produce adverse effects I am particularly angry at this type of advertising that is promoting the sale of a neurotoxin in the childhood age group." [Nov 2, 1987]

Neurosurgeon Russell Blaylock, MD, declares Aspartame is a toxin like arsenic and cyanide that causes confusion, disorientation, seizures, cancer, pancreatic, uterine, ovarian and brain tumors and leads to Alzheimer's. Read "Excitotoxins, the Taste That Kills"[505-474-0303]. Hear Dr. Blaylock's radio interview on http://www.dorway.com/' Courageous whistleblowers like these have spoken in three congressional hearings, but industry's lobbying and political action keep the poison in the foods of the world. Our recourse as consumers is personal communication since the media is paid by advertising to push Nutrasweet/Equal/Diet Coke, etc.

1996, 27 June without public notice, the FDA removed all restrictions from aspartame allowing it to be used in everything, including all heated and baked goods. The truth about aspartame's toxicity is far different than what the NutraSweet Company would have you readers believe.

203-2
203-3

203-4   THEY'RE COMING TO TAKE ME AWAY

"It also gives us a very special, secret pleasure to see how unaware the people around us are of what is really happening to them."   ~Adolf Hitler

Stanley Kubrick's film "2001 A Space Odessy" is memorable for many things, among them is that opening sequence involving the pre-human "ape" creatures. It was intended for the viewers to learn or glean some information from, and there are indeed many lessons within that sequence.

One interesting view is another way of defining the "golden rule". Perhaps more important than the usual "those that got the gold makes the rules" would be "those that have a monopoly on the weapons make all the rules" and that includes deciding not only who gets the gold, but how it is shared and where it's kept.

As well illustrated in those scenes of the movie we learn that if one having weapons, even if only a bone club (still used in the world today) then one can overpower, dispossess, or slaughter who he will providing they are not equally or better armed. And pardon the pun, let's make no bones about it, it is surely a basic element in the makeup of man to want everything for himself alone.

The success to be had in attacking an unarmed group (nation or whatever) or disarming them before an attack is obviously well known since the "beginning".

The United States of America was founded because its resident population having access to arms could thus boldly declare independence from the oppressive British rule. The British not liking that idea sent in its armies and a war of independence ensued. Each side called up their allies and things got very nasty. The former colonists in America won the war, ousted the British and vowed never again to be subject to non local, non resident foreign rule. Recognizing that victory was had because the citizens could take up arms, a constitution was framed declaring a citizen's right to carry arms and the citizens were to be responsible for the government. The citizens were not responsible to the government. Huge big differences there. In any true democracy the people are responsible for the government and the government is responsible to the people. It is when a situation arises that a people fear their government, and that government knowing that, fears its people and is scared of them that scary things happen and are done. By the above definitions there are very few democracies in the world today.

In this world today we find most nations comprised of totally unarmed civilians not only deprived of arms, but also forbidden ownership under various penalties. Such people do NOT control their government but are totally controlled by them and more so by the "departments" that administer the "policy" underlying governments. Departmental bureaucrats are not elected and most often survive changes of government.

Now tying up the matters of large groups or nations of unarmed civilians and mans basic nature, let's look at just recent history to learn some more lessons. Just before we look at case histories, let us ask ourselves just why our governments are so hell bent on disarming its citizens and making ownership of arms so difficult. Globally governments virtually without exception want a monopoly on weapons, and if limited and restricted weapons are permitted insist on knowing who has them and where they are. Had those citizens in the miniseries "V" been as well armed as the American colonists those reptiles would never had achieved what they did. Ask, are we being set up? For what? Let's look at history.

THEY CAME AND THEY TOOK THEM AWAY.

In these examples not only did "they" come and take them away, but there was little if anything anyone was able to do about it. Citizens had been stripped of armaments. These are in no specific order except perhaps chronological order.

<u>USA:</u> We have dealt with how the USA came into being largely because its citizens were allowed to carry arms, but this right did not apply equally to everyone. By the late 1800s there were some 4 million slaves in the USA and about one quarter million free blacks. Disarmament laws were created across the land but were designed to allow only 1 race to freely possess weapons. "No slave may use firearms even in self defence" Louisiana 1806. "Free Negroes may not carry firearms." Florida 1831, Mississippi 1852, Alabama 1866, Louisiana post civil war. "White citizen patrols shall enter into all Negro homes … and lawfully seize … arms, weapons, and ammunition." Florida 1825. "It shall not be lawful for any freed man, Malatto, or free person of color … to own firearms … or other deadly weapons…." Alabama 1866. "Dealers must

record the race of all buyers of pistols and ammunition." Mississippi 1906. Current gun laws still require race to be stated and recorded.

Between 1880 and 1965 (See it's not all "stuff" that happened over 100 years ago.) mobs of citizens forcibly took and lynched some 3,500 defenceless unarmed black people. Consider one case where one intended lynch victim was saved because of the presence of just one handgun. A local sheriff was holding a man in his cell and left the jail for a while leaving his 14 year old daughter "in charge". A mob gathered intent on taking the man by force and murdering him by common called lynching. The girl took up a handgun and confronted the mob, vowing to shoot anyone who stepped forward to make good the threats. Not one coward in the mob stood forward. The sheriff returned and the mob disbanded. What a lifesaving difference just one gun can make.

In 1864 those who had the only guns, US troops, gunned down 150 Indians at Sand Creek Colorado, almost all women, children and old men.

December 1890 the US troops caught up with a group of Souix Indian Ghost Dancers at Wounded Knee and forced them to surrender their weapons. Subsequently every Indian was gunned down, some having fled up to 3 miles away.

Couldn't or wouldn't happen now or today you think? During World War 2 the US rounded up its Japanese citizens, many born in the USA. Some 110,000 were taken away and placed in remote "camps" under armed guards. A similar thing happened to US citizens of Italian and German descent. These were men, women, and children, guilty of nothing, disarmed, detained, and placed under armed guard. There for their own safety you think? That's the apologist line.

TURKEY: The events in Turkey involving the Armenian population seems to be lost and forgotten about, drowned out by the horrors of World War 1. It is a tale of willfully premeditated genocide. By 1915 a new government was in power taking over from the old Ottoman Empire. They wanted to rid the country of "wrong and lawless ideas", and to protect "national security". Oh the crimes against humanity committed in the pursuit of such ill defined and often used phrases.

In this case the "wrong and lawless ideas" were held to be those of the Armenians, a Christian minority in a mostly Moslem country. It was decreed that "Since the collective society is endangered … they must all be killed, men, women, and children without discrimination." And to this end a well-established and proven method was used in the genocide. (I will always refuse to grace mass murder and genocide with the words "ethnic cleansing". It is cold-blooded methodical and systematic slaughter on a massive scale. Sadly it is done so often.)

The targeted group were separated from society, this after they had been forced to surrender all weapons after a brutal forced search of their homes. It is said some obtained weapons illegally just to be able to surrender them to the searching troops and hopefully spare their households from the associated brutality.

On 26 June 1915 an order was made to deport them and they were ordered to report 5 days later bearing only what they could carry. As all weapons had been taken the remaining civilians were forced to assemble into groups of from 200 to 4000 and sent off on forced marches under armed troops. I say "remaining civilians" because almost all able bodied men had been forced into the army. They were then completely disposed of out of sight and knowledge of the common civilian within the confines of the army. The groups were then forced to march through the desert were 90% are said to have died. They were simply cut down, shot, butchered, women, children, and the aged and infirm, all defenceless. The small percentage of survivors who finished the march was then also butchered.

Some 1,500,000 Armenian souls perished in that organized massacre of unarmed and defenceless people by their own government.

SOVIET UNION: After the Communists came into power in 1917 following the armed revolution, new and strict laws were put in place to control the ownership and use of firearms. It became almost impossible for ordinary Soviet civilians who were non-Party members to own or access firearms.

Strict licensing laws recorded who had guns and where they were. The country was now defenceless and under the control of a government out of control.

Between 1929 and 1934 the Ukraine was singled out for a purge, and grain production quotas that were impossible to meet were enforced by armed soldiers. After 10 years of forced disarmament and weapons confiscation the civilians were powerless and when food, distribution of which was also controlled by the government, was withheld they were faced with certain starvation. They could not move away from the

Ukraine as travel, yet again rigidly controlled and restricted by the government, was not an option. In effect they were imprisoned within one huge country sized concentration camp under armed guard by soldiers. Their isolation was complete hidden from the world behind an Iron Curtain, and the ensuing starvation, executions, and cannibalism that began took a toll of an estimated 10,000,000. 10 million people killed by their own government.

Worse massacres were to come, but this time at the hands of a former ally, one who would have full knowledge of the unarmed state of the civilians before they treacherously invaded. The Nazi hordes swept almost unopposed across the Soviet territory and mercilessly massacred everyone before them. Nazi intent was to totally eliminate all Russians and take and use an empty country. I believe over 20,000,000 Russian civilians died.

GERMANY: Early in 1933 Hitler was elected into power. Firearm registration laws had been put into effect some 5 years earlier and thus his regime had access to the records of who had the guns and where those people were. It always seems that this is vital information to have to begin to implement the various plans to "rule the world."

The first stage for total control was already in place and stage two was very soon implemented. A mass seizure of guns and weapons from any remotely considered as political opponents, or for those matter undesirables, was started. As a result of raids carried out and obedient civilians surrender of guns, the population was almost totally unarmed and defenceless by 1938.

In 1938 new and very specific gun laws were effected. No Jews were allowed to have ownership or access to guns. It was decreed that no Jew be in possession of weapons, guns, clubs, knives, sharp edged weapons, and those found with such were to be sent immediately to already established concentration camps. Remaining weapons were surrendered. In November of 1938 the so-called "night of broken glass" followed by massive persecution was unleashed upon the defenceless Jews. A "holocaust" followed and millions of European Jews were slaughtered in specially designed death camps and factories. One rare example of resistance arose when some in the Warsaw ghetto, a holding "pen" where people were forced to wait for their turn before transportation to the death factories, got hold of some weapons and said "no more" to the Nazis. Without population disarmament and specifically Jewish disarmament things could have been so very different and so many innocents may not have been mercilessly slaughtered.

Now whereas everywhere else in Europe the populations were able and capable of rising up with arms to resist the Nazi oppression, this was not so in Germany. The government had the monopoly of weapons and the people entirely at its mercy.

Between 1933 and 1945 some 3 million Germans considered political opponents were sent to concentration camps. How could this be? How could this happen? Gun control enabled it.

Over 11,000,000 died in concentration camps. In most cases these were deaths at the hands of their own government.

Over 21,000,000 civilians died in Europe at Nazi hands, a government out of control. Things could have been different.

CHINA: In 1935 a Nationalist government was in power and made the possession of guns "without a good cause" or for military use punishable with imprisonment. The population was of course then disarmed.

1937 to 1939 witnessed the Sino Japanese war and the civilian population was forced into the army. It is estimated 4,000,000 died at both the hands of their own army and that of the invading Japanese. Those refusing to fight for whatever reason were summarily killed. In 1937 the city of Nanking was defended by 300,000 Chinese troops, but they threw down their weapons in the face of an invading army of 225,000 Japanese troops. The unarmed civilians of the city now lay helplessly before the invaders. Hundreds of thousands of unarmed civilians died, having no defence as weapons were forbidden. Their own government and its army were solely to blame.

Between 1942 and 1944 an estimated 4,000,000 died in famine and starvation caused by government troops confiscating crops. An unarmed population is powerless to resist and survive.

In 1949 it was the turn of the Communists to take over. Anyone who supplied their enemy, (opponents) either domestic or foreign, arms or ammunition faced immediate death. Ownership of armaments was strictly forbidden. The communists wanted a smooth ride into power unhindered by an armed citizenry such as hindered the British in its war with American colonists.

Somewhere between 35 and 100 million Chinese perished between 1935 and 1970. It could have been different. (Chairman) Mao stated "political power grows out of the barrel of a gun.

UGANDA: In 1971 Idi Amin led a successful armed revolution against the Obote government and seized power. World leaders thought that was good, as Obote was left wing and "bad". Idi Amin re-defined "bad". In such a country gun control laws were already in place of course. Bad governments take care of that first step as just that, the "first step". Obote's existing laws prohibited the carrying, ownership, or selling of firearms to civilians. Government troops exclusively thank you.

Immediately on gaining control Amin began doing things his way and for him. He began with the slaughter of all or any troops whose loyalty could be doubted. 16,000 were murdered for that cause. He then decreed that all Asians be ejected from Uganda. That causing no immediate problems for him he then selected all English to join them out of Uganda. As the population was unarmed and totally at his mercy, he began his persecution of Christians, and rival tribe's people.

It was illegal for more than 3 people to gather if one had a weapon. The persecutions and killings began.

Somewhere in all this time, a group of non-Ugandans were detained and held at an airport in Entebbe. Their fate looked very bleak indeed, but help came at the hands of a raiding party of Israeli commandos flown in just for the occasion. They were all rescued and flown to safety. Cowards back down or take no action in the face of capable opposition, even if it is a 14 year old girl with just one gun.

After 8 years of slaughter with the worlds governments and powers just watching it happen "over there" in "that place got no oil and don't matter" Uganda, over 300,000 had been murdered by their own government and troops. Finally Amin himself outwore his welcome and had to flee. He went to Saudi Arabia with untold wealth, and lived in luxury, unhindered by thoughts of justice, being held accountable or any conscience.

CAMBODIA: Definitely not the place to be between 1975 and 1979, or even now possibly. This had been a French colony and in 1975 after 5 years of war, communists took control with its Khmer Rouge under Pol Pot. He was a man with a dream. His dream was everyone else's nightmare for it aimed at definite population reduction from 7 million people to around just 1 million people.

He would eliminate all religion and its leaders, all political opponents, all city dwellers, all non-Cambodian ethnic groups, all Western culture, all traces and forms of capitalism, all students and intellectuals (That's anyone with better than a 7th grade level.), professionals of all types, all people who spoke French or English, even people who wore eye glasses. That has to be a bad start.

He imposed worse than tight gun and weapon control from the start of course, and any permits allowed stated that even the lending of a weapon within a family was forbidden. No guns were to be owned, no self-defence allowed, and everyone forced to disarm, except the Khmir rouge of course. Once the disarmament was in place the troubles began.

Total and mass evacuations of cities was ordered and enforced with the entire population forced onto collective farms. Like the Ukraine decades before the entire country became one huge concentration camp. Farming was inadequate and unable to support the entire population of the country. Result, same as Ukraine and China before this, famine and starvation. The administration was brutal. There was no mail, no telephones, no media, no books, no medical care of any sort, family units broken up and disallowed. Common kindness was not only discouraged, but also punishable by immediate death if witnessed. The manner of death was unspeakably and unimaginably brutal and cruel. Special death camps were set up within the greater concentration camp that the country had become.

This out of control insanity endured for 4 years unhindered by the western world or its governments. Over 2,000,000 died in the land at the hands of its own government before a neighboring country took the initiative to end it all. Vietnam invaded "its over there and not important, got no oil" Cambodia and crushed the Khmir within just 1 month. There is an important lesson to be learned here if you can just figure it out.

BANGLADESH (PAKISTAN): In 1971 after President Yahya Khan stated of the "troublemakers", namely Hindus, students, and intellectuals, "kill 3 million of them and the rest will eat out of our hands" 1,500,000 civilians died. Those deaths must be attributed to their own government.

GUATEMALA: Target group: the country's own Mayan Indians. 1981 firearm laws and restrictions provide "only government officials may carry firearms." Now that is very definitely disarming the civilians. Further laws stated that "firearms, even sharp pointed tools or farming implements are forbidden outside of town."

The population was forbidden arms, disarmed by its own government and in the 1980s some 200,000 Mayans died at the hands of their own government.

RWANDA: Herein lies another harrowing tale of government incited mass murder of its own civilians. This incident is more terrible than most if that is possible in as much as government openly broadcast the intent and both government agencies and the public did the mass killings openly together.

In this former Belgian colony the departing government gave all control to the minority Tutsi tribe. 9% of the population were Tutsi, and some 90% were of the Hutu tribe and by 1994 the Hutu had control of power. In that year the Hutu government declared all Tutsi to be rebels and called for the extermination of all Tutsi. In April 1994 it began, and civilians were urged to murder all Tutsi people with army troops participating.

The Ministry of Defence forbids the Tutsi tribe's people to own or carry weapons, and that same department organized the campaign of extermination and total mass murder. In one incident a large group of 5,500 people held out against murderous mobs for a week, holed up in a Christian church complex. It is reported that their defensive weapons included only one gun that had been seized from a soldier. This would indicate that had the Tutsi not been so completely disarmed, such massacres as ensued might not have happened. After one-week grenade using soldiers broke the siege and the entire group were slaughtered without mercy even to babies.

In one town its mayor urged civilians to fully disarm and surrender all weapons. When they failed to do this for obvious reasons he then ordered police to shoot them all. 20,000 Tutsi residents were mercilessly slaughtered in an horrific three-day killing frenzy. Roads were blocked and sealed off, ID cards were in use and checked, and Tutsi people were singled out for murder on the spot. I don't thing the average reader would be able to imagine the horror and terror of such events.

800,000 men women and children were singled out and brutally butchered over a period of just 100 days by fellow civilians and their own government and its agencies.

THE LESSONS TO LEARN

There are many lessons to be learned from the above incidents; some are obvious and some not so obvious. The first and most basic lesson is that no one is really safe from their own government, agencies, or troops when things go "bad". Who would think that merely wearing spectacles, or being a health professional would automatically guarantee your death? Who would imagine that your own country's soldiers of a so-called Ministry of Defence would be ordered to kill their own civilians, yet alone actually carry out that order? Most civilians have no idea that military personnel are carefully trained not to think but to become "automated" killing machines. I was somewhat stunned after I joined one military force that on the first day of training our course NCO yelled at us that he didn't give an "F" why we thought we had joined the service, but that we were now government property, his personal property and that he would teach us how to kill. Rule one therefore, no one is out of possible harm's way when things go bad.

The next rule is probably that warning signs are there for all to see as evidence of a government with the ability to go bad. These signs to not guarantee things will turn bad, but the potential is there and "machinery" is being put into place.

In all of the above cases the civilians are either totally disarmed or forbidden ownership or the right to carry weapons. Additionally any armaments that may be allowed must be registered so that government and its agencies know who has the weapons and where they are. Further and in most cases they will also know the ethnic groups and the numbers of each group in possession of armaments. The possible danger to the people is escalated when those people become required to physically surrender up those weapons to government. There will generally be prosecutions and penalties for breaching firearm laws. And red lights are flashing, sirens screaming, when specific ethnic groups are singled out and discriminated against for ownership of armaments. That would indicate they are marked for some form of special and probably not good attention from government. Never forget that a public without armaments is a vulnerable population, unable to defend itself, and that government or defence forces cannot be totally relied upon for their safety. Nanking found itself deserted by army, and its population was massacred. Ukraine, Tutsi and many others found to their horror that their own army became the instrument of their death.

Then there is the entire issue of citizens being required to use and carry ID cards. I remember decades ago associating the requirement for populations to carry "papers", identity papers that revealed all the information governments demand that enable effective population control including movement, with a total loss of freedom experienced in Nazi occupied Europe or communist Russia. It was simply just not a democratic way of life. We all now compliantly carry ID regardless that our various governments vow that the cards we carry are not intended for or not really ID cards. They are. Effectively our governments know who we all are, where we are, our ages, state of health, our ethnic groups, most likely our religious persuasions, our financial status, and our work classification and certainly if we possess armaments. That's a lot of information that in "bad" government or other hands could spell TROUBLE. But the governments or powers that be know assuredly that as long as the vast majority keep drinking the local tap water, keep watching the TV and media and endlessly consuming products while eating modern foods that we are as controllable as any herd of cattle.

WHAT IT MEANS

When people accept being disarmed they become surprisingly easy to control and to kill. They have surrendered not only any weapons they may have had, but they also surrender their freedom and independence. They become totally dependent on their government and its military. History shows this is not really a safe or good practice. When innocent populations become so defenseless others can slaughter them in mass with the most ordinary of weapons, guns, knives, pitchforks, clubs, or even simple box cutters.

I marveled at the report that a mere handful of alleged highjackers took planes and caused so much havoc and death in the USA, and that there was not a single armed person who could have speedily resolved the issue and brought them down. Likewise I marvel at more recent reports of some rogue going on a shooting and killing spree, generally in schools, in the USA. A single gunman is wandering around and killing at random, often over a fairly lengthy period of time. Gun control alone is responsible for all those sort of deaths as there was not a single person with a gun to resolve the issue by simply bringing the killer down.

Vital lesson: gun control and disarmament of the civilians is not about eliminating crime, or getting guns out of the hands of criminals or the simply crazy. The criminals and the insane will always have and get guns. Recently I saw a documentary about police conducting raids on marihuana growers in New Zealand. Mostly these were simple residential affairs and not large-scale producers in a mega-buck illegal operation, yet in a large number of cases firearms were found, and those invariably unregistered and undeclared. The criminally minded have the guns and will not give them up. It's the trustworthy and honest citizens who lose the firearms and the ability to rightfully defend themselves and their family, or for that matter the community if necessary. I ask what is the point of allowing a situation where a crazed gunman is randomly killing people and a cowering population must either wait their turn or until police with a gun can be located and then arrive on the scene. You think this is emotive claptrap? Tell that to the survivors of any of the above historical and other similar situations.

The way to preserve freedom is to never give any person or persons more power than the people have. If that situation is not adhered to then there is a loss of freedom. It is said that the main reason for the USA forces to be overseas is that other governments have gone "bad" and started killing their people. Those people fear their government and cannot control it, they have no weapons nor access to them. Intervention is needed.

People should not have to live in fear of their government, and there is danger in downplaying the importance of self-defence, or in giving over of all defence, even at a local community level, to a central governmental authority.

None of the above situations or circumstances are now ever likely to change, so don't think that they will. The purpose of this writing is to open your eyes to what is really going on out there in our world, and some of the events are absolute horrifying but could have been prevented. This is how humans play the game of power and how dictatorships come into power. As a final word on this matter let's ask one question.

If we humans treat our own species and race with such ruthless callousness, how and what could we expect from those not of our species, the "not-us" that probably exist?

204-MEET OUR TRUE LEADERS

"Knowledge makes a man unfit to be a slave."
Frederick Douglass

No our true leaders, owners if you will, are not the various governments around the globe, of whatever professed colour, democratic, fascist, communist, etc. Simple thinking and reasoning should expose this self-evident truth. If you haven't already thought about the above claim consider this: Governments of all nations and countries come and go, even the great communist Soviet Union has been disbanded. Their various leaders change even more frequently, whereas those who have almost total control over all governments remain forever, unchanged with the exceptions of becoming wealthier, more powerful, and greedier.

When we consider the position and state of the world's corporate bodies we should not forget to include in our thinking that most, if not all, of the bureaucratic governmental or semi-government institutions are basically the same. They are non-elected ruling bodies with effective direct control over a country's population. They control health, housing, defence, economy, in fact just about everything you can name that has some or any effects upon mankind.

Now let me ask, if you wanted to rule the world, you would want the powerful corporates on your side wouldn't you? Or is there something really basically wrong with that question? Should it read, If you were the corporate bodies **already** ruling the world you would want ownership of governments, and all government departments and bureaucrats totally under your control, wouldn't you? Yes start to squirm uncomfortably right now, because it is probably too late to change anything now. We can only hope that for some brief time in perhaps a post-apocalyptic future, some of humanity may live in freedom for a brief time before yet another new empire is set up.

The article below records some facts about such bodies and is freely available on the Internet. Again, this is but one sample of a great wealth and abundance of material available.

A History of Corporate Rule
and Popular Protest

A new populist movement has emerged to challenge corporate power and call for a more equitable economic order that protects traditional cultures and ecosystems and promotes sustainability.

by Richard Heinberg © 2002
Editor/Publisher
MuseLetter
1604 Jennings Avenue
Santa Rosa, CA 95401, USA
Email: heinberg@museletter.com
Website: http://www.museletter.com/

The corporation was invented early in the colonial era as a grant of privilege extended by the Crown to a group of investors, usually to finance a trade expedition. The corporation limited the liability of investors to the amount of their investment--a right not held by ordinary citizens. Corporate charters set out the specific rights and obligations of the individual corporation, including the amount to be paid to the Crown in return for the privilege granted.

Thus were born the East India Company, which led the British colonisation of India, and Hudson's Bay Company, which accomplished the same purpose in Canada. Almost from the beginning, Britain deployed state military power to further corporate interests--a practice that has continued to the present. Also from the outset, corporations began pressuring government to expand corporate rights and to limit corporate responsibilities.

The corporation was a legal invention - a socio-economic mechanism for concentrating and deploying human and economic power. The purpose of the corporation was and is to generate profits for its investors. As an entity, it has no other purpose; it acknowledges no higher value.

Many people understood early on that since corporations do not serve society as a whole, but only their investors, there is therefore always a danger that the interests of corporations and those of the general populace will come into conflict. Indeed, the United States was born of a revolution not just against the British monarchy but against the power of corporations. Many of the American colonies had been chartered as corporations (the Virginia Company, the Carolina Company, the Maryland Company, etc.) and were granted monopoly power over lands and industries considered crucial to the interests of the Crown.

Much of the literature of the revolutionaries was filled with denunciations of the "long train of abuses" of the Crown and its instruments of dominance, the corporations. As the yoke of the Crown corporations was being thrown off, Thomas Jefferson railed against "the general prey of the rich on the poor". Later, he warned the new nation against the creation of "immortal persons" in the form of corporations. The American revolutionaries resolved that the authority to charter corporations should lie not with governors, judges or generals, but only with elected legislatures.

At first, such charters as were granted were for a fixed time, and legislatures spelled out the rules each business should follow. Profit-making corporations were chartered to build turnpikes, canals and bridges, to operate banks and to engage in industrial manufacture. Some citizens argued against even these few, limited charters, on the grounds that no business should be granted special privileges and that owners should not be allowed to hide behind legal shields. Thus the requests for many charters were denied, and existing charters were often revoked. Banks were kept on a short leash, and (in most states) investors were held liable for the debts and harms caused by their corporations.

All of this began to change in the mid-19th century. According to Richard Grossman and Frank Adams in Taking Care of Business: "Corporations were abusing their charters to become conglomerates and trusts. They were converting the nation's treasures into private fortunes, creating factory systems and company towns. Political power began flowing to absentee owners intent upon dominating people and nature."1

Grossman and Adams note that: "In factory towns, corporations set wages, hours, production processes and machine speeds. They kept blacklists of labour organisers and workers who spoke up for their rights. Corporate officials forced employees to accept humiliating conditions, while the corporations agreed to nothing."

The authors quote Julianna, a Lowell, Massachusetts, factory worker, who wrote: "Incarcerated within the walls of a factory, while as yet mere children, drilled there from five till seven o'clock, year after year what, we would ask, are we to expect, the same system of labour prevailing, will be the mental and intellectual character of future generations a race fit only for corporation tools and time-serving slaves?... Shall we not hear the response from every hill and vale: 'Equal rights, or death to the corporations'?"

Industrialists and bankers hired private armies to keep workers in line, bought newspapers and (quoting Grossman and Adams again): "painted politicians as villains and businessmen as heroes. Bribing state legislators, they then announced legislators were corrupt, that they used too much of the public's resources and time to scrutinise every charter application and corporate operation. Corporate advocates campaigned to replace existing chartering laws with general incorporation laws that set up simple administrative procedures, claiming this would be more efficient. What they really wanted was the end of legislative authority over charters."

During the Civil War, government spending brought corporations unprecedented wealth. "Corporate managers developed the techniques and the ability to organise production on an ever grander scale," according to Grossman and Adams. "Many corporations used their wealth to take advantage of war and Reconstruction years to get the tariff, banking, railroad, labour, and public lands legislation they wanted."

In 1886, the US Supreme Court declared that corporations were henceforth to be considered "persons" under the law, with all of the constitutional rights that designation implies.

The Fourteenth Amendment to the Constitution, passed to give former slaves equal rights, has been invoked approximately ten times more frequently on behalf of corporations than on behalf of African Americans. Likewise the First Amendment, guaranteeing free speech, has been invoked to guarantee corporations the "right" to influence the political process through campaign contributions, which the courts have equated with "speech".

If corporations are "persons", they are persons with qualities and powers that no flesh-and-blood human could ever possess--immortality, the ability to be in many places at once, and (increasingly) the ability to avoid liability. They are also "persons" with no sense of moral responsibility, since their only legal mandate is to produce profits for their investors.

Throughout the late 19th and early 20th centuries, corporations reshaped every aspect of life in America and much of the rest of the world. The factory system turned self-sufficient small farmers into wage earners and transformed the family from an interdependent economic production unit to a consumption-oriented collection of individuals with separate jobs.

Advertising turned productive citizens into "consumers". Business leaders campaigned to create public schools to train children in factory-system obedience to schedules and in the performance of isolated, meaningless tasks. Meanwhile, corporations came to own and dominate sources of information and entertainment, and to control politicians and judges.

During two periods, corporations faced a challenge: the 1890s (a depression period when Populists demanded regulation of railroad rates, heavy taxation of land held only for speculation, and an increase in the money supply), and the 1930s (when a profound crisis of capitalism led hundreds of thousands of workers and armies of the unemployed to demand government regulation of the economy and to win a 40-hour week, a minimum-wage law, the right to organise, and the outlawing of child labour). But in both cases, corporate capitalism emerged intact.

In the words of historian Howard Zinn: "The rich still controlled the nation's wealth, as well as its laws, courts, police, newspapers, churches, colleges. Enough help had been given to enough people to make Roosevelt a hero to millions, but the same system that had brought depression and crisis remained."2

World War II, like previous wars, brought huge profits to corporations via government contracts. But following this war, military spending was institutionalised, ostensibly to fight the "Cold War". Despite occasional regulatory setbacks, corporations seized ever more power, and increasingly transcended national boundaries, loyalties and sovereignties altogether.

GLOBAL PILLAGE

In the 1970s, capitalism faced yet another challenge as post-war growth subsided and profits fell. The US was losing its dominant position in world markets; the production of oil from its domestic wells was peaking and beginning to fall, thus making America increasingly dependent upon oil imports from Arab countries; the Vietnam War had weakened the American economy; and Third World countries were demanding a "North & South dialogue" leading towards greater self-reliance for poorer countries. President Nixon responded by doing away with fixed currency exchange rates and devaluing the dollar, largely erasing US war debts to other countries. Later, newly elected President Reagan, at the 1981 Cancún, Mexico, meeting of 22 heads of state, refused to discuss new financial arrangements with the Third World, thus effectively endorsing their further exploitation by corporations.

Meanwhile, the corporations themselves also responded with a new strategy. Increased capital mobility (made possible by floating exchange rates and new transportation, communication and production technologies) allowed US corporations to move production offshore to "export processing zones" in poorer countries. Corporations also undertook a restructuring process, moving toward "networked production"--in which big firms, while retaining and consolidating power, hired smaller firms to take over aspects of supply, manufacture, accounting and transport. (Economist Bennett Harrison defined networked production as "concentration of control combined with decentralisation of production".) This restructuring process is also known as "downsizing", because it results in the shedding of higher-paid employees by large corporations and the hiring of low-wage contingent workers by smaller subcontractors.

Jeremy Brecher and Tim Costello write in Global Village or Global Pillage that: "As the economic crisis deepened, there gradually evolved a 'supra-national policy arena' which included new organisations like the Group of Seven (G7) industrial nations and NAFTA and new roles for established international organisations like EU, IMF, World Bank, and GATT. The policies adopted by these international institutions allowed corporations to lower their costs in several ways. They reduced consumer, environmental, health, labour, and other standards. They reduced business taxes. They facilitated the move to lower wage areas and threat of such movement. And they encouraged the expansion of markets and the 'economies of scale' provided by larger-scale production."3

All of this has led to a globalised economy in which (again quoting Brecher and Costello): "All over the world, people are being pitted against each other to see who will offer global corporations the lowest labour, social, and environmental costs. Their jobs are being moved to places with inferior wages, lower business taxes, and more freedom to pollute. Their employers are using the threat of 'foreign competition' to hold down wages, salaries, taxes, and environmental protections and to replace high-quality jobs with temporary, part-time, insecure, and low-quality jobs. Their government officials are justifying cuts in education, health, and other services as necessary to reduce business taxes in order to keep or attract jobs."

Corporations, no longer bound by national laws, prowl the world looking for the best deals on labour and raw materials. **Of the world's top 120** *economies, nearly half are corporations, not countries. Thus the power of citizens in any nation to control corporations through whatever democratic processes are available to them is receding quickly.*

In November 1999, tens of thousands of students, union members and indigenous peoples gathered in Seattle to protest a meeting of the World Trade Organisation (WTO). This mass demonstration seemed to signal the birth of a new global populist uprising against corporate globalization. In the three years since then, more mass demonstrations - some larger, many smaller – have occurred in Genoa, Melbourne, Milan, Montreal, Philadelphia, Washington and other cities.

In January 2001, George W. Bush and Dick Cheney took office, following a deeply flawed US election. With strong ties to the oil industry and to the huge energy-trading corporation Enron, the new administration quickly proposed a national energy policy that focused on opening federally protected lands for oil exploration and on further subsidising the oil industry.

Enron, George W. Bush's largest campaign contributor, was the seventh largest corporation in the US and the 16th largest in the world. Despite its reported massive profits, it had paid no taxes in four out of the previous five years. The company had thousands of offshore partnerships, through which it had hidden over a billion dollars in debt. When this hidden debt was disclosed in October 2001, the company imploded. Its share price collapsed and its credit rating was slashed. Its executives resigned in disgrace, taking with them multimillion-dollar bonuses, while employees and stockholders shouldered the immense financial loss. Enron's bankruptcy was the largest in corporate history up to that time, but its creative accounting practices appear to be far from unique, with dozens of other corporations poised for a similar collapse.

Following the outrageous and tragic attacks of September 11, Bush launched a "War on Terror", raising the listed number of potential target countries from three to nearly 50, most having exportable energy resources. With Iraq (holder of the world's second-largest proven petroleum reserves) high on the list of enemy regimes to be violently overthrown, the Bush administration's Terror War appeared to be geared toward making the world safe for the expanded reach of US oil corporations. Meanwhile, new laws and executive orders curtailed constitutional rights and erected screens of secrecy around government actions and decision-making processes.

It remains to be seen how the American populace will react to these new developments. Here again, a little history may help us understand the options available.

HURDLES IN THE PATH

The Populism of the 1890s failed for two main reasons: divisiveness within, and co-optation from without. While many Populist leaders saw the need for unity among people of different racial and ethnic backgrounds in attacking corporate power, racism was strong among many whites. Most of the Alliance leaders were white farm owners who failed in many instances to support the organising efforts of poor rural blacks, and poor whites as well, thus dividing the movement.

"On top of the serious failures to unite blacks and whites, city workers and country farmers," writes Howard Zinn, "there was the lure of electoral politics. Once allied with the Democratic party in supporting William Jennings Bryan for President in 1896 the pressure for electoral victory led Populism to make deals with the major parties in city after city. If the Democrats won, it would be absorbed. If the Democrats lost, it would disintegrate. Electoral politics brought into the top leadership the political brokers instead of the agrarian radicals... In the election of 1896, with the Populist movement enticed into the Democratic party, Bryan, the Democratic candidate, was defeated by William McKinley, for whom the corporations and the press mobilised, in the first massive use of money in an election campaign."4

Today, a new populist movement could easily fall prey to the same internal divisions and tactical errors that destroyed its counterpart a century ago. In the recent American presidential election, populists faced the choice of supporting their own candidate (Ralph Nader) and thereby contributing to the election of the far-right, pro-corporate Republican candidate (Bush), or supporting the centrist Gore and seeing their movement co-opted by pro-corporate Democrats.

Meanwhile, though African Americans, Asian Americans, Hispanic Americans, European Americans and Native Americans have all been victimised by corporations, class divisions and historical resentments often prevent them from organising to further their common interests. In recent elections, ultra-right candidate Pat Buchanan appealed simultaneously to "populist" anti-corporate and anti-government sentiments among the working class, as well as to xenophobic white racism. Buchanan's critique of corporate power was shallow, but it was often the only such critique permitted in the corporate controlled media. One cannot help but wonder: were the corporations looking for a lightning rod to rechannel the anger building against them?

While Buchanan had no chance of winning the presidency, his candidacy did raise the spectre of another kind of solution to the emerging crisis of popular resentment against the system - a solution that again has roots in the history of the past century.

A FALSE REVOLUTION

In the early 1900s, workers in Italy and Germany built strong unions and won substantial concessions in wages and work conditions; still, after World War I they suffered under a disastrous post-war economy, which fanned unrest. During the early 1920s, heavy industry and big finance were in a state of near-total collapse. Bankers and agribusiness associations offered financial support to Mussolini -who had been a socialist before the war - to seize state power, which he effectively did in 1922 following his march on Rome. Within two years, the Fascist Party (from the Latin fasces, meaning a bundle of rods and an axe, symbolising Roman state power) had shut down all opposition newspapers, crushed the socialist, liberal, Catholic, democratic and republican parties (which had together commanded about 80 per cent of the vote), abolished unions, outlawed strikes and privatised farm co-operatives.

In Germany, Hitler led the Nazi Party to power, then cut wages and subsidised industries.

In both countries, corporate profits ballooned. Understandably, given their friendliness to big business, Fascism and Nazism were popular among some prominent American industrialists (such as Henry Ford) and opinion shapers (like William Randolph Hearst).

Fascism and Nazism relied on centrally controlled propaganda campaigns that cleverly co-opted the language of the Left (the Nazis called themselves the National Socialist German Workers Party while persecuting socialists and curtailing workers' rights). Both movements also made calculated use of emotionally charged symbolism: scapegoating minorities, appealing to mythic images of a glorious national past, building a leader cult, glorifying war and conquest, and preaching that the only proper role of women is as wives and mothers.

As political theorist Michael Parenti points out, historians often overlook Fascism's economic agenda - the partnership between Big Capital and Big Government - in their analysis of its authoritarian social program. Indeed, according to Bertram Gross in his startlingly prescient Friendly Fascism (1980), it is possible to achieve fascist goals within an ostensibly democratic society. 5 Corporations themselves, after all, are internally authoritarian (courts have ruled that citizens give up their constitutional rights to free speech, freedom of assembly, etc., when they are at work on corporate-owned property); and as corporations increasingly dominate politics, media and economy, they can mould an entire society to serve the interests of a powerful elite without ever resorting to stormtroopers and concentration camps. No deliberate conspiracy is necessary, either: each corporation merely acts to further its own economic interests. If the populace shows signs of restlessness, politicians can be hired to appeal to racial resentments and memories of national glory, dividing popular opposition and inspiring loyalty.

In the current situation, "friendly fascism" works somewhat as follows. Corporations drive down wages and pay a dwindling share of taxes (through mechanisms outlined above), gradually impoverishing the middle class and creating unrest. As corporate taxes are cut, politicians (whose election was funded by corporate donors) argue that it is necessary to reduce government services in order to balance the budget. Meanwhile, the same politicians argue for an increase in the repressive functions of government (more prisons, harsher laws, more executions, more military spending). Politicians channel the middle class's rising resentment away from corporations and toward the government (which, after all, is now less helpful and more repressive than it used to be) and against social groups easy to scapegoat (criminals, minorities, teenagers, women, gays, immigrants).

Meanwhile, debate in the media is kept superficial *(elections are treated as sporting contests),* and right-wing commentators are subsidised while left-of-centre ones are marginalised. **People who feel cheated by the system turn to the Right for solace, and vote for politicians who further subsidise corporations, cut government services, expand the repressive power of the state and offer irrelevant scapegoats for social problems with economic roots. The process feeds on itself.**

Within this scenario, George W. Bush (and similar ultra-right figures in other countries) are not anomalies but, rather, predictable products of a strategy adopted by economic elites - harbingers of a less-than-friendly futures - the more "moderate" tactics for the maintenance and *consolidation of power founder under the weight of corporate greed and resource exhaustion.*

CAUSE FOR HOPE?

These circumstances are, in their details, unprecedented; but in broad outline we are seeing the re-enactment of a story that goes back at least to the beginning of civilisation. Those with power are always looking for ways to protect and extend it, and to make their power seem legitimate, necessary or invisible so that popular protest seems unnecessary or futile. If protest comes, the powerful always try to deflect anger away from themselves. The leaders of the new populist movement appear to have a good grasp of both the current circumstances and the historical ground from which these circumstances emerge. They seem to have realised that, in order to succeed, the new populism will have to:
¥ avoid being co-opted by existing political parties;
¥ heal race, class and gender divisions and actively resist any campaign to scapegoat disempowered social groups;
¥ avoid being identified with an ideological category - "communist", "socialist" or "anarchist" - against which most of the public is already well inoculated by corporate propaganda;
¥ direct public discussion toward the most vulnerable link in the corporate chain of power: the legal basis of the corporation;
¥ internationalise the movement so that corporations cannot undermine it merely by shifting their base of operations from one country to another.

As Lawrence Goodwyn noted in his definitive work, The Populist Moment, the original Populists were "attempting to construct, within the framework of American capitalism, some variety of co-operative commonwealth". This was "the last substantial effort at structural alteration of hierarchical economic forms in modern America".6

In announcing the formation of the Alliance for Democracy, in an article in the August 14, 1996 issue of The Nation, activist Ronnie Dugger compiled a list of policy suggestions which comprise some of the core demands of the new populist movement. These include: a prohibition of contributions or any other political activity by corporations; single-payer national health insurance with automatic universal coverage; a doubling of the minimum wage, indexed to inflation; a generic low-interest-rate national policy, entailing the abolition of the Federal Reserve System; statutory reversal of the court-made law that corporations are "persons"; establishment of a national public oil company; limitations on ownership of newspapers, magazines, radio and TV stations to one of any kind per person or owning entity; and the halving of military spending. The new populists are, in Ronnie Dugger's words, "ready to resume the cool eyeing of the corporations with a collective will to take back the powers they have seized from us".7

The new populism draws some of its inspiration from the work of the Program on Corporations, Law and Democracy (POCLAD), a populist "think-tank" that explores the legal basis of corporate power. POCLAD believes that it is possible to control - and, if necessary, dismantle corporations by amending or revoking their charters.8

Since the largest corporations are now transnational in scope, the new populism must confront their abuses globally. The International Forum on Globalization (IFG) was founded for this purpose in 1994, as an alliance of 60 activists, scholars, economists and writers (including Jerry Mander, Vandana Shiva, Richard Grossman, Ralph Nader, Helena Norberg-Hodge, Jeremy Rifkin and Kirkpatrick Sale), to stimulate new thinking and joint action along these lines.

In a position statement drafted in 1995, the International Forum on Globalization said that it: "views international trade and investment agreements, including the GATT, the WTO, Maastricht and NAFTA, combined with the structural adjustment policies of the International Monetary Fund and the World Bank, to be direct stimulants to the processes that weaken democracy, create a world order in the control of transnational corporations and devastate the natural world. The IFG will study, publish and actively advocate in opposition to the current rush toward economic globalization, and will seek to reverse its direction. Simultaneously, we will advocate on behalf of a far more diversified, locally controlled, community-based economics. We believe that the creation of a more equitable economic order-based on principles of diversity, democracy, community and ecological sustainability will require new international agreements that place the needs of people, local economies and the natural world ahead of the interests of corporations."9

*Leaders of the new populism appear to realise that anti-corporatism is not a complete solution to the world's problems; that the necessary initial focus on corporate power must eventually be supplemented by a more general critique of centralising and unsustainable technologies, money-based economics and current nation-state governmental structures, by efforts to protect traditional cultures and ecosystems, **and by a renewal of culture and spirituality.***

It would be foolish to underestimate the immense challenges to the new populism from the current US administration and from the jingoistic, bellicose post September 11 public sentiment fostered by the corporate media. Nevertheless, POCLAD, the Alliance for Democracy and the IFG (along with dozens of human rights, environmental and anti-war organisations around the world) provide important rallying points for citizens' self-defence against tyranny in its most modern, invisible, effective and even seductive forms.

Endnotes:

1. Grossman, Richard and Frank Adams, Taking Care of Business: Citizenship and the Charter of Incorporation, pamphlet, 1993, available at http://www.poclad.org/resources.html.
2. Zinn, Howard, A People's History of the United States: 1492 to Present, Harper Perennial, 2001.
3. Brecher, Jeremy and Tim Costello, Global Village or Global Pillage: Economic Reconstruction from the Bottom Up, South End Press, 1998.
4. Zinn, op. cit.
5. Gross, Bertram, Friendly Fascism: The New Face of Power in America, South End Press, 1998.
6. Goodwyn, Lawrence, The Populist Moment: A Short History of the Agrarian Revolt in America, Oxford University Press, 1978.
7. The Alliance for Democracy website, http://www.thealliancefordemocracy.org/.
8. POCLAD website, http://www.poclad.org/.
9. IFG pamphlet, 1995; revised position statement at IFG website, http://www.ifg.org/.

About the Author:

Richard Heinberg is a journalist, educator, editor, lecturer and musician. He has lectured widely and appeared on national radio and TV in five countries. He is a core faculty member of New College of California, where he teaches courses on Culture, Ecology and Sustainable Community.

He is the author of: "Memories and Visions of Paradise"; "Celebrate the Solstice"; "A New Covenant with Nature"; and "Cloning the Buddha: the Moral Impact of Biotechnology". His next book, "The Party's Over: Oil, War and the Fate of Industrial Societies", is to be published by New Society in March 2003. His essays have been featured in The Futurist, Intuition, Brain/Mind Bulletin, Magical Blend, New Dawn and elsewhere.

Richard is also author/editor/publisher of MuseLetter, a highly regarded monthly, subscription-only, alternative newsletter which is now in its tenth year of publication. MuseLetter's purpose is "to offer a continuing critique of corporate-capitalist industrial civilisation and a re-visioning of humanity's prospects for the next millennium". His article, "A History of Corporate Rule and Popular Protest", was originally published in MuseLetter in 1996 as "The New Populism", and was revised in August 2002. Visit the MuseLetter website at http://www.museletter.com/.

205-EDUCATION

What good fortune for those in power that the people do not think."
~Adolf Hitler

The following article presents a recent history of education in a most succinct, clear, and readable manner and some real issues and problems in dealing with it. It is of course straight off the Internet and is unchanged and unedited from how it appears there. Please note the source and authorship at the foot of the article. That site and source is 100% recommended for everyone, and is an excellent launching pad for additional research not only on the issues of this section, but of this entire book.

The Public School Nightmare:

Why fix a system designed to destroy individual thought?

by John Taylor Gatto [Two time New York State "Teacher of the Year"]

I want you to consider the frightening possibility that we are spending far too much money on schooling, not too little. I want you to consider that we have too many people employed in interfering with the way children grow up -- and that all this money and all these people, all the time we take out of children's lives and away from their homes and families and neighborhoods and private explorations -- gets in the way of education.

That seems radical, I know. Surely in modern technological society it is the quantity of schooling and the amount of money you spend on it that buys value.

And yet last year in St. Louis, I heard a vice-president of IBM tell an audience of people assembled to redesign the process of teacher certification that in his opinion this country became computer-literate by self-teaching, not through any action of schools. He said 45 million people were comfortable with computers who had learned through dozens of non-systematic strategies, none of them very formal; if schools had pre-empted the right to teach computer use we would be in a horrible mess right now instead of leading the world in this literacy.

Now think about **Sweden**, a beautiful, healthy, prosperous and up-to-date country with a spectacular reputation for quality in everything it produces. It makes sense to think their schools must have something to do with that.

Then what do you make of the fact that you can't go to school in Sweden until you are 7 years old? The reason the unsentimental Swedes have wiped out what would be first and seconds grades here is that they don't want to pay the large social bill that quickly comes due when boys and girls are ripped away from their best teachers at home too early. It just isn't worth the price, say the Swedes, to provide jobs for teachers and therapists if the result is sick, incomplete kids who can't be put back together again very easily.

The entire Swedish school sequence isn't 12 years, either -- it's nine. Less schooling, not more. The direct savings of such a step in the US would be $75-100 billion, a lot of unforeclosed home mortgages, a lot of time freed up with which to seek an education.

Who was it that decided to force your attention onto **Japan** instead of Sweden? Japan with its long school year and state compulsion, instead of Sweden with its short school year, short school sequence, and free choice where your kid is schooled? Who decided you should know about Japan and not **Hong Kong**, an Asian neighbour with a short school year that outperforms Japan across the board in math and science? Whose interests are served by hiding that from you?

One of the principal reasons we got into the mess we're in is that we allowed schooling to become a very profitable monopoly, guaranteed its customers by the police power of the state. Systematic schooling attracts increased investment only when it does poorly, and since there are no penalties at all for such performance, the temptation not to do well is overwhelming. That's because school staffs, both line and management, are involved in a **guild system**. And in that ancient form of association no single member is allowed to outperform any other member, none are allowed to advertise or to introduce new technology or improvise without the advance consent of the guild. Violation of these precepts is severely sanctioned--as Marva Collins, Jaime Escalante and a large number of once-brilliant teachers found out.

The guild reality cannot be broken without returning primary decision-making to parents, letting them buy what they want to buy in schooling, and encouraging the entrepreneurial reality that existed until 1852. That is why I urge any business to think twice before entering a cooperative relationship with the schools we currently have. Cooperating with these places will only make them worse.

The structure of American schooling, 20th century style, began in 1806 when **Napoleon's** amateur soldiers beat the professional soldiers of Prussia at the battle of Jena. When your business is selling soldiers, losing a battle like that is serious. Almost immediately afterwards a German philosopher named **Fichte** delivered his famous "Address to the German Nation" which became one of the most influential documents in modern history.

In effect he told the Prussian people that the party was over, that the nation would have to shape up through a new Utopian institution of forced schooling in which everyone would **learn to take orders.**

So the world got compulsion schooling at the end of a state bayonet for the first time in human history; modern forced schooling started in Prussia in 1819 with a clear vision of what centralized schools could deliver:

1. Obedient soldiers to the army;

2. Obedient workers to the mines;

3. Well subordinated civil servants to government;

4. Well subordinated clerks to industry

5. Citizens who thought alike about major issues.

Schools should create an artificial national consensus on matters that had been worked out in advance by leading German families and the head of institutions. Schools should create unity among all the German states, eventually unifying them into Greater Prussia.

Prussian industry boomed from the beginning. She was successful in warfare and her reputation in international affairs was very high. Twenty-six years after this form of schooling began, the King of Prussia was invited to North America to determine the boundary between the United States and Canada. Thirty-three years after that fateful invention of the central school institution, as the behest of Horace Mann and many other leading citizens, we borrowed the style of Prussian schooling as our own.

You need to know this because over the first 50 years, our school's Prussian design -- which was to create a form of state socialism -- gradually forced out our traditional American design, which in most minds was to prepare the individual to be **self-reliant**.

In Prussia the purpose of the Volksshule [work school], which educated 92 percent of the children, was not intellectual development at all, but socialisation in obedience and subordination. Thinking was left to the Real Schulen, [Real School] in which 8 percent of the kids participated. But for the great mass, intellectual development was regarded with managerial horror, as something that caused armies to lose battles.

Prussia concocted a method based on complex fragmentation to ensure that its school products would fit the grand social design. Some of this method involved dividing whole ideas into school subjects, each further divisible, some of it involved short periods punctuated by a horn so that self-motivation in study would be muted by ceaseless interruptions.

There were many more techniques of training, but all were built around the premise that isolation from first-hand information, and fragmentation of the abstract information presented by teachers, would result in obedient and subordinate graduates, properly respectful of arbitrary orders.

"Lesser" men would be unable to interfere with policy makers because, while they could still complain, **they could not manage sustained or comprehensive thought. Well-schooled children cannot think critically, cannot argue effectively.**

One of the most interesting by-products of Prussian schooling turned out to be the two most devastating wars of modern history.

Erich Maria Ramarque, in his classic "All Quiet on the Western Front" tells us that the **First World War** was caused by the tricks of schoolmasters, and the famous Protestant theologian Dietrich Bonhoeffer said that the **Second World War** was the inevitable product of good schooling.

It's important to underline that Bonhoeffer meant that literally, not metaphorically -- schooling after the Prussian fashion **removes the ability of the mind to think for itself.** It teaches people to wait for a teacher to tell them what to do and if what they have done is good or bad.

Prussian teaching paralyses the moral will as well as the intellect. It's true that sometimes well-schooled students sound smart, because they **memorise** many opinions of great thinkers, but they actually are badly damaged because their own ability to think is left rudimentary and undeveloped.

We got from the United States to Prussia and back because a small number of very passionate ideological leaders visited Prussia in the first half of the 19th century, and fell in love with the order, obedience and efficiency of its system and relentlessly proselytised for a translation of Prussian vision onto these shores.

If Prussia's ultimate goal was the unification of Germany, our major goal, so these men thought, was the unification of hordes of immigrant Catholics into a national consensus based on a northern European cultural model. To do that children would have to be removed from their parents and from inappropriate cultural influence.

In this fashion, compulsion schooling, a bad idea that had been around at least since Plato's Republic, a bad idea that New England had tried to enforce in 1650 without any success, was finally rammed through the Massachusetts legislature in 1852.

It was, of course, the famous "Know-Nothing" legislature that passed this law, a legislature that was the leading edge of a famous secret society which flourished at that time known as "The Order of the Star Spangled Banner," whose password was the simple sentence, "I know nothing" -- hence the popular label attached to the secret society's political arm, "The American Party."

Over the next 50 years state after state followed suit, ending schools of choice and ceding the field to a new government monopoly. There was one powerful exception to this -- the children who could afford to be privately educated. [Although it may be relevant that not ALL private schools are geared to a "real" education, but are simply more of the same as the public schools, but are promoted as being for the elite.]

It's important to note that the underlying premise of Prussian schooling is that the government is the true parent of children -- the State is sovereign over the family. At the most extreme pole of this notion is the idea that biological parents are really the enemies of their own children, not to be trusted.

How did a Prussian system of **dumbing children down** take hold in American schools?

Thousands and thousands of young men from prominent American families journeyed to Prussia and other parts of Germany during the 19th century and brought home the Ph. D. degree to a nation in which such a credential was unknown. These men pre-empted the top positions in the academic world, in corporate research, and in government, to the point where opportunity was almost closed to those who had not studied in Germany, or who were not the direct disciples of a German PhD, as John Dewey was the disciple of G. Stanley Hall at Johns Hopkins. Virtually every single one of the founders of American schooling had made the pilgrimage to Germany, and many of these men wrote widely circulated reports praising the Teutonic methods. Horace Mann's famous 7th Report of 1844, still available in large libraries, was perhaps the most important of these.

By 1889, a little more than 100 years ago, the crop was ready for harvest. It that year the US Commissioner of Education, William Torrey Harris, assured a railroad magnate, Collis Huntington, that American schools were "scientifically designed" to prevent "over-education" from happening. The average American would be content with his humble role in life, said the commissioner, because he would not be tempted to think about any other role.

My guess is that Harris meant he would not be able to think about any other role.

In 1896 the famous John Dewey, then at the University of Chicago, said that independent, self-reliant people were a counter-productive anachronism in the collective society of the future. In modern society, said Dewey, people would be defined by their associations --not by their own individual accomplishments. In such a world **people who read too well or too early are dangerous because they become privately empowered, they know too much, and know how to find out what they don't know by themselves, without consulting experts. [emphasis added]**

Dewey said the great mistake of traditional pedagogy was to make reading and writing constitute the bulk of early schoolwork. He advocated the phonics method of teaching reading be abandoned and replaced by the whole word method, not because the latter was more efficient (he admitted that it was less efficient), but because

independent thinkers were produced by hard books, thinkers who cannot be socialised very easily.

By socialisation Dewey meant a program of social objectives administered by the best social thinkers in government. This was a giant step on the road to state socialism, the form pioneered in Prussia, and it is a vision radically disconnected with the American past, its historic hopes and dreams.

Dewey's former professor and close friend, G. Stanley Hall, said this at about the same time, "Reading should no longer be a fetish. **Little attention should be paid to reading."**

Hall was one of the three men most responsible for building a gigantic administrative infrastructure over the classroom. How enormous that structure really became can only be understood by comparisons: New York State, for instance, employs more school administrators than all of the European Economic Community nations combined.

Once you think that the control of conduct is what schools are about, the word "reform" takes on a very particular meaning. It means making adjustments to the machine so that young subjects will not twist and turn so, while their minds and bodies are being scientifically controlled. Helping kids to use their minds better is beside the point.

Bertrand Russell once said that American schooling was among the most radical experiments in human history, that **America was deliberately denying its children the tools of critical thinking.**

When you want to teach children to think, you begin by treating them seriously when they are little, giving them responsibilities, talking to them candidly, providing privacy and solitude for them, and making them readers and thinkers of significant thoughts from the beginning. That's if you want to teach them to think. There is no evidence that this has been a State purpose since the start of compulsion schooling.

When Frederich Froebel, the inventor of kindergarten in 19th century Germany, fashioned his idea he did not have a "garden for children" in mind, but a metaphor of teachers as gardeners and children as the vegetables.

Kindergarten was created to be a way to break the influence of mothers on their children. I note with interest the growth of daycare in the US and the repeated urgings to extend school downward to include 4-year-olds. The movement toward state socialism is not some historical curiosity, but a powerful dynamic force in the world around us.

The state socialism movement is fighting for its life against those forces which would, through vouchers or tax credits, deprive it of financial lifeblood, and it has countered this thrust with a demand for even more control over children's lives, and even more money to pay for the extended school day and year that this control requires. A movement as visibly destructive to individuality, family and community as government-system schooling has been, might be expected to collapse in the face of its dismal record, coupled with an increasingly aggressive shake down of the taxpayer, but this has not happened.

The explanation is largely found in the transformation of schooling from a simple service to families and towns to an enormous, centralized corporate enterprise. While this development has had a markedly adverse effect on people and on our democratic traditions, it has made schooling the single largest employer in the United States, and the largest grantor of contracts next to the Defense Department.

Both of these low-visibility phenomena provide monopoly schooling with powerful political friends, publicists, advocates and other useful allies. This is a large part of the explanation **why no amount of failure ever changes things in schools**, or changes them for very long. **School people are in a position to outlast any storm and to keep short-attention-span public scrutiny thoroughly confused.**

An overview of the short history of this institution reveals a pattern marked by intervals of public outrage, followed by enlargement of the monopoly in every case. After nearly 30 years spent inside a number of public schools, some considered good, some bad, I feel certain that management cannot clean its own house. It relentlessly marginalizes all significant change.

There are no incentives for the "owners" of the structure to reform it, nor can there be without outside competition. What is needed for several decades is the kind of wildly-swinging free market we had at the beginning of our national history.

It cannot be overemphasised that no body of theory exists to accurately define the way children learn, or which learning is of most worth. By pretending the existence of such we have cut ourselves off from the information and innovation that only a real market can provide. Fortunately our national situation has been so favourable, so dominant through most of our history, that the margin of error afforded has been vast.

But the future is not so clear. Violence, narcotic addictions, divorce, alcoholism, loneliness... all these are but tangible measures of a poverty in education.   Surely schools, as the institutions monopolising the daytimes of childhood, can be called to account for this. In a democracy the final judges cannot be experts, but only the people.

Trust the people, give them choices, and the school nightmare will vanish in a generation.

****

This article is not a favourite among public school teachers. Unless, of course, they are truly interested in teaching, and much more importantly, their students learning to be self-reliant, thinking human beings -- as was Mr. Gatto, before his voluntary departure from the system. Teachers of the latter stripe, of course, have very little options when school administrators and bureaucrats dictate in the tradition of evil dictators. It is, of course, the latter who are so excessively compensated, while the front line teachers are just attempting to make ends meet.   Perhaps parents should consider joining forces, finding good teachers, and hiring them on a private basis for a multiple home schooling scenario.

The Library of ialexandriah

And elsewhere on the Internet the following is found.

I would go so far as to say that all the "world problems/solutions" derive from a stupid populace, one who has no chance for freedom because they don't know the truth, or even suspect that they don't know it. There is, in fact, no effort being made to continually question everything, including one's old opinions and Paradigms. Even if one solved a world problem -- e.g. outlawed vaccinations -- within a couple of generations, the same problem would rear its head again, and because the children's education was such a low priority, they would not know the history of why the people did away with it before.

If, for example, one indoctrinates children into believing that "Father Knows Best", that all Vaccines are good for you, that the "authorities" really know what they're doing, and will always do things with your best interests in mind... Then there's no hope for freedom. Just keep in mind that freedom includes the right to fail, to get burned by the stove.

It is no wonder every State arrogates to itself the power to oversee and influence the education of its citizens. Compulsory education is the premiere means by which change for the better (for the citizens) can be nipped in the bud, and thereby imbue to the benefit of the State. It is those individuals in charge of the state, and who wish to maintain absolute dominance, that the educational system is inevitably designed to protect. Compulsory education is mind-control par excellence. In Western so-called "democracies" it is a subtle part of the system that few intellectuals -- let alone the masses -- can or are willing to see (the latter being, effectively, wilful ignorance), and therefore no remedy is thought by the so-called intellectual elite to be needed.

****

Judith: Janus, would you consider that what needs to be compulsory is not a State-supervised education system, but a State-supervised minimum education standard? By this, I mean, that the State is strictly LIMITED to administering tests to ensure that all "young minds" are acquainted with certain fundamentals -- such as reading, writing, mathematics, basic understandings of human rights and the constitution, and so forth. The idea is to ensure that education is not withheld by parents or groups to some minimum basis, but at the same time, to place the actual educational process itself -- along with all the other materials deemed appropriate by the student's parents and community -- in the hands (control) of the parents and community. ....

Judith: I find it curious that communists, religious fundamentalists, and other very-control-oriented groups have invariably adopted the strategy that the best idea (i.e. the highest priority) is to educate children in such a way that within a generation (say 15 years), they will have a group of · fanatic, true believers that will do anything but exercise critical thinking, discriminate between conflicting ideas, and so forth. They will thus avoid touching the stove, not because of its inadvisability, but because of a traumatic order.

206-RELIGION 1

If you think that something is right just because everyone believes it, then you are not thinking" - Vievienne Westwood

The following is an article taken off the Internet. My thoughts and comments on religion follow as "Religion 2". As this article is so well written and cannot be improved upon I use it "as is". Please note the copyright notes at its conclusion and use this site for additional materials.

Why Have Religion?

Updated -- 11 November 2006

In today's world and throughout history, religion has played a predominant role in the affairs of men and women and the groups with which they associate. Probably more than any other single factor, religion has had an influence which far outweighs virtually everything else. The manner in which people have lived their lives, fought their wars, sought peace and tried to pursue happiness have all been heavily influenced by the religious dictates of the time and place in which these people have lived.

But is religion really needed for such pursuits as happiness, sociability, war and peace? Are there, perhaps, better alternatives?

On the most basic level anyone professing to the beliefs and lifestyles of any religion must ultimately ask the question: Why have religion? What justifies its existence, especially in lieu of having other alternative devices with which we might prefer to use in order to motivate ourselves and to create our own reality? One might even question the role religion might ideally play within a society which claims to be civilized or humane. Ultimately, it comes down to the most fundamental (pardon the pun) of questions: Why even bother with religion?

If this seems sacrilegious... well... why not? Is there a reason that religion should enjoy some kind of immunity from inquiry? David Koepsell [6] has noted, for example, "the reason religious conservatives fear too much inquiry: it leads to doubt."

"Religion is one of the most powerful social phenomena in the world. It guides nations, wars, societies, even whole eras; it has catalyzed climactic moments in history. As such, it should be studied -- and thoroughly. Religions hinge on truth claims, usually embodied in texts and carried out through social practices and belief sets that are often highly institutionalised and structured. The texts, truth claims, belief sets, and structures of religion can and should all be put to the sort of tests to which other institutionalised phenomena are subject, namely: tests for **internal logical consistency** in belief sets, tests of **corroboration** for truth claims, and examinations of the **efficacy** of institutions and other structures within the boundaries of religions. We do this with ideologies in political science. We do this with theories in economics. We do this with nontheistic philosophies. Scholarly integrity and academic honesty demand that the same level of criticism be employed for religions and their institutions as for other social phenomena." [6]

One reason such a question is asked is that bloody and **horrific wars** have been fought over religious differences. This is the case wherein essentially the fundamentalists of one sect or cult were arrayed against the fundamentalists of another sect or cult, and a whole host of seemingly innocent people invariably got in harm's way. The fact that the higher ranking members of either fundamentalist sect or cult pretty much escaped the ravages of wars and devastation they were so instrumental in initiating, proliferating, or profiting thereby is... well... another matter altogether.

Wars, of course, have been waged for purposes other than religious differences, but the purveyors of such wars have in countless cases used religion to rally the troops -- not to mention the society which supports the troops. Religion may not always generate war, but it readily accedes to being used to justify and sanctify war, and attempt to lift the purely materialistic reasons "to a transmaterial level in which killing in war often takes the form of religious duty." [3]

Said religious duty is supported by the fact that "Killing in the name of God as sacrifice and worship, as an act expressive of religious devotion, is one of the most enduring and universal features of religion. Near the core of religion lies a grand, cosmic battle between order -- equated with all that is righteous and good -- and chaos --equated with all that is evil, sinful, and bad -- along with all the heroes, martyrs, and holy warriors who maim, kill, and die fighting the foes of the cherished divinities and receive vast and eternal rewards." [3]

It is in fact a fundamental -- there's that word again -- tenet of war to use religion to motivate anyone and everyone to go out and commit all manner of atrocity and heinous crimes. Curiously, the religions used to justify such atrocities and heinous crimes are typically opposed in principle to these horrendous and inhumane acts as a matter of their most basic and sacred beliefs. Or at least opposed to such atrocities and heinous crimes on their own people.

What is absolutely astounding is that so many people -- ostensibly good, loving, and religiously dedicated souls -- have enthusiastically accepted inane and incredulous religious justifications for untold and unlimited destruction, killing, maiming, and torturing. It has always been the height of irony that all the dictates of religions advocating righteousness and correct living have been so easily ignored by those religions who have been more than eager to condone any action in "defense of the faith", but which are diametrically opposed to the religions' dogmas, laws, and allegedly ethical standards.

Inevitably, wars and conflicts have always been portrayed as being between "the good guys and the bad guys", with the applicable religions more often than not aiding in the identification of who gets to wear the white hats (as opposed to the black hats). This identification is further predicated upon the concept that one religion is good and everyone else's religion is wrong. This technique does have the quality that at least it's simple, and thus ideal for the simple minded folk who will be the primary fodder in pursuing the war's agenda.

In view of the immense pain and suffering caused by religions over the millennia - said pain and suffering incurred in the fanatical quest of religious fundamentalists to impose their antiquated, narrow, limited and irrational views on others (using techniques ranging from inquisitions to holocausts to jihads to making the world safe for democracy to avoiding meat on Fridays), and so forth and so... One must ask the question again and again as to why should we as human beings want to have such an anti-ethical, immoral, and inhumane force in any human civilisation worthy of the name?

In view of the historical horrors associated with them, why even have religions?

****

This webpage is one attempt to answer that question. Its thesis is that the answer can be summarised in what might be thought of as The Seven Purposes of Religion. These seven purposes are:

Guidance in the daily and societal lives of individuals,

Societal bonding of certain segments of society,

Understanding of purpose (both individual, group and/or species),

Comfort

Connection/communication with a higher power (for whatever reason),

External Control, and

A Discussion Topic for various websites, commentators, and fund raisers.

Unlike the Seven Deadly Sins, the 99 names of God, or the Three Attributes of the Truly Demented Mind, the Seven Purposes (or at least the first six) may suffice to identify any redeeming quality of religion. We'll take them one at a time.

Guidance in Daily Living

Religion can be used, ideally, to provide its adherents with a set of principles or rules by which they can live their lives to the fullest, and at the same time to allow for them to live with other people in a civilised, caring society. Said rules can also be used to provide the means to live in an uncivilised, uncaring society, but inasmuch as most religions appeal to the downtrodden by claiming attributes of the civilised, caring bit, we will assume that the better road to travel (or at least the first one) is the one leading toward a caring civilised life. The attributes of the Klingon Empire can be, for the moment, debated elsewhere.

On the one hand, religions have always claimed responsibility for providing the very foundations of civilised society. However, as Thomas Mates [7] has noted,

"Instead of straining to show that the Bible is not the foundation of our democracy, [progressives] should challenge the Right to show how it ever could have been."

"No one taking the New Testament seriously could view it as a template for governance, and it's high time that American secularists compelled conservative American believers to treat their religion like a religion, instead of a weapon or a tool."

"It takes the institutionalisation of a bold set of lies to make an apocalyptic religion seem compatible with procreation and 401k plans and to make a pacifist religion compatible with war."

Victor Stenger [8] has also noted that, "Only three of the Ten Commandments are codified into modern law, and those rules -- against killing, stealing, and bearing false witness -- predate the time of Moses." Mr. Stenger has also written:

"The Judeo-Christian and Islamic scriptures contain many passages that teach noble ideals, which the human race has done well to adopt as norms of behaviour and, where appropriate, to codify into law. Without exception, these principles developed in earlier cultures, and history indicates that they were adopted by -- rather than learned from -- religion. While it is fine that religions preach moral precepts, they have no basis to claim that these precepts were **authored** by their particular deity, or, indeed, any deity at all."

"In The Doctrine of the Mean 13, written about 500 B.C.E., Confucius says, 'What you do not want others to do to you, do not do to others.'

"Isocrates (c. 375 B.C.E.) said, 'Do not do to others what would anger you if done to you by others.'

"The Hindu Mahabharata, written around 150 B.C.E., teaches, 'This is the sum of all true righteousness: deal with others as thou wouldst thyself be dealt by.'"

"'I treat those who are good with goodness. And I also treat those who are not good with goodness. Thus goodness is attained. I am honest with those who are honest. And I am also honest with those who are dishonest. Thus honesty is attained.' (Taoism: Tao Te Ching 49).

"'Conquer anger by love. Conquer evil by good. Conquer the stingy by giving. Conquer the liar by truth.' (Buddhism: Dhammapada 223)."

[It's curious but so many of the noble ideals by which we might govern ourselves came into widespread belief not long after 600 B.C.E.]

Any common set of rules and principles constitutes a mutual societal contract, the **Common Law**, wherein individuals and groups with wildly different agendas, goals, pursuits, and aspirations can be encouraged and even enabled to function in a tolerant, cooperative and/or competitive environment. Religion can serve the purpose, the bedrock, of providing the defining structure of what is "right" and what is "wrong".

More accurately, religion in its highest calling can define what is acceptable and what is unacceptable in a society which promotes the maximum freedom for its members, their individual pursuits of happiness, and the destinies or paths which they have chosen for their individual enlightenment. In brief, religion can identify, promote, and motivate people to: 1) participate in activities which are conducive to mutual peace and harmony, 2) or to avoid engaging in those other activities which are not conducive to such goals.

This common law has been perpetuated throughout history in two distinct forms. One is akin to the **Sumerian Me**, a set of precepts which promote standards on how to live a life which is beneficial to both the individual and the society which surrounds him or her. Things like, the art of kindness, or the Golden Rule, or even the making of beer. One might think of these as the "carrot" approach. All the standards of the Me and similar rules for living are based on what one should do or not do. Period.

A second form of motivating people to obey the rules is the very basic: Do it this way or else! Instead of describing what is good, and then leaving it alone, the second form includes not just the rules, but also the consequences of not following the rules. This is definitely the "stick" approach. It includes as its primary motivators, **punishments** or **enforcements** for a failure to not lead a "righteous" life. Instead of an appeal to do right, there is a very real threat on what happens if the appeal fails. The difficulty in this form is, of course, the fact that it inevitably degrades to "Do it my way or else", where the "my" is an extremely narrow view with a tendency toward fashionable changes on a whim.

One might argue as to the appropriateness in a civilised society of the Carrot and/or Stick approaches. In either case, however, there are rules or standards which seem pretty straight-forward and thus logically or rationally a good idea to which one might wish to adhere. For example, rules or standards such as "thou shalt not kill" are seemingly unquestionable - even when such rules are tossed aside when it comes to being applied to "enemies of the state". Other rules, such as "thou shalt honour thy father and mother", are less intuitively obvious. On the one hand, they make sense, but may clearly, for any number of reasons, not be applicable or justified in all cases or situations. Many fathers and mothers are clearly not worthy of being honoured.

Many religious rules (aka commandments) become even stranger when critical terms in the rule are undefined - as in "thou shalt love thy God." The problem is that even though "God" may be defined elsewhere in a very narrow manner, there is still room for considerable debate on just what or who the word, "God", means. Furthermore, such definitions (and the implications of identifying a particular "God") can be -- and often have been -- hotly debated to the point of all out war. [There is also the curious aside of why would any "God" worthy of the name require his creations to love him or her. Such a neediness implies a degree of dysfunctional behaviour.]

Another fascinating ingredient is that there exists a commonality in virtually all religions worthy of the name. This commonality includes the principles by which people can live in a mutually beneficial society. One possible example is what one might define as the Golden Rule, i.e. "Do unto others what you would have them do unto you." There are many variations, but the gist of the rule is fundamentally the same. The appeal of this dictum is that it does not involve punishment, it provides a sense of an inherent reward for following the rule, and it seems particularly desirable in a world where we must all get along collectively in order to get along individually.

[The notion that the rule should read: "Do unto others what you would have them do unto themselves" is generally perceived to be without merit among civilised folk, although it was the manner in which the first draft of this page was inadvertently written. <grin>]

An enormously less appealing dictate is "And if a man lie with his daughter in law, both of them shall surely be put to death; they have wrought confusion; their blood shall be upon them." [Leviticus 20:12] The problem here (and in most of Leviticus and similar books in other religions) is that death is the punishment for a whole host of actions which violate a very narrow view of life. Too many people have been burnt alive for actions which in another time and place are entirely acceptable.

It is one thing for an individual to choose a religion which has such strict rules and thereafter be expected to follow them. It is an entirely different matter for someone to have such rules imposed upon her or him by individuals who condemn the actions of others in order to justify the most unspeakable crimes of their own religions. Most major religions in fact have words to the effect that one should not kill another, and then has hundreds of rules about killing others who somehow avoid offending some antiquated rule, some anal retentive, or some alleged divinity concocted by a truly demented mind.

[Note: The first Attribute of the Truly Demented Mind is concocting a preposterous divinity on which to inflict such a fantasy upon everyone else within reach.]

For examples, in order to guide the faithful in the conduct of their daily lives:

"And when the Lord their god shall deliver them before thee; thou shalt smite them, and utterly destroy them; thou shalt make no covenant with them, nor shew mercy unto them." -- Deuteronomy 7:2

"Those kings who, seeking to slay each other, fight with the utmost exertion and do not turn back, go to heaven." -- ancient Hindu code, the Law of Manu [3]

"It is necessary for all one hundred million subjects [of the emperor] to be prepared to die with honour... If you see the enemy, you must kill him, you must destroy the false and establish the true... these are the cardinal points of Zen." -- Harada Sogaku [3]

Despite the gross misuse of religions by various control freaks throughout history (and up until the modern day), religions can offer an excellent regimen in providing voluntary guidance on how best to live one's life. Ideally, such a regimen will be promulgated for the purpose of maximizing the long term happiness of the individual. On the other hand, it is critical that this religious underpinning of regimens be stripped down to the essential ingredients - and thereby avoid the side effects of madness-inspired attempts to kill others for victimless alleged crimes. [One might notice, parenthetically, the constant linkages between religion and politics/government.]

It must be pointed out, however, that such bare bones regimens or guidance never require a belief or adherence to the other tenets of a religion. The good news (the "gospel") is that doing things which are inherently beneficial for all concerned does not require a religious base. The bad news is that religions have all too often linked what might be a set of acceptable and understandable principles of living with a whole host of other belief requirements, the latter which are neither acceptable nor even understandable. What in the world, for example, does the alleged "virginity" of a mother in the ancient past have to do with treating others with respect and dignity?

Sad to say as we come to the end of discussing the first possible purpose of religion, that we are now facing the implication that **religion is not needed in order to promulgate guidance for living.** It might have occasionally done so in the past, but the side effects of such an opiate is simply not conducive to one's physical, mental, emotional, and/or spiritual health.

But not to worry, there are five (or six) other possible justifications for having religions.

Societal Bonding

Religions by their very nature tend to foster the idea that "birds of a feather tend to flock together." There is something enormously comforting in the idea that someone who might otherwise be a stranger to you can be counted on for certain behaviours by virtue of your knowing their religion and what is therefore expected of them in dealing with others. There is a marvellous sense of security in knowing that major surprises are unlikely to arise, and that rules for aiding travellers, for example, can be relied upon.

Furthermore, the inclusiveness of many religious relationships is very appealing, and allows for a sense of bonding which is often lacking in our lives. A stranger, for example, upon arrival in town might immediately go to the church, synagogue, mosque, or run-down pad of his or her choice, and be welcomed with open arms by the locals as one of their own. One can sit down and pray together or smoke pot in a friendly (albeit foggy) atmosphere. Such cohesiveness and common lifestyles makes for a higher quality of living for everyone.

[Of course as the hint of humour indirectly suggests in the above, one does not need a religion in order to connect with the pot smoking hippies -- except as a matter of making certain that one or more individuals are not narcotics cops.]

The two-headed nature of this particular religious sword, of course, is the fact that such societal bonding also includes a distinct **exclusiveness,** and strangers who profess other beliefs, even merely dress differently, are many times not only not welcome, but are in fact prohibited by force from interacting with the locals. It is said that the essence of community (including religious communities) is knowing a little dirt on everyone else. This **mutually assured destruction** (MAD) against anyone daring to fire the first shot, gives many people a weird sense of comfort. But a stranger in the midst, of whom nothing is known, is a decided threat inasmuch as they might discover the dirt on someone else without the MAD option on the part of the dirtee. One clear example of this is that Muslims on their way to Mecca will form a wonderfully cohesive grouping, whereas a Christian or Jew on the same trek would have to be considered suicidal.

Another two-edged sword aspect is the alleged added benefit of inclusiveness for those who profess the same faith or ideals, and the exclusiveness - something of a country club snobbery - which tends to make the in-crowd feel exalted and superior to those not included. This is the strange logic which says that someone who does not agree with me cannot possibly possess the intellect and enlightenment that I do as an insider. This logic of a sought-after exclusivity cannot be considered a desirable quality, but it may nevertheless provide many members of the Society for the Willfully Ignorant with a false sense of security, importance, and/or **self-righteousness**. Whatever floats their boat. Or Yacht. Whatever.

Does such a societal bonding require religion, however? Obviously not as country club members whose only religion is the worship of the intricate movements of small, white, dimpled balls might attest. One can feel decidedly bonded with those of equal wealth, status, celebrity, ego, arrogance, and so forth and so on. Just knowing that one lives in a red state or a blue state, or that one subscribes to a particular magazine, may be sufficient to place one in a hopefully privileged position within society.

The choice of one's religion is therefore merely another entrance exam (among many), a prerequisite for joining a club. Unfortunately, it is a poorly defined threshold as calling oneself a Christian, Jew, Muslim, Hindu, Buddhist, Lord of Creation, or some such... never really says much about one's beliefs. Such labels are as notoriously lacking in precision as political labels. (On the other hand, wealth or the net worth of individuals is much more mathematically precise, and is thus sought by the more precision oriented individuals of taste and breeding. Being a billionaire, for example, speaks volumes!)

Another important factor is the common belief that "all religious fundamentalists share: worship of God and obedience to his laws are essential for a peaceful, healthy society. From Orthodox rabbis in the occupied West Bank to Wahhabi sheiks in Saudi Arabia, from the pope in Vatican City to Mormons in Salt Lake City, the lament is the same: God and his will must be at the center of everyone's lives in order to ensure a moral, prosperous, safe, collective existence.

"Furthermore, fundamentalists agree that, when large numbers of people in a society reject God or fail to make him the center of their lives, societal disintegration is sure to follow. Every societal ill -- whether crime, poverty, poor public education, or AIDS -- is thus blamed of a lack of piety." [4] Essentially the use of Scapegoatology to demand that everyone think in the same demented manner as the perpetrators of the religion.

"In reality, the most secular countries -- those with the highest proportion of atheists and agnostics -- are among the most stable, peaceful, free, wealthy, and healthy societies." "And the most religious nations -- wherein worship of God is in abundance -- are among the most unstable, violent, oppressive, poor, and destitute." The secular nations have "the lowest homicide rates, infant mortality rates, poverty rates, and illiteracy rates and among the highest levels of wealth, life expectancy, educational attainment, and gender equality in the world." [4] A noteworthy point is that there are fewer suicides in religious countries.

Clearly, such correlations do not prove that higher percentages of atheism cause societal health. And while it may be true: "high levels of irreligion do not automatically result in a breakdown of civilisation, a rise in immoral behaviour, or in 'sick societies'." [4] It is in fact quite probable that living in relative comfort in a stable and healthy society generates a lackadaisical attitude, and thus there is no pressing need for religion. It is the society which spawns a lack of attention to an involved deity. When life is good, there is reason to limit oneself to the dictates of an ancient religion. It is only when conditions become horrendous (or just moderately lousy) that one is apt to wonder just why life is just a bummer, and that therefore in order for things to get better, we will require divine intervention to set things right again.

It is plausible one might judge the health of various societies on the relative importance of religious doctrines among the populace -- except that instead of more religion suggesting greater health, the converse is true. But truth be told, there does not seem to be, strictly speaking, a causal relationship between the two. Rather, the extent of a religious fervour might be more of a symptom of a sick society than a causal factor.

Consider, for example, the idea that attributes of healthy societies include: gender equality, low poverty rates, low homicide rates, high literacy, tolerance of homosexuality, and the highest medium levels of wealth. If this is the case, then more and more people are experiencing a relatively high quality of life, and are accordingly less prone to look to religion for providing any of their needs. Religion is thus not just the opiate for the masses, but the opiate for the poor, the downtrodden, and those seeking to be free.

However... if there is wealth, comfort, and quality of life for the vast majority of the members of a given society, there will simply be no need whatsoever for religion. The only societal need for religion is when the society has problems which are not open to being alleviated short of divine intervention.

The bad news, of course, is that once again religion has failed to justify its existence. It may provide a type of societal bonding, but the alternatives are much less difficult to deal with. Church socials may be all the rage in some locales, but inevitably the horrible lack or perceived lack of other alternative socials is very likely the only thing keeping the church social a going enterprise. There is a reason, for example, why Christian church socials are almost never on a Saturday night.

Understanding of Purpose

Finally, we encounter something by which religion - or more strictly speaking, **philosophy** - can be thought of as perhaps being integral to the task at hand. Making sense of one's destiny, one's ideal purpose during their sojourn in their space suit of a body on a less than hospitable planet, and finding some reason for bothering with the entire mess called life, is something to which religion would seem to be all too eager to address. Any philosophy, for example, which can provide someone with the all important answer to the "why" question - as opposed to the "how" question of rules to live by - has an interesting and undeniable appeal. The fact religions have an unfortunate tendency to insist everyone is in the same boat, with the same desires, etc.... That's the bad news.

The worst news is that religions have often avoided the issue of why we must - as Douglas Adams has noted - put up with the "inconvenience" of living on Earth. In fact, religions have instead decided to blame the whole mess on us. This seeming irrationality of why we're on earth might be, for example, because we have **"fallen from grace"**. Worst yet, we have taken this fall ostensibly due to our own shortcomings, or better yet because of the sex of someone long ago who really, really blew it and thereafter doomed us all to wretchedness. Such teaching is of course the ultimate example of **Scapegoatology**, but does have the advantage of removing for all time any personal responsibility for creating one's own reality.

In some respects, this attempt by religions to pass the buck to some dualistic form of good and evil is very practical. Having dark forces about provides scapegoats for all manner of otherwise inexplicable happenings -- happenings which religions are loath to even attempt to explain. More importantly, however, such religions don't seem to have a clue as to how one might actually extricate themselves from the situation - short of doing what certain authorities (for their own purposes) have deemed appropriate. Thus by a process of elimination religions have determined that there's really nothing to do but go along with the party platform (however much it changes over time and between elections).

It might be thought that science and the scientific method might be able to provide religion with some clever ideas and means of understanding what in the world is going on around here. Unfortunately, **science** tends to have its own priesthood, which has traditionally limited the purview of science to matters decidedly **not involved with the "why" question**. Mainstream science in fact tends to be something of a religion in and of itself - filled with faith in the peer-reviewed method, obedience to the dictates of the Lords of Funding, and the most basic anathema to all things apparently inexplicable or simply metaphysical (i.e. "beyond physics").

Religion, meanwhile, has never really reconciled itself to new discoveries in science and their inevitably deleterious effect on traditional values. Keep in mind that religions are the ultimate conservatives in avoiding change at all cost, and science is dedicated to discovering new things and thus changing our minds about what's what. This duality is not likely to benefit from "opposites attract), or even suffice as the ultimate odd couple... and/or bedfellows. [Religion, in fact, inevitably does not like odd couples, strange bedfellows, or for that matter any other kind of bedfellows.]

Ultimately, understanding of one's individual purpose - which just might be one among a whole host of very diverse and varied possibilities - does not seem to be the ideal religious construct. Finding one's purpose involves research, investigation, or searching (soul or otherwise). It's looking for something new -- if only a new insight. It, like science, is about change; i.e. the antithesis of religious conservatism. Furthermore, any alleged **understanding of purpose is the purview of philosophy**, which does not require the inclusion of religious' tenets such as the number of angels on a pinhead.

Understanding of a purpose for an entire species might appear to be a bit more compatible with the religious "every size fits all" modus operandi. However, the difficulty here is that inevitably faith is absolutely required in order to make any sense of anything. But inasmuch as having faith is tantamount to resorting to wilful ignorance in order to avoid nagging questions, even the group purpose understanding seems out of reach of the religious zealots.

Comfort

Understanding the purpose of existence has a counterpart which is far less intellectual or just so much mind stuff. Instead of some profound philosophy -- one derived from scientific method and rational evidence which can be replicated, peer-reviewed, and demonstrated to the most ardent sceptic -- there is the intuitive, personal, and very often wholly outrageous philosophical paradigm upon which many place their undying faith.

A good portion of the motivation for such (pardon the pun) undying **faith** is what might be called the "transcendental temptation", i.e. "a quest for an unseen spiritual reality behind this world. That temptation explains in part the recurrent persistence of religiosity. It has deep roots in cultural history and genetic disposition. The transcendental temptation is expressed by human beings overcome by the fragility of life and yearning for a deeper purpose to the universe. A common fear of death and nonbeing gnaws at the innards, goading humans to seek balm for the aching heart and to find solace in the promise of deliverance. The 'quest of certainty', as John Dewey called it, seems to offer a secure anchor in a contingent universe for those seeking such security." [5]

It would seem likely that those who are not viewing life as particularly fragile, i.e. the young and healthy, are unlikely give up immediate gratification methods in order to seek and adhere to beliefs which promise something on the other side of death. It is likely that the higher percentages of atheism are among those who perceive themselves furtherest from death. These denizens do not really need religious faith.

Such faith is not necessarily one of expecting the sun to rise in the morning in the east and later that day set in the west. That might seem somewhat self-evident - even though on one notable occasion, the sun rose in the east, almost immediately set in the east, and then an hour or so later rose for a second time in the east before proceeding westward.

No, the kind of **faith** that often provides the greatest degree of comfort, solace, and/or relief is the kind **which is based on no evidence,** and which is in fact contradicted by mountains of evidence gathered from the religion of science, the shrines of logic, and the temples of rationality. We're talking about the kind of faith which assures one that a benevolent higher power will always come to one's aid, and preferably in the most dramatic fashion imaginable.

In this regard one is reminded of the very devout man who found himself on the roof of his home as it slowly lifted itself off its foundation and began to float away in rapidly rising flood waters. The man, however, was not even slightly worried as he knew that his god would soon answer his prayers and come to his rescue. He was so confident, however, that he waved away a rescue boat which approached him, even passed on taking a ride on a helicopter which had offered to save him. Soon, however, the house began to break up and eventually the man died by drowning. Upon arrival in heaven, he was just a bit put out, having put all his faith in his god and clearly, god had failed him. But then his god pointed out that he had sent a boat and a helicopter in answer to the man's prayers. What did he expect?

The real benefit of such **wilfully ignorant faith**, the kind where the adherent **never questions the source of his paradigm** or beliefs is an intuitive sense that everything will be just fine in the final reel. It's a deep seated belief in Hollywood style justice - **despite the horrific examples of injustice in the world**, particularly in regards to the histories of religions. It's an extraordinary sense that any and everything from living a good life to blowing oneself to bits in a crowd of innocents will result in rewards almost beyond imagining in the afterlife. Such faith is almost as unrealistic as working extremely hard for forty five years- all to the extreme detriment of one's mental and physical health -- and then retiring to the land of alligators and oranges and expecting a carefree, healthy and stimulating retirement.

And yet there is another kind of **faith**. This is a faith in things which can never be rationalized, but instead depend upon some weird intuitive sense, something in the DNA which promotes a sense of calm and peace in the midst of utter chaos (the latter as exemplified when Mel's Holstein wasn't milked in time). It is a faith or confidence that love and compassion are major players in the universe. It is even the security of knowing that one can always use **the Force** - as in metaphors be with you.

In fact, faith in the general sense of the word is incredibly diverse and almost invariably arises as a means to find comfort and serenity in the midst of the decidedly weird and/or traumatic events of our lives. People simply want to feel good - or at least better -- and one of the best means imaginable is a strong faith in... well... something! Anything! This same faith can also provide comfort in the here and now, wherein we begin to judge things from a distance - and where ultimately everything becomes enormously funny.

The irony is that the use of faith to make one feel good is almost antithetical to many of the tenets of mainstream religions. **When women, homosexuals, non-believers, infidels, critics, clerics and priests of other religions, stuffed animals, novels about magic, et al are condemned and degraded by a religion, one really has to wonder.** Clearly, none of these religious claims of evil support the intent to feel good - that is without making others feel decidedly bad. Faith in order to feel good is not part and parcel of most religions. Religious faith is, on the contrary, about feeling remorse, guilt, and pain.

There are clearly examples where people of a particular religious persuasion have done marvellous things of clear benefit to others. But inevitably their good deeds have been acts which did not include an imposition of their religious beliefs on the recipients of their largess. What, for example, was the religion of the Good Samaritan? His religion is in fact totally irrelevant. Only his actions speak of his philosophy.

Higher Power Communications

The world, as most have come to understand, is not, as has been alluded to, a "garden of Eden." Just like River City, we've got troubles and they're not limited to the game of pool being played hereabouts. There are constant obstacles in our pursuit of whatever, seemingly catastrophic events to endure, and all manner of challenges to overcome (or fail at doing so). What is often needed along life's journey is a good, up-to-date road map, or better yet a guide who really knows the lay of the land. Even better yet, a facilitator, someone who can pull rank and part the waters that stand between us and our chosen paths. In short, we need the telephone number, the e-mail address, and/or a direct link to a higher power who can make things happen for us.

Religion has leaped into the communications with a higher power market place with what can only be described as a vengeance. For as any entrepreneur can attest, **this is where the profit is, this is where money and power can be accumulated on a grand scale.** This is where "show me the money" takes on a whole new dimension.

The key to the money and power angle, of course, is that it is essential that the money and power brokers insert an intermediary into the communication link between the individual and the alleged higher power. Be it a cleric, a rabbi, a priest, a channel, a soothsayer, an operator, a wedding planner, whatever!... the critical ingredient is someone to interpret, explain, perform rituals, or just collect from the seeker the necessary consulting fees and excessive reimbursements of expenses. Religions must, of necessity, rely on their sole and exclusive ability to prescribe non-prescription drugs and procedures for the needy in order to really maximize the financial returns and power accumulation.

Alas, there is the possibility that communication with a higher power can be accomplished via means which do not include an intermediary. There is, for example, the power of **prayer** - both individual prayer and like-minded group prayer which do not require a leader, facilitator, or religious professional. People at home alone can participate at the drop of a hat or the drop in their enthusiasm for whatever is happening to or around them. **You don't have to be accredited to be effective in prayer.**

In fact the ability of focused intentions in the form of prayer, meditation, chants, songs, and all manner of describing intentions has become in recent years inescapably effective in terms of achieving results. One can create realities limited only by one's most benighted imagination. And all without intermediaries! One doesn't even require advice or guidance in how one should maximize their prayer results. "Believe that it is already so" and it is! Shazzam! Bingo! Wow!

There have also been alleged **visitations** by higher powers to select individuals - which unsurprisingly, involve individuals who are inevitably not professional religious intermediaries. These visitations may prompt a degree of scepticism, but it seems clear that all socially accepted prophets and sages have historically been poorly dressed, downcast, and for lack of a better classification, down on their luck individuals. Well-fed fat cats of the religious persuasion, on the other hand, have a distinctly poor track record on revelations via higher power connections.

Neale Donald Walsh in his Conversations with God began his process, for example, when he was down on most everything. He also came to believe that despite his financial success since then, that anyone has access to direct communications with divinity. His perspective is that it's just a matter of listening. The fact that the world tends to provide all manner of distraction and background noise (including religious rituals) does suggest that one needs to be alone and in an almost desperate focus in order to hear anything other than the pipes banging, and the heated arguments next door. But taking the time to listen, or observe what's happening, can be enormously gratifying. It stands to reason for example that one needs to be able to see the boat or helicopter which has been sent to retrieve you from your precarious perch amidst the flood waters.

A sceptic might question the very existence of communications with higher powers - or even the higher powers themselves - but it is clear that focused intentions by individuals and groups do have an uncommon effectiveness. This may or may not include replies in the language of our choice, but it almost certainly does not include the need for an intermediary. Religion can therefore not hang its justification for existence on this particular point. Religion, in fact, does not even have a good track record for teaching methods of effective prayers and the like.

External Control

The average religious advocate might find themselves becoming discouraged at this point. Or planning an insightful and stunning feedback to this essay. Either way, the problem is that of the seven purported reasons for having religion in our lives, five have thus far not done well. There is in fact the distinct suggestion that no matter what reason might be advanced as a justification for religion, there is also the very real possibility that religion is simply not needed and can be replaced with such things as commonly accepted moral principles, societal groupings of common interests, philosophies which might explain universal principles, methods, and implications, and helping hands which tend to reside at the end of our arms -- or in the recesses of our consciousness. This leaves only External Control as a truly viable reason for religion to exist. [We're already pretty much discounting the seventh purpose as anything but comedy relief.]

Religion has, it must be admitted, done more to impose control on the many by the few than any other means of external control. Religions have in fact outdone themselves in forcing the vast bulk of society to obey the dictates of the governing elite. Religions have, furthermore, been outrageously successful in maintaining control of the masses by the most incredible of fantasies, incredulous tales, and fundamental deceits. Control has in fact been the overriding mission of religions since time immemorial, and they've done it with spectacular results.

Admittedly, there have been other organisations, individuals, and groups which have imposed external controls over the vast bulk of mankind by means of lies, deceit, and just simple force of arms. It's just that religion has taken the threat of bodily injury for not rendering unto Caesar whatever is due Caesar to much greater links. **Bodily injury has become in fact something of a minor threat when compared to the eternal damnation threat of religions.**

Ah, yes... This latter threat is truly the genius of religion, whereby religions have threatened what can never be shown to even exist as a punishment, in order to coerce others to do the bidding of a select elite intent upon attaining or maintaining power by any means whatsoever.

Therefore, while religion may have a few Johnny-come-lately copycats in terms of control of the non-elite classes, religion is unlikely to be seriously challenged by any contenders for King of the Controllers title. Religion has brought external control to its current and ultimate pinnacle.

This then is the REASON for religions. External control of the many by the few. It may fail the test of being caring and/or civilised, but the bottom line is that it has worked! One can even add "Q.E.D." ("thus, it is conclusively demonstrated") to the mix.

Purposes of the Seventh Kind

It has been noted herein that there is little or no justification for having religions -- other than perhaps to impose control over the many by the few.

On the other hand, maybe, just maybe the problem is with having religionS! It is possible, for example, that having a unitary, singular religion might be okay -- such that this lone religion might never have to defend itself from other religions, and thus be spared the angst of having to justify actions which could never be rationally justified? Probably not, but it was worth mentioning -- if only for comedy relief.

As for the Seventh grand purpose, the interminable discussions of religion could easily be replaced with the latest news concerning Jennifer, Brad, and Angelina. For example, many writers have leaped into the fray of questioning religion in recent times. Many of these thoughts are included under Thoughts on Religion.

Summary

The reader is likely to assume that this essay is attempting to suggest that religion's only justification for existence is as a means of control of most of humanity, and that this control madness is a bad thing. Curiously, that may not necessarily be the case. One can, for example, make the argument that a great deal of humanity desperately needs some form of control when the self-control of so many seems so decidedly lacking.

It should be clear that many members of the human race are only marginally Homo sapiens (i.e. "wise"), and routinely exhibit behaviour which is decidedly in contradiction with the Golden Rule. One might even call it Neanderthal, animalistic, or mind boggling on the level of dumb as a fencepost.

Furthermore, those people who are willing to exercise self-control and who are not intent upon controlling others for the sheer delight of their very own power trip, can without the aid of some form of external control, find themselves at a serious disadvantage. This disadvantage stems from the fact that those who adhere to responsible behaviour will have a hard time competing with the non-responsible members who are more than willing to do anything to accomplish their aims. Historical reality suggests **that those with scruples are at a decided disadvantage in competing with those without any limiting scruples.** There does not, for example, seem to exist any limits to the crimes, monstrous behaviours, or horrifying actions of which some humans are so obviously capable. And I'm not just talking about the Bush Administration.

It has been noted [1], for example, that "Seattle, a city of highly educated progressives, 'has 45 percent more dogs than children.' Traditional Salt Lake City has '19 percent more kids than dogs.'" Inasmuch as "Fertility is now highly correlated to political and religious beliefs." The old "be fruitful and multiply and subdue the earth" mentality of religions suggests that those people feeling responsible for not continuing the gross overpopulation of the earth will soon find themselves in ever increasing disadvantage with respect to the number of voters on any given issue. The 'Responsibles" are a minority who should be placed on the endangered species list.

The astounding fact, however, is that these same sub-humans [for example, the Bush Administration] often take particular delight in **using the vestiges of some religion or another to justify their acts.** What is even more appalling is that the vast majority of religious leaders upon whose religious authority the despicable acts have been committed, are loath to suggest anything whatsoever amiss. The sub-humans actions are thus excused, exonerated, even praised by the religious hierarchy, despite that religion's strict edicts against such actions. One suspects that religious leaders may recognise that anyone in government willing to commit atrocities might very well commit an atrocity against... heaven forbid... the religious leaders who speak out against them!

In other words, violating religious ethics does not imply condemnation by religious leaders, such that external control by religions is rapidly becoming a thing of the past. Thank God! (Does this imply that God had a hand in correcting the situation? <grin>.)

In any case, one must ultimately conclude... that there are really no good reasons to have religion. Except, maybe, for dramatic license and/or comedy relief.

On the other hand, it might be a very good idea for all of the religions of the world to come together for a Grant Ecumenical Council, figure out their commonality in terms of how to live a good and rewarding life, and then agree to promote this set of standards as a means for everyone to get along. This might be just slightly better than the situation laughingly portrayed in The Kingston Trio's Merry Little Minuet :

They're rioting in Africa. They're starving in Spain. There's hurricanes in Florida. And Texas needs rain. The whole world is festering with unhappy souls. The French hate the Germans, the Germans hate the Poles. Italians hate Yugoslaves, South Africans hate the Dutch, and I don't like anybody very much.

But we can be tranquil and thankful and proud, for man has been endowed with a mushroomed shaped cloud. And we know for certain that some lovely day, some one will set the spark off and we will all be blown away.

They're rioting in Africa. They're strikes in Iran. What nature doesn't do to us. Will be done by our fellow man.

Late Breaking News: Something which for the incurable optimist might suggest is good news: There are now reports [2] of slight ripples on the horizon to suggest that certain evangelicals of a particularly fundamentalist persuasion have suddenly had an epiphany with regards to Global Warming. These traditional anti-environmentalists have apparently come to the conclusion that it might not be nice to fool mother nature, and/or mess up God's creation.

Religion just might have find a calling worth mentioning!

BTW, just in case you're wondering whose team(s) are ahead in the game of being the biggest religion on the block, http://www.mindspring.com/~hellfire/bishop/ has provided us with this pie chart:

What would be even more interesting would be something showing how these numbers and percentages are changing over time.

References:

[1] Phillip Longman, "Will liberals become extinct?", (as reported in) The Week, News, March 24, 2006, page 14.

[2] Jim Wallis, "The Religious Right is losing control," www.sojo.net, 22 March 2006.

[3] Gabriel Palmer-Fernandez, "Contemporary Religious Terrorism," Free Inquiry, http://www.secularhumanism.org, August/September 2006.

[4] Phil Zuckerman, "Is Faith Good for Us?", Free Inquiry, August/September 2006.

[5] Paul Kurtz, "Creating Secular and Humanist Alternatives to Religion," Free Inquiry, August/September 2006.

[6] David Koepsell, "New Threats to Academic Freedom," Free Inquiry, August/September 2006.

[7] Thomas E. Mates, "Throwing the Book at Them," Free Inquiry, August/September 2006.

[8] Victor J. Stenger, "Do Our Values Come from God? The Evidence Says No," Free Inquiry, August/September 2006.

The Library of ialexandriah

207-RELIGION 2

Earlier I said that I have no time for religions, but please do not be personally offended by that statement. Again do not confuse the fact that there is a vast difference between "religion, religious" and "spiritual". Later we look more at what "spiritual" involves and how it may be awakened.

Obviously what I think or write will have little or no effect on the world at large or possibly even you, the reader, and will certainly not empty the churches. Forgetfulness is an inbuilt element of our mortal make up, and things deemed very important at one time are often totally forgotten and lost to the mind later. This element of humanity was one of the reasons I stated for writing the first book. It was to be for my benefit, so that at some future time I may be able to learn again what I once knew. I expect most people will forget what is written in these books, and resume the "old" way of thinking.

These materials are compiled so that you may become aware that all is not necessarily as it seems, and that your mind and eyes may see religion and things as they really are. Most religions are indeed as the whited sepulchre, nice on the outside appearance, but filled with death and decay within.

We are now on a subject that is so vast that entire libraries would be needed to contain all the information and history of even just Christianity. However I am not against Christianity, but only the religions that supposedly devolve from it. The principles of Christianity are indeed an acceptable philosophy, and to be encouraged. Trouble is that the churches, the forefront of religions, do not adhere to those principles. So its "churchism" more than religion, its "sectarianism" wherein lies the true cause for objection.

In the previous article taken off the Internet, one will notice that its writer on no occasion spoke against the man Jesus Christ, his teachings or the underlying philosophies. On the contrary he commended those principles. He also stands against organized churches and sectarian groups that now define "religion". His analysis was to the effect that the only thing at which organized religions, or churches, were successful was in the area of group control. He also noted merit in the social function played by churches but points out that even the local "whatever" group or club was equally effective. He mentions grievous atrocities that can only be laid at the hands of church leaders and thus the church.

In this chapter I will mention and point out many unforgivable flaws within the structure of "Christian" churches without going into inexhaustible details. You can get that level of detail from the Internet and from your own research.

Now I am aware that any **apologist** worth the title will be able to perform a plausible "**spin**" on many individual items. I have heard many myself. (Oh that happened "x" hundred years ago, and of course was wrong, but it doesn't happen now and you cannot judge us by what happened then… blah blah blah.) Two thoughts come to mind immediately. First, yes I can judge today by what happened "x" hundred years ago, even if today's people are not the ones responsible. Point is the immortal institution of the church is unchanged and accountable. Second, whereas one may be able to plausibly put a spin on one named deficiency, there are still innumerable other deficiencies for which to account. An army of spin-doctors would be needed to patch up the rotting structure, and alas, all plausibility soon is lost and the ship sinks under its own weight of defects. If similar sins or acts were to be held accountable to any one individual, such a one would have been hanged after just one or two such charges.

Lets start off with just a small amount of reason and logic.

There are by now probably thousands of individual and different sectarian groups within the framework of "Christianity". It would follow that such exist because they each have some disagreement with others, some different dogma, creed, belief, scripture, interpretations or practices. If so, then most of them must be in error, assuming there is such a thing as "error free". Further, if one is in error a possibility exists that all are in error.

All such have a foundation in the "Bible". If it is in error, there is no hope for credibility in any such sect or church group. All devolve from **Judaism**, if it is not valid, again all fall. Although it may be disputed, all devolve from the **Church of Rome**, and if it is severely defective, all must fall. I think we will see that looking at the very foundations of today's Christianity, its churches are built upon a most dubious and shaky foundation. Big bad news comes with the absolute fact that all are based on the god of the old testament, one **Jehovah** (by whatever spelling) and if that one is no valid god, then the entire Jehovah based structure is without any substance.

I have given my thoughts concerning Jehovah in "201-What of God". If the god is false, then any organization based on the acceptance of validity or worship of that god must be in vain.

Now I know millions will go all defensive and many on the offensive. "But what about the miracles, the healings, the good works, the charity, the Mother Theresa's etc.?" But that is not addressing the issue raised, that is playing the game commonly called "bait and switch". Such a response is "duck shoving" the issue and allegation raised, and substituting it, or trying so to do, with a more palatable and favourable issue. And in any case, I am not for one moment saying that the works of individuals must fall, become questionable or less meritorious merely because the church or religion to which they subscribed is in error. The author of the article in the preceding chapter also raised that issue and dealt with it. No, the "church" must be judged alone and not attempt to validate itself by the good works of the few.

A major fault that I find is at the most fundamental level. The churches of Christianity generally exhibit a total failure to understand even the basic nature of man. This effectively makes their entire paradigm faulty and is the cause why so many Christians, sectarianists really, have such a fear and terror of death.

It was in fact this issue that really set me off on the journey of discovery, I had to ask why the man in the bed next to me in hospital was so terrified of death. What had happened that his religion had not prepared him for this inevitability?

The major (and almost certainly minor) churches lead us to believe or understand that we are mortal human beings of flesh and blood, living on earth, originally created by "god" and that as "the good book" says, we will die and return to the earth. Fair enough so far. But most erroneously teach that we **have** a spirit and that it may or will live on in variously claimed confusing ways. Some teach physical resurrection and thus re-union of flesh and blood with this vaguely defined and less understood "spirit". Major confusion and variety of claims and teachings exist.

There is a universe of difference between the teachings and understanding of the "religious" churchgoers and what is real. For a start we are not mortal human beings of flesh and blood living on earth, and being such "have" a spirit. We are in fact individual Intelligence's, elements of the omnific fabric of the universe, called "spirit", "souls", or other ambiguous and confusing names. In that native state we are not mortals to this world, and what we "have" is in fact a body of flesh and blood assigned to us (by some method as yet unknown by me) for our brief tour of duty in this world. That body is of the elements of the earth and will of course return to the earth.

In short the whole paradigm of the churches is wrong. The issues of our true nature have been dealt with more extensively elsewhere in this book and will not be further explored here.

I have serious problems understanding the rigid claims by Christendom regarding resurrection. I have heard it said the very same elements of the body will be reclaimed and restored and to me that defies any logic or reason. My current body is now aged 64 earth years, has been re-arranged by surgery, has bits missing, and rebuilds or replaces itself completely I understand (with the exception of a few component pieces) about every 7 years. All the component elements of it have their origin in the few inches of topsoil that recycles endlessly. Which elements would be finally be allocated to little old me when they have been endlessly used for countless millions of years? I see no reason or need for such a "miracle".

What also is illustrated by this fault is the fact that if said religion and churches were based on a valid god, and thus, or alternatively vehicles for the dissemination of divine wisdom and word, they should have got it right, or at least come close.

A major area of mental indigestion is caused by the claims by the churches that we are all "sinners", and have departed from "the ways or word of god". It does not take a degree in intelligence to figure out just what this "all are sinners" is all about or to where it is leading. The next claims are obvious and predictable. The claims are that "we can save you". This saving from our ill-defined sins can be had through the church and one church at one time actually accepted money in return for forgiveness including future sins not yet committed. Nice racket. Ah but that is not all nor the end of it.

If one accepts that one is a sinner needing forgiveness, and if one accepts that such can be had through the church, and further, if one submits to the dictates of said church and humbly obeys the rules and proscribed penance then and only then will one become eligible for the reward. In effect your unstated sins can be forgiven and overlooked, all you have to do is obediently confess, submit, obey, pay the price because if you don't you will rot in hell forever and be prodded with pitchforks while you are eternally roasted and tormented.

Protection racket it's called. I do not accept that one has to obey any laws or ordinances or religious dictates in order to get a reward that in reality is already ours. In any case according to the books used by the churches there should be no form of priesthood held or used by mere mortal men, for the book of Hebrews in the New Testament makes it clear that the intention was for man to live free from any form of priesthood.

Being an individual "spirit" intelligence, a part of and substance of the very fabric of the universe that is confused with and often called "god" we are already immortal, possibly eternal, beings that need no forgiveness nor salvation to reach a status we already have. Although philosophers have long known this, the churches cannot and do not teach it, for there can be neither control nor profit in confirming what is already ours.

Let me briefly enumerate a few other areas of gross deficiency with the established religions of Christendom, of which virtually any one of them should spell lack of any credibility.

The claim of **papal infallibility**. Yet those who discovered the world was not flat, nor the centre of all things were persecuted or put to death at their hands.

Celibacy for the priesthood when the New Testament states that a deacon should be married. (1 Tim. 3:12, 4:1-3)

There has been a history of denying **women** basic equality, and in fact even persecution of women. This is illustrated even today in the Church of Rome which still deny women ecclestiacal position, and have **Mary** forever clothed in **blue** so that she may not be associated or confused with priesthood authority.

Women were the most numerous of those murdered in various **witch-hunts**. *"Over the 160 years from 1500 to 1660, Europe saw between 50,000 and 80,000 suspected witches executed. **About 80% of those killed were women**."* I think this evidences prejudice against women, their persecution if they are in any way "different" (independent, intelligent, superior to the average intellect, etc.) and their subjugation.

But this raises a double issue for the very idea or issue of "witch hunts" is surely anathema to reality. Yet it still goes on in some church groups.

In August 1999, Jack Harvey, pastor of Tabernacle Independent Baptist Church in Killeen, Texas, allegedly arranged for at least one member of his church to carry a handgun during religious services, "in case a warlock tries to grab one of our kids [...]. I've heard they drink blood, eat babies. They have fires, they probably cook them [...]." During the speeches which preceded his church's demonstration against Wiccans, Rev. Harvey allegedly stated that the U.S. Army should napalm Witches. One of the protesters carried a sign which read "Witchcraft is an abomination" on one side and "Burn the witches off Ft. Hood" on the other. A Wiccan faith group is active at Ft. Hood, a large army base near Killeen.[28]

In 2008, Jim Piculas, a substitute teacher at Charles S. Rushe Middle School in Land O' Lakes, Florida, was reported to have lost his job for "wizardry." Piculas performed a sleight of hand trick in front of students, making a toothpick seem to disappear using concealed adhesive tape. In a phone conversation with Piculas, an administrator is claimed to have told Piculas that he had been "accused of wizardry." School officials later informed reporters that wizardry was "just one of the reasons Piculas was let go."[29]

These latter issues also raise that ugly facet of religion and the churches, which is **persecution**, and killings on small and very large scales. Individuals have died at the hands of the unholy church, groups have been killed, entire cities have been slaughtered (as in the **crusades**) and whole races have been singled out for special attention. The frequency and death tolls from numerous **pogroms** (organised massacre, especially of Russian Jews) testify of that, as does the unfortunate fate of the American natives.

All of these things testify of gross error, total injustice, disregard for individual or human rights, and frankly of unspeakable evil. Now how is one supposed to sustain the churches and religion of Christendom as "of god"? If god were Enlil and a human hating entity then that would resolve such a seeming inconsistency.

We have not looked into the suppression and book burning conducted in god's name by the church nor of some of the ridiculous doctrines (for instance virgin birth, transubstantiation, etc.) and frankly I am too disgusted and disturbed to do so at the moment. There are too many faults to ever justify, patch up, or to warrant any claim for acceptability as truth and "gods way" for mankind.

These are but a few reasons why I am against religion. But not against spirituality. Against churches but not the principles of Christianity.

WHAT WAS THE CHURCH TRYING TO HIDE?

In 1415, the Church of Rome took an extraordinary step to destroy all knowledge of two second-century Jewish books that it said contained "the true name of Jesus Christ". The antipope Benedict XIII firstly singled out for condemnation a secret Latin treatise called Mar Yesu, and then issued instructions to destroy all copies of the Book of Elxai. No editions of these writings now publicly exist, but Church archives recorded that they were once in popular circulation and known to the early presbyters. Knowledge of these writings survived from quotations made by Bishop Hippolytus of Rome (176-236) and St Epiphanius of Salamis (315-403), along with references in some early editions of the Talmud of Palestine and of Babylonia. The Rabbinic fraternity once held the destroyed manuscripts with great reverence, for they were comprehensive original records reporting "the life of Rabbi Jesus".

Later, in a similar manner, Pope Alexander VI (1492-1503) ordered all copies of the Talmud destroyed. The Council of the Inquisition required as many Jewish writings as possible to be burned, with the Spanish Grand Inquisitor Tomas de Torquemada (1420-98) responsible for the elimination of 6,000 volumes at Salamanca. In 1550, Cardinal Caraffa, the Inquisitor-General, procured a Bull from the Pope, repealing all previous permission for priests to read the Talmud which he said contained "hostile stories about Jesus Christ". Bursting forth with fury at the head of his minions, he seized every copy he could find in Rome and burned them. Solomon Romano (1554) also burned many thousands of Hebrew scrolls, and in 1559 every Hebrew book in the city of Prague was confiscated. The mass destruction of Jewish books included hundreds of copies of the Old Testament and caused the irretrievable loss of many original handwritten documents.

THE WISE WHO KNOWS THE SELF AS BODILESS WITHIN THE BODIES, AS UNCHANGING AMONG CHANGING THINGS, AS GREAT AND OMNIPOTENT, DOES NOT GRIEVE.

WHAT GRIEF OR ATTACHMENT CAN THERE BE FOR A REALIZED SOUL – A MAN OF WISDOM – WHEN ALL THE ANIMATE AND INANIMATE OBJECTS OF THE WORLD HAVE BECOME HIS SELF, WHEN HE SEES ONENESS EVERYWHERE?

The "I" that is me – you cannot see
You see only the form
that you think is me

The form that you see will not
always be; but the "I"
that is me – lives eternally.
****

We are a spirit in a body, not a body
with a spirit.
****

Everything in the universe is nothing
more than energy. Life can change form
but it cannot be destroyed.

****

The illuminated soul…
Thinks always: "I am doing nothing."
No matter what he sees,
hears, touches, smells, eats…
This he knows always:
"I am not seeing, I am not hearing:
it is the senses that see and hear
and touch the things of the senses."

PART FOUR

300- RECLAIMING LIFE

01-RECLAIMING LIFE

When the conventional or orthodox Christian "god", commonly known as **Jehovah**, (with it's infinite variations of names, symbols, and words,) and associated religion no longer become part of your normal "everyday" life, then you may find a need to evaluate and validate your life.

Once such belief paradigms are abandoned, it could be either wise or necessary to find some suitable substitute or alternative path, or develop ones own inner strength to a level of total impregnable independence.

CAUSES OF DEPRESSION

For a time will come, if it has not already, when one will feel or experience a painful separation, a loss or void, and recognize the need for either support or comfort or else depend upon ones own inner strength. If one has not sufficient inner strength or extraneous support, then the result will be distress with various symptoms, or even depression. When (sectarian) religion is given up it is at times like these when one will be tempted to, or will return to ones former way of life, associates, or group. Some may call that "backsliding", but people also often "go back" because of the lack of social life, recognition, or to rekindle friendship with former associates who now shun them. They feel ostracized and rejected.

Other causes will also prove most difficult and likewise, without external support or sufficient inner strength may cause an emotional spiral ending in depression. The list of causes is almost endless, but will include the following, and I am sorry if you think I should have mentioned other things.

Existing depression, recent death of someone "close", serious illness of self or someone close, life threatening trauma, medical crisis, alcohol drug or substance addiction, loss of employment status or friends, loneliness, lack of affection from others, substantial monitory or property loss, being victim of crime or thoughtless external actions, lack of ability to self-actualize, rejection, frustration with some failure, frustration with life or inability to understand, realization of immanent death, recognition that beliefs held are unfounded, recognition that your ability to advance or progress is barred, financial or relationship difficulty or hardship, poverty, physical injury of self or someone close, deemed failure or "loser" status. Yes the list is endless. Sometimes one may simply become tired of life because of age or infirmity and feel like "just letting go".

IN THE FACE OF DEATH

Although death is the one absolute certainly and inevitability in everyone's life, very few are reconciled to that fact and able to approach their own demise with grace or dignity. Because we are so much alive, and mentally and emotionally consumed with this life, world, and all in it, we scarcely give it a thought, yet alone any serious preparation. I am speaking of mental and emotional preparation.

I think generally it takes years, even decades for the "average" person to even concede their own mortality, and then generally immediately dismiss the train of thought as something that is in the far distant future. But it sneaks up on us if unprepared. I read or heard somewhere that the most commonly spoken words facing those with immanent death (evidenced by cockpit recorders in 'plane crashes etc.) are the words "oh shit" or similar.

I have recounted the personal experience faced in September 2004 awaiting surgery in a cardio-thoracic ward. A man in the bed next to me was visibly terrified of the prospect of almost immediate death, as he had to go back to theatre because his new wound would not stop bleeding. I realized his dismal plight, and felt concern for his total terror and failure to be ready for death. I then asked myself if I was ready for death this week, as my turn for open heart surgery could be counted as within a few days at most. Survival odds are not brilliant, and are only acceptable to one who is not an inpatient, shaved like a plucked chicken, and ready to roll into the theatre. Naturally I then had to go over my own mental and emotional checklist and ask, "am I ready for permanent death now"?

I had to admit that although I had some degree of "inner peace" (having survived and returned after two cardiac arrests in one day previously in May 2003) and tremendous (forced?) faith in the medical staff and procedures, many question marks still remained. I found on analysis that I did not have a satisfactory understanding of life and death and all things involve. I figured it would be very nice to be able to *fully understand* all that there is some time before I left this world. I started asking questions. More importantly, I believed there were answers to all and any questions I could frame, and those answers could be found and understood. I had not found all answers in "religion", rather, I found lots of confusion and conflicting ideas and "teachings".

It is preferable, even necessary for ones own self to be able to understand what it is all about, exactly who or what you are, and to be able to walk away from this life and world without fear and trembling. This becomes even more vital if one is living without "religion", or worse, even without "spirituality". Whatever ones status or attitude regarding belief systems or lack of them, the same conditions apply and it will be of tremendous comfort to understand them before ones time of passing. Without that understanding one may develop the classic trauma and symptoms of those not ready to die. (The anger, denial, bargaining etc.)

KNOW AND UNDERSTAND THE BASICS

Never lose sight of the basics. The basics are contained in many parts of this book, and reveal that you are not only that body of flesh and bone that everyone else perceives as "you" with their physical senses. You are a "god stuff", non-mortal, and non-earth "cosmic stuff" individual intelligence here for a short time only.

That mortal physical body is deceptive and a source of confusion. You are the "software", the "program", the mind and the intelligent entity that animates that outwardly visible body of meat and bone. It is your vehicle for this earth only. It is of this earth and when one leaves this earth it must be left behind. It is left behind just like your car, earthly possessions, clothes etc. because being "crude" elements of this earth, you will be unable to take them with you or use them when you pass over into the next stage of "life" or existence that operates at a different level. Think about it as similar to the fact that you do not take your physical earth body or possessions with you when you enter into the "dream world", for in like manner they are of no use there. So just as you take no "earth" possessions into the dream world, including your actual physical earth body, yet continue to exist as an intelligent individual being, so it continues after "passing" mortality. One concludes there is a different "dimension" of existence that continues without the mortal body. (I do appreciate that some will claim that such a dream is merely a mental construct created by "mind" but still anchored in the physical body. That claim is not being discussed here or at this point.)

We have dealt at length with the nature of this earth and all in it earlier in this book. Remember always that this universe, and all that is in this world is an unsubstantial illusion, as substantial as a hologram, and of no true substance. "Solid" is simply illusion. This is not only a claim of "nutters" and mystics, but also adequately verified in quantum physics. Your individual intelligence, your personality and identity have absolutely no physical source or natural place and do not originate within the "material" manifest universe.

Just as the manifest and material universe is rooted in and bathing in the fabric of the universe, so is your intelligence, your individual identity, but at different levels or "vibrations". They are as distinctly different as stage and actors.

THE FACE IN THE MIRROR

Our problems in this world have their foundation in our confusing the face we see in the mirror as actually being "us". We see that face get older and believe we are getting older. In reality the true individual behind the face in the mirror, the one who uses those eyes to see that reflected face, is ageless and not of this world. It's not that we're not human, we are wearing a human "suit" for a short time only, and are far more than solely mortal creatures of this earth. If you ever forget that, and believe that you ARE the face in the mirror, then you will become subject to all the ills and "evils" of that body and this world.

If you accept the body that you and others see as the one and only you, then you will undoubtedly also accept or select some particular role to play while on this earth. A particular role may be selected and imposed on you by others, depending on where or when, or into which race or family the body taken up at mortal birth was born. **Forgetfulness of who you really are condemns you to that role for the term of your natural life** on earth. Do not confuse your current circumstances, health, wealth, or any of a thousand such things as defining "you". At best or worst they just indicate your then current state, the result of the role you choose to play or that was imposed upon you.

Reference to my essay "Here and Now" fully discusses that very issue of the state and condition of "self" relative to time and space.

There are always alternatives available. You can change all things.

LEARN THE ADVANCED COURSE, FINDING "US".

There are two ways of proceeding with ones life. (Minimally speaking) One is the "spiritual" way; the other would be the "material" way. Regardless of which way you choose, the underlying basic facts as above are unchanging facts. Remember your mortal body while alive and animated is a **gestalt**. The sum total is vastly more than the sum of all the component parts.

After considerable thought and in view of the information or data available, I came to the conclusion that even now while this intelligent "us" seems firmly anchored in this prison of a world, **we are multidimensional entities or beings. Just as mistaking the face in the mirror as "us", so mistaking the body and the "us" occupying, animating, and using it, as the only manifestation of "us" is also a mistake.**

I think that even if one determines they are totally materialistic, there can be no escape from the conclusion that we are at a minimum a separable non-physical fleshless being living generally within the confines of such a meat body. And that puts "paid" to any further limiting materialist restrictions. It does not mean you have to become all "touchy feely" spiritualistic or religious. It does mean that you will need to re-think all your opinions, beliefs, thoughts and attitudes relative to life and your tenure in it in this world.

A "GOD" BY ANY NAME

One of the major problems facing us on this earth is our use of *languages* and the misunderstandings that come as a result of our not understanding what another person intends or means when using a word. By way of example: Recently I picked up a book with the title *"There's a Spiritual Solution to Every Problem,"* written by **Wayne W Dyer**. It sounded like a "new age" type of book that I immediately mentally categorised as probably of little use. I assumed from the words of the title that it would babble on about the love of god and his forgiveness of us sinner's... blah blah. Let me share a definition Mr Dyer gives on page 4 of his book. *"Spirit is what I have chosen to call the formless, invisible energy which is the source of all life on this planet. This force, no matter what name we give it, can solve every problem that we encounter...."* (This definition will clearly find its role as the "force", as is "Use the force Luke", of "Star Wars" fame.)

That certainly makes the book quite different from what I had assumed and judged. Oh yes, do get hold of a copy of that book and make it essential reading. Throughout that book Mr. Dyer talks of and mentions "spirit" and "god" often. However his use of the words clearly mean and are stated as intending something a bit different from what the average sectarian Christian would infer. (Imagine confusion of intention and meaning if his text is quoted totally out of context.)

He is talking about the fabric of the universe and as a convenience, giving it the name and calling it "spirit". Earlier I mentioned my aversion to using that word as it does invoke various preconceived ideas, usually all wrong. Whereas one may deny the existence of "spirit" just as surely as one may deny the existence of "ectoplasm", one *cannot* deny the existence and actuality of the fabric of the universe. It's just that some call it "spirit". Clear?

FABRIC OF UNIVERSE & QUANTUM PHYSICS

Another grand word that invokes countless varieties of pre-conceived ideas is the word "god". It cannot be reasonably or logically denied that the fabric of the universe is in fact actual reality and is omnific, omnipresent, and omniscient. It exists within even the sub-atomic particles as well as between them. It is in fact making and manifesting the sub-atomic particles and thence all that exists in countless dimensions. This is no longer subject to question or doubt, it is fact. It is also fact that it is omniscient. Now before this fabric of the universe was identified, proclaimed, and accepted, those characteristics were exclusively used to describe some of the natures of what or who religions called or named as "god". Unfortunately because of false understanding and imposition of "religion", that common insignificant noun became itself considered sacred and "holy".

There is absolute evidence of the non-reality or relevance of distance, space or time as we understand or use those principles when dealing with this fabric of the universe. It "knows" what is happening everywhere at the same instance in time. It is always "now", and past and future do not "exist". In short there is "knowing" and intelligence underlying everything. In exactly like manner **quantum physics** states that subatomic particles always know what other particles are doing regardless to what we think of as spatial distance or time.

Bear in mind this fabric of the universe is also making us, manifesting us, totally throughout every fibre of our physical, mental, emotional, thinking, living selves, gives us all that we are, and we are hopefully demonstrably intelligent. Pray tell, how could that which gives, is the source, be less than that which is given or made from it?

This is the force and source of all that generates the electromagnetic energy vibrations and the fields that make things appear visible and manifest. It writes the "hologram" that we see and assume to be reality. **It is the mirror, it is the face in the mirror, and it is the intelligence that sees the face in the mirror looking back at the person who is not "in" the mirror. It is everything. It is intelligent. Allow us to call it "god" for simplicity, but do not misunderstand such use with the meanings inherent with the word when used by religion.**

In summary, the advanced course tells us that we are not the source of our own nor of others intelligence. This means that there really is a power and source beyond ourselves.

USE OF WORDS AND FORMAT IN THIS ARTICLE.

Because of the limitations of our English language and the propensity for people to see only words devoid of intended meaning or of context, it is necessary to implement a procedure to make my intention as clear as possible. Hopefully this will help eliminate misunderstanding, intentional or by their frequent use of the same or similar words within some interpretation or manner not intended by me. I have already alluded to the use of such words as "spirit", "god" and so forth, and could well add other words subject to probable immediate use by other alternative intended meaning. (faith, miracle, heaven and such come to mind.)

For this reason I will endeavor to use a different format for words that I would consider as possibly "dodgy" to use without drawing attention to a meaning probably not commonly assumed.

*Thus henceforth, **when words appear in italics** it is to be taken as meaning the word is not intended to be taken on simple face value and assumed to mean what may usually be inferred by say people of religious nature.*

Safely assume all words such as "god", "spirit", "heaven", and associated words or pronouns (such as "who", "he", "his" etc) do not refer to a god etc of religious interpretation, but to use the words as a simple convenience for "fabric of the universe", or the universal force thereof. As stated, the use and interpretation of English words is sadly easy to misunderstand.

CHOOSE CAREFULLY A PARADIGM

If you have chosen any of the various flavors of Christianity to follow in your life it's a fair probability that you have a lot of erroneous ideas or beliefs clogging up your mind and thinking.

Bear in mind that there are now hundreds of different Christian churches alone, all teaching different doctrines, beliefs, and to a large extent, different ideas, teaching and principles. It is therefore very obvious that they cannot ALL be correct, and thus most, being in disagreement with each other, you will be exposed to a vast amount of conflicting errors. Assuming that there is any measure of truth in the entire Christianity paradigm. If there is NO truth or reality in Christianity, as in the "Jehovah" concept is totally in error, then obviously 100% of such religions are in error. I cover this in other essays.

Almost certainly you will follow the incorrect old paradigm that holds that you may "have" a vaguely defined and little understood "spirit". You will probably also have been told, and probably accept, that we are all "sinners" and separated from "God". To resolve this problem you will have learned that we must seek forgiveness, repent, pay the "dues" in various ways (confession private or public, obey various ordinances, submit totally to some form of "one up on you" priesthood, pay money generally in large amounts, probably a designated percentage of earnings, and henceforth obey and refrain from various things or activities. Hard isn't it?) and only then will you have a good or perhaps merely possible chance of being re-united with "God" one day. Some vaguely suggest that their god is still somehow with us, or in our presence still and continuously.

That is the conventional Christian paradigm. Considerable variations exist between rival sects, be it Roman Catholic, protestant, Latter Day Saints to Jehovah's Witness etc.

GETTING IT RIGHT

Step one is to recognize that you are not limited to your body and the circumstances in which you now find yourself in this life. That idea is just not true. **You are a very part of the fabric of the universe,** call that god if you wish, but you are an alive and active intelligent part of it. This means that **you are not, and never were separated from god. That *god* is even now within every part of your total being.**

Know that this *god* or power within you is the essential and same power that creates all universes, governs all things and it always was within you. Start thinking about that claim and in time you will **recognize** the truth and reality of it. Once you recognize and **acknowledge** that truth, your life can begin to seriously change. A natural form of *spirituality* such as you may never imagined will develop within you as the awakening develops. I am not talking about "religious" fervor or whatever you may call the arm waving mantra singing variety of "righteousness". There will develop a natural and wonderfully health giving change in some of your thinking patterns.

Please do not become confused thinking this is merely some form of **gnosticism**, and then dismiss it without any understanding. Any Christian priest would recognize the similarity and with no further question or thought, dismiss and merely say, "Yes well that was wrong, wasn't it!"

The big secret however is not to lose it once you have this awareness, and know of its reality. **Backsliding** as mentioned and defined above is a very serious and real risk. For this reason it is wise to keep away from adverse and "negative" influences and focus on "positive" things. For that reason I have made some recommendations in this book. Some Internet web sites have been mentioned and the book named above by Wayne W Dyer. You will soon be able to sort out books that are conducive and that magnify your "enlightenment".

Knowing that **this "fabric of the universe" is generally confused and known by Christendom and its sects as "God"** (As defined by them and their creeds.) will create an awareness of many errors fundamental to most religions. Let's start by listing and briefly discussing some of the more important issues.

In the following matters the use of the word "*god*" in all lower case (small letters) *italics* is intended to refer to the "fabric of the universe" only, and does in no way refer to any god or concept of god such as religions of any brand may interpreted the word.

We are not sinners, and do not need any forgiveness.

When we entered this world we effectively entered as newly born "blanks". It cannot reasonably be said that such newly born are or can be guilty of any error or sin. The newborn are surely totally blameless, guiltless, and without "sin" of any sort. Yet churchism vows we are born in sin and into sin. Apart from laying the foundations for a "good" racket, I see no reason and certainly no validity for such claims. (It does not matter what the Christian "fathers", saints, or popes have said nor how long ago it was said and subsequently believed. It is wrong regardless of what any mortal has said.)

It therefore defies all logic and reason to think or assume that we are collectively held as ill-defined sinners as a result of anything that may have "happened" prior to, or at our mortal birth. Any sins of the fathers (or mothers) cannot justly be held accountable to the children, and any inference that this is so simply denies any claim of justness on the part of the one supposedly holding us accountable and condemned as sinners. (I.e. the Christian God)

(It is noted however that centuries ago children could be held accountable, enslaved or even imprisoned as "repayment" for sins or debts incurred by a parent. It should be self evident that such a practice is not only immoral, but a grievous error. Yet church doctrine proclaims like doctrine.)

The phrase heading this little section and in bold refers only to the concept as held out by religions that we mortals have sinned against some "god" of theirs, and thus need "his" forgiveness. I hold this to be total error. Some flavours of Christendom hold this "all guilty and condemned" so rigidly as to claim that "un-forgiven" meaning their "un-baptized" babies, children or other humans will forever be denied (their) god's acceptance and future company. Rubbish. (The chapters on "Religion" establish this sort of claim as one of the underlying claims for a lucrative and enslaving racket.)(In previous books of mine.)

We are all a component part of the *god* who, being the fabric of the universe, is the source of **all things.** To say we have sinned against this true *god* is to claim sin against ones actual and true self. If this were possible or so, then a remedy is simple and immediate. **Forgive yourself.** Stop beating yourself up and carrying some burden of guilt around with you. Know that this is true and try it if you have never done so already. It is tragic to see the extent to which some people go, or suffer, in a futile effort to gain this vague or improbable "forgiveness", then later believe they gain it by submission to priest craft and their words saying such is then given consequent to submission.

(There was a time, and may well be again, when priests and their craft held control and power of life and death over all people. With such nefarious control compulsion of submission could and well did determine ones actual fate in mortality. Over countless centuries mankind became conditioned to their rule.)

However it is possible that we are all sinners in that we have "sinned" against some fellow mortal/s. This is entirely possible of course, and the only way to resolve any guilt or remorse there is to sort it out with the other party involved. Now I cannot say what such sorting out may involve, but if it is a problem it will need to be resolved so that ill will, guilt, resentment, and any other negative feelings or thoughts are dissipated. This will allow one to continue life with a clear conscience and a mind uncluttered with remorse, guilt or avoidance. (All those negative thoughts)

Simply affirm to yourself that *"I am indeed a part of the fabric of god, and am thus perfect, faultless, and blameless in "his" sight. Any real issues are therefore limited to this earth only, and yes, I can sort out and resolve those issues that may exist. I need no religion or church to do this for me. I already have the ability, strength and resolve to sort out all problems and negative issues."*

Determine to identify any emotional baggage, clutter, or guilt you may be harboring, clearly identify it, and determine to get rid of it.

We are not being punished in any way. Neutral *god*.

The *god* as defined in this chapter could be said to be entirely **neutral** concerning any of our actions or thoughts. It is quite wrong to think that **"a god"** is carefully noting all our actions, judging, and marking some sort of scorecard on which you will inevitable come up short of good works. There is however a valid principle in operation that must or should be understood.

Never forget that we all are literally part of *god* as our entire being, even including the mortal body of the earth, is formed from the very fabric of the universe. As such we all have the ability and intelligence to know what is "right" and what is "wrong", or what is "good" and what is "not as good". **(As expressed in the universal "golden rule" philosophy,**

"do unto others….) That is assuming we are of sound mind. Don't laugh yet; as there are degrees of "sound mind" that you may not initially envisage. There are many walking among us who are genuine or borderline "psychopaths" who cannot be deemed fully of sound mind. There are also habitual "criminals" (kleptomaniacs, serial killers, serial "whatever", addicts of all sorts) who have their minds or consciences so blunted that they also could not be deemed to be fully of sound mind.

Having that ability and very element of *god* as part of our very make-up effectively gives us the ability to be **continually judging ourselves, and indeed sentencing ourselves.** In other words any misfortune that we have blamed on **"a god"** or his judgment, may just possibly be self inflicted, or even self-accepted, even if most probably at a subconscious level.

Therefore do not look to *god* as the source of any misfortune or evil in which you find yourself, but look for the cause more locally with yourself first then other fellow mortals next. Once you have identified the real source or cause of your affliction, then you can set about correcting it. Your first step after soul-searching analysis will probably involve a "confession" to yourself alone, then a forgiveness of yourself. Once that is sorted out by use of reason and analysis you can sort out how to extricate yourself from the problem.

Never accept or believe you are "evil" or "bad" and are thus being punished by any "god". **God** does not punish himself or any individual facet of *himself. He* is not a masochist. That is a non-valid Christian sectarian way of thinking and a cause of lots of unnecessary grief.

Later in this chapter we will deal with the subjects of "karma" and its variants. It is closely related to the matter just covered.

We cannot influence "god" (a.k.a. fabric of the universe) – what can be achieved.

Understanding that *god* is not an "individual" as we use and understand that word should give us pause for thought about the entire subject of petitioning "god" for favours etc. as most churches would have us believe is how things are done. It will all become quite clear as we gain understanding of precisely what is involved and who in fact we are at all times, that we are not merely or just a plain flesh and bone mortal petitioning a vast cosmic god who we presume is "listening" to us.

Also understand that it is extremely unlikely that in response to a prayer or petition that any manifestation of a god will appear to deal with your concerns. This regardless of what is written in the book of Genesis. However the good news is that the force and power, the *god*, *that* IS the very fabric of the universe, *that* as such is the origin or source of all that is or can be, is already within yourself. You are a manifest localized "piece" of that very power or "*being*" right here and now on planet earth in this dimension. The only thing really anthropomorphic about *god* or *his* attributes is that which is expressed in each of our personal beings.

(You may possibly "create" a "vision" or "revelation" effected by your own mind or thought process. Your mind does have such an ability and power. But it is almost certainly not a result of an independent and/or individual god, regardless of what you may think, conclude, or believe. Indeed the power exists by oneself to externalize, even create effects considered "miracles" etc. However there also exists a rarely encountered ability for individual or groups of others to directly influence an individual, this even at an unconscious level to those causing the effect. It has been concluded that some cases of "hauntings" can only come from such a source.)

Specify what is wanted.

The first element of effectiveness and efficiency in prayer and petition is in the focusing of attention on what is required or desired, in other words getting very specific. Simply put we must be most clear, explicit and specific on our desires. (For example, "I want a red car, about 1300cc, automatic, probably a Nissan or Mazda or similar." Is infinitely more effective than "I would like to get a car." Think about it, unless you know exactly what you want how would you know where or how to find it, or recognize opportunity for fulfillment when it appears?)

Individual or group. Principle of "expectation".

The second element for effectiveness of prayer is the focusing of our *spiritual* energy (which is that part of divine cosmic power that is possessed by us individually and in groups.) and generating the strength of will and desire to actually make, change, or organize things to conform according to our individual or collective will. As sacrilegious or insane as that may sound at first, kind of like "using the force (Luke)", that is the underlying reality. In this manner "miracles", healing, etc. become manifest. **There is a principle of expectation that is little understood that may be invoked.** Once one has a clear mental image of what is desired, has focused *spiritual* attention upon it, and develops an expectation that it will be fulfilled, then unless it is a completely futile desire, it probably will become manifest. I do not say that the red Nissan will simply materialize, but in knowing what is wanted, and being positively expectant that it will turn up, it's bound to be found. Among other things, **expectation sharpens awareness**. **Awareness sees and recognizes opportunity** and takes advantage of opportunity while others just wonder what is happening or if things will ever even happen.

Earlier in this book and the previous one we looked at the issue and claim that "we become what we think about" and such statements like "whatever the mind can conceive and believe, the mind can achieve". These are a sample from millions of similar statements and sentiments that say it is us and our minds once clear and focused that can cause the effect we are seeking.

"God" does not withhold anything.

"All things whatsoever you ask in my name will be given to you" or words meaning exactly that are afforded to Jesus. ("How dare a heathen like me quote Jesus"? Quite easily. Self-evident truths are not the exclusive property of those who claim to be his sole heirs with exclusive use of words, and a pox on all others.) Jesus also told the story of the "prodigal son" who, when he returned home was a cause of concern by the other brother. The other son was told that "all that I have is thine." In other words the older brother, thinking he was being deprived of some part of inheritance was told he **already** had it in full. Your priests will not spell out that part of the story.

Think about it this way: Imagine you have and control a super abundance of all that could ever be needed by your children to make them safe, secure, healthy, happy, independent or even prosperous. You could also give them dignity and a feeling of deserved worthiness. You have all this, but it is sitting idle and not being used in any way at all. Your children are visibly distressed and in some difficulty. (It could be health, need for direction, any of the things listed in the cause of depression listings above.) Would you be withholding from your children? Would you refuse an insignificant portion of the unused bounty if they did not act in some specific manner, or grovel and beg help from you? No? What sort of god then would withhold anything or predicate it upon humiliating conditions being met?

The fact is simple. Whereas a god of a religion may so withhold, the *god* of all, the very fabric of the universe is freely giving. This is the real one that says "ask...receive", "seek...find".

Understanding that we are indeed elements of the power and bounty of the creative force of the entire universe will rid our minds of thoughts of the need to humiliate ourselves before a false god in order to access our natural inheritance. It is ours already. All we have to do is "learn the ropes" not "pay the dues", and all is freely accessible. This does not mean or infer that "*god*" will provide you with winning lotto numbers. Anyone can get those from last week's results.

"*God*" does not "overcome" anything, nor is at war.

At **the ultimate reality level**, there is a self-consistent field of information and intelligence, a field of pure energy that is the sum total of all that exists and can exist. That source is also undoubtedly a gestalt just as we in mortality define a gestalt by reason or our intelligence. There is nothing else that is not PART of this field. There is nothing that is or can exist outside of this field. Thus every thing we can name, see, or imagine is also part of the same field, or *god* as we will call it for sake of simplicity. **It is unbounded and unrestricted in any way whatsoever.**

For these reasons long ago I determined the "ultimate" or highest "god", (having recognized that there are various interpretations or understanding of levels of gods, real or imagined.) the one at the very top of the "food chain" could **not be an individual as we use the word**, and this *god* essentially had to be **"neutral"**. (To not be neutral must infer prejudices as well as likes and dislikes, favorites etc., a concept surely foreign to any solo creative energy or source.) The force or power, the fabric of the universe being neutral could not be fighting an ongoing and never ending battle within itself between "good" and "evil". To think such is to fail to recognize the nature of the absolute origin and source of all that can be. "Good" and "evil" therefore must be purely constructs and not "real".

("Good" and "evil" may well exist and certainly be "allowable" between the independent components within the Fabric of the universe. In other words, humans may well create or imagine such concepts and attempt to invoke judgment as such and then attempt to fight, resist, and so forth the decision.)

If I had the ability to reason out that the source of miracles is not to be found in a few cases only at the hands of *god's* elect and select few "priests" or "saints" and all else of the "devil" then any one can come to the same conclusions without the need for a degree or qualification in theology or philosophy. These are self-evident truths. It is not "me" saying or avowing what is written herein.

Any determination of what is "good" or "evil" must be subjective and in the same order as judgments as to what is "beautiful" or what is "ugly". Concepts of right or wrong fall within the same category. (Is it "right" for us to eat chicken, fish, or meat, but "wrong" for say a lion or shark to eat us?) This has all been long and well known out there in our world. But it would seem religions have a strong vested interest in fostering a belief in actual reality of "good" and "evil" and of an ongoing war between their god and some form of entity that is a devil or Satan.

Man, what sort of power could sustain such an alleged entity that is able to withstand the sole "god" for untold millennia? Surely that would require a completely separate independent universe with its own underlying power and fabric. The entire concept becomes unsustainable. (Logically, it would be probable that both the "god" and the opposing entity are bogus or false.)

It seems then that the story of the devil or Satan may be a construct designed by religion to create and corner another lucrative market. If such an entity is real, then what hope could any church or priest have in withstanding or casting out one that "god", after millennia of conflict, seems to be incapable of defeating? Think about it logically. But hey, come along any Sunday, put your money down and get some assurance that the devil won't get you if….

I have covered just what and who this serpent referred to starting with Genesis chapter 3 may well be. We noted also Job 1:6-7 concerning "Satan" and see that there was then no obvious conflict involved with the early Old Testament god and "Satan". Job records they met together in council and had their discussions. Sounds like **Enki and Enlil** et al to me. The symbol of Enki was the **serpent**.

No, there is nothing for our *god* as defined in this chapter to have to fight against, resist, or overcome. And again to think this is to deny that the source is all-powerful self-consistent and an harmonious whole.

You cannot fight or resist evil.

May sound strange or wrong initially, but following the above section, it becomes a logical extension that we are mistaken if we believe that we also have to overcome an extraneous enemy that is the source of evil. "Evil" as such does not exist and cannot exist because all that is and can be is of the same fabric of the universe, of *god*. We are misdirecting our energy and resources if we think to resist "evil".

More correctly what must be identified and then resisted are all those many **causes and sources** of things and results which we judge as "evil" or not right, conducive to harmony, peace, justice etc. If we put on our correct glasses and see what really is, then we will see most human misery, war, and suffering of all sorts can be laid squarely at the feet of human (or corporate and government) causes. In many cases those that we have been conditioned to trust, believe in, and to whom we have given power and authority are the cause of the "evil". Small wonder that the churches promote belief in an ideal scapegoat (Satan) and find support from other "powers that be". Blame squarely shifted because "it wasn't me" it was the devil, or "he made me do it". Nice racket, good cop out, cover our tracks, blame something else, earn money, excellent deception. No reality.

Asking the right question.

Always ask yourself "what is really going on here? What are the possible causes of all this trouble, and how can I identify the real and true cause?" An old wise saying is that the one with the most to gain is the most likely cause if it's beneficial to them. The "war against terrorism" led to the occupation of what could be the richest oil producing real estate on the planet, strange co-incidence that. Others just say "follow the money". Do the research.

"God" will not intervene personally in your life.

This is probably fairly self-evident by now, but it does not mean you are all alone or without help or back-up in dealing with your problems, troubles, worries or woes. So even though the heavens may not part, and there be a massive sounding of trumpets and divine beings bathed in light become manifest, do not lose heart, for there is a way to activate divine help as may be needed.

"Here and Now".

God is doing the same now as *he* was 100 years ago and doubtless will be doing 100 years hence. And that is sustaining the universe of which you are a part. **At the "level" of the fabric of the universe time and space as we understand it and live by in this dimension and earth have no meaning. There is only an eternal "here and now" that exists,** and that is how and why superposition (ability to be in two or more places at the same time) omnipresence (being everywhere at the same time) and omniscience (knowing what is happening or going on everywhere in the same instance.) work and apply. There is no application of "linear time". Your and my concept of something in the past or future does not compute, but something in the "here and now" does compute. Effective prayer uses "here and now" to set up conditions, resolutions, expectations etc. that will remain established in our ever-changing "now" state, and that is what will facilitate change from what else might have been.

You can use your inherent power, which is of the substance of *god* and the universe to effectively control your life.

"*God*" is not found in a "church" of any sort.

Well *he* is of course, but then *he* is everywhere for everything is of the same fabric and source. What is meant is that the various churches by whatever name or title are not the exclusive or particularly favoured or special places set aside for *his* "presence". That "presence" is everywhere, omnipresent and that means it is within your very "body-space" and being as well. Of necessity therefore, if you think about it, *"his"* presence must also be within your presumed personal mind and thoughts.

If you wish to "communicate" with *god*, simply find a quiet place, or at least develop a quiet state of mind, to enable and allow the focus of your thoughts. Your thoughts access *god*.

True prayer and the power of focus and asking.

Before one can begin any journey one must have some idea of where they are going. Before one opens the mouth to speak one must have some idea of what they are going to say. (Hopefully) I once had a saying: *"A true professional knows what to do and what to say, and how to do it and how to say it, under any conceivable circumstances."* I guess I still have that saying really.

Now regarding prayer, we do not need to manifest all those elements that define the "true professional", but we certainly do need to be clear in our understanding of what we are seeking to achieve. **Rule one** for getting what you want is to know what you want, in fact down to the finest details. Then you can focus your *god* given powers on attracting or attaining those wishes.

I do not intend to re-write the details of the mechanics of the transmuting of desires into reality here, as all those details are out there in books such as "Think and Grow Rich" etc. Self-help or motivational books will give all the principles and details of what is involved. It is all quite easy and simple enough.

Ideally you need to internalize your thoughts, in other words know and understand what you want or seek with every "fibre" of your being. Let your thoughts fully understand and visualize the objects of your petition and **emotionalize** them. Get to want it with a real fervor, then verbalize or speak out loud your wishes. Express it in clear unambiguous words. You do not need to make them public, but hearing yourself say the words adds literally a touch of empowering magic to the project.

"The Whispering trees …."

The whispering trees will hear you and tell it to the birds etc. Then the very fabric of the universe in which you alone secretly held your petition is now privy to your desire and needs. Remember the words "omnipresent" and "omnipotent" used to define *god,* which is the underlying fabric and power of the universe? Or if you prefer, in **quantum physics**, it's the fact that any particle knows what is happening with any other particle regardless of what we consider spatial distance.

In short it is an easy thing to get your message "out there" and **shared literally with every element of the universe**. You do not have to attempt to mollify, influence nor make any bargains with any "god". You do not need to shout or do anything other than the above to get *his* attention, nor do you have to be of a certain colour, creed, or class.

You already have all the power.

We have covered this ground fairly comprehensively but it is mentioned here purely to reiterate it in this summary. You need no power, authority, or source extraneous to yourself to get your

message or petition to the "attention" of *god* and to attain reasonable fulfillment.

"Fate", "Destiny", "predestination" are non-existent.
What "karma" is really all about.

As mentioned earlier "*god*" is doing the same now that he was doing 100 years ago and will be doing 100 years hence. The neutral fabric of the universe does not play favorites, withhold from any, and all are equal. The concept of fate, destiny and all associated thoughts are a cop out and avoidance of thinking things through correctly and then taking steps to remedy or modify any conditions or circumstances that we may be tempted to deem fate etc.

Random nature of universe and events.

There is seemingly an untold and unimaginably vast amount of random events at large in this universe of ours. I strongly suspect, even believe, that the circumstances of our birth into it are purely random. If that were not so then one would be forced to accept or agree that this omnific source, this fabric... or *god* is the author of a script wherein infants are stillborn, born defective enough to die almost instantly, or be born into the world wherein their condition from birth makes for an almost pointless existence. Apologists may come up with a good and credible "spin" along the lines that such a one was so perfect before birth (necessarily in some former state of being) that life on earth was not really necessary for them and all they needed to do was merely put in a brief appearance to get the "mortality badge" and points. Religions love this "cop out".

There is little doubt that random events, or a series of random events often seemingly unrelated, (not related to cause and effect.) come together and can affect individual lives in a most dramatic way. In the movie "The Curious ... Benjamin Button" we see a remarkable construction of just such a chain of individually insignificant events playing together in a way that changed forever the lives of many. If any of some 10 "lead up" events had not happened or had occurred just seconds later the results would have been totally different. Why is this? Is this random or are we to believe such minutiae are all script-written and pre-destined?

It is not fate, destiny, predestination, fore-ordination of events nor karma, it is truly random events interweaving and playing out the fundamental

laws of cause and effect. It is a well-known principle and stated in the old philosophy of "a butterfly falls in the Amazon and a star explodes somewhere in the galaxy". Everything really is interconnected.

Yet some people still use the "(if) it was meant to be" chain of thought with reckless abandon. Or the similar and interesting variation of "I wont do/get (the thing in question) now, but if it's still (there, available etc.) tomorrow/later/next time **I'll know it was meant to be and I'll (do it, get it, take it, etc.) then**." The problem is that many people really accept thinking like this as based on reality and the way their life and the universe around them actually works. Thankfully every minutiae of our lives is not authored at the level of the fabric of the universe, or at the "hand" of *god*. Don't look for involvement of "angels" either.

Law of "attraction".

This all leads into karma. There is a law or principal of cause and effect, and another **law of attraction.** With just those few words it probably becomes apparent wherein is the cause for coining the word "karma". "Evil begets evil", "like things attract each other", "birds of a feather flock together" these and numerous similar phrases simply illustrate and state the law of attraction. I recall a movie (yes again another one) called "Waterhole Number 3" wherein the law was put to song and music called the "code of the west", which was "do unto others before they do it unto you". The habitual wrong doer, the one who disregards others often becomes well known for his actions, and it will be a certainty that one day such a one will meet a like minded person who, knowing of his mannerisms, will do unto him before he does it unto them. His getting his **"just desserts"** ("just deserves") is the effect and result caused by his continual actions. Cause and effect in action. A law of cause and effect will of course be greatly magnified when a group of like people associate one with another. "No honour among thieves" has been said of such groups, and payback is close at hand for such.

APPLYING AND MAKING IT PERSONAL

No matter what is the nature of ones problems, troubles, worries or woes a way exists to enable us to resolve those issues.

You can fully reclaim your life and become free from fear and worry, free from addiction or despair. Equally important you can become free from the dictates and demands of religion and "churchism" with its laws and creeds. I do not say that you will be able to dip your hand into the fabric of the universe, or another dimension and produce your wealth or dreams, but be aware that this is not impossible and seems to be a reality recorded and reportedly achieved by some. Nor do I say that you will never be able to do that sort of thing. (The double negative in a sentence above is intentional, as "not impossible" is vastly different to "possible".)

It is possible that some truly unavoidable or inescapable obstacle is in front of you and what may really be desirable is freedom from fear, and the ability to maintain your dignity, self-respect and manifest those personal characteristics. Know that genuine unavoidable obstacles or "things" are realities that some of us may confront at some time.

Our passing from this world in death is just one such unavoidable event and to be able to face it with dignity and calmness will probably require more than just an understanding of it.

What is of supreme importance is to know and understand that you are already the best equipped to find your solution and implement it. Alternatively you may first have to identify any help and assistance you may need to help achieve what is desired. Once help is found and enlisted you may then be able to work together with others to achieve your end result. Unless your issues are shared, you will carry them alone. I have already mentioned there is far greater power available when a group is involved for the use of a common cause or purpose, and although this may appear and seem to be common sense, it is surprising just how many people "muddle along" alone, struggling to sort out their troubles, worries, and woes.

A *prayer* for guidance and direction in finding the ability or path to enable the resolution of your problems will get best results. To pray and ask *god* to solve or remove your problems or issues is most likely **totally futile**. Remember that effectively you ARE your *god* on earth, you have the powers, the "force" is with you, and it is you who will find the way and the solution. You may need just a little bit of guidance and a bit of help from fellow mortals.

Sometimes you may find your solution requires that you change your circumstances, lifestyle, and circle of friends or acquaintances so as to avoid continuance of certain undesirable situations or future events. This may well be your solution to a lot of despair and hopeless feelings associated with most sorts of addictions. Be aware of all possibilities and do not short pay the wisdom or insights found or "popping into your awareness" after *prayerful* consideration of your issues and a request for guidance. Also it may help to get some other perspective involved in the matter.

A message in and of the mirror.

Look in the mirror and remind yourself that these troubles or issues are effecting that person in the mirror. They belong or appear to belong to the mortal person that others think of **as** really being you. In fact this world and all in it is illusion. Very few people indeed will know the true "you", but only know and see the person who you can see when you look in the mirror. **That "man in the mirror" of course is NOT "you".** You are actually on "this" side of the mirror, the observer, the non-illusion reality side, and you are really untroubled by the issues.

Troubles are even more transitory and temporary than life itself. Being the observer and neutral you can be perfectly placed and poised to be totally objective and help that person (The "you" that the real you sees in the mirror.) out of difficulty. As is often said but little used or understood, "ask and it shall be given you; seek and ye shall find; knock and it will be opened unto you." (Matt 7:7 Luke 11:9 James 1:5) Remember and know that although those words are in the bible, they are not exclusive to Christendom, they are universally applicable cosmic truths, and they are very true and real in their promise and application.

NOT "THE SECRET" BUT THE "HIDDEN"

To effectively implement "change" we need to look at our thinking. Yes, our thinking, and how we express our thinking in our words.

In this book I have said that the fabric of the universe, the source of all that is and can be, a.k.a. *"god",* only operates in a "now" state. There is no "past" and there is no "future", linear time as we understand it does not exist at the level of the source, the force.

Follow this carefully if you wish to understand fully why it so frequently said and claimed that we "become what we think about", which is of recent times called "the secret".

Most importantly we are going to shout out loud and clearly why it "always" seems to work only for **some** and why your and my efforts to use this vouched for source and "secret" is so often frustrated, so futile. We may have said "well yes I believed, I tried, but it didn't/doesn't work for me".

Sound familiar?

If you can understand what follows, that will change and it will "work" for you. Or rather, you will work for you.

Understand that it's not about changing anything except your understanding. It probably does not even matter if you do understand or accept that there is an omnific fabric of the universe, a.k.a. *god* and that there is no linear time at that level but only an eternal "now" state. How could such an understanding of those things really matter or be a key element if so few know of or understand it. Also how many have used the principle effectively with no thought of any thing involved whatsoever other than their own natural thoughts. See, it's only our own way of thinking that makes anything complicated or frustrates our efforts. Once we understand we will laugh at how simple a thing it is, and how strange it is that we missed the whole point, the simple understanding and reasons for failure with so many of our endeavors.

COMMON EXAMPLES

"We are absolutely *broke* till next pay. We are always broke till next pay." "We never have any spare money or savings." "We can never afford or go on a holiday." "Our car is always breaking down and we can never afford to get it fixed or get a good one." Or a few variations of the same subject: "I wish we could earn more money, get a better job, win the lottery, be as rich as the ZZZ family." And yet another variation of the same theme of poverty: "Please God, help us get more wealth, I will …(bargain) if you … please. Oh God help me get a better job, car, house, whatever."

THE REAL ISSUE OR PROBLEM.

We are acknowledging a problem and not only thinking about it but we are also verbalizing it. We are really "whispering it to the trees"…. (We have very recently covered just what the result of 'whispering it to the trees' causes.) We may think we are addressing the issue, and petitioning our all-powerful god for help and think that has to be a positive step. Goodness, we even promise to give half or whatever to charity and good works to seal the deal with some god.

The reality is that we are really whining and complaining. All we are really doing is stating the obvious and confirming our **current status**, that of **poverty**. But is it really our "current status", or is it more correctly a condition that is really belonging to our "past"? But - there is no "past" with the fabric of the universe, a.k.a. *god*. Did I just hear a proverbial penny drop?

With such remonstrations and verbalizing all we are really doing is **re-affirming** that we are whining and poor people. Note that those words and thoughts are how we believe and see ourselves as what we **ARE** in the "now" state. The "force", being neutral, will allow continuance of the "now" state, which of course is our overt statement of **being** a whining poor individual. No, *"God"* does not *give* us anything, and is not sweetened by the bargain of charity. You have unwittingly just given yourself a continuance of an unchanged future.

When we complain about our ***work or jobs***, about how we are unhappy and unsatisfied with our boss or fellow workers, what are we doing? We are **re-affirming** that we are unhappy and dissatisfied workers, and that we like to whine about it all. In such conditions little if anything will ever change. In whining and complaining we are not giving any thought or energy to **change or solutions**.

The real issue and fault is that we have accepted and believe that this is our current and now condition based on what was in the past. Then we re-affirm that condition by whining about it. We have overlooked or never knew that *"god"* only operates **NOW** because that is all there is at the source. If *god* could speak he may say "yes I hear you, you say you are poor and miserable, OK fine, no problem, you are having a satisfying whine, so be it."

We may be stressed to the max because of some ***addiction***. It could be an addiction to almost anything, and not only the usual things like alcohol, drugs, tobacco, foods or gambling. We have seen above how even a prayer can be phrased in an inappropriate or ill advised manner. An inappropriate manner is one that will not get, or more accurately, **cause** *god* (a.k.a. fabric of…) to implement a divine correction. So long as we whine about the fact that we **ARE** an addict of whatever, and wish we **could** change, give it up, or that we will **TRY** to give it up, we are probably doomed to failure and retain our confessed and accepted status-quo. (Phrases like those just illustrated are future tense wishes. Figure out what is wrong.) Again we are merely **re-affirming** that sad status quo. Yoda said, **"there is no try, there is only do or not do"**. **To *god* there is no "future"**.

The absolute reality is <u>not</u> that "we become what we think about", but that "we <u>ARE</u> what we think about". This is what is hidden or not spelled out clearly.

Thus when we whine or verbalize our problems we are simply stating what we accept, judge or believe we ARE. Because at the source, the fabric level, there is no past etc. we remain as what we think about as being us "now" and that condition will not change. Poverty remains, Addiction remains, the bad work relations remain. Our resentment and self-conviction remain. **All remain and will remain until we change our thinking and spoken words** till they are no longer confirmation of those thoughts that judge us and then condemn us to the continuance of the same conditions in that eternal now.

Law of attraction takes charge.

Every time we say, whine, think (or pray) about "not having", "needing", "hating", "disliking" etc. that is what we are defining ourselves as; a wanter, needer, hater, etc. Remember that **law of attraction** to which we referred earlier? It goes to work to fulfill our dominant thoughts by finding the circumstances and conditions that best express them, especially if they have been emotionalized. Like attracts like, misery loves misery. Later we can really wallow in it and refuel the cycle.

Notice when you complain how often you will be joined by others who will even try to outdo you in your misery, whining, and tales of woe. It is sad but true that in a group of people the tendency is generally to sink to the level of the "lowest" individual. That is how **"mob" mentality** operates.

If you think about hating being overweight, you will be forced to act on what you are thinking, and more "hating being overweight" will continue to show up often, (almost endlessly?) in your life. If you have not allowed or stated some positive alternative there is no choice. You have said you are overweight, and that you are a person who hates something. **Those are the motivating and enabling thoughts that will activate the force and power that is yours as part of that *god* a.k.a. fabric...that in fact IS you.**

Summary: every time we say "I hate..." "I wish..." it's a reaffirmation of what we think or accept that we are. We strengthen our acceptance of our desperate state. If we pray to a god by whatever name or concept along the lines of asking to heal, give me, remove, strengthen, etc. we are confessing that we are in this fallen sad lacking and needful state NOW.

Try this to change your thinking.

Decades ago I learned somewhere that in prayer one should never ask anything of *god* till one had run out of things for which to express and give thanks. There is much wisdom there, as it switches off the negative emotions and starts one on a chain of positive thoughts. Once you realize for just how much you have to be thankful, you may well forget your problems, troubles worries and woes, or at least see them as less a burden.

What is needful is a total change in the way we deal with and how we think about things that may not be desirable in our lives. Of course it is natural to identify less than ideal conditions and to desire to change them. We need to begin to **think a little differently** that's all. This is exemplified in the Kennedy saying, *"some men see things as they are and say why, I dream things that never were and say why not."*

Starting now, you are not an addict (or whatever is the affliction) and the *god* who is in you can now begin to change things from what they "were". Ask for **guidance** not direct help. Ask to be led or for help to find whatever is wanted. I am sure you can see the importance difference. With a little thought and careful editing of your thinking you can change your attitudes and outlook entirely.

There really is magic in positive **self-affirmations**. Self-affirmations will affect attitude and belief. Actions will also affect attitude. To become enthusiastic act enthusiastic. To become happy act happy. Add happy and enthusiastic together and try it. Think about something absolutely crazy funny and have a good laugh <u>out loud</u>. (Try the "fake it" till you "make it" routine, but give it a real go. I knew one sales group decades ago that were taught, and were compelled, to shout the following at meetings. "I feel healthy, I feel happy, I feel terrific!" If the leader did not feel it loud or enthusiastic enough, he demanded they do it again. (and then again if needed.) It did and does work.)

Laughter just may be one of the best medicines. Above all else, guard very carefully what you say and think about your current status, attitudes, words and thoughts. Yes, think about your thoughts, and what it is that you think about most of the time, because chances are that is the state in which you will spend the rest of your life.

You can reclaim your life and **live it the way you choose**. You must get a clear picture of what it is you want, focus on that, and eliminate all foggy thinking that would have you believe you are other than that already. Remember *god* is not only with you, but is within you.

May you live long and prosper. May the force be with you.

*The game we play is let's pretend
and pretend we're not pretending.
We choose to forget who we are
and then forget that we have forgotten.
Who are we really?
(we are) the centre that watches
and runs the show
that chooses which way it will go
the "I AM" consciousness -
that powerful loving perfect reflection
of the cosmos.
But in our attempt to cope with early
situations we chose or were hypnotised
into a passive situation to avoid
punishment - or the loss of love.
We chose to deny our response/ability
pretending that things just happened
or that we were being controlled -
taken over.
We put ourselves down, and have become
used to this masochistic posture, this
weakness, this indecisiveness...
but we are in reality free,
a centre of cosmic energy.
Your will is your power - don't pretend
you don't have it - or you wont.
(Bernard Gunther)*

(First printed and published in Book 3, "I Can See Clearly Now" in October 2010. Extensively revised and re-written Feb 2013.)

INTERLUDE –

POINTS TO PONDER

- When functioning "in the body" in the temporal waking world it is difficult to always remember and remain aware of that status – that one is just functioning in a temporary illusionary world in a similar temporary body.

- The "gods" (and others) "reach" into the quantum soup, the fabric of the universe and its information (data etc.) and manipulate that information.

  The resulting data manipulation, an apparent "miracle" is thus not performed in this physical 4-dimension world. It is only manifest here. The "work" is performed in another dimension within the field of the universe.

- (Thoughts on waking up) The information or data must be the same, synchronized in all dimensions to exist in them and as a manifestation in this 4-dimension universe.

- People generally become too focused on the 4 dimensional physical world and even believe the physical body is really and actually them.

- Religion is for those who fear death and/or hell. Spirituality is for those who have been there or seen them.

- What if "energy" is just the manifest tool of "intelligence" and the means of cosmic intelligence's getting things done or accomplished.

- When one awakens the intelligence, the consciousness, reverts back to the mortal body, abandoning the dream body and world, sometimes with retained memory of its experiences there.

  Now why should this be significant or important? Probably because on dying (physical death) the consciousness, the intelligence, reverts back to the multidimensional body. Who knows if it will retain memories of this (mortal) life, or even they are of sufficient importance. Are thoughts or memories of this life as memorable long term as are or dreams or memories of childhood?

- On mortal death things of this temporal world cease to exist for and to us, they pass from us as do the events, experiences and people in a dream also pass from us on awaking. Our "new" dimension will come into focus and awareness for us just as this world emerges and comes into focus after a sleep and dreaming.

  Question: Does the dream world continue in its dimension without our presence when we have left it in awaking?

- In the grander cosmic scale of things this mortal life span and experiences must be so insignificant it could hardly be of any ultimate purpose or everlasting value. It is as a short dream of a short lived seemingly insignificant "being" who is but a temporary manifestation on a temporary world in one dimension of the "quantum soup".

- Just as the dream body does not have the capacity to manifest itself to or in our waking world, so the "waking self" and body lack the capacity to manifest itself (in its standard state) in or use "privileges" of dimensions beyond this temporal dimension.

- Probably the "hyperspace" with its predicted (10 or more) dimensions is very real, and "mortality" (or this temporal world and universe) is just one of those dimensions. The "dream world" merely another, and our individual consciousness and intelligence can move "between" them at times. This would allow adequate explanation of dreams, waking, death and the dead, aliens, etc.

- Do we meet those dead to mortality in dreams because they still exist and can access that reality level or dimension?

- **Speed of light issue.** As far as light goes, possibly "nothing" is actually moving, (more likely if the fabric of the universe really does only exist and operate in an eternal "here and now" state.) but it's vibrations or waves of energy that move. (Like waves in the sea, the sea-water is not moving, but only a wave of energy is moving through the water.) The wave movement is energy and constant to the observer, it is a reality of observation. The information or data is transmitted in and by the energy wave in the fabric of the universe. (At a rate or "speed" constant to an observer and not a fixed spatial point, thus observer movement is irrelavent.)

Consider the energy wave as a "pulse", a pulse of information, a "thought" (etc.) a stream of data coming from the fabric of the universe and manifesting itself into our 4D space/time. The transmission of that data, thought (etc.) comes into our dimension at a speed we know as the speed of light, "c" the ultimate speed limit. Anything beyond that is simply beyond the capacity or physics of this dimension we know as our universe and is not discernable. (As are thoughts, dreams, and other paraphysical manifestations.) But our inability to discern data beyond our comprehension range does not remotely deny the reality of their possibility or existence. Were this so we must deny thought itself.

SUPPLEMENTARY

READING

(OR THINGS YOU REALLY

SHOULD KNOW ABOUT)

ANNALS OF EARTH

© 1995, 2003 Dan Sewell Ward

Episode V -- The Anunnaki

In our last Episode, there was the hint that we were about to welcome Man and his history in these Annals of Earth. Moreover, Man's arrival on the scene, supposedly in a starring role, promised to be a dramatic event, complete with controversy and wonderment. It was a tense moment, mitigated only by the realization that there were a lot of unanswered questions still on the books. The good news is that it's now time -- in this very episode -- to welcome Man onto the scene, begin his history (and include a fair amount of herstory as well), and at the same time, answer all the piddling little questions.

In order to accomplish in one Episode all of these tasks, it is necessary to backtrack once again in our dating (but probably for the last time), in order to bring the relevant histories of the rest of the major characters into our drama. In doing this we will initially resort to an assortment of Sumerian texts, coupled with just enough Biblical quotes to add spice to the arguments. We will also recall to the stage, a major character who has received little mention in the latest Episodes: Nibiru.

For while life has been merrily evolving along on the planet Earth circa 1 million years B.C.E., back on the ranch on the planet Nibiru -- that currently distant member of our solar system -- evolution has marched and/or accelerated to the beat of a different (and possibly hyper) drummer. Nibiru has, according to the texts of Sumeria, not only developed an intelligent civilization, but has even managed to develop blood feuds and space flight, and inevitably to acquire imperialistic ambitions.

c. 485,000 B.C.E. In a Hittite version of a Sumerian text entitled by modern scholars Kingship in Heaven, the story is told of the descendents of LAMA. The text, after elaborating on their ancestry, "the fathers and mothers of the gods", tells the tale of Anu and Alalu, "the mighty olden gods, the gods of the olden days". When the time of succession had arrived on Nibiru, it was not Anshargal, Anu's father and the heir apparent, who had ascended the throne. Instead, a relative named Alalu (or Alalush in the Hittite version) became the ruler. Then in a gesture of reconciliation (or possibly by custom), Alalu appointed Anu to be his royal cup-bearer, an honored and trusted position. But after nine Nibiruan years (known as Sars, where 1 Sar = 3600 Earth years), Anu "gave battle to Alalu" and deposed him (so much for the honored and trusted bit).

"Once in the olden days, ALALU was king in Heaven, ALALU was seated on the throne; The mighty ANU, first among the gods, was standing before him: He would bow to his feet, set the drinking cup in his hand.

For nine counted periods [Sars], ALALU was king in Heaven.

In the ninth counted period, ANU gave battle to ALALU. ALALU was defeated, he fled before ANU -- Down he descended to the dark-hued Earth.

ANU took his seat upon the throne."

Noted the phrase: "Descended to the dark-hued Earth." Ah yes, the critical connection.

Mind you, the texts did not say that Alalu came from Nibiru, but rather from Heaven -- what we now recognize -- at least in these Annals -- as being periodically located in the environs of the asteroid belt. Was Alalu a fallen angel? By no means. Man, at the time, was only a gleam in the eye of Homo erectus. He was not ready for gods yet. And Alalu was not destined to be one of the major characters in our drama anyway. But his arrival on Earth began the process, the initiation of all the events that would be detailed within the Sumerian texts.

The House of Anu had put an end to the rival house by deposing its ruler Alalu, who in the best tradition of deposed rulers escaped the planet of his birth and chose exile. Nibiru, apparently, was not big enough for the both of them. Alalu was thus forced to find greener pastures (and what greener pastures can one find in the solar system, than Earth?). By descending to dark-hued (Nibiruan for greener pastures) Earth, one assumes that Alalu made the trip in a spaceship, probably with a retinue of aides and supporters, and thereafter found refuge on an unexplored planet.

c. 450,000 B.C.E. After many, many moons, or roughly ten orbits of Nibiru, during which Alalu, et al made the best of it in their exile domicile, a momentous event occurred. According to the Sumerian texts, Alalu **discovered gold**, a commodity apparently in great demand on the planet Nibiru. Why the gold was so valuable to Nibiru's inhabitants is not made clear in the texts, but as the narrative continues we will soon realize that this was a discovery of immense importance. Furthermore, Alalu, even though deposed, was sufficiently concerned for Nibiru's need for gold, he advised Anu that he had found the precious metal in Earth's oceans. This momentous discovery apparently had a major impact, in that a reconciliation of sorts then ensued with Anu appointing KUMARBI, a grandson of Alalu, to be his royal cup-bearer. Alalu then, it is assumed, was allowed to return to Nibiru for a more genteel exile.

All the evidence suggests that at this juncture the Nibiruans launched into a space program of some magnitude [pardon the pun]. It was probably a crash program (or rather a hurried up program where it was hoped there would be no crash). But the process nevertheless took some 7,000 years. This may sound a trifle long, but keep in mind that it was two orbits of Nibiru, or only two of their years.

As will become apparent in reading this Episode, the inhabitants of Nibiru were extremely long-lived. If one is to take the Sumerian texts literally, one would have to suspect they had a Nibiruan-normal life-time in excess of some 500,000 Earth years, about 140-150 orbits of Nibiru. But they were not immortal! As time will tell, they were quite capable of dying young, having their life taken by dismemberment and other bloody deeds, and other forms of accidental or homicidal death. Of course, from the viewpoint of any human with a life expectancy of less than 100 years, such long-lived creatures would appear immortal.

A related and highly speculative corollary to their long lives is the question as to whether or not such creatures would progress at an equally slow rate. As we will see, different factions of the Nibiruans created and maintained a family feud worthy of the Hatfields and the McCoys, and one which lasted for more than 400,000 years. This would hardly be considered progress from any species' point of view, where the species had less tenure than a tenth the length of the feud.

Furthermore, all progress, improvements, or advances in the Nibiruan technology seem to also proceed at an incredibly slow rate. The fact that it took them 7,000 Earth years to take advantage of Alalu's discovery would attest to this rather laid-back way of life. One could also speculate on whether or not their Earth-daily lives were quite leisurely by human standards, and whether or not a good night's sleep for them was on the order of Earth weeks or months. The Sumerian texts do not address this question (nor for that matter the personal traits of the Nibiruans which do not affect the human race), but one wonders if extreme longevity might be coupled with extremely slow transformational rates, both personal and cultural. And vice versa for the very short-lived species. E. g. not cleaning a toilet for a month might allow the bacteria therein to reach the state of a civilization advanced enough to be capable of achieving spaceflight. A thought to ponder.

But eventually, the Nibiruans began their imperialistic conquest of the Earth.

c. 443,000 B.C.E. The Sumerians considered Nibiru to be a twelfth member of the solar system -- after the Sun, Moon, and the nine other planets that modern science recognizes. The texts also revealed that Nibiru's orbit took the planet to a "station" in the distant heavens, then brought it back to Earth's vicinity, crossing between Mars and Jupiter.

In the latter position, the planet obtained its name Nibiru ("crossing") and its symbol, the cross. The inhabitants of the planet, the "Righteous Ones", were known as the Anunnaki ("Those Who From Heaven to Earth Came"). The inhabitants of Nibiru who stayed home (supposedly the overwhelming majority of the population) were still Nibiruans, but the astronaut-wing were known by a very specific name -- the one we will hereafter use. Keep in mind also that Heaven has been identified as the asteroid belt located between Mars and Jupiter, the exact location of the "crossing" point, the perihelion (closest approach to the Sun) of Nibiru in its highly elliptical orbit. The Anunnaki of the planet Nibiru, then, quite literally came from Heaven.

For reasons we will discuss in future Episodes, the Biblical Deluge, the torrential covering of the Earth with water in ancient times, has been dated to circa 11,000 B.C.E. This date is not without controversy, but is well supported by evidence from several diverse sources. In any case, the date of the arrival of the Anunnaki on Earth is calculated by back dating from the Deluge. According to the Sumerian texts, the all-important arrival of the Anunnaki occurred 120 Sars, or -- inasmuch as one Sar equals 3,600 Earth years -- 432,000 years before the Deluge. 432,000 years! Hmmmmmm.

For those who were wondering where the Hindu traditions (Episode III) came up with their figure for the 432,000 year Yuga... Well, now you know! And even if you're not convinced about which came first, the

Anunnaki or the Hindus, there nevertheless is a clear connection. And if you consider the fact that 432,000 years is a very long time for Hindu humans to keep track of, then perhaps the Anunnaki have the best claim to originating the dating. In any case...

Exactly one **Yuga (432,000 years)** prior to the Deluge, the DIN.GIR ("Righteous Ones of the Rocketships") came down to Earth from their own planet. ["Rocketships" might be pushing the translation a bit, but as Zecharia Sitchin continues his interpretation of the Sumerian texts, the term makes more and more sense.] The first major expedition of the Anunnaki was let by E.A ("Whose House is Water"). After landing and establishing a base at Eridu, located at the headwaters of the Persian Gulf, this eldest son of Anu, assumed the title: EN.KI ("Lord of Earth"). According to his first-person report:

"When I approached Earth, there was much flooding.
When I approached its green meadows, heaps and mounds were piled up at my command.
    I built my house in a pure place... My house -- its shade stretches over the Snake Marsh."

Ea / Enki was well chosen for the mission. He was a brilliant scientist and engineer whose nickname was NU.DIM.MUD ("He Who Fashions Things"). His plan was to extract gold from the waters of the Persian Gulf and the adjoining shallow marshlands. In this regard Sumerian depictions showed Enki as the lord of flowing waters, sitting in a laboratory and surrounded by interconnected flasks. Enki was also destined to be one of the two major players in the history of our race. Keep him in mind. His place in the early parts of Genesis are of the highest significance.

The extraction by Enki and his followers of gold is of critical importance. The whole purpose of the imperialistic intentions of the Anunnaki was to accumulate gold. But apparently, not for any vain purposes. It is noteworthy, for example, that at no time during the millennia that followed were the Anunnaki ever shown trading in gold or wearing golden jewelry. There was no hint of a monetary role either. The Anunnaki apparently had much higher purposes for the precious metal. (There is, however, absolutely no evidence for the Anunnaki having higher porpoises.)

Gold may have been required for their space craft (as does our modern day space program), and as noted in Hindu texts, references to the celestial chariots of the gods refer to them being covered with gold. But there is little need for spacecraft except as a means to acquire gold from Earth, and thus this idea is probably not correct. Instead, there appears to be a much more important need of the metal, with its unique properties, possibly some vital need back home on Nibiru, a need conceivably affecting the very survival of life on Nibiru. One theory Sitchin seemed fond of was that the Nibiruans needed the precious metal in order to suspend gold particles in Nibiru's waning atmosphere and thus shield it from a critical dissipation. Sitchin, however, has not been willing to defend this idea to any great extent. The question must remain mute for a bit longer. But we shall return to this all important detail a bit later in the narrative.

Another factor worth mentioning is the genealogy of the leaders of the Anunnaki and their relationship to the planets. First of all there is the matriarch LAMA, who is responsible for both lineages of the warring houses of ANSHARGAL and ALALU. Anshargal is identified with Anshar (Saturn). His mate is KISHAR (Jupiter). Their son is ANU (Uranus). By NAMMU or ID, a concubine of Anu's, Anu "begot his twin and equal" NUDIMMUD, EA or ENKI (Neptune).

In the Sumerian traditions, Anu is generally considered the Sky God, the head of the Sumerian pantheon of gods and goddesses. Enki is considered the God of Wisdom and the God of Waters (Nammu, his mother, was the Goddess of the Watery Deep --"Deep Space"?). At the same time, Enki is Anu's "twin and equal", and Enki's planet Neptune is at the gateway to the solar system, such that the solar system is Ea's (Enki's) "abode".

As already mentioned, Enki will become one of the most important gods in the saga of Man. He is also the father of Marduk, the latter being Enki's first born son. This makes sense, inasmuch as it was Neptune's gravitational pull that first brought Nibiru (Marduk) into the solar system. Marduk also plays a very major part later on, particularly during the time of Babylon. Meanwhile, at this stage, Enki, the equal of Anu is on Earth, prospecting in the Persian Gulf waters for gold.

The Sumerian texts also note that Nibiru (or Marduk) made for himself two abodes: One in the "Firmament"; the other, "in the Deep" -- the latter being called the "Great Distant Abode", as well as E.SHARRA ("Abode/Home of the Ruler/Prince"). The abode in the Firmament is not entirely clear as to its exact name, location, address, and/or zip code, but there is a possibility this abode was on the planet Mars. This rather outrageous suggestion will be revisited more than once as we progress in these Annals.

The sea we today call the Arabian Sea, the body of water between the Persian Gulf and the Indian Ocean was called in antiquity the Sea of Erythrea, from whence we derive the word, Earth. The first settlement of the Anunnaki on Earth was at a place called E.RI.DU ("Home In a Faraway place"). The Sumerian term for Earth's globe and its firm surface was KI. Note, for example, that the word, Anunnaki breaks down into ANU, N, NA, and KI. ANU is thought of as heaven and KI, Earth. In the same fashion, EA, after having established the first five of the seven original settlements on Earth, was given the title of EN.KI ("Lord of Earth"). KI also conveys the meaning "to cut off, to sever, to hollow out." Its derivatives illustrate this. For example: KI.LA meant "excavation", KI.MAH "tomb", and KI.IN.DAR "crevice, fissure." In Sumerian astronomical texts, the term KI was prefixed with the determinative MUL ("celestial body"). Thus MUL.KI meant "the celestial body that had been cleaved apart", a reference to the creation of Earth from Tiamat. Over the years, the pronunciation of KI change to GI, and ultimately to "geo" (as in geo-graphy, geo-metry, geo-logy, etcetera).

The cosmology of the Sumerian gods and their related planets has its counterpart in the Greek version. In the eighth century B.C.E., Hesiod began the divine tale of events that ultimately led to the supremacy of Zeus with:

"Verily, at first Chaos came to be, and next the wide-bosomed Gaia,
She who created all the immortal ones; Who hold the peaks of snowy Olympus:
Dim Tartarus, wide-pathed in the depths, and Eros, fairest among the divine immortals...
From Chaos came forth Erebus and black Nyx; and of Nyx were born Aether and Hemera."

It seems apparent that Gaia was the Greek equivalent of Tiamat, and the divine pairs of Tartarus and Eros, Erebus and Nyx, Aether and Hemera were the Romans' Mars and Venus, Jupiter and Saturn, Uranus and Neptune, just as in the Sumerian version. At the same time, Ouranos ("Heaven") came about, according to Hesiod's Theogony, in a similar way as well:

"And Gaia then bare starry Ouranos -- equal to herself --

To envelop her on every side, to be an everlasting abode place for the gods."

Later on after the battle, Hesiod spoke of Gaia as being the half equivalent to Heaven: on one side she bore Urea, who "brought forth long hills, graceful haunts of the goddess-Nymphs"; and on the other side "she bore Pontus, the fruitless deep with its raging swell." The former would be on the side the firm lands had formed from the crust of Tiamat; while on the other side there was a hollow, an immense cleft into which the waters of the erstwhile Tiamat must have poured. In effect, the fruitless Pontus was the Pacific Ocean (where no fruit grows in the extensive salt water). Apparently, the authors or compilers of the Book of Genesis were not the only ones accepting the Sumerian cosmogony (and also editing it to outline the derivation of their own gods and Olympic dynasties).

c. 429,000 B.C.E. Four Sars later, more Anunnaki arrive on Earth, among them a Chief Medical Officer, Enki's half-sister Ninharsag, (also referred to as NINTI). The Anunnaki came in groups of fifty, as attested to by one of these groups led by Enki's firstborn son, MAR.DUK. Marduk describes to his father an "attack" on his spacecraft by one of the solar system's larger planets (possibly Jupiter):

"It has been created like a weapon;
It has charged forward like death...
The Anunnaki who are fifty it has smitten...
The flying, birdlike Supreme Orbiter it has smitten on the breast."

It's relevant that these "gods" were not exactly omnipotent... They could certainly get smitten, and space travel was not to the level of being routine. In fact, as will become more and more apparent in these Annals, just getting from place to place on the Earth had a degree of adventure.

There is also the suggestion from the Sumerian artifacts that Marduk may have landed on Mars on the way to Earth, that Mars may have been a way station between Nibiru's crossing in the asteroid belt and Earth. This clue comes from a depiction on a Sumerian cylinder seal. It also makes sense in that Nibiru making its perihelion approach to the Solar System may have been a lot closer to Mars at the time in its orbit than to Earth (which might easily have been on the other side of the Sun at the time).

Other more indirect evidence includes photographs by the NASA's Mars probe, Mariner 9, which shows what has come to be called "The Face on

Mars." The photo includes the "Face" and what appears to be an extensive area of pyramids and other allegedly artificial structures, all faintly reminiscent of ancient cities and major religious areas on Earth. Any one of the latter might easily be attributed to the Anunnaki, at least in terms of their design and layout.

c. 414,000 B.C.E. Four Sars later -- about 15,000 Earth years -- it finally becomes apparent to the Anunnaki that the gold production from seawater is failing to live up to expectations. More significantly, these primeval prospectors were now faced with a decision to either abandon the project -- essentially out of the question -- or try to obtain the gold by other means, for example, by mining. The Anunnaki had by this time become aware that gold was available in abundance in the AB.ZU, "The Primeval Source". Scholars, such as Sitchin, interpret this to mean South Africa. But such deep mining in "the place of the shining lodes", would necessitate expanding the processing facilities and fabricating ore vessels (MA.GUR UR.NU AB.ZU -- "Ships for Ores of the Abzu"). It was major decision time!

And as in all major decision times, the ones on the front lines, Enki and the Gang, were not going to be allowed to make the decision. This was one for the Big Guy. And so, eight Sars and 28,800 Earth years after Enki's landing, the Supreme Anu arrived on Earth for a closer inspection. His gold train had been threatened! It was time to step in and act authoritative.

Anu arrived on the scene, however, with considerable baggage. His retinue included his heir apparent, ENLIL ("Lord of the Command"), and the young Kumarbi (the grandson of the same Alalu whom Anu had deposed). One can rationalize Anu's decision to include Kumarbi on the basis that it might have been unwise to have left the young contender back home, close to the throne. As for Enlil, Anu may already decided there needed to be a shake-up in the Earth bureaucracy. As heir apparent, Enlil was the son of Anu and his half-sister ANTUM (or KI or URASH, later considered an Earth goddess). Enlil was someone whom Anu could trust, while Enki was the disenfranchised son who just might have a grudge or genteel upset toward Anu and the powers that be. Note in this regard that Enki was Anu's first-born son, but that Enlil was Anu's first-born son by his half-sister, and thus the legal heir apparent! This is the same situation on which is based the saga of Abraham, Sarah, Ishmael, and Isaac. In some respects, the Ishmael/Isaac rivalry was just a rerun of the Enki/Enlil one. But in the latter case, as we shall see, the stakes were much greater. It was the Earth that was up for grabs!

We might note in passing a fundamental factor in the succession code of the Anunnaki. The heir apparent is first and foremost the first-born son by a half-sister. Only if no such son exists do we drop down to the subsequent levels on which Enki found himself. Later on, we will see that Enki finds himself strongly attracted to Ninti, his half-sister, whose union could produce an heir that would have even more clout than Enlil's son by any other woman. The epic of this romantic interlude, we will return to in a later episode. For the moment, suffice it to say that the half-sister-wife rule of the Anunnaki surfaces in all of its glory with Abraham, who went to some lengths to emphasize Sarah's status as his half-sister and wife. From Genesis 20: 12:

"And yet indeed she is my sister; she is the daughter of my father, but not the daughter of my mother; and she became my wife."

Curiously, scientists in 1980 found that given a choice, female monkeys preferred to mate with half-brothers. These preferred half-brothers shared the same father, but had different mothers. Other reports [Discover, December 1988] showed that "male wasps ordinarily mate with their sisters, but preferentially mate with half-sisters, those with the same father but different mother." One might wonder if the succession code of the Anunnaki is more than just whim. Or if these older and wiser gods have determined in their near omniscience that: Incest really is best!

The importance of lineage and genealogy with the Anunnaki cannot be stressed enough, as it will be intimately involved in the struggles for succession and supremacy in the coming millennia. Much of the ferocity of these later wars stemmed from a code of sexual behavior based not on morality but on considerations of genetic purity; that-is-to-say, sexual acts were judged not by their tenderness or violence, but by their purpose and outcome. Furthermore, while the code prohibited marriage (but not lovemaking) between full brother and sister, marriage with a half-sister was not only allowed, but the male progeny by a half-sister even had precedence in the hierarchical order. And while rape was condemned, sex -- even irregular and violent -- was condoned if done for the sake of succession to the throne. Finally, the same code which condemned rape did not prohibit extramarital affairs per se.

Meanwhile back at the gold-producing crisis, Anu took stock of the situation, showed why he was on the throne, and made the command decisions: Enlil would take command of the Earth operations and organize the gold deliveries back to Nibiru. At the same time, Enki was to be demoted as Lord of Earth, and given a lesser command, the actual mining in the Abzu; and would be allowed to keep his abode in Eridu (housing prices, at the time being at an all time low). But the latter gesture wasn't sufficient to prevent heated arguments from Enki, who threatened to return to Nibiru. More than the loss of the command of Earth, there was the fact Enki had lost it to Enlil!

The choice of Enlil for command of the Earth mission might have been a necessary one, but it greatly sharpened the rivalry and jealously between the two half-brothers. Enki had already had to deal with being disenfranchised as heir apparent when Anu's half-sister wife Antum had bore Enlil. Anu, thus, had to deal with Enki's outrage at having to step down in favor of Enlil, as well as being chastised for the lack of gold-production. As the scientist-engineer in charge, Enki could easily have taken it as a professional insult to have his plans be universally acknowledged as failing to meet expectations. Ultimately, it was decided to draw lots; allow chance to determine how it would be.

"The gods clasped hands together, then cast lots and divided: Anu to heaven went up; To Enlil the Earth was made subject; That which the sea as a loop encloses [South Africa?], They gave to the prince Enki.

To the Abzu Enki went down, assumed the rulership of the Abzu."

Unfortunately, for Anu, the drama was not yet over. Kumarbi had been left by Anu on the space platform orbiting the Earth. When Anu returned "up to heaven" (or at least, enroute), the two "gave battle" to one another. As Kumarbi momentarily bested Anu in the wrestling (the Anunnaki's preferred method for settling differences), "Anu struggled free from the hands of Kumarbi". But then Kumarbi managed to grab Anu by his feet, and "bit between his knees", hurting Anu in his "manhood". Ouch, that must have hurt. (This, if you can believe it, was a typical "hold" in Anunnaki wrestling.) Anu then took off for Nibiru, disgraced and in pain, leaving Kumarbi behind with the IGIGI manning the space platform. Thus was delivered in the classic fashion of the Anunnaki the first blow that would ultimately pave the way for the "War of the Olden Gods." In the interim...

c. 400,000 B.C.E. The Anunnaki begin arriving on Earth in larger numbers. Ultimately as many as six or seven hundred resided at any one time somewhere on Earth. Some were assigned to the "Lower World" to help Enki mine the gold, some manned the ore ships between the Abzu and Mesopotamia, some remained on the space platform orbiting the

Earth, and some stayed with Enlil in Mesopotamia -- the latter controlling the all important spaceport. According to the Sumerian texts, Enlil established settlements according to a master plan:

"He perfected the procedures, the divine ordinances; established five cities in perfect places, called them by name, laid them out as centers,

The first of these cities, Eridu, he granted to Nudimmud, the pioneer."

(Sounds like Enlil is doing a bit of revisionist history himself, claiming his generosity in "granting to Nudimmud" the city of Eridu, when Anu had already done it! Ah well, such is imperial life.)

Meanwhile, each city was given a specific function. E.RI.DU ("House in Faraway Built"), continued as the gold-extracting facility by the water's edge (and which for all time remained Enki's home away from home). The others included BAD.TIBIRA ("Bright Place Where the Ores Are Made Final"), the metallurgical center for smelting and refining; LA.RA.AK ("Seeing the Bright Glow"), a beacon-city to guide the landing shuttlecraft; SIPPAR ("Bird City"), the Landing Place; and SHU.RUP.PAK ("The Place of Utmost Well Being"). The latter was considered the medical center and was placed under the control of SUD / NINHARSAG / NINTI ("She Who Resuscitates"), a half-sister of both Enki and Enlil.

Later, other cities were established including LA.AR.SA ("Seeing the Red Light") and NIBIRU.KI -- Nippur in Akkadian -- ("The Earth-Place of Nibiru"), essentially the mission control center. As such, Nippur was complete with a DIR.GA ("Dark, Glowing Chamber") where space charts ("the emblems of the stars") were displayed and where the DUR.AN.KI ("Bond Heaven-Earth") was maintained. Finally, the IGI.GI ("Those Who See and Observe") remained on the space platform in constant Earth orbit. Refined metal from the smelters at Badtibira was sent aloft to the Igigi, until such time as the gold was transferred via spaceships periodically to Nibiru. Were these Anunnaki organized, or what!? Of course it took them 10,000 to 20,000 Earth years to get things running smoothly, but hey, it worked! But then, just when it looked as if things could become routine, things became very complicated again.

c. 380,000 B.C.E. In the quintessential example of how the Anunnaki and Nibiruans take forever to progress in any meaningful way (at least in terms of Earth years), the lingering and bitter struggle between the House of Anu and the House of Alalu broke out in the "War of the Olden Gods".

This war, upon which the Greek "War of the Titans" is undoubtedly based, pitted "the gods who are in heaven" against the "gods who are upon dark-hued Earth". (What was going on back on Nibiru is not addressed by the Sumerian texts -- the texts almost always restricting themselves to only those portions of the conflicts and events which directly affect the Earth.)

Gaining the support of the Igigi (who had been going around in circles in their space platforms and were probably bored, as well as possibly atrophying from the weightlessness), Alalu's grandson Kumarbi tossed aside his effectively tenured job as cup-bearer, and attempted to seize mastery over Earth. Kumarbi first attempted to enlist Enki in his cause -- thinking, obviously, that Enki just might still be a little bitter about the "recent" demotion. The Anunnaki do, after all, know how to carry a grudge... For millennia!

Subsequently, Kumarbi attempted to seek help from Lama, "mother of the two gods". But as we all know, the plans of mice, men and Anunnaki oft times go astray, and Anu got wind of the activity. Deciding once and for all that enough was enough, Anu ordered Enlil's son to find Kumarbi and kill him. Ferocious battles then ensued between the terrestrial gods led by Enlil's son and the sky-borne gods led by Kumarbi. In one battle, no less than 70 gods participated, all riding in "celestial chariots". It was Star Wars in the very neighborhood of Earth! In the end, the son of Enlil (and grandson of Anu) prevailed against Kumarbi.

There is some question as to which of Enlil's son was the avenging god. In the Hittite text entitled by modern scholars, The Kumarbi Cycle, the avenging god is identified as Enlil's youngest son, ADAD (also known as the Storm God Teshub and the principal Hittite deity). However, in the Sumerian version, in the tale known as The Myth of Zu, the hero is NINURTA, Enlil's first born son by his half-sister Ninharsag (and therefore the Heir Apparent to Enlil). Even in the Hittite version, though, Adad is assisted by his older brother.

For our purposes, it appears that the Sumerian version is more pertinent, in that it provides additional detail to the war, in particular to the attempts by Zu / Kumarbi to take control of Enlil's Mission Control Center in Nippur. For it was there in the DIR.GA room, the most restricted, holy-of-holies room, where the vital celestial charts and orbital data panels -- the "Tablets of Destinies" -- were installed and maintained. Control of this sacred chamber could conceivably be used to control the fate of the Anunnaki on Earth as well as on Nibiru. In getting there, Zu apparently had help from Enki (who was never loath to put a bee in Enlil's bonnet). Enki, aware of Zu's ancestry (the grandson of Alalu), suggested to Enlil that Zu be allowed into his service.

"Your service let him enter, in the sanctuary, to the innermost seat, Let him be the one to block the way.

To the words that Enki spoke to him, the god [Enlil] consented. At the sanctuary Zu took up his position at the entrance to the chamber."

As Zu stayed by his post, he "constantly viewed Enlil, the father of the gods, the god of the Bond-Heaven-Earth [communications post?]... his celestial Tablet of Destinies Zu constantly viewed." Soon a scheme took shape. "The removal of Enlilship he conceives."

"I will take the celestial Tablet of Destinies; The decrees of the gods I will govern;
I will establish my throne, be master of the Heavenly Decrees; The IGIGI in their space I will command!"

"His heart having thus plotted aggression," Zu saw his chance one day as Enlil went to take a cooling swim. "He seized the Tablet of Destinies in his hands" and in his Bird "took off and flew to safety in the HUR.SAG.MU ("Mountain of the Sky-Chambers"). No sooner had this happened than everything came to a standstill:

"Suspended were the divine formulas; The lighted brightness petered out; silence prevailed.
In space, the IGIGI were confounded; The sanctuary's brilliance was taken off."

At first, "father Enlil was speechless", the latter a possible reference to communications being cut. But when Anu on Nibiru was informed of the coup, the order to capture Zu was clear. (It was a Zu coup!) There were, however, few volunteers to go chasing after Zu. The apparent reason was that Zu had also taken "Enlil's brilliance", a powerful weapon. It's not altogether clear what the weapon was, but one must suspect it was a bit more than a polished sling shot, something that the average Anunnaki might be loath to challenge.

But then, in the true spirit of a futuristic Hollywood script, the young hero, Ninurta stepped forward, ready to do battle for god Anu, country Earth, and Mom. Of course, he was given the slightest of

motivations by his mother who pointed out Enlil's loss of the throne was ultimately Ninurta's loss! Mom armed Ninurta with weapons equal to Zu's stolen weapons, including a few of her own design. (There's nothing like having a mother who keeps a lethal arsenal in her broom closet!)

The ensuing battle had all the earmarks of nuclear weapons, guided missiles, and fighter aircraft. Had Homo erectus occasioned to look up, he would undoubtedly have been impressed -- even if he hadn't had the slightest idea of what was going on. Ultimately, Ninurta defeated Zu, and in a subsequent trial was given the right to cut Zu's throat -- which he did. Forthwith.

However... As a condition for his volunteering to go after Zu, wily old Ninurta had extracted from the other Anunnaki, a promise to ensure that the vanquisher of Zu was appropriately rewarded:

"Thy name shall be the greatest in the Assembly of the Great Gods;
　　Among the gods, thy brothers, thou shall have no equal;
　　Glorified before the gods and potent shall be thy name."

While this is all well and good for the war hero, it had an unintended, undesirable effect. It planted the seed for future conflict by establishing Ninurta higher in the hierarchical order than even Enki. And while Ninurta was indeed Enlil's Legal Heir on Nibiru, having been born there, he was not necessarily the next in line on Earth! Thus the son of Enlil and a son of Enki were ultimately destined in the future to battle for control of the Earth. But such is still in the future. Try to be patient.

Meanwhile, back at the zoo, Zu (Kumarbi?), prior to his demise, had managed to impregnate a goddess of the mountain. It's the old soldier-off-to-the-war trick -- works almost every time. And in typical fashion, this dalliance led to the birth of a possible avenger, the "Stone God ULLIKUMMI.

Ullikummi grew up in secret, but eventually, the Sumerian Sun God UTU, a grandson of both Enki and Enlil, saw Ullikummi roaming the skies one day and informed Ninurta. Enlil's son promptly attacked Ullikummi, but at first to no avail. Even when his brother Adad joining the battle, Ninurta continued to be unsuccessful. The two then went to Enki in the Abzu, to seek an oracle according to "the old tablets with the words of fate". (Essentially they wanted some advice from the uncle known as the God of Wisdom.)

Enki realized that Zu / Kumarbi had created a monster, and Enki, himself, went to Enlil to warn him of the danger. Enki also brought a solution: "let them bring out the Olden Metal Cutter, and cut under the feet of Ullikummi the Stone God". Crippled, the Stone God was still defiant, even to the end when Ninurta caught up with him at sea and engaged him in a final battle. Ultimately, the Enlilites won this final phase of the War of the Olden Gods, what the Greeks called the Battle of the Titans. The meaning of the Greek word "Titan", incidentally, may appear obvious, but it is worth noting that the word, TI.TA.AN, in Sumerian means "Those Who in Heaven Live". This is rather precisely the designation of the Igigi led by Zu / Kumarbi.

****

Up to this point, other than references to Anunnaki colonies in the Tigris-Euphrates valley and South Africa, much of these Sumerian tales could apply to any number of locales. There is, for example, only minimal mention of any activity that might definitely connect the Anunnaki antics to the Annals of Earth. However, that is about to change. Suddenly the lives of Anunnaki and mankind are about to become irrevocably entwined. Suddenly, our very concept of what it means to be human and from whence we came, is about to be severely challenged. It all began with a mutiny. Not on the Bounty, mind you, but at the source of all the activity, the gold mines.

c. 270,000 B.C.E. Something on the order of 30 Sars (110,000 years) later, or about 40 Sars (144,000 years or 40 "counted periods") after the mining of the Abzu began, the Anunnaki toiling the minds did something quite extraordinary: They mutinied! From The Alta-Hasis Epic, we find:

"Inside the mountains, in the deeply cut shafts, the Anunnaki suffered the toil; excessive was their toil for forty counted periods.

[The Anunnaki] suffered the toil day and night, they were complaining, backbiting, grumbling in the excavations."

The Sumerian texts go on to relate in vivid detail the fact that the miners mutinied, and marched on Enlil's quarters in the middle of the night (apparently receiving night visitors being one of the joys of being Top Gun on Earth). Taking Enlil prisoner, the mutineers then demanded that Anu be sent a message and asked to come to Earth to negotiate. Enlil quickly obliged them, but upon Anu's arrival, Enlil called for a court-martial before the Great Anunnaki to be convened. Enlil, rather clearly, was not one of those diplomatic facilitators with consummate skills of negotiation and compromise.

At the court-martial, according to the texts, "Enki, Ruler of the Abzu, was also present." Enlil took this opportunity to accuse Enki of being the instigator of the mutiny. This didn't fly with the Great Anunnaki, even though it was certainly not beyond Enki to have planted a few seeds of discontent in order to get Enlil's goat (Enlil's goat being an award-winning goat, one that all the Anunnaki coveted). But then, not getting the support of Anu, Enlil offered his resignation: "Noble one, take away the office, take away the power; to Heaven will I ascend with you."

Anu, however, did not bite. Instead, he calmed Enlil, while at the same time expressed his understanding of the miner's hardships. Anu was, of course, playing the role of ruler/diplomat, attempting to offend no one and managing to take both sides at the same time. Not unexpectedly, he thus created a situation with little or no hope of a solution: Someone had to mine the gold, it was really tough on the Anunnaki miners, the mining process was indeed arduous, and yet, still, someone had to mine the gold. Ye olde vicious circle. The problem would simply not go away. Then, into this quandary, rushed Enki.

Enki "opened his mouth and addressed the gods." He and his Chief Medical Officer, his half- sister Ninti, had a plan: a brilliant, and simultaneously, brazen and outrageous plan:

"Let her create a Primitive Worker; and let him bear the yoke...
Let the Worker carry the toil of the gods, let him bear the yoke!

In the following one hundred lines of the Alta-Hasis text, and in several other "Creation of Man" texts that have been discovered in various states of preservation, the tale of the genetic engineering of Homo Sapiens has been told in amazing detail. Man, Homo sapiens sapiens, was to be created through the wonders of genetic engineering for the sole purpose of mining gold for the Anunnaki. The yoke was on Man! (Somehow, we always suspected something like this.)

To achieve this feat, Enki suggested that a "Being that already exists" -- Apewoman -- be used to create the Lulu Amelu ("The Mixed Worker"). This would be done by "binding" upon the less evolved beings, "the mold of the gods." It was time to mold the mitochondrial and nucleic DNA of Homo erectus (or possibly Archaic Homo sapiens) to evolve the Ape-man into a gold miner, complete, no doubt, with a jaw full of chewing tobacco and a pickax.

Where have we heard of this scenario before?

"And God said, Let us make man in our image, after our likeness...

"So God created man in his own image, in the image of God created he him; male and female created he them." [Genesis 1:26, 27]

If you've ever wondered why God said, Let "us" make man in "our" image... Now you know. Suddenly, the verse which makes absolutely no sense, becomes crystal clear. The "us" was Enki and Ninti, while the "our" was that of the Anunnaki. The Biblical version, therefore agrees with the Sumerian. And on the scientific front, the agreement is similarly precise. The Sumerian timing, for example, was perfect, the evolution of mankind beginning some 270,000 years ago. This, of course, is an agreeable compromise date between the different geneticists and paleoanthropologists immersed in the mtDNA debate.

Sumerian, Biblical, and Scientific sources agree on the beginning of mankind!

But before you identify the God of Genesis with Enki (whose "abode" is our solar system), note that it was the goddess Ninti who purified the "essence" of a young male Anunnaki and mixed it into the egg of an Apewoman." It was the goddess that implanted the fertilized egg into the womb of a female Anunnaki, and then when the "mixed creature" was born, it was Ninti who lifted him up and shouted: "I have created it! My hands have made it!" Not surprisingly, Enki and Ninti called their creation, Adapa, similar to the biblical, Adama. Eve, apparently, was the female Anunnaki! Maybe.

Irregardless of the exact identity of Adam and Eve, the "primitive worker" -- Homo sapiens -- had come onto the scene through a feat of genetic engineering and embryo-implant techniques. In effect the Anunnaki had taken a hand in the long process of evolution, jump-starting it and "creating" Man sooner than he might otherwise have evolved on his own. In effect the "missing link" in man's evolution turns out to be a feat of genetic engineering performed in an ancient laboratory of the Anunnaki ("Those who from heaven to earth came"). Suddenly we can explain why the progenitor of both Neanderthal and Cro-Magnon Man (Homo sapiens sapiens) appeared so soon on the scene, a mere million years after Homo erectus' initial foray into the wilds of Africa, Asia, and Australia.

It is, of course, worth mentioning that the creation of the "primitive worker" was easily 100,000 years before Neanderthal Man. As for Cro-Magnon Man's appearance, circa 90,000 B.C.E., the time frame is even later. The mitochondrial DNA dating is right on target, but the fossil remains of both Neanderthal and Cro-Magnon Man simply do not go back that far.

This variance, however, does not imply a serious problem, in that the "primitive worker", potentially the first in the Neanderthal-line, would not have left a lot of fossil remains for the benefit of paleoanthropologists in a later era, in that they would have been working (and probably dying) in the deep mines of South Africa. Furthermore their remains might have been disposed of by the Anunnaki in a fashion not conducive to becoming fossils later on. For these reasons, it is reasonable to assume that the "quantum leap" from Homo erectus to Neanderthal may have been due to the intervention of Enki, Ninti, and the Anunnaki.

One should also keep in mind that it is unlikely that God-Enki-Ninti would get it right on the first try. The first experiments in producing the "primitive worker" may very well have failed, but yielded enough information to continue the process, improving on each new attempt. According to the Sumerian texts, several kinks did in fact occur in the process. But then, after considerable trial and error, a mass-production process was launched, with fourteen at-a-time "birth goddesses" (female Anunnaki) being implanted with the genetically manipulated eggs of the Apewoman. Eventually, the process provided sufficient workers in the mines for the Anunnaki to retire (except for supervisory roles), and then later to work the land in Sumeria, the land between the Tigris and Euphrates rivers.

At the time, the "primitive workers" were still pretty crude: "When Mankind was first created, they knew not the eating of bread, knew not the dressing of garments, ate plants with their mouth like sheep, drank water from the ditch..." (Reminds me of some people I know in New

York City.) The workers were good enough for the purposes of the mines, but they were not a thing of beauty and joy forever. They still lacked the all-essential style and grace of later years.

But Enki was not yet finished. It was clear to him and Ninti that the use of young female Anunnaki to perform the roles of "birth goddesses" was not a long term solution. The Anunnaki were not eager to work in the mines, but giving birth in an assembly line fashion did not have a great deal more glory or desirability. Accordingly, unbeknownst to Enlil, and with the connivance of Ninti, Enki contrived to improve upon the "primitive worker", and give the new creature one more genetic twist: granting to the hybrid beings -- incapable of procreating, as all hybrids are (mules, e.g.) -- the ability to have offspring, the sexual "Knowing" for having children. And while the original Sumerian text of this tale has not yet been found, a number of Sumerian depictions of the event were discovered.

"And God blessed them, and God said unto them, Be fruitful and multiply, and replenish the earth, and subdue it..." [Genesis 1:28]

There is the suspicion that Enki continued the work of improving (i.e. evolving) the primitive worker over a long period of time. It is entirely conceivable that his and Ninti's first efforts produced mule-like Neanderthals (hybrids who were not procreating without the aid of the Anunnaki laboratory workers and female birth goddesses), then Neanderthals with the capability of procreating, and then in a second quantum leap, Cro-Magnon Man. The superior model might have then caused the first industrial lay off in human history with the Cro-Magnon Man replacing the Neanderthals in the mines, and with the early version of Homo sapiens sapiens discovering the distinct lack of unemployment benefits in the archaic world.

The Neanderthals (and later the Cro-Magnons) might also have occasionally left the mines of their own accord. In any case, the Neanderthals were soon roaming free in Africa, migrating, and then popping up all over in the fossil records, as they proceeded to "conquer" the rest of the world. And with their infusion of Anunnaki talents, skills, and genes (and quite possibly, tools), they probably had a much longer life expectancy than the other Homo erectus. The tools could easily have brought them into the Upper Paleolithic (blades, etc.), or just the Middle Paleolithic (when the newly freed workers would be aware of blades, and attempt to fashion a substitute). The paleontological evidence of Homo sapiens sapiens "outliving" and outperforming Homo erectus thus becomes clear.

It is also clear that the issue of "no intermixing" between the conquering Neanderthal (and later the Cro-Magnon invaders) -- with their superior genes, tools, etcetera -- and the conquered Homo erectus is quickly resolved as well. The Anunnaki had caused in the evolution of mankind a quantum leap, a clear distinction between what had gone before and a new breed. And this distinct difference was sufficient to keep any sexual intermixing to a minimum -- conceivably, even zero. Let's face it: How many humans develop a sexual yearning for chimpanzees?

The differences could, at least in the eyes of the Neanderthals and Cro-Magnons, have been as great. Furthermore, the lack of evidence of warfare between the species also makes sense, in that the vast superiority of the invaders made it clear to them that there was no competition, no fear of the Homo erectus as competitors, and thus no need for warfare. Moving onto an island prolific with monkeys is not likely to motivate a modern human inhabitant to declare war on the monkey population, i.e. no monkey holocaust. But the monkey population will just as surely go into serious decline as the human development of the island proceeds.

As this theory of an Enki/Ninti/Anunnaki genetic manipulation of the human species begins to register in your mind, you might take note of how many questions it answers. For example, in the twelve questions proposed at the end of the last Episode, note that virtually all are answered! (1) The Sumerians could have known about the cosmology of our solar system, because at some later date, the Anunnaki told their miners their history. Simple. (2) The concept that Nibiru somehow planted the "seed of life" on Earth is not as clear, but one at least recognizes that Nibiru did have life on it at the time. (There is also the realization that the Anunnaki may have had no motivation -- and there's no record that they ever did -- to confide in the Sumerians as to their thinking and private lives). Had the Nibiruans deliberately planted the seed of life on Earth, they may have chosen not to say why.

(3) The unusually slow mtDNA mutation rate of humans (as compared to other related species) could come from an infusion of Anunnaki genes. Furthermore, we have already commented on the longevity-implying-slow-progress theory as directly affecting the Anunnaki, and this would suggest a slow mtDNA mutation rate for the Anunnaki. It all falls together rather well. One can even quickly visualize the meaning of the phrase in Genesis 6:2: "the sons of God". In effect, this is a literal

statement! And, as we will soon discover, most of Genesis becomes literal in this way!

(4) The question of the Neanderthal and Cro-Magnon "outliving" the Homo erectus they replaced is answered (see above). (5) Homo sapiens sapiens migrating Out of Africa (sounds like a movie title) and "denying their ancestry" becomes clear. One can easily visualize a "primitive worker" visiting the local career counselor and learning that mining is just not his bag -- no real chance for advancement or meeting his innermost needs. And at the same time, dashing off to become a big-game hunter, a prolific gatherer, or real estate tycoon, such a creature might have been embarrassed at his ancestry and former employment. Small wonder he or she kept it a secret (even from the fossil hunters of a later era).

(6) The no-intermixing issue has also been resolved (see above), and (7) one can even give credence to man evolving the ability to speak. Certainly, the genes for the physical equipment to be able to speak could have come from the Anunnaki, and there is also the possibility that speech would be encouraged in the mines (at least, discussions on the conduct of work, and the dire need for the development of the world's first employee suggestion box).

(8) The Anunnaki creating Man for work in the South African mines clearly locates mtDNA Eve in southern Africa (Botswana, for example), and allows for any subsequent migration from this central point. Shortly, we will point out that a secondary, and on a time scale, later, focal point will be generated in the Middle East -- just as the modern scientists of such topics would find evidence for. (9) There is even the possibility that Becky Cann's statement that the migrating Homo sapiens sapiens in leaving on a jet plane for Australia "knew exactly where they were going", can be explained. The Anunnaki could easily have told them.

The question (10) on races has not quite been answered, but there is the possibility that the different models of "primitive worker" created by Man may have resulted in significant variations, which later became type cast. There is also the possibility that some races did not make it (not to mention the fact that many offshoots might have been eliminated by the Deluge -- the latter subject to be discussed in great detail in a subsequent Episode). There is, finally, the "Tower of Babel" biblical episode which may account for a great deal of linguistic variations.

(11) Also, the potential for Cro-Magnon having superior evolutionary staying power over the Neanderthal may easily have derived from their acquiring such superiority from Enki and Ninti's tweaking of the "primitive worker". As to exactly what happened some 40,000 to 35,000 years ago to account for the rather abrupt disappearance of Neanderthal Man... Well, we can't give all the answers away. Besides, it's still in the future. There much more of a story to tell.

(12) But before we proceed, let us not forget that the half-sister rule of Abraham and Sarah's era clearly derives directly from the Anunnaki's rules of succession. As to the why of such rules, the Anunnaki were not into explaining themselves to their slaves.

Meanwhile, back at the mines, the Anunnaki who had been laid off from their work, were a bit at loose ends. Enlil, recognizing that an idle Anunnaki mind is an authority-questioning Anunnaki mind, took immediate action. Inviting the unemployed Anunnaki back to Mesopotamia, a virtual vacation paradise after the Abzu, Enlil thoughtfully put them to work digging ditches, raising dikes, and deepening canals. Theoretically, this was a fast improvement over their lot in Africa. However, it didn't take the Anunnaki long to yearn for another version of "undocumented workers" for whom they could assign all the dirty jobs (and at the same time, avoid paying social security taxes). Enlil (no longer a fan of house arrest) was quick to agree with the Mesopotamian Anunnaki that the creatures with the thick black hair (man) were sorely needed in Mesopotamia as well as in the Abzu.

Naturally, Enlil was not allowed to just take the "primitive workers" from Enki's mines without a fight from the ruler of the Abzu. But eventually Enlil did his own version of a pre-emptive strike, and took many of the workers back to his place in Mesopotamia. You'll never guess what Enlil (and the Sumerian texts) called their little paradise-away-from-home! You guessed E.DIN? Okay, so you're beginning to catch onto the strange logic of all of this. But!!! If you're so smart...

Did you ever wonder why there are two creation of man epics in the Bible? If not, why not? Obviously, in addition to the latter verses of the first chapter of Genesis, there follows another version in the second chapter of Genesis, after God had taken to resting on the seventh day. It would appear that the first creation was for the miners of the Abzu, those created by Enki and Ninti in the image of the Anunnaki. The second creation of man was based on another motivation:

"And every plant of the field before it was in the earth, and every herb of the field before it grew: for the Lord God had not caused it to rain upon the earth [apparently spending all his time irrigating where it didn't rain], and there was not a man to till the ground." [Genesis 2: 5]

Rather precisely, the Bible makes it clear in this verse that Enlil's E.DIN did not have the slave labor for which the Anunnaki craved. The solution? A little raiding party, a man-rustling foray into the Abzu, to acquire someone other than the Anunnaki to "till the ground" of E.DIN.

"And the Lord God planted a garden eastward in Eden; and there he put the man whom he had formed [i.e. stolen from Enki's camp]. And out of the ground made the Lord God to grow every tree that is pleasant to the sight [with man tilling the soil, obviously it takes man and God to make a tree], and good for food; the tree of life also in the midst of the garden, and the tree of knowledge of good and evil." [Genesis 2:8-9]

This raises one of the most important aspects of the Sumerian and Genesis versions of the earliest times of man. In the Sumerian version, it was the Lord God, Enki (with help from his half-sister Ninti), who created man and woman in their image, and it was the Lord God, Enlil, who planted a garden eastward in Eden! There are, as a minimum, two gods, whose adventures are described in Genesis. The Hebrews, in their quest to attribute all creation to a single god, condensed the activities of the GODS into the character of a single deity.

As will become even more apparent in the continuing of these Annals, there are really TWO gods of Genesis. Only by understanding this can one hope to understand the early chapters of Genesis. The simple truth is that if one demands that there be only one god of Genesis, then one is faced with a picture of that same god, who is continually reversing himself.

For example, according to the Bible, God made man and placed him in Eden. Then he threw him and his spouse out for no good reason (more on this later). Then God repented "that he had made man" [Genesis 6:6] and determined to destroy him and his progeny. Then God changed his mind and decided to let Noah and his brood survive. Then God became upset with Noah's descendants and felt compelled to confuse his language. And so forth. As one progresses through the Bible, one is forced to question if the Biblical god has a multiple personality. Or is just psychotic. For the described Biblical god flips back and forth, is notorious for taking sides, and is radically unpredictable.

BUT! If there is more than one god in the proceedings, then things begin to make sense. Different peoples might choose one god as their favorite deity, and then defend his alleged superiority to the death. Which is precisely what the Hebrews did. They picked one God (as we shall see, Enlil and his heirs), attributed all of the good deeds of other gods to their god (in effect, ignoring the contributions of Enlil's rival, Enki et al), and then even went to the extreme to deny that any other gods ever existed.

The single-god hypothesis proposed by Genesis just doesn't make it! Once we let go of this artifact of a life-long brain-washing by the single-god fanatics, we find ourselves able to derive from the Biblical accounts a wealth of information. There's nothing like a basic truth to lighten our load.

Keep in mind one thing, however: A belief in a single deity, a supreme, divine being who created the universe, is NOT being questioned here. What is being questioned is that the "God of Genesis" is a single god. In fact, what is being strongly suggested (as a means of understanding the Book of Genesis) is that the God of Genesis is really an edited condensation of the "gods": Enki, Enlil, and possibly Ninti. Other Anunnaki also occasionally play a role, but primarily, it is the rival camps of Enki and Enlil that get all of the press in Genesis and the later books of the Bible.

Before we press on, we might note that nestled between Genesis 2:9 (when God made Eden) and Genesis 2:15 (when God "took the man, and put him into the garden of Eden to dress it and keep it.") there is the following very important and puzzling group of verses:

"And a river went out of Eden to water the garden: and from thence it was parted, and became into four heads. The name of the first is Pison: that is it which compasseth the whole land of Havilah, where there is gold; And the gold of that land is good; there is bdellium and the onyx stone. And the name of the second river is Gihon; the same is it that compasseth the whole land of Ethiopia. And the name of the third river is Hiddekel; that is it which goeth toward the east of Assyria. And the fourth river is Euphrates." [Genesis 2:10-14]

Let's see if we've got this right:

God created the Heaven and the Earth, created the flowers and the herbs, established night and day, created the creatures, formed man "of the dust of the ground", planted a garden in Eden, and then announced with great fanfare: "There's gold in them thar hills!"

Does this strike you as God having a strange sense of priorities? Does the God of creation seem overly concerned with the yellow metal? Is mentioning the rivers a means by which God suggests that Man pan for gold? Why is it that gold seems to play such an important part in the Annals of Man?

Of course, it all makes sense if one buys into the Sumerian texts and recalls that the "Prime Cause" for the Anunnaki to be on the Earth in the first place was for the location, mining, processing and shipping to Nibiru of gold in large quantities. What exactly "bdellium" constitutes is not clear from the text, but I would suggest it is the Elixir of Life, while the onyx stone is the Philosopher's Stone (the most sought-after elements of the Alchemists' trade). Bdellium" might also include the "rare earth elements" closely associated with gold in the Periodic Table of Chemistry, i.e. Ruthenium, Rhodium, Palladium, Silver, Osmium, Iridium, and Platinum. It is these seven additional elements, found in the same ores as gold, which may constitute the all important quest for gold. This is the same "gold fever" initiated by the Anunnaki, and carried on down through the ages by Man.

Stop and think about it: Why is gold so incredibly important to Man and his history? No other precious metal has the appeal, even though elements such as silver may have improved industrial uses. The fact remains that gold is the premier substance on which most of history revolves. The Sumerian texts do not explain why the Anunnaki were so gold hungry, but the evidence is prolific that they were after it in spades (the preferred means of mining gold). Furthermore, the Abzu was the place to get it, and the current residents of South Africa were not the first to work the mines.

In fact, realizing that sites of abandoned ancient mines might indicate where gold could be found, the Anglo-American Corporation, South Africa's leading mining corporation, in the 1970s (of the current era, C.E.) engaged archaeologists to look for such mines. Discoveries in Swaziland and other sites in South Africa indicated extensive mining areas with shafts to depths of fifty feet. Stone objects and charcoal remains established dates of 35,000, 46,000, and 60,000 B.C.E. for these sites! The archaeologists and anthropologists who joined in dating the finds came to the conclusion that mining technology was used in southern Africa "during much of the period subsequent to 100,000 B.C.E.!" In

September 1988, a team of international physicists came to South Africa to verify the age of human habitats in Swaziland and Zululand. The most modern dating techniques indicated an age of 80,000 to 115,000 years for those areas with evidence of ancient mining.

If this doesn't fortify your resolve in believing the Anunnaki and their gold quest were for real, consider the fact that Zulu legends of the most ancient gold mines of Monotapa in southern Zimbabwe claim these mines were worked by "artificially produced flesh and blood slaves created by the First People." These slaves, the Zulu legends recount, "went into battle with the Ape-Man" when "the great war star appeared in the sky." [Indaba My Children, by the Zulu medicine man Credo Vusamazulu Mutwa.]

It doesn't take a creative or imaginative rocket scientist to conjecture Nibiru to be "the great war star", that the "artificially produced flesh and blood slaves" were the jump-started Homo erectus, or that "the First People" were the Anunnaki. Everything just fits!

There are, however, despite our honest endeavor to answer all of the questions prompted by the first four Episodes of these Annals, additional questions arising from our newly found knowledge:

1.   What happened some 40,000 to 35,000 years ago to account for the demise of the Neanderthals and the unchallenged ascendency of the Cro-Magnons? Were the Neanderthals part of an Anunnaki factory recall? Is there any possibility of another recall in our own immediate future?

2.   Will the black haired humans enjoy their sojourn in E.DIN? Will they pine away for the mines back home in Swaziland? Will they find farming and the glories of dressing and keeping E.DIN to their taste? Will they freely eat of every tree of the garden, save one? Will they get their forest merit badge?

3.   Will Enlil find out that his newly acquired slaves, the advanced models of Homo sapiens sapiens, have the ability to create little sapiens of their own? Can Enlil possibly miss the fact that there are all these little sapiens running about? Will Enlil insist on being called their Godfather? Will the art of puns be introduced in time for the reader to understand the last joke? (*)

4.   Will Enki and Ninti get into trouble for their creativity creating creative creatures such as man and woman? Will Anu ground them? Will Enlil have a cat? Will the female get blamed for everything?

5.   Why is it Man and Woman can eat of every tree of the garden save two, "the tree of life and the tree of knowledge of good and evil"? Why are the trees with the most intriguing names, off-limits to the gardeners who are maintaining them? And why is it, immediately after mentioning for the first time these wondrous trees, that the Book of Genesis then launches off into a discussion of rivers and the fact that "thar's gold in them thar hills!"? Is there a connection here? Or are we barking up the wrong tree?

6.   Why was gold so important to the Anunnaki? Could mankind similarly benefit by wise use of the gold? Are the Anunnaki likely to share it with us?

7.   And in looking ahead to the next exciting Episode, who in the world are the Nefilim of Genesis 6: 4? Giants!? What about the Yankees? Don't they deserve some mention as well? What in the world am I talking about!?

8.   Will there be no end to these questions?

For the answers to these and other exciting possibilities, stay tuned for the next thrill-packed Episode. Rest assured that if you thought the above was intriguing, the next Episodes will be even more astounding! To paraphrase John Paul Jones, "We have not yet begun to rattle the cages of outrageous fortune!"

(*) "Hanging is too good for anyone who makes puns. They should be drawn and quoted." [Fred Allen]

The Library of ialexandriah

The following articles are off the Internet, and some are copyright as per notices with the articles. They are a sample of what is available on these matters.

Genesis

The first book of the Bible is a fascinating document. On the one hand, it is the basis for many religions -- either as a matter of faith or one of historical precedence. At the same time, it is a complete history spanning eons, but still capable of telling unique stories of individuals. In the original Hebrew, it is a masterpiece of Sacred Geometry -- wherein it incorporates the Geometry of Alphabets while recreating the story of mankind. But it is also the subject of a massive number of interpretations (and probably misinterpretations as well). In this latter respect, it is often more that of "a puzzle wrapped in an enigma."

There is, for example, in the King James version a distinction between "God" and the "Lord God". Chapter One is exclusively the province of "God", the creator of the heaven and the earth, while beginning at Genesis 2:4, the Lord God is supposedly in charge. It is almost as if "God" was the universal creator, while the "Lord God" was an earth-based deity. In fact, it was when (or after) God was resting on the "seventh day" that the Lord God began the "generations" on a whole new regimen. God created man in his image, and the Lord God used a dusty clay model. It's possible they're the same being, but the evidence is not strong in that regard. On the contrary...

There are the paradoxes, the apparent contradictions, the strange twists and turns of first one thing, and then, curiously, the seemingly opposite. Consider one the most obvious:

"And God said, Let us make man in our image, after our likeness..." "So God created man in his own image, in the image of God created he him; male and female created he them." -- Genesis 1: 26-27 [emphasis added]

Why the plural tense? Are we talking about the "royal we"? If so, then why was the proposal to make man in the plural tense, but the actual act, in the singular? Basically, we must ask, "What do you mean, "we", white man?" All of which is also applicable to:

"And the Lord God said, Behold the man is become as one of us, to know good and evil; and now, lest he put forth his hand, and take also of the tree of life, and eat, and live for ever;" -- Genesis 3: 22 [emphasis added]

Become one of us, become a God? Man? Eat of the Tree of Life and live forever? It might be justifiable as punishment to send Man packing, but why bring up the tree of life thing? Obviously the tree's fruit was an eye opener for the naked couple, but...?

"And it came to pass, when men began to multiply on the face of the earth, [and presumably to do long division as well] and daughters were born unto them, That the sons of God saw the daughters of men that they were fair; and they took them wives of all which they chose." -- Genesis 6: 1-2

I can appreciate the daughters being fair, but "the sons of God" is not at all clear -- at least in the context of there being only one god. But if there were two or more... Then the "us" is clear, even if only one "he" was the final version of created man. And if more than two, why not have sons of God? (And presumably daughters?) A pantheon!

Biblical Scholars, including the Jesuits of the Catholic Church, have reluctantly had to admit that there must have been at least two gods in the story of Genesis. In fact, if the role model for Genesis was the Sumerian Epic of Creation, then it's pretty much of a done deal that there was a whole flock of Gods and Goddesses in the time before man. Not necessarily before the Chapter One Creator God, but by the time of the Garden, Adam and Eve, and so forth. This group of "lesser" gods and goddesses -- as distinct from the Creator God -- may indeed have been troubled by the possibility of man inadvertently joining their ranks by eating of the Tree of Life. They might have also been concerned about man's attempts to build new and wondrous things, such as:

"And the Lord said, Behold, the people is one, and they have all one language; and this they begin to do; and now nothing will be restrained from them, which they have imagined to do. Go to, let us go down, and there confound their language, that they may not understand one another's speech." -- Genesis 11: 6-7

If the local gods and goddesses are not omnipotent, but simply superior beings, then the concern for man's getting "uppity" makes sense. Otherwise, why would a tower built to reach heaven give any concern to a true Supreme Being. Did God actually think the Tower of Babel might reach the heavens? If your kid tells you of his or her decision to build a Giza size pyramid in the backyard, is this going to cause you a great deal of worry?

Alternatively, was it simply a "tower" or something a bit more? Like a means of lifting off the planet? Ah, then, now there's a case of concern! Because the key phrase is: "nothing will be restrained from them, which they have imagined to do."

This latter phrase hasn't received a lot of press, even though it has been echoed in the words of Jesus Christ, i.e.

"Therefore I say unto you, What things soever ye desire, when ye pray, believe that ye receive them, and ye shall have them." -- Mark 11:24

But the idea is probably noteworthy. [The latter statement is the Grand Prize Winner for the Biggest Understatement within this website! Congratulations to the winner!]

Obviously, much of the early chapters in Genesis are perplexing in their interpretation. If one ignores the two creation of man stories -- Genesis 1:27 (the image thing) and Genesis 2:7 (the dust one) -- you've still got a lot of reversals and inconsistencies. For example:

[God placed Man in the Garden of Eden -- then threw him out. In the process, He blessed Man (Genesis 1:28), and then cursed him (Genesis 3:17-19), as in:

"...cursed is the ground for thy sake; in sorrow shalt thou eat of it all the days of thy life; Thorns also and thistles shall it bring forth to thee; and thou shalt eat the herb of the field; In the sweat of thy face shalt thou eat bread, till thou return unto the ground; for out of it wast thou taken; for dust thou art, and unto dust shalt thou return."

Hey man, you're dirt! On the other hand...

"Unto Adam also and to his wife did the Lord God make coats of skins, and clothed them." Genesis 3:21

Just as God show Adam and Eve the door, He gives them a door prize!?

[He cursed Cain...

"Now art thou cursed from the earth... When thou tillest the ground; it shall not henceforth yield unto thee her strength; a fugitive and vagabond shalt thou be in the earth." -- Genesis 4:11-12

And then He protected Cain!!!

"...Therefore whosoever slayeth Cain, vengeance shall be taken on him sevenfold. And the Lord set a mark upon Cain, lest any finding him should kill him." -- Genesis 4:15

[Man fell out of favor...

"And it repented the Lord that he had made man on the earth, and it grieved him at his heart." -- Genesis 6:6

But then...

"But Noah found grace in the eyes of the Lord." -- Genesis 6:8

We're either talking about a very inconsistent God -- even one possibly schizophrenic. Either than or something else.

The simplest answer is often the best. Therefore, how about the idea that there was more than one local god? This does not discount the possibility of a truly Supreme, Singular Being from creating the heaven and the earth, but the down-to-earth activities are inevitably the work -- and possibly the conflict -- of two or more gods.

Over the last fifty years or so, there have been found and interpreted, libraries of clay tablets from the Sumerian Civilization, circa 4,000 to 2,000 B.C.E. The Sumerian texts, specifically the Epic of Creation is essentially the long version of Genesis (or Genesis is the edited, condensed Reader's Digest version, or the executive summary of the Sumerian account. The Sumerian texts are on six tablets, with a 7th glorifying God -- akin to the 7 days of Genesis. The Epic details the creation of the planets (aka the firmament), and the separation of the "waters". (Keep in mind also that the Sumerian texts described the creation and some characteristics of Uranus, Neptune and Pluto -- with modern astronomy finding these planets only in the last 150 years or so.)

The latter brings up the critical question of: "How was the Sumerian knowledge obtained (who told them!)?

According to the texts: the Anunnaki (i.e. "Those who from Heaven to Earth Came").

Are there any more questions?

Okay. But pay attention here. This is a crash course. According to the Sumerian texts, a deposed leader of a planet called Nibiru discovered gold on Earth. This might not sound like a big deal for a species obviously capable of long range interplanetary travel, but gold figures heavily into the situation. Recall that:

In Genesis, after God made the heaven (the firmament) and the Earth, divided the waters, created grass, herbs and trees, placed lights in the firmament, created the fishes, the fowl, the great whales and animals, made man in his image, rested on the seventh day; after which he watered the earth (Genesis 2:6), formed man (again?) of the dust of the ground and breathed life into him (such that he became a living soul -- Genesis 2:7), created the Garden of Eden and placed man in it (Genesis 2:8), then grew the tree of life in the midst of the garden, and the tree of knowledge of good and evil (Genesis 2:9), arranged for four rivers, one to irrigate the garden (Genesis 2:10), and immediately thereafter (Genesis 2:11) announced, "Thar's Gold in Them Thar Hills"!

Strange. There is no mention of copper, aluminum, or carbon... Just... gold. Gold, apparently, is very important! Biblically, as well as to the Anunnaki -- the latter apparently spacefarers from the planet, Nibiru.

Again, according to the texts, thousands of years after the earth gold discovery, the gold rush began in earnest. The Anunnaki in charge was named EA (Nudimmud), or Enki ("Lord of Earth" -- EN, lord; KI, earth). Enki was an engineer/scientist. He established a base at the headwaters of the Persian Gulf, at Eridu (now considerably inland due to the sediment build up), in order to acquire gold from sea water.

[The fact the Anunnaki put an engineer in charge should give us considerable pause.]

Roughly 29,000 years later (greater than the time for the precession of the equinoxes -- and a strong implication of the Anunnaki extremely long lifetimes), it became apparent that acquiring gold from sea water was not living up to expectations. Anu (the head honcho of Nibiru) and his heir-

apparent, Enlil ("Lord of the Command") arrived on the scene to set things straight.

Therein begin the earth portion of the continuing sibling rivalry saga of Enki and Enlil. One was the first-born son of Anu, and the other the first-born son of Anu and his half-sister. Remember the tale of Abraham, Sarah, Ismael, and Isaac? Same drill. Enlil had it over Enki (just as Isaac had it over Ismael), and their rivalry would last for some 450,000 years -- give or take an eon. Talk about carrying a grudge!

The Compromise Plan was to mine the gold. Enki was placed in charge of mining South Africa, while Enlil took over the administrative duties in Sumer. Thousands of years later, more Anunnaki began arriving, opening mines, and creating boom towns. (See the movie: Paint Your Spaceship.)

This was not a sterling plan, however. [pardon the pun] There were wars and mutinies. Turns out the Anunnaki are not into tens of thousands of years of working the mines -- even for gold. Enlil was then taken hostage, whereupon he blamed Enki (naturally!). But Anu knew better (it's the "Father knows best" syndrome). The problem was that mining was hard work -- and no fringe benefits for the last 130,000 years or so.

But Enki had a solution. He proposed to cross breed the Anunnaki with some local beasts known as Homo erectus, and make them do the work. Everybody agreed. (Well, all of the Anunnaki.) Enki's proposal was to combine DNAs -- i.e. create man in the image of the Anunnaki. Enki and his half-sister, Ninhursag (Ninti) began a program of genetic engineering and created ADAPA ("the mixed worker") or ADAMA. Ninti, given the job of carrying the creation to term, was able to announce, "I have created it!"

After Ninti's first born, the team resorted to 14 Birth Goddesses to begin an assembly line birthing operation for the new mixed workers. Unfortunately, the ADAPA was a hybrid -- i.e., he could not procreate. So this plan worked for a while.

But the assembly line goddesses found the program somewhat arduous. Assembly line birthing has never been what it's cracked up to be. For the goddesses it was less than appealing -- not a whole lot better than mining. Thus in a second act of creation of man [Ah, so! Two creation stories!], Enki and Ninti created a man and woman who could procreate. Enki just didn't tell Enlil about the new models. [The plot thickens.]

Meanwhile, Enlil had decided he wanted his own undocumented workers to do the ditch digging and crop raising in Mesopotamia. So he placed some of Enki and Ninti's creations in a place called in the Sumerian texts, E.DIN. To tend the garden, and the trees. Enlil, however, still thought they were hybrids and incapable of procreating, whereas Enki had sold him the new models. Boy was Enlil surprised! For, of course, the new state of (love) affairs eventually became obvious! These two had been eating of the Tree of Life! And for this crime, Enlil threw them out of the Garden -- the ultimate act in party pooping.

This then is the key! The solution to the Biblical paradoxes is that there were (at least) two gods -- and for the most part, working from contradictory agendas. In fact, most of the following history is based on the rivalry between Enki and Enlil, with the rest of the Anunnaki being split in their agendas as to who to support next.

According to the Sumerian texts, the Number One God was Anu (MARDUK in the Babylonian version), while in the creation of Man, Enki was God. The Lord God referred to either Enlil ("Lord of the Command") or Enki ("Lord of Earth"). Enki made man, Enlil created the Garden of Eden. Enki was the "serpent" who genetically engineered man so he could procreate (eat of the tree of knowledge of good and evil). Enlil is the God who threw man out of the garden, and Enki who clothed him. Enlil took Abel's offering, but ignored Cain's, cast Cain out and cursed him; Enki gave him his passport to freedom. The other players are identified in the Sumerian Family Tree.

The "sons of God" (not the Lord God), the "giants in the earth", were the Anunnaki who found the female half-breeds to their liking. Sumerian texts talk about the Anunnaki sons breeding with human women, and creating "mighty men of renown." Enlil hated it and vowed to kill off man. As luck would have it, he got help. The Deluge and Flood.

Roughly 11,600 B.C.E., Nibiru had a close encounter of the most important kind with Earth, triggering the ice cap of Antarctica to slide off and swamp the place. The Anunnaki had seen it coming and hauled ass while Enlil demanded that the humans not be forewarned! Enki by subterfuge saved Noah, the latter also known as Ziusudra (Sumerian) or Utnapishtim (Babylonian). Noah also saved the animals, the fowl, his family, and a fair number of laborers on the Ark. Enki told Noah to tell the city folk that he's building a boat to journey away from Enlil, who is mad at him and is causing untold misery -- and the town folk are only too eager to help build the Ark. ("Noah," by the way, means Respite. Things had been altogether too dry on earth prior to the Deluge and Flood.)

And of course, it was Enlil who did the Tower of Babel gig (about 3400 B.C.E.). Enlil is definitely not a fan of man! Even the stories of Abraham begin to make sense. Isaac and Ishmael are simply a reprise of the Enlil and Enki drama -- the drama which about 2000 B.C.E. flourished into all out war.

Abraham (as noted in the Chronicles of Earth) was the commander of an elite military, calvary force. In rescuing Lot, with his 318 well trained and armed men, Abraham was in the employ of Enlil. And with such credentials, Abraham, upon arriving in Egypt was able to immediately go before the Pharaoh -- which was not the privilege of most shepherds!

But the dramatic climax came at Sodom and Gomorrah, where Enlil's son went over the edge and used nuclear weapons to obliterate two cities in conflict with Enlil (a "grievous sin" from one point of view). The result was not only their fiery end, but anyone exposed to the blast was either incinerated or turned into a pillar of salt. Unfortunately, the fallout was even more grievous, in that the Sumerian Civilization met its end as a result of its being downwind from ground zero.

Now... Is any of the above, legitimate?

Basically, yes. The entire scenario is based on the Sumerian texts, and the thoughtful and insightful consideration of numerous scholars, including Zecharia Sitchin, Laurence Gardner, and many others. It is also based on hard science. In the latter category there is the evidence concerning:

The advent of Neanderthals and Cro-Magnon man (particularly in the timing of their appearances and evolutionary timescales);

The identification of the ancestry of Adam and Eve, from mitochondria DNA and the male equivalent;

An understanding of the varying lifetimes of The Adam's Family and their descendants, and the Sumerian King List ("Before the Flood" and thereafter); Comparative Religions

The identification of Adam as "Adama"; E.DIN as Eden, Enoch as Enmendaranna; Lamech as Ubar-tutu; Noah as Ziusudra, etceteras;

The fact of the Sumerian Civilization suddenly having all of the firsts: (aka The Me, which included: writing, law, proverbs, priests, animal husbandry, and genetic engineering of crops), and agriculture returning after the Flood (around 11,500 B.C.E.) in the highlands instead of the -- flooded -- valleys).

The gods of the ancient Egyptian Civilization: Ptah, Ra, Shu and Tefnut, Geb, Seth and Nephtys, Osiris and Isis, Horus, Thoth -- all being identical with their Sumerian counterparts, and the dating of Ra after the flood, Ptah's rebuilding, the creation of the Sphinx circa 10,000 B.C.E. (the Great Pyramid having been constructed earlier); and even

The early MesoAmerican Civilization, where the precursors to the Incas (the latter being the race immediately preceding the Dinkas and the Dos) created in what must have been a hell-of-a-place to start one, a civilization. The Andes was not an agricultural region, such as the Tigris, Euphrates, Nile, Indus valleys, but on the other hand, there was in abundance: gold and tin (the latter a critical ingredient in bronze). The Andes location was also at a high elevation in case of high water!

There is just too much evidence not to believe the plausibility of the above. But if you want more detail, simply refer to the Annals of Earth. The evidence is astounding!

But there is also an unanswered question in all of the above. What is so all-fired important about gold? (Besides the fact that it's "god" with an "l" inserted.)

In a word (or two), gold is the source for the ORME, the Star Fire, the "What is it?" of the Egyptian Book of the Dead, the "white powder of gold" of the Ha Qabala, the key ingredient in the long lives and powers of the Anunnaki -- and by implication of their step-children, the members of the human race. Gold is one route to the Tree of Life, as well as The Tree of Knowledge of Good and Evil. Gold is the premier example of the Precious Metals (gold, silver, rhodium, iridium, platinum, palladium, osmium, and ruthenium).

Genesis, therefore, is the story of such magnitude and majesty as to stun the imagination.

Genesis is, truly, "the origin, or mode of formation or generation," of humans for whom "nothing will be restrained from them, which they have imagined to do."

Library of ialexandriah

Anunnaki

Updated 22 August 2003

Genesis 6:1-4 reads:

"And it came to pass, when men began to multiply on the face of the earth, and daughters were born unto them, That the sons of God saw the daughters of men that they were fair; and they took them wives of all which they chose... There were nephilim in the earth in those days; and also after that, when the sons of God came in unto the daughters of men, and they bare children to them, the same became mighty men which were of old, men of renown." [emphasis added]

Nephilim is often translated as "giants", a legitimate and appropriate interpretation, but one which may be only partially accurate. A better definition might be "those who came down", "those who descended", or "those who were cast down." The Anunnaki of ancient Sumerian texts is similarly defined as "those who from heaven to earth came". Sitchin [1], Gardner [2], and Bramley [3] have all identified the Nephilim as the Anunnaki, more specifically, essentially the rank and file.

Virtually all open-minded historical and theological scholars agree the Old Testament's book of Genesis was extracted from the older Sumerian records, if only because of the similarity in their Comparative Religions. The Enuma Elish, the Sumerian Epic of Creation, and Genesis have a variety of common elements. Stories of a Great Flood and Deluge, among other stories, are also common to both Sumerian and Biblical accounts. An inevitable conclusion is that the Anunnaki were as real as Noah, Moses or Abraham.

Laurence Gardner [2] has written: "Every item of written and pictorial attestation confirms that the ancient Sumerians were absolutely sincere about the existence of the Anunnaki, and those such as Enki, Enlil, Nin-khursag and Inanna fulfilled earthly functions with designated community duties. They were patrons and founders; they were teachers and justices; they were technologists and kingmakers. They were jointly and severally venerated as archons and masters, but there were certainly not idols of religious worship as the ritualistic gods of subsequent cultures became. In fact, the word which was eventually translated to become 'worship' was avod, which meant quite simply, 'work'. The Anunnaki presence may baffle historians, their language may confuse linguists and their advanced techniques may bewilder scientists, but to dismiss them is foolish. The Sumerians have themselves told us precisely who the Anunnaki were, and neither history nor science can prove otherwise."

The Sumerian records recorded in great detail the stories of the Anunnaki, and among these, that of Enki, Enlil, Ninki, Inanna, Utu, Ningishzida, Marduk, and many others. Chief among these stories was the continuing conflict between Enki and Enlil, the sons of the supreme god of the time, Anu. Much of ancient human history, and the Biblical Genesis, can be explained as the militant differences between these two half-brothers, and how they affected the life of all sentient beings on Earth.

But the Anunnaki were more than just a pair of squabbling half-brothers. They were the council of Gods and Goddesses, who periodically met to consider their future actions with respect to each other, and probably as a smaller, nondescript item on their agenda, the fate of mankind. The Anunnaki, depending upon the context, were the Nephilim, the gods that Abraham's father, Terah, (according to the book of Joshua) was reputed to have served, the fallen angels, the lesser individuals of the race from which Anu, Enki, Enlil, Inanna and the other notables had sprung, and the "judges" over the question of life and death. They were in fact the bene ha-elohim, which translates as "the sons of the gods", or equally likely, "the sons of the goddesses." For example, from Psalm 82:

> *"Jehovah takes his stand at the Council of El to deliver judgment among the elohim." "You too are gods, sons of El Elyon, all of you."*

The Anunnaki have also been equated with the "Watchers" (who are also mentioned in the books of Daniel and Jubilees), i.e. "Behold a watcher and an holy one came down from heaven." -- Daniel 4:13

According to Zecharia Sitchin [1] and his interpretation of ancient Sumerian texts, the Anunnaki were extraterrestrials (aka "angels"?), who were an extremely long-lived race, potentially living as long as 500,000 years. Laurence Gardner [2] reduces this to more on the order of 50,000 years, and notes specifically that the Anunnaki were not immortal. He point out that no records are currently extant which relates to their natural deaths, but the violent deaths of Apsu, Tiamat, Mummu, and Dumu-zi are provided in some detail. (Sitchin and Gardner also disagree on the date of the Great Deluge/Flood; Sitchin assuming a time frame of 11,000 B.C.E., while Gardner assumes one of 4,000 B.C.E.)

Sitchin's book, The 12th Planet, published in 1976 was the first modern volume to begin to describe the Anunnaki, their arrival on Earth supposedly some 485,000 years ago, and from where they had come -- a planet called Nibiru. Sitchin believes Nibiru to be in an orbit about our sun, but in a strongly elliptical orbit which requires 3,600 Earth years to make a complete orbit. Nibiru's perihelion (closest point of approach to the Sun) is thought to be within the main asteroid belt between Mars and Jupiter, at a distance from the Sun of approximately 2.75 A.U. (an A.U. being the distance from the Sun to the Earth). (the Annals of Earth include a detailed description of how Nibiru created the asteroid belt by destroying a planet, Tiamat, in roughly the same orbit, and which created the Earth in the aftermath, the Earth being a remnant of the greater, destroyed planet.)

Nibiru is not known to modern astronomy primarily due to the extreme elliptical nature of its orbit and the fact its aphelion (furthest point in the planet's orbit from the Sun) is more than eight times the distance from the Sun to the planet Pluto (the latter being some 40 A.U. away, and thus the former, some 320 A.U. distant). Furthermore, Nibiru may be now far out in deep space and unlikely to be detected. (Or close by, e.g. Planet X.)

While Sitchin and Gardner may disagree with the extent of the long lives of the Anunnaki, it is clear that these gods and goddesses, baring accidents or "Anunnaki-cide", lived a very long time. It has also been theorized that because of their long lives, they do not quite move in "the fast lane" -- at least to the extent humans do.

This could be fundamentally important in that, quite possibly, the human life span, while enormously brief as compared to the Anunnaki gods and goddesses, might nevertheless be compensated by the humans possessing the ability to achieve a great deal in a relatively short time. The creativity of a shortened, and thus highly motivated lifespan is likely to be enormously greater than that of a god or semi-god resting on their laurels. This may also relate to the idea of why the gods and goddesses of the Anunnaki even bother with mankind. Humans may, on the one hand, act as workers to accomplish the Anunnaki's agenda, but an accelerated creativity may be well worth the trouble for the Anunnaki to manage a crew as motley as the human race.

But the connection between humans and the Anunnaki is much more profound than that of masters and slaves. All the evidence strongly advocates the concept that Adam and Eve and their ancestors, cousins, and what-have-you were created by genetic engineering and mixing the

DNA of Anunnaki with that of Homo erectus, the reigning progenitor of man at the time. Fundamentally, this was because the Anunnaki needed someone to work the mines in search of gold and other Precious Metals, and in all likelihood the ORME.

http://www.vibrani.com/Anunnaki.htm provides what just may be an insider view of the Anunnaki -- but from the perspective of Enki. The advantage of this link is that it provides extensive details on pre-Anunnaki history. While such channeled information is always speculative, it is nevertheless worthy of serious consideration.

The most fundamental question with respect to the Anunnaki is whether or not they're still on Earth! Sitchin [1] has pointed out that he never said they left (and there is no evidence that they did). There was, however, an apparently fundamental Anunnaki policy shift circa 600 B.C.E. wherein the overt, day-to-day interference in human affairs by the Anunnaki disappeared. There is also the scenario encapsulated in Richard Wagner's classic opera The Ring of the Nibelung, which included Night Falls on the Gods and the Entrance of the Gods Into Vahalla -- titles which are suggestive of possible changes in status of the Anunnaki. Finally, there is evidence to suggest that this state of affairs may be temporary, and may be scheduled to end with the end of the Mayan Calendar on or about 2012. A.D.

From mankind's point of view, the dysfunctional nature of the Anunnaki family, and the continuing rivalry of Enki and Enlil, may still be ongoing and having enormous effects on the quality of our physical, emotional, mental and spiritual lives. It's a very important question, and one that needs to be answered by each of us.

References:

[1] Zecharia Sitchin, The 12th Planet, 1976, The Wars of Gods and Men, 1985, Genesis Revisited, 1990, Divine Encounters, 1995, Avon Books, New York.

[2] Laurence Gardner, Genesis of the Grail Kings, Bantam Press, New York, 1999.

[3]   Bramley, William, The Gods of Eden, Avon Books, New York, 1989, 1990.

The Library of ialexandriah

Adam and Eve

The story of Adam and Eve is often treated as an allegory, but in reality is quite likely a great deal closer to factual history, a story of genetic manipulations at the Dawn of Man, by a group of extraterrestrials who commit the ultimate in "Prime Directive" Violations.

According to ancient Sumerian texts, as interpreted by Laurence Gardner [1], Zecharia Sitchin [2], and others, the Anunnaki ("those who from heaven to earth came") are extraterrestrials who arrived on the planet Earth after the discovery of gold by a deposed ruler of their race, named

Alalu. The discovery eventually led to an Anunnaki mission to Earth to recover as much of this noteworthy example of the Precious Metals as possible.

The initial effort was led by Ea; whose title, Enki, meant "Lord of Earth", and who was the son of the new ruler, Anu. Enki (or Ea) set up shop at Eridu, near the northwest end of the Persian Gulf at the point where the Tigris and Euphrates Rivers meet the Gulf -- and at a time long before the silting of the two great rivers had extended the shoreline many miles to the southeast. At Eridu, Enki began to recover gold from sea water.

After this initial effort failed to produce the expected quantities of gold, an enlarged effort was commenced, this time under the command of Enlil ("Lord of the Command"), another son of Anu, and a half-brother to Enki. The new plan was to shift the operation from Mesopotamia to southern Africa (referred to in the Sumerian texts as Ab-zu), ship the gold back to Mesopotamia, and then lift it off the planet for trans-shipment to the home planet of the Anunnaki, Nibiru. (Nibiru is also a member of Earth's solar system, but has an extremely elliptical orbit and only reaches perihelion every 3600 years or so.)

At this juncture, there were supposedly 600 Anunnaki in the Netherworld (i.e. working the mines) and 300 in the heavens (doing the trans-shipments and minding the store). After a long period of time (Sitchin reckons the date as 300,000 B.C.E.), the Anunnaki who were laboriously mining the gold from the South African mines, mutinied! The mutiny and the difficulties the Anunnaki had encountered in working the mines were resolved, however, when Enki proposed to create a "primitive worker" to work the mines in lieu of the Anunnaki. Enki's proposal was, "Let us make man in our image, after our likeness."

Given the go-ahead, Enki and his half-sister, Ninki (Nin-khursag) created man, Homo sapiens, using genetic manipulation. They did so, allegedly, for the sole purpose of having workers to mine the gold for the Anunnaki, and thereby to quell the mutiny! The actual creation of Homo sapiens, as depicted in the ancient Sumerian texts in detail, was done by cross-breeding Homo erectus with that of the extraterrestrial Anunnaki! In other words, we're all half-breeds! (Except for a few notable personalities such as described in the Epic of Gilgamesh, who might better be described as one-third breeds. No kidding.)

Ninki, the Lady of Life (now we know where she received her title!), carried the first "mixed worker" to term and gave birth to a being she called the "Lulu." Later, fourteen "birth goddesses" (female Anunnaki) were used to produce additional workers. This solution was only a moderate success in that the Lulu was a hybrid and incapable of procreation (just as the mule, a cross between horse and donkey, cannot reproduce itself).

In addition, the "birth goddesses" had become weary of continually being pregnant!

Accordingly, it was back to the drawing board for Enki and Ninki. More work had to be done in genetically engineering a self-replicating, humanoid creature to be used as a slave. In the process, they may have encountered more than one dead end. It is possible, for example, that the legends of strange creatures and mythological monsters (from a Cyclops to a Hydra) may have arisen from the early experiments in genetic engineering, those which did not quite work quite so well. Cyclops, for example, was listed as the son of Neptune, the God of the Ocean -- another likely name or title for Enki (who was given the oceans as his bailiwick, and who was identified in the Sumerian texts with the planet Neptune. There is also the possibility that both the Neanderthal and Cro-Magnon species were simply different "models" of the genetic engineering project, and created for different forms of work -- ostensibly the Neanderthal being the mine workers, and Cro-Magnon being the new, improved version of Homo sapiens for the purposes of housework and domestic servants. The latter may also have been the precursor of Homo sapiens sapiens.

Eventually, Enki and Ninki were able to modify the genetic structure of the Lulu in order for it to be able to produce itself. Yea! They thus created the "Adama".

Significantly, they did so without Enlil's knowledge or approval! (Enki and Enlil did not really get along, a conflict stretching over eons.)

Once the interbreeding began to show some significant results, several Lulus were taken to Mesopotamia to work in agriculture (in Enlil's backyard, so to speak). There, they aided the Anunnaki efforts to raise food for themselves and their new workers. According to the Sumerian texts, Enlil created an E.DIN, a special place where new strains of edible crops could be developed and later implemented. Lulus were placed inside Edin, but without Enlil having learned of the Lulu's recently acquired talent for procreation.

When the obvious result becoming obvious even to Enlil -- when the Lulu's had in effect eaten from the Tree of Knowledge of Good and Evil (e.g., "sexual knowing"), the result was the Adamas' expulsion from Edin. At the same time, Enki, their paternal "creator", became the god who clothed the now homeless Adam and Eve on their way out the door.

The apparent duality of God in the book of Genesis is thus explained by the often opposing actions of Enki and Enlil. Enlil expels Adam and Eve; Enki clothes them. Enlil gives the old heave ho to Cain; Enki protects him. Enlil brings about a flood; Enki assists a Noah in building an ark. And so forth and so on. Even the Jesuits of the Catholic Church have begun to acknowledge the reality of at least two gods in the story of Genesis. Considering what we know of the Anunnaki and the elohim, there are a whole slew of Gods and Goddesses in the story of Genesis.

The scientific confirmation for the creation of mankind from Homo erectus comes in part from two sources. The first is the result of research by Cann, et al [3], where it was shown that mitochondria DNA (a form of DNA transmitted only maternally] could be shown to postulate a single woman living in Africa approximately 250,000 years ago who became the mother of every human being now living on the planet. Later, Dorit, et al [4] found no intraspecific polymorphism whatsoever in a gene paternally inherited, and concluded a date of the last common male ancestor to be roughly 270,000 B.C.E. These dates tie in well with Sitchin's argument, and tend to conflict with a purely evolutionary theory of humans evolving naturally from a survival of the fitness type scenario.

The conclusion is that Adam and Eve were real, possibly Lunatics, and were created by the genetic manipulation of cross-breeding Homo erectus with extraterrestrials from the planet, Nibiru. As such, they began a dynasty (i.e. The Adam's Family) of beings who lived to a much riper age than Homo sapiens sapiens are generally expected -- just part of their genetic heritage from the Anunnaki, who apparently live for hundreds of thousands of years. (There are, apparently, advantages to being a half-breed.)

References:
[1] Gardner, Laurence, Genesis of the Grail Kings, Bantam Press, NY, 1999.

[2] Sitchin, Zecharia, The 12th Planet, 1976, The Wars of Gods and Men, 1985, The Lost Realms, 1990, Avon Books, New York.

[3] Cann, R. L., Stoneking, M., and Wilson, A. C., "Mitochondrial DNA and human evolution", Nature, Vol 325, January 1, 1987.

[4] Dorit, R. L., Akashi, H., Gilbert, W., "Absence of Polymorphism at the ZFY Locus on the Human Y Chromosome," Science, Vol 268, May 26, 1995.
The Library of ialexandriah

Gods and Goddesses

It should be readily obvious that the "God" who has been identified as the "Creator of Heaven and Earth" is by definition an extraterrestrial -- inasmuch as creating Earth implies both predating the Earth and not being "of Earth" at the time it was created. This Creator God, however, is not necessarily the God of Genesis, nor the gods and goddesses of the other religions of the ancient world. In fact, mankind may have very little traditional literature which describes this Creator God.

As for the "local gods and goddesses", numerous authors have discussed in great detail the stories of their lives (Mythologies, Ancient Myths, Descent into the Underworld), personality characteristics (Archetypes), the dysfunctional relationships between them, and to a lesser degree, their origin. Zecharia Sitchin [1], on the other hand, has argued in seven exhaustively researched books that the so-called gods and goddesses of the ancient world (including the god(s) of Genesis) were almost certainly extraterrestrials -- more specifically: mortal beings from another planet. Sitchin's work explains the particulars of the arrival of the Anunnaki ("those who from heaven to earth came"), and why these extraterrestrials are believed to come from a 12th planet called Nibiru.

Sitchin also describes the genetic experiments to create mankind, the story of Adam and Eve, the Garden of Eden, the events surrounding the biblical Flood and Deluge, and the early history of the world up until the time of Abraham (circa 2000 B.C.E.), including the reality of what happened at Sodom and Gomorrah and the Tower of Babel. Laurence Gardner [2] has independently described many of these same events, and also discussed the importance of Monoatomic Elements, the ORME, Star Fire, and related subjects. In Lost Secrets of the Sacred Ark, Gardner, in fact, goes into considerable detail about how the Anunnaki are connected to the all important subject of Gold. [This book is really a must read!]

The work of Gardner, Sitchin, and others makes it clear that the extraterrestrial "gods and goddesses" were intervening and lording over the human species with a vengeance! The Anunnaki, specifically Enki and his half-sister Ninki, were responsible for the genetic experiments which combined Anunnaki DNA with that of Homo erectus in order to create Homo sapiens sapiens, thus placing the human evolution far ahead of schedule and with the added ingredient of extraterrestrial DNA.

There is also the possibility that these experiments may have been responsible for the creation of Neanderthals (perhaps the early version), and even certain mythical creatures (in terms of genetic mishaps). While some of the later generation of Anunnaki were born on Earth (thus making them "terrestrials"), the "Prime Directive" Violations by these Anunnaki were extensive and far-reaching.

One of the best examples of interventions is the long lifetimes of The Adam's Family, the Biblical Patriarchs from Adam to Abraham. Prior to the Flood and Deluge, all of the patriarchs lived for roughly nine hundred years. (One exception is Enoch who did not die, but was taken up to heaven by "God". The other is Lamech, the father of Noah who lived a "mere 777 years".)

After the Flood and Deluge, however, there was a step wise reduction in the patriarch's lifetimes, from Shem (600 years) to roughly 450 years for the next three patriarchs, to an average of 222 years for the next six -- including Abraham. A curious result is that the five generations between Eber and Abraham were already dead and presumably buried, at a time when the four generations beginning with the son of Noah, Shem, were still alive (and presumably kicking). [Waiting for an inheritance must have been a lost art!]

Today, of course, average lifetimes are far less than a hundred years. This suggests a very directed and specific extraterrestrial intervention. This intervention is likely due to denying humans the ORME, Star Fire, or Monoatomic Elements, which may have been the key ingredients in keeping the patriarchs and their kin living to very ripe old ages.

One might also mention that there is nothing in Gardner's, Sitchin's or any other author's works to suggest that these extraterrestrials ever left the Earth! Just so you'll know.

On the other side of the planet, American Indian traditions have asserted that there are hundreds of extraterrestrial races which have routinely involved themselves in the affairs of Earth (and who are apparently continuing to do so). Specifics include: Jesus Christ allegedly being a Star Man [3], White Buffalo Calf Woman being an extraterrestrial -- who incidentally is returning in the immediate future [4], extraterrestrials being heavily involved in Iroquois traditions for tens of thousands of years [5], and 12 extraterrestrial cultures currently interested in the Earth, including the Pleiadians, Sirians, and Orions [6].

Other authors, such as Graham Hancock [7], William Bramley [8] and Erich Von Daniken in Chariots of the Gods have provided extensive documentation of advanced technologies in the Chronicles of Earth being held or wielded by peoples, who are now considered members of pre-historical and ancient civilizations -- and who supposedly had no such technologies. All of these authors have concluded, either mankind's previous civilizations were remarkably well advanced (and then later dissolved for some unknown reason), or that Earth was being visited on a regular basis -- and quite probably interfered with -- by extraterrestrials of one or more different cultures.

The evidence from ancient histories of extraterrestrials representing themselves as gods and goddesses is massive and virtually without alternative explanations. A review, for example, of such works as The

Egyptian Book of the Dead [9] makes it clear that strange-looking, non-human beings were actively involved in terrestrial affairs. The traditional view that such depictions were based on mythological archetypes or fantasies of the allegedly backward ancients is nothing more than mainstream science burying its head in the traditional sand. Quite deeply, in fact.

Tricia McCannon [6] has stated explicitly, "All the ancient pictures are of real beings!" Beings from the constellation Pegasus, for example, are supposedly flyers. The Egyptian goddess, Isis, was, according to McCannon, a Sirian, while those from Sirius B had their mouths on top and looked to be a cross between a human and a fish. Drunvalo Melchizedek [10] places the Hathors (Hippo-like beings) as being from Venus. McCannon [6] also believes that Jehovah was definitely an extraterrestrial, but suspects that Yawyeh was more likely the "true God".

In effect, we already have picture galleries of extraterrestrials, and ample evidence of multiple "Close Encounters" of the most far-reaching kind. As Barbara Marcinak [11] once said, "The best secrets are carved in stone or on the ceilings."
References:

[1] Sitchin, Zecharia, The Wars of Gods and Men, Avon Books, New York, 1985; Genesis Revisited, Avon Books, New York, 1990; and others.

[2] Gardner, Laurence, Genesis of the Grail Kings, Bantam Press, New York, 1990; Lost Secrets of the Sacred Ark, HarperCollins, London, 2003.

[3] Standing Elk, Lecture at the Star Knowledge Conference, Lakota Indian Reservation, South Dakota, June, 1996.

[4] Hand, Floyd, Lecture at the Star Knowledge Conference, Lakota Indian Reservation, South Dakota, June, 1996.

[5] Underwood, Paula, Lecture at the Star Knowledge Conference, Lakota Indian Reservation, South Dakota, June, 1996.

[6] McCannon, Tricia, Lecture at the Star Knowledge Conference, Lakota Indian Reservation, South Dakota, June, 1996.

[7] Hancock, Graham, *Fingerprints of the Gods*, Crown Publishers, New York, 1995.

[8] Bramley, William, *The Gods of Eden*, Avon Books, New York, 1990.

[9] Faulkner, Raymond, *The Egyptian Book of the Dead, The Book of Going Forth by Day*, Chronicle Books, San Francisco, 1994.

[10] Melchizedek, Drunvalo, Lecture at the Star Knowledge Conference, Lakota Indian Reservation, South Dakota, June, 1996.

[11] Marchinak, Barbara, Lecture at the Star Knowledge Conference, Lakota Indian Reservation, South Dakota, June, 1996.

The Library of ialexandriah

In an earlier section I wondered where the gods are now, and put forth the idea that the Jehovah of Israel did not and could not surely be more than just a "local god", and one that has now long departed or abandoned his godly duties. It all comes together now and starts to make big sense. Of interest is the fact that the human race were obliged to give tribute to the gods, and this will come up again later as a major issue that is still ongoing, or so it would seem.

Now is certainly the time to forget and abandon the whole dogma of religion, open the eyes and the mind, lose that awe and fearful reverence that has been engendered for millenia by those proclaimed as priests and leaders.

In recent history, the Sphinx was covered at least twice to its neck in sand, which means there was no time for the rain water to do this kind of damage, unless we go much farther back in time. When was the last time there was enough rain in the Sahara desert to cause such an extensive amount of erosion? It wasn't just a couple of years to create the depth and detail we see here. Computer models and geologists say that 10,000 - 12,000 years ago was the last time the Sahara had that much rain.

806-Archaeological Cover-ups
-- A Plot to Control History? --

The scientific establishment tends to reject, suppress or ignore evidence that conflicts with accepted theories, while denigrating or persecuting the messenger.

by Will Hart © 2002
Email: Wrtsearch1@aol.com

"THE BRAIN POLICE" AND "THE BIG LIE"

Any time you allege a conspiracy is afoot, especially in the field of science, you are treading on thin ice. We tend to be very sceptical about conspiracies--unless the Mafia or some Muslim radicals are behind the alleged plot. But the evidence is overwhelming and the irony is that much of it is in plain view.

The good news is that the players are obvious. Their game plan and even their play-by-play tactics are transparent, once you learn to spot them. However, it is not so easy to penetrate through the smokescreen of propaganda and disinformation to get to their underlying motives and goals. It would be convenient if we could point to a plumber's unit and a boldface liar like Richard Nixon, but this is a more subtle operation.

The bad news: the conspiracy is global and there are many vested interest groups. A cursory investigation yields the usual suspects: scientists with a theoretical axe to grind, careers to further and the status quo to maintain. Their modus operandi is "The Big Lie"--and the bigger and more widely publicised, the better. They rely on invoking their academic credentials to support their arguments, and the presumption is that no one has the right to question their authoritarian pronouncements that:
1. there is no mystery about who built the Great Pyramid or what the methods of construction were, and the Sphinx shows no signs of water damage;
2. there were no humans in the Americas before 20,000 BC;
3. the first civilisation dates back no further than 6000 BC;
4. there are no documented anomalous, unexplained or enigmatic data to take into account;
5. there are no lost or unaccounted-for civilisations.
Let the evidence to the contrary be damned!

Personal Attacks: Dispute over Age of the Sphinx and Great Pyramid

In 1993, NBC in the USA aired The Mysteries of the Sphinx, which presented geological evidence showing that the Sphinx was at least twice as old (9,000 years) as Egyptologists claimed. It has become well known as the "water erosion controversy". An examination of the politicking that Egyptologists deployed to combat this undermining of their turf is instructive.

Self-taught Egyptologist John Anthony West brought the water erosion issue to the attention of geologist Dr Robert Schoch. They went to Egypt and launched an intensive on-site investigation. After thoroughly studying the Sphinx first hand, the geologist came to share West's preliminary conclusion and they announced their findings.

Dr Zahi Hawass, the Giza Monuments chief, wasted no time in firing a barrage of public criticism at the pair. Renowned Egyptologist Dr Mark Lehner, who is regarded as the world's foremost expert on the Sphinx, joined his attack. He charged West and Schoch with being "ignorant and insensitive". That was a curious accusation which took the matter off the professional level and put the whole affair on a personal plane. It did not address the facts or issues at all and it was highly unscientific.

But we must note the standard tactic of discrediting anyone who dares to call the accepted theories into question. Shifting the focus away from the issues and "personalising" the debate is a highly effective strategy--one which is often used by politicians who feel insecure about their positions. Hawass and Lehner invoked their untouchable status and presumed authority. (One would think that a geologist's assessment would hold more weight on this particular point.)

A short time later, Schoch, Hawass and Lehner were invited to debate the issue at the American Association for the Advancement of Science. West was not allowed to participate because he lacked the required credentials.

This points to a questionable assumption that is part of the establishment's arsenal: only degreed scientists can practise science. Two filters keep the uncredentialled, independent researcher out of the loop: (1) credentials, and (2) peer review. You do not get to number two unless you have number one.

Science is a method that anyone can learn and apply. It does not require a degree to observe and record facts and think critically about them, especially in the non-technical social sciences. In a free and open society, science has to be a democratic process.

Be that as it may, West was barred. The elements of the debate have been batted back and forth since then without resolution. It is similar to the controversy over who built the Giza pyramids and how.

This brings up the issue of The Big Lie and how it has been promoted for generations in front of God and everyone. The controversy over how the Great Pyramid was constructed is one example. It could be easily settled if Egyptologists wanted to resolve the dispute. A simple test could be designed and arranged by impartial engineers that would either prove or disprove their longstanding disputed theory--that it was built using the primitive tools and methods of the day, circa 2500 BC.

Why hasn't this been done? The answer is so obvious, it seems impossible: they know that the theory is bogus. Could a trained, highly educated scientist really believe that 2.3 million tons of stone, some blocks weighing 70 tons, could have been transported and lifted by primitive methods? That seems improbable, though they have no compunction against lying to the public, writing textbooks and defending this theory against alternative theories. However, we must note that they will not subject themselves to the bottom-line test.

We think it is incumbent upon any scientist to bear the burden of proof of his/her thesis; however, the social scientists who make these claims have never stood up to that kind of scrutiny. That is why we must suspect a conspiracy. No other scientific discipline would get away with bending the rules of science. All that Egyptologists have ever done is bat down alternative theories using underhanded tactics. It is time to insist that they prove their own proposals.

Why would scientists try to hide the truth and avoid any test of their hypothesis? Their motivations are equally transparent. If it can be proved that the Egyptians did not build the Great Pyramid in 2500 BC using primitive methods, or if the Sphinx can be dated to 9000 BC, the whole house of cards comes tumbling down. Orthodox views of cultural evolution are based upon a chronology of civilisation having started in Sumeria no earlier than 4000 BC. The theory does not permit an advanced civilisation to have existed prior to that time. End of discussion.

Archaeology and history lose their meaning without a fixed timeline as a point of reference.

Since the theory of "cultural evolution" has been tied to Darwin's general theory of evolution, even more is at stake. Does this explain why facts, anomalies and enigmas are denied, suppressed and/or ignored? Yes, it does. The biological sciences today are based on Darwinism.

Pressure Tactics: The Ica Stones of Peru

Now we turn to another, very different case. In 1966, Dr Javier Cabrera received a stone as a gift from a poor local farmer in his native Ica, Peru. A fish was carved on the stone, which would not have meant much to the average villager but it did mean a lot to the educated Dr Cabrera. He recognised it as a long-extinct species. This aroused his curiosity. He purchased more stones from the farmer, who said he had collected them near the river after a flood.

Dr Cabrera accumulated more and more stones, and word of their existence and potential import reached the archaeological community. Soon, the doctor had amassed thousands of "Ica stones". The sophisticated carvings were as enigmatic as they were fascinating. Someone had carved men fighting with dinosaurs, men with telescopes and men performing operations with surgical equipment. They also contained drawings of lost continents.

Several of the stones were sent to Germany and the etchings were dated to remote antiquity. But we all know that men could not have lived at the time of dinosaurs; Homo sapiens has only existed for about 100,000 years.

The BBC got wind of this discovery and swooped down to produce a documentary about the Ica stones. The media exposure ignited a storm of controversy. Archaeologists criticised the Peruvian government for being lax about enforcing antiquities laws (but that was not their real concern). Pressure was applied to government officials.

The farmer who had been selling the stones to Cabrera was arrested; he claimed to have found them in a cave but refused to disclose the exact location to authorities, or so they claimed.

This case was disposed of so artfully that it would do any corrupt politician proud. The Peruvian government threatened to prosecute and imprison the farmer. He was offered and accepted a plea bargain; he then recanted his story and "admitted" to having carved the stones himself. That seems highly implausible, since he was uneducated and unskilled and there were 11,000 stones in all. Some were fairly large and intricately carved with animals and scenes that the farmer would not have had knowledge of without being a palaeontologist. He would have needed to work every day for several decades to produce that volume of stones. However, the underlying facts were neither here nor there. The Ica stones were labelled "hoax" and forgotten.

The case did not require a head-to-head confrontation or public discrediting of non-scientists by scientists; it was taken care of with invisible pressure tactics. Since it was filed under "hoax", the enigmatic evidence never had to be dealt with, as it did in the next example.

Censorship of "Forbidden" Thinking: Evidence for Mankind's Great Antiquity

The case of author Michael Cremo is well documented, and it also demonstrates how the scientific establishment openly uses pressure tactics on the media and government. His book Forbidden Archeology examines many previously ignored examples of artifacts that prove modern man's antiquity far exceeds the age given in accepted chronologies.

The examples which he and his co-author present are controversial, but the book became far more controversial than the contents when it was used in a documentary.

In 1996, NBC broadcast a special called The Mysterious Origins of Man, which featured material from Cremo's book. The reaction from the scientific community went off the Richter scale. NBC was deluged with letters from irate scientists who called the producer "a fraud" and the whole program "a hoax".

But the scientists went further than this--a lot further. In an extremely unconscionable sequence of bizarre moves, they tried to force NBC not to rebroadcast the popular program, but that effort failed. Then they took the most radical step of all: they presented their case to the federal government and requested the Federal Communications Commission to step in and bar NBC from airing the program again.

This was not only an apparent infringement of free speech and a blatant attempt to thwart commerce, it was an unprecedented effort to censor intellectual discourse. If the public or any government agency made an attempt to handcuff the scientific establishment, the public would never hear the end of it.

The letter to the FCC written by Dr Allison Palmer, President of the Institute for Cambrian Studies, is revealing:

At the very least, NBC should be required to make substantial prime-time apologies to their viewing audience for a sufficient period of time so that the audience clearly gets the message that they were duped. In addition, NBC should perhaps be fined sufficiently so that a major fund for public science education can be established.

I think we have some good leads on who "the Brain Police" are. And I really do not think "conspiracy" is too strong a word--because for every case of this kind of attempted suppression that is exposed, 10 others are going on successfully. We have no idea how many enigmatic artifacts or dates have been labelled "error" and tucked away in storage warehouses or circular files, never to see the light of day.

Data Rejection: Inconvenient Dating in Mexico

Then there is the high-profile case of Dr Virginia Steen-McIntyre, a geologist working for the US Geological Survey (USGS), who was dispatched to an archaeological site in Mexico to date a group of artifacts in the 1970s. This travesty also illustrates how far established scientists will go to guard orthodox tenets.

McIntyre used state-of-the-art equipment and backed up her results by using four different methods, but her results were off the chart. The lead archaeologist expected a date of 25,000 years or less, and the geologist's finding was 250,000 years or more.

The figure of 25,000 years or less was critical to the Bering Strait "crossing" theory, and it was the motivation behind the head archaeologist's tossing Steen-McIntyre's results in the circular file and asking for a new series of dating tests. This sort of reaction does not occur when dates match the expected chronological model that supports accepted theories.

Steen-McIntyre was given a chance to retract her conclusions, but she refused. She found it hard thereafter to get her papers published and she lost a teaching job at an American university.

Government Suppression and Ethnocentrism: Avoiding Anomalous Evidence in NZ, China and Mexico

In New Zealand, the government actually stepped in and enacted a law forbidding the public from entering a controversial archaeological zone. This story appeared in the book, Ancient Celtic New Zealand, by Mark Doutré.

However, as we will find (and as I promised at the beginning of the article), this is a complicated conspiracy. Scientists trying to protect their "hallowed" theories while furthering their careers are not the only ones who want artifacts and data suppressed. This is where the situation gets sticky.

The Waipoua Forest became a controversial site in New Zealand because an archaeological dig apparently showed evidence of a non-Polynesian culture that preceded the Maori--a fact that the tribe was not happy with. They learned of the results of the excavations before the general public did and complained to the government. According to Doutré, the outcome was "an official archival document, which clearly showed an intention by New Zealand government departments to withhold archaeological information from public scrutiny for 75 years".

The public got wind of this fiasco but the government denied the claim. However, official documents show that an embargo had been placed on the site. Doutré is a student of New Zealand history and archaeology. He is concerned because he says that artifacts proving that there was an earlier culture which preceded the Maori are missing from museums. He asks what happened to several anomalous remains:

Where are the ancient Indo-European hair samples (wavy red brown hair), originally obtained from a rock shelter near Watakere, that were on display at the Auckland War Memorial Museum for many years? Where is the giant skeleton found near Mitimati?

Unfortunately this is not the only such incident. Ethnocentrism has become a factor in the conspiracy to hide mankind's true history. Author Graham Hancock has been attacked by various ethnic groups for reporting similar enigmatic findings.

The problem for researchers concerned with establishing humanity's true history is that the goals of nationalists or ethnic groups who want to lay claim to having been in a particular place first, often dovetail with the goals of cultural evolutionists.

Archaeologists are quick to go along with suppressing these kinds of anomalous finds. One reason Egyptologists so jealously guard the Great Pyramid's construction date has to do with the issue of national pride.

The case of the Takla Makan Desert mummies in western China is another example of this phenomenon. In the 1970s and 1980s, an unaccounted-for Caucasian culture was suddenly unearthed in China. The arid environment preserved the remains of a blond-haired, blue-eyed people who lived in pre-dynastic China. They wore colourful robes, boots, stockings and hats. The Chinese were not happy about this revelation and they have downplayed the enigmatic find, even though Asians were found buried alongside the Caucasian mummies.

National Geographic writer Thomas B. Allen mused in a 1996 article about his finding a potsherd bearing a fingerprint of the potter. When he inquired if he could take the fragment to a forensic anthropologist, the Chinese scientist asked whether he "would be able to tell if the potter was a white man". Allen said he was not sure, and the official pocketed the fragment and quietly walked away. It appears that many things get in the way of scientific discovery and disclosure.

The existence of the Olmec culture in Old Mexico has always posed a problem. Where did the Negroid people depicted on the colossal heads come from? Why are there Caucasians carved on the stele in what is Mexico's seed civilisation? What is worse, why aren't the indigenous Mexican people found on the Olmec artifacts? Recently a Mexican archaeologist solved the problem by making a fantastic claim: that the Olmec heads--which generations of people of all ethnic groups have agreed bear a striking resemblance to Africans--were really representations of the local tribe.

STORMTROOPERS FOR DARWINISM

The public does not seem at all aware of the fact that the scientific establishment has a double standard when it comes to the free flow of information. In essence, it goes like this... Scientists are highly educated, well trained and intellectually capable of processing all types of information, and they can make the correct critical distinctions between fact and fiction, reality and fantasy. The unwashed public is simply incapable of functioning on this high mental plane.

The noble ideal of the scientist as a highly trained, impartial, apolitical observer and assembler of established facts into a useful body of knowledge seems to have been shredded under the pressures and demands of the real world. Science has produced many positive benefits for society; but we should know by now that science has a dark, negative side. Didn't those meek fellows in the clean lab coats give us nuclear bombs and biological weapons? The age of innocence ended in World War II.

That the scientific community has an attitude of intellectual superiority is thinly veiled under a carefully orchestrated public relations guise. We always see Science and Progress walking hand in hand. Science as an institution in a democratic society has to function in the same way as the society at large; it should be open to debate, argument and counter-argument. There is no place for unquestioned authoritarianism. Is modern science meeting these standards?

In the Fall of 2001, PBS aired a seven-part series, titled Evolution. Taken at face value, that seems harmless enough. However, while the program was presented as pure, objective, investigative science journalism, it completely failed to meet even minimum standards of impartial reporting. The series was heavily weighted towards the view that the theory of evolution is "a science fact" that is accepted by "virtually all reputable scientists in the world", and not a theory that has weaknesses and strong scientific critics.

The series did not even bother to interview scientists who have criticisms of Darwinism: not "creationists" but bona fide scientists. To correct this deficiency, a group of 100 dissenting scientists felt compelled to issue a press release, "A Scientific Dissent on Darwinism", on the day the first program was scheduled to go to air. Nobel nominee Henry "Fritz" Schaefer was among them. He encouraged open public debate of Darwin's theory:

Some defenders of Darwinism embrace standards of evidence for evolution that as scientists they would never accept in other circumstances.

We have seen this same "unscientific" approach applied to archaeology and anthropology, where "scientists" simply refuse to prove their theories yet appoint themselves as the final arbiters of "the facts". It would be naive to think that the scientists who co-operated in the production of the series were unaware that there would be no counter-balancing presentation by critics of Darwin's theory.

Richard Milton is a science journalist. He had been an ardent true believer in Darwinian doctrine until his investigative instincts kicked in one day. After 20 years of studying and writing about evolution, he suddenly realised that there were many disconcerting holes in the theory. He decided to try to allay his doubts and prove the theory to himself by using the standard methods of investigative journalism.

Milton became a regular visitor to London's famed Natural History Museum. He painstakingly put every main tenet and classic proof of Darwinism to the test. The results shocked him. He found that the theory could not even stand up to the rigours of routine investigative journalism.

The veteran science writer took a bold step and published a book titled The Facts of Life: Shattering the Myths of Darwinism. It is clear that the Darwinian myth had been shattered for him, but many more myths about science would also be crushed after his book came out. Milton says:

I experienced the witch-hunting activity of the Darwinist police at first hand, it was deeply disappointing to find myself being described by a prominent Oxford zoologist [Richard Dawkins] as "loony", "stupid" and "in need of psychiatric help" in response to purely scientific reporting.

(Does this sound like stories that came out of the Soviet Union 20 years ago when dissident scientists there started speaking out?)

Dawkins launched a letter-writing campaign to newspaper editors, implying that Milton was a "mole" creationist whose work should be dismissed. Anyone at all familiar with politics will recognise this as a standard Machiavellian by-the-book "character assassination" tactic. Dawkins is a highly respected scientist, whose reputation and standing in the scientific community carry a great deal of weight.

According to Milton, the process came to a head when the London Times Higher Education Supplement commissioned him to write a critique of Darwinism. The publication foreshadowed his coming piece: "Next Week: Darwinism - Richard Milton goes on the attack". Dawkins caught wind of this and wasted no time in nipping this heresy in the bud. He contacted the editor, Auriol Stevens, and accused Milton of being a "creationist", and prevailed upon Stevens to pull the plug on the article. Milton learned of this behind-the-scenes back-stabbing and wrote a letter of appeal to Stevens. In the end, she caved in to Dawkins and scratched the piece.

Imagine what would happen if a politician or bureaucrat used such pressure tactics to kill a story in the mass media. It would ignite a huge scandal. Not so with scientists, who seem to be regarded as "sacred cows" and beyond reproach. There are many disturbing facts related to these cases. Darwin's theory of evolution is the only theory routinely taught in our public school system that has never been subjected to rigorous scrutiny; nor have any of the criticisms been allowed into the curriculum.

This is an interesting fact, because a recent poll showed that the American public wants the theory of evolution taught to their children; however, "71 per cent of the respondents say biology teachers should teach both Darwinism and scientific evidence against Darwinian theory". Nevertheless, there are no plans to implement this balanced approach.

It is ironic that Richard Dawkins has been appointed to the position of Professor of the Public Understanding of Science at Oxford University. He is a classic "Brain Police" stormtrooper, patrolling the neurological front lines. The Western scientific establishment and mass media pride themselves on being open public forums devoid of prejudice or censorship. However, no television program examining the flaws and weaknesses of Darwinism has ever been aired in Darwin's home country or in America. A scientist who opposes the theory cannot get a paper published.

The Mysterious Origins of Man was not a frontal attack on Darwinism; it merely presented evidence that is considered anomalous by the precepts of his theory of evolution.

Returning to our bastions of intellectual integrity, Forest Mims was a solid and skilled science journalist. He had never been the centre of any controversy and so he was invited to write the most-read column in the prestigious Scientific American, "The Amateur Scientist", a task he gladly accepted. According to Mims, the magazine's editor Jonathan Piel then learned that he also wrote articles for a number of Christian magazines. The editor called Mims into his office and confronted him.

"Do you believe in the theory of evolution?" Piel asked.

Mims replied, "No, and neither does Stephen Jay Gould."

His response did not affect Piel's decision to bump Mims off the popular column after just three articles.

This has the unpleasant odour of a witch-hunt. The writer never publicly broadcast his private views or beliefs, so it would appear that the "stormtroopers" now believe they have orders to make sure "unapproved" thoughts are never publicly disclosed.

TABOO OR NOT TABOO?

So, the monitors of "good thinking" are not just the elite of the scientific community, as we have seen in several cases; they are television producers and magazine editors as well. It seems clear that they are all driven by the singular imperative of furthering "public science education", as the president of the Cambrian Institute so aptly phrased it.

However, there is a second item on the agenda, and that is to protect the public from "unscientific" thoughts and ideas that might infect the mass mind. We outlined some of those taboo subjects at the beginning of the article; now we should add that it is also "unwholesome" and "unacceptable" to engage in any of the following research pursuits: paranormal phenomena, UFOs, cold fusion, free energy and all the rest of the "pseudo-sciences". Does this have a familiar ring to it? Are we hearing the faint echoes of religious zealotry?

Who ever gave science the mission of engineering and directing the inquisitive pursuits of the citizenry of the free world? It is all but impossible for any scientific paper that has anti-Darwinian ramifications to be published in a mainstream scientific journal. It is also just as impossible to get the "taboo" subjects even to the review table, and you can forget about finding your name under the title of any article in Nature unless you are a credentialled scientist, even if you are the next Albert Einstein.

To restate how this conspiracy begins, it is with two filters: credentials and peer review. Modern science is now a maze of such filters set up to promote certain orthodox theories and at the same time filter out that data already prejudged to be unacceptable. Evidence and merit are not the guiding principles; conformity and position within the established community have replaced objectivity, access and openness.

Scientists do not hesitate to launch the most outrageous personal attacks against those they perceive to be the enemy. Eminent palaeontologist Louis Leakey penned this acid one-liner about Forbidden Archeology: "Your book is pure humbug and does not deserve to be taken seriously by anyone but a fool." Once again, we see the thrust of a personal attack; the merits of the evidence presented in the book are not examined or debated. It is a blunt, authoritarian pronouncement.

In a forthcoming instalment, we will examine some more documented cases and delve deeper into the subtler dimensions of the conspiracy.

References and Resources:

¥ Cremo, Michael A. and Richard L. Thompson, Forbidden Archeology, Govardhan Hill, USA, 1993.

¥ Cremo, Michael A., "The Controversy over 'The Mysterious Origins of Man'", NEXUS 5/04, 1998; Forbidden Archeology's Impact, Bhaktivedanta Book Publishing, USA, 1998, website http://www.mcremo.com/.

¥ Doore, Kathy, "The Nazca Spaceport & the Ica Stones of Peru", http://www.labyrinthina.com/ica.htm; see website for copy of Dr Javier Cabrera's book, The Message of the Engraved Stones.

¥ Doutré, Mark, Ancient Celtic New Zealand, Dé Danann, New Zealand, 1999, website http://www.celticnz.co.nz/.

¥ Milton, Richard, The Facts of Life: Shattering the Myths of Darwinism, Corgi, UK, 1993, http://www.alternativescience.com/.

¥ Steen-McIntyre, Virginia, "Suppressed Evidence for Ancient Man in Mexico", NEXUS 5/05, 1998.

¥ Sunfellow, David, "The Great Pyramid & The Sphinx", November 25, 1994, at http://www.nhne.com/specialrepots/spyramid.html.

¥ Tampa Bay Tribune, October 12, 2001 (Darwinism/evolution quote), http://www.tampatrib.com/.

About the Author:

Will Hart is a freelance journalist, book author, nature photographer and documentary filmmaker. He lives and does much of his research in the Lake Tahoe area in the USA, and writes a column titled "The Tahoe Naturalist" for a regional publication. He has produced and directed films about wolves and wild horses.

807-The Population Control Agenda
by Bob Lee • Sunday January 20, 2002 at 07:26 PM

Stay armed, stay free!
Rense.com

The Population Control
Agenda - A Timeline
From Bob Lee <rboblee@home.com>
http://www.fortunecity.com/roswell/daniken/443/populationcontrolagenda2. htm
Robert E. Lee, M.S., M.S.W., L.C.S.W.
Author "AIDS: An Explosion of the Biological Time-bomb?" c2000
Author "AIDS in America: Our Chances, Our Choices" c1987
website: http://www.bhc.edu/eas tcampus/leeb/aids/index.html
11-15-00

1963 The mass vaccination campaigns of the 1950s and '60s may be causing hundreds of deaths a year because of a cancer-causing virus that contaminated the first polio vaccine, according to scientists. Known as SV40, the virus came from dead monkeys whose kidney cells were used to culture the first Salk vaccines. Doctors estimate that the virus was injected into tens of millions during the vaccination campaigns, including several million in Canada, before being detected and screened out in 1963. Those born between 1941 and 1961 are thought to be most at risk of having been infected.

...Humanity must drastically scale down its industrial activities on Earth, change its consumption lifestyles, stabilize and then reduce the size of the human population by humane means, and protect and restore wild ecosystems and the remaining wildlife on the planet." The Wildlands Project

Chemtrails Lab Analysis -Virulent Bio-Toxin Soup

"Inasmuch as ye have done it unto the least of these my brethren, ye have done it unto Me." (Matthew 25:40)

A History Timeline Of Population Control
By Robert Howard

The Tartars had the idea of infecting the enemy by catapulting bodies infected with bubonic plague over the walls of the city of Kaffa. Some historians believe that this event was the cause of the epidemic of plague that swept across medieval Europe killing 25 million.

1763 The British during the French-Indian War. The Native Americans greatly outnumbered the British and were suspected of being on the side of the French. As an "act of good will" the British give blankets to the Indians, but the blankets came from a hospital that was treating smallpox victims and consequently smallpox raged through the Native American community and devastated their numbers.

1814 Andrew Jackson, whose portrait appears on the U.S. $20 bill today, supervised the mutilation of 800 or more Creek Indian corpses, the bodies of men, women and children that his troops had massacred, cutting off their noses to count and preserve a record of the dead, slicing long strips of flesh from their bodies to tan and turn into bridle reins.
(Historian Ward Churchill, A LITTLE MATTER OF GENOCIDE; HOLOCAUST AND DENIAL IN THE AMERICAS, 1492 TO THE PRESENT
(San Francisco: City Lights Books, 1997).
ISBN 0-87286-323-9. pg.186)
U.S. Presidents And The Masonic Power Structure

1911, Turkey established gun control. From 1915-1917, 1.5 million Armenians, unable to defend themselves, were rounded up and exterminated.

1918 The modern history of Biological Warfare (BW) starts in 1918 with the Japanese formation of a special section of the Army (Unit 731) dedicated to BW. The thought at the time was "Science and Technology are the Key's to Winning War and BW is the most cost effective."

1918-1919 Flu pandemic that killed over 20 million worldwide and over 500,000 here in the US.

1920's Unlike the malignant twists of nature, ranging from bubonic plague through to potato blight, which have killed masses throughout the ages, both the beef and pituitary hormone CJD crises were manmade. Scrapie, the sheep equivalent of BSE and CJD, has been around for more than two centuries. Somewhat differently, human spongiform encephalopathy was unheard of before two German physicians, Creutzfeldt and Jakob, independently reported the initial cases in the 1920s. BSE, too, was unheard of until a decade after cattle began to be fed the protein-rich remains of scrapie-infected sheep to accelerate their growth.

1929 The Soviet Union established gun control. From 1929 to 1953, approximately 20 million dissidents, unable to defend themselves, were rounded up and exterminated.

1930's Less known to the public is that fluoride also accumulates in bones. "The teeth are windows to what's happening in the bones," explained Paul Connett, Professor of Chemistry at St Lawrence University, New York, to these reporters. In recent years, pediatric bone specialists have expressed alarm about an increase in stress fractures among young people in the US. Connett and other scientists are concerned that fluoride-linked to bone damage in studies since the 1930s- may be a contributing factor. Link

1931 Japan expanded its territory by taking over part of Manchuria and Unit 731 moved in to secure "an endless supply of human experiment materials." Essentially all prisoners of war were available for Biological Warfare (BW) experiments.

1931 Dr. Cornelius Rhoads, under the auspices of the Rockefeller Institute for Medical Investigations, infects human subjects with cancer cells. He later goes on to establish the U.S. Army Biological Warfare facilities in Maryland, Utah, and Panama, and is named to the U.S. Atomic Energy Commission. While there, he begins a series of radiation exposure experiments on American soldiers and civilian hospital patients. Link

1932 The Infamous Tuskegee Study In recent history, we have seen the influence of occult population control advocates here in America. Nowhere is that influence better demonstrated than in the Tuskegee Study, a scientific research program in which 400 syphilis-infected black men were recruited by the U.S. Public Health Service back in 1932. The participants were all told that they would be treated for their infections, but instead of treating their illness, all medicines were withheld. The black men were then actively prevented from obtaining treatment elsewhere as their bodies, and the bodies of their wives and children, were systematically ravaged by disease. The evil men who conceived that Nazi-style study justified their atrocity by alleging that scientists needed to learn how untreated syphilis progressed in the human body. For a period of forty years, between 1932 and 1972, the genocidal Tuskegee Study continued. It was not until 1972, when one newspaper finally had

the courage to break the story to the public, that the Tuskegee Study was finally terminated.
The Population Control Agenda

1934 The original lesson about the infectious nature of these brain diseases mad cow disease" or bovine spongiform encephalopathy (BSE) in cattle, and Creutzfeldt-Jakob disease (CJD) in humans) came from a 1934 vaccine catastrophe in the UK which brought scrapie, or "mad sheep disease", to almost 5,000 out of 18,000 lambs within two years of their immunization against louping-ill virus infection. Tracing back, scientists discovered that the vaccine serum was prepared from a number of lambs whose dams had subsequently developed scrapie, but the significance of scrapie passing vertically from ewes to their lambs, and horizontally from lamb to lamb by virtue of the vaccine injections, was kept from international eyes by a series of egotistical carry-ons which prevented the data from reaching the pages of the scientific literature for a further 15 years.

1935 The Pellagra Incident. After millions of individuals die from Pellagra over a span of two decades, the U.S. Public Health Service finally acts to stem the disease. The director of the agency admits it had known for at least 20 years that Pellagra is caused by a niacin deficiency but failed to act since most of the deaths occured within poverty-striken black populations.
Link

1935 China established gun control. From 1948 to 1952, 20 million political dissidents, unable to defend themselves, were rounded up and exterminated.

1938 Germany established gun control in 1938 and from 1939 to 1945, 6 to 7 million Jews, gypsies, homosexuals, the mentally ill, and 12 million Christians who were unable to defend themselves, were rounded up and exterminated.

1939 Margaret Sanger organized her "Negro project," a program designed to eliminate members of what she believed to be an "inferior race." Margaret Sanger justified her proposal because she believed that: "The masses of Negroes ...particularly in the South, still breed carelessly and disastrously, with the result that the increase among Negroes, even more than among whites, is from that portion of the population least intelligent and fit..."
The Population Control Agenda

1940 Four hundred prisoners in Chicago are infected with Malaria in order to study the effects of new and experimental drugs to combat the disease. Nazi doctors later on trial at Nuremberg cite this American study to defend their own actions during the Holocaust. Link

1941 Japanese planes sprayed bubonic plague over parts of China. At least 5 separate instances of this occurring have been documented. In 1942 "bacterial bombs" were deployed on mainland China but these attacks were determined to be ineffective.

1942 The United States (US) becomes aware of the Japanese efforts in Biological Warfare (BW) and decided to start its own program. These acts were not the only atrocities committed, however. The Japanese released thousands of plague infested rats prior to their surrender, with unknown consequences. They also tested on American POW's during the war and the U.S. Government apparently knew about it, but did nothing (perhaps a worse atrocity). These people killed over 3000 POWs, including many Americans, in a variety of grisly experiments. What they did instead was to offer immunity to would-be war criminals in exchange for the information the Japanese learned from these experiments!

1942 Chemical Warfare Services begins mustard gas experiments on approximately 4,000 servicemen. The experiments continue until 1945 and made use of Seventh Day Adventists who chose to become human guinea pigs rather than serve on active duty. Link

1942 Great Britain was also developing a program in Biological Warfare (BW). The program focused on anthrax spores and their viability and "range of spread" when delivered with a conventional bomb. The fateful **Gruinard Island** off the coast of Scotland was chosen as the site for this testing. It was thought that it was far enough off the coast as too prevent any contamination of the mainland, which later turned out to be false. The data gathered from these experiments was used by both Great Britain and the U.S. to develop bombs that were better able to effectively disperse spores.

1943 After an outbreak of anthrax in sheep and cattle in 1943 on the coast of Scotland that directly faced Gruinard, the British decided to stop testing. A tragic consequence of this testing is that even today Gruinard Island is contaminated with Bacillus anthracis spores. The original idea for decontamination was to start a brushfire that burned off the top of the soil and killed all traces of the organisms. Unfortunately, the spores unexpectedly embedded themselves in the soil so total decontamination of the island was/is impossible. As long as no ground is disturbed, we are supposedly safe, but birds that travel back and forth from mainland to island probably don't know this!

1943 Planning began in1943 with the appointment of a special New York State Health Department committee to study the advisability of adding **fluoride** to Newburgh's drinking water. The chairman of the committee was, again, Dr Harold C. Hodge, then chief of fluoride toxicity studies for the Manhattan Project. Subsequent members of the committee included Henry L. Barnett, a captain in the Project's Medical Section, and John W. Fertig, in 1944 with the Office of Scientific Research and Development- the super-secret Pentagon group which sired the Manhattan Project. Their military affiliations were kept secret. Hodge was described as a pharmacologist, Barnett as a pediatrician. Placed in charge of the Newburgh project was David B. Ast, chief dental officer of the New York State Health Department. Ast had participated in a key secret wartime conference on fluoride, held by the Manhattan Project in January 1944, and later worked with Dr Hodge on the Project's investigation of human injury in the New Jersey incident, according to once-secret memos.

1944 A Manhattan Project memorandum of 29 April 1944 states: "Clinical evidence suggests that uranium hexafluoride may have a rather marked central nervous system effect... It seems most likely that the F [code for fluoride] component rather than the T [code for uranium] is the causative factor." The memo, from a captain in the medical corps, is stamped SECRET and is addressed to Colonel Stafford Warren, head of the Manhattan Project's Medical Section. Colonel Warren is asked to approve a program of animal research on CNS effects. "Since work with these compounds is essential, it will be necessary to know in advance what mental effects may occur after exposure... This is important not only to protect a given individual, but also to prevent a confused workman from injuring others by improperly performing his duties. The author of the 1944 CNS research proposal attached to the 29 April memo was Dr Harold C. Hodge-at the time, chief of fluoride toxicology studies for the University of Rochester division of the Manhattan Project.

1944 When a severe pollution incident occurred downwind of the E.I. DuPont de Nemours Company chemical factory in Deepwater, New Jersey. The factory was then producing millions of pounds of fluoride for the Manhattan Project whose scientists were racing to produce the world's first atomic bomb. The farms downwind in Gloucester and Salem counties were famous for their high-quality produce. Their peaches went

directly to the Waldorf Astoria Hotel in New York City; their tomatoes were bought up by Campbell's Soup. But in the summer of 1944 the farmers began reporting that their crops were blighted: "Something is burning up the peach crops around here." They said that poultry died after an all-night thunderstorm, and that farm workers who ate produce they'd picked would sometimes vomit all night and into the next day. "I remember our horses looked sick and were too stiff to work," Mildred Giordano, a teenager at the time, told these reporters. Some cows were so crippled that they could not stand up; they could only graze by crawling on their bellies. The account was confirmed in taped interviews with Philip Sadtler (shortly before he died), of Sadtler Laboratories of Philadelphia, one of the nation's oldest chemical consulting firms. Sadtler had personally conducted the initial investigation of the damage. The farmers were stonewalled in their search for information about fluoride's effects on their health, and **their complaints have long since been forgotten**. But they unknowingly left their imprint on history: their complaints of injury to their health reverberated through the corridors of power in Washington and triggered intensive, secret, bomb program research on the health effects of fluoride.
Link

1944 U.S. Navy uses human subjects to test gas masks and clothing. Individuals were locked in a gas chamber and exposed to mustard gas and lewisite.
Link

1945 May. Newburgh's water was fluoridated, and over the next 10 years its residents were studied by the New York State Health Department.

1945-1955 Much of the original proof that fluoride is safe for humans in low doses was generated by A-bomb program scientists who had been secretly ordered to provide "evidence useful in litigation" against defense contractors for fluoride injury to citizens. The first lawsuits against the American A-bomb program were not over radiation, but over fluoride damage, the documents show. Human studies were required. Bomb program researchers played a leading role in the design and implementation of the most extensive US study of the health effects of fluoridating public drinking water, conducted in Newburgh, New York, from 1945 to 1955. Then, in a classified operation code-named "Program F", they secretly gathered and analyzed blood and tissue samples from Newburgh citizens with the cooperation of New York State Health Department personnel. The original, secret version (obtained by these reporters) of a study published by Program F scientists in the August

1948 Journal of the American Dental Association1 shows that evidence of adverse health effects from fluoride was censored by the US Atomic Energy Commission (AEC)-considered the most powerful of Cold War agencies-for reasons of "national security". The bomb program's fluoride safety studies were conducted at the University of Rochester-site of one of the most notorious human radiation experiments of the Cold War, in which unsuspecting hospital patients were injected with toxic doses of radioactive plutonium. The fluoride studies were conducted with the same ethical mindset, in which "national security" was paramount.
Link
Hitler claimed to have gotten his inspiration for the "final solution" from the extermination of Native Americans in the U.S.

1947 By then, as the 1950s dawned, mad sheep disease was shown in the United States to jump the species barrier when a scrapie-infected food supplement brought a similar brain illness to farm-raised mink in 1947. By this stage, the medico-scientific fraternity was intensely preoccupied with another incurable brain illness, kuru, which had reached epidemic proportions amongst the Fore people living in the highlands of New Guinea. Anthropologists from the University of Adelaide unraveled a chain of events to trace the origin of kuru back to the reverent consumption of deceased tribal members' bodies. Kuru was essentially eradicated by New Guinean authorities acting in 1959 on the anthropological clue to outlaw the eating of human flesh.

1947 The CIA begins its study of LSD as a potential weapon for use by American intelligence. Human subjects (both civilian and military) are used with and without their knowledge.

1949 U.S. Army begins 20 years of simulated germ warfare attacks against American cities, conducting at least 239 open air tests.

1950 Sept. 20-26. One of the biggest experiments involved the use of Serratia marcescens and bacillus globigi being sprayed over 117 square miles of the San Francisco area, causing pneumonia-like infections in many of the residents. The family of one elderly man who died in the test sued the government, but lost. To this day, syraceus is a leading cause of death among the elderly in the San Francisco area.

1950 Department of Defense begins plans to detonate nuclear weapons in desert areas and monitor downwind residents for medical problems and mortality rates

1953 U.S. military releases clouds of zinc cadmium sulfide gas over Winnipeg, St. Louis, Minneapolis, Fort Wayne, the Monocacy River Valley in Maryland, and Leesburg, Virginia. Their intent is to determine how efficiently they could disperse chemical agents.

1953 CIA initiates Project **MKULTRA**. This is an eleven year research program designed to produce and test drugs and biological agents that would be used for mind control and behavior modification. Six of the sub-projects involved testing the agents on unwitting human beings.

1955 Another case was the joint Army-CIA BW test in 1955, still classified, in which an undisclosed bacteria was released in the Tampa Bay region of Florida, causing a dramatic increase in whooping cough infections, including twelve deaths.

1956 The Soviet Union accused the U.S. of using biological weapons in Korea, which lead them to threaten future use of Chemical and Biological weapons. This changed the focus of the U.S. program to a more defensive one. Before this, the bulk of the research was based at Ft. Detrick and used "surrogate biological agents" to model more deadly organisms. Most of the offensive tests were based on "secret spraying" of organisms over populated areas. This program was (supposedly) shut down in 1969.

1956 Cambodia established gun control. From 1975 to 1977, one million "educated" people, unable to defend themselves, were rounded up and exterminated.
Other experiments included tests on Minneapolis that were disguised as "smoke screen tests" because residents were told a harmless smoke was being tested so that cities might be 'hidden' from radar guided missiles.

1956 U.S. military releases mosquitoes infected with Yellow Fever over Savannah, Ga and Avon Park, Fl. Following each test, Army agents posing as public health officials test victims for effects.

1958 LSD is tested on 95 volunteers at the Army's Chemical Warfare Laboratories for its effect on intelligence.

1960 The Army Assistant Chief-of-Staff for Intelligence (ACSI) authorizes field testing of LSD in Europe and the Far East. Testing of the European population is code named Project THIRD CHANCE; testing of the Asian population is code named Project DERBY HAT.

1963 The mass **vaccination** campaigns of the 1950s and '60s may be causing hundreds of deaths a year because of a cancer-causing virus that contaminated the first polio vaccine, according to scientists. Known as SV40, the virus came from dead monkeys whose kidney cells were used to culture the first Salk vaccines. Doctors estimate that the virus was injected into tens of millions during the vaccination campaigns, including several million in Canada, before being detected and screened out in 1963. Those born between 1941 and 1961 are thought to be most at risk of having been infected.

1964 Guatemala established gun control. From 1964 to 1981, 100,000 Mayan Indians, unable to defend themselves, were rounded up and exterminated.

1965 **Aspartame** is the technical name for the brand names, NutraSweet, Equal, Spoonful, and Equal-Measure. Aspartame was discovered by accident in 1965, when James Schlatter, a chemist of G.D. Searle Company was testing an anti-ulcer drug. Aspartame was approved for dry goods in 1981 and for carbonated beverages in 1983.

1965 Project CIA and Department of Defense begin Project MKSEARCH, a program to develop a capability to manipulate human behavior through the use of mind-altering drugs.

1965 Prisoners at the Holmesburg State Prison in Philadelphia are subjected to **dioxin**, the highly toxic chemical component of **Agent Orange** used in Viet Nam. The men are later studied for development of cancer, which indicates that Agent Orange had been a suspected carcinogen all along.

1966 CIA initiates Project MKOFTEN, a program to test the toxicological effects of certain drugs on humans and animals.

1966 July 7-10, The virus Bacillus subtilis was released throughout the New York subway system, conducted by the U.S. Army's Special Operations Division. Due to the vast number of people exposed it would virtually impossible to identify, let alone prove, and specific health problems resulting directly from this test.

1967 CIA and Department of Defense implement Project MKNAOMI, successor to MKULTRA and designed to maintain, stockpile and test biological and chemical weapons.

1968 CIA experiments with the possibility of poisoning drinking water by injecting chemicals into the water supply of the FDA in Washington, D.C.

1968 - 69 The Hong Kong flu, which was influenza A type H3N2, killed over 30,000 people in the U.S. alone. That was a fortuitous learning event for some because it taught them that the flu could still conceivably be used to wipe out a population. But at the same time, it pointed out the need to precondition the populace so that those who might normally be resistant could be rendered susceptible. Hence the development of the vaccine program and the aerial spraying procedures to condition the population. The purpose of the chemicals in the chemtrails is to help the viral envelope fuse with lung cells, permitting easier penetration and infection.

1969 At a House Appropriations hearing, the Defense Department's Biological Warfare (BW) division requested funds to develop through gene-splicing a new disease that would both resist and break down a victim's immune system. "Within the next 5 to 10 years it would probably be possible to make a new infective micro-organism which could differ in certain important respects from any known disease-causing organisms. Most important of these is that it might be refractory to the immunological and therapeutic processes upon which we depend to maintain our relative freedom from infectious diseases." The funds were approved. AIDS appeared within the requested time frame, and has the exact characteristics specified.

1970 Uganda established gun control. From 1971 to 1979, 300,000 Christians, unable to defend themselves, were rounded up and exterminated.

1972 The World Health Organization (W.H.O.) published a similar proposal: "An attempt should be made to ascertain whether viruses can in fact exert selective effects on immune function, e.g., by ...affecting T cell function as opposed to B cell function. The possibility should also be looked into that the immune response to the virus itself may be impaired if the infecting virus damages more or less selectively the cells responding to the viral antigens." (Bulletin of the W.H.O., vol. 47, p 257-274.) This is a clinical description of the function of the AIDS virus.

1972 It was discovered that black children as young as age five were having psychosurgery performed on them at the University of Mississippi in Jackson in order to control "hyperactive" and "aggressive" behavior.

Their brains were being implanted with electrodes that were heated up to melt areas of the brain that regulate emotion and intellect. When we first opposed these experiments, and eventually stopped them, we did so despite resistance from organized psychiatry and the research community.

Mid-1970's The incidence of AIDS infections in Africa coincides exactly with the locations of the W.H.O. smallpox vaccination program in the mid-1970's (London Times, May 11, 1987). Some 14,000 Haitians then on UN secondment to Central Africa were also vaccinated in this campaign. Personnel actually conducting the vaccinations may have been completely unaware that the vaccine was anything other than what they were told.

1975 Two neuroscientists, Laura and (the late) Eli Manuelides, from Yale University in the US, went on to illustrate by 1975 that injections of human blood, like injections of brain taken from kuru and CJD victims, transmitted the disease across the species barrier to laboratory animals. Their prophetic, but unheeded, message implied that blood was the vehicle that carried the agent of CJD around the body until it chanced upon an hospitable residence like the brain. This meant that the blood route was the key to the transmission of CJD from a primary host to a secondary host.

1975 The virus section of Fort Detrick's Center for Biological Warfare Research is renamed the Fredrick Cancer Research Facilities and placed under the supervision of the National Cancer Institute (NCI) . It is here that a special virus cancer program is initiated by the U.S. Navy, purportedly to develop cancer-causing viruses. It is also here that retrovirologists isolate a virus to which no immunity exists. It is lat er named HTLV (Human T-cell Leukemia Virus).

1976 Nobel Prize went to American scientist Carleton Gajdusek for his experiments demonstrating that injections of kuru brain (1967) and CJD brain (1969) reproduced similar illnesses in chimpanzees.
A striking feature of AIDS is that it's ethno-selective. The rate of infection is twice as high among Blacks, Latinos and Native Americans as among whites, with death coming two to three times as swiftly. And over 80% of the children with AIDS and 90% of infants born with it are among these minorities. "Ethnic weapons" that would strike certain racial groups more heavily than others have been a long-standing U.S. Army BW objective. (Harris and Paxman, p 265)
The "discovery" of the AIDS virus (HTLV3) was announced by Dr. Robert Gallo at the National Cancer Institute, which is on the grounds of

Fort Detrick, Maryland, a primary U.S. Army biological warfare research facility.

1977 Senate hearings on Health and Scientific Research confirm that 239 populated areas had been contaminated with biological agents between 1949 and 1969. Some of the areas included San Francisco, Washington, D.C., Key West, Panama City, Minneapolis, and St. Louis.

1978 The Hepatitis B vaccine study appears to have been the initial means of planting the infection in New York City. The test protocol specified non-monogamous males only, and homosexuals received a different vaccine from heterosexuals. At least 25-50% of the first reported New York AIDS cases in 1981 had received the Hepatitis B test vaccine in 1978. By 1984, 64% of the vaccine recipients had AIDS, and the figures on the current infection rate for the participants of that study are held by the U.S. Department of Justice, and "unavailable."

1978-1987 Even as the understanding of spongiform encephalopathy increased, various human pituitary hormone programs in countries such as Australia, France, New Zealand, the United Kingdom and United States were attracting hefty government sponsorships. Few of the programs' stalwarts caught on to the implications of the Manuelides' experiments, and unsuccessful attempts between the years of 1978 and 1987 to filter the CJD agent out of the pituitary hormones being injected into unsuspecting short-statured children and infertile women were left to one of this era's rare visionaries, British scrapie expert Alan Dickinson. At about the same time, a British Royal Commission on Environmental Pollution in 1979 raised the possibility that the unregulated cycling of protein-rich sheep remains back into animal feed might spread scrapie to cattle, as it had done to farm mink in the US three decades beforehand, via the oral route.

1979 There was an explosion at a Soviet plant in Sverdlosk and an outbreak of anthrax followed. At the time, all accusations of BW research were vigorously denied by Soviet officials, with the explanation that anthrax outbreaks can occur naturally and that the explosion was merely a coincidence.

1979 June , a well-dressed, articulate stranger visited the office of the Elberton Granite Finishing Company and announced that he wanted to build an edifice to transmit a message to mankind. He identified himself as R. C. Christian, but it soon became apparent that was not his real name. He said that he represented a group of men who wanted to offer direction to humanity, but to date, almost two decades later, no one knows who R. C. Christian really was, or the names of those he represented. Several things are apparent. The messages engraved on the Georgia Guidestones deal with four major fields: (1) Governance and the establishment of a world government, (2) Population and reproduction control, (3) The environment and man's relationship to nature, and (4) Spirituality. In the public library in Elberton, I found a book written by the man who called himself R.C. Christian. I discovered that the monument he commissioned had been erected in recognition of Thomas Paine and the occult philosophy he espoused. Indeed, the Georgia Guidestones are used for occult ceremonies and mystic celebrations to this very day. Tragically, only one religious leader in the area had the courage to speak out against the American Stonehenge, and he has recently relocated his ministry.

The Georgia Guidestones

1981 Aspartame was invented by the G D Searle Co. acquired by Monsanto in 1985. For 16 years FDA refused to approve it until 1981 when Commissioner Arthur Hayes overruled the objections of a Public Board of Inquiry and the protests of the American Soft Drink Association and blessed it. The tests submitted by Searle were so bad the Department of Justice, initiated prosecution of Searle for fraud. Then the defense lawyers hired the prosecutors, Sam Skinner and Wm. Conlon, and the case expired when the statute of limitations ran out. Aspartame/Nutrasweet, a toxin that blinds, drops intelligence, eradicates memory, grows brain tumors and other cancers, brings fatigue. Depression, ADD, panic, rage, paranoia, diabetes, seizures, suicide and death. This toxin is supported by unlimited advertising and the manufacturers pay off the American Diatetics Association, the American Diabetics Association, the AMA, and whomever else, to convince us its safe as rain. These lies are backed by a Federal Bureaucracy knowing it may kill your child, but the bureaucrat who approved the poison got a fat job as have many of his successors. Suppose this government watchdog, ignoring thousands of consumer complaints, has become an Attack Dog protecting corporate corruption. This is the bitter reality of Aspartame/Nutrasweet, Monsanto, the FDA, Coca Cola, Pepsi, and the hundreds of food, drink and drug makers who add to their products a known poison Conceived in Fraud and Dedicated to the Proposition that Profit is all that Matters! (They're Poisoning Our Kids - Aspartame Warning The Facts From Betty Martin <mailto:Mission-Possible-USA@altavista.netMission-Possible-USA@altavista.net< /FONT>

352

Dr Miguel A. Baret of the Dominican Republic removed milk from 360 children's diets, because cow's milk has a specific protein that can cause diabetes, especially in children. They drank juice laced with aspartame instead and many developed "abnormal restlessness, lack of concentration, irritability and depression." When Dr Baret removed it: "The results were astonishing. Their symptoms disappeared in 4-6 days in ALL of them!" Thank you, Dr Baret, for this study showing what aspartame does to the brains of our kids!

1984, July 4. The first detailed charges regarding AIDS as a BW weapon were published in the Patriot newspaper in New Delhi, India. It is hard to say where the investigations of this story in the Indian press might have led, if they had not been sidetracked by two major domestic disasters shortly thereafter: the assassination of Indira Gandhi on Oct. 31 and the Bhopal Union Carbide plant "accident" that killed several thousand and injured over 200,000 on Dec. 3.

1985 The first of the fatal legacies of this form of medical madness emerged with four cases of CJD in human pituitary growth hormone-treated children.

1986 According to the Proceedings of the National Academy of Sciences (83:4007-4011), HIV and VISNA are highly similar and share all structural elements, except for a small segment which is nearly identical to HTLV. This leads to speculation that HTLV and VISNA may have been linked to produce a new retrovirus to which no natural immunity exists.

1987 Dr Louis Elsas, Professor of Pediatrics & Genetics at Emory University, testified before Congress; "Aspartame is in fact a well known neurotoxin and teratogen [triggers birth defects] which in some undefined dose will irreversibly in the developing child or fetal brain, produce adverse effects I am particularly angry at this type of advertising that is promoting the sale of a neurotoxin in the childhood age group." [Nov 2, 1987]

Neurosurgeon Russell Blaylock, MD, declares Aspartame is a toxin like arsenic and cyanide that causes confusion, disorientation, seizures, cancer, pancreatic, uterine, ovarian and brain tumors and leads to Alzheimer's. Read Excitotoxins, the Taste That Kills [505-474-0303]. Hear Dr. Blaylock's radio interview on http://www.dorway.com/' Courageous whistleblowers like these have spoken in three congressional hearings, but industry's lobbying and political action keep the poison in the foods of the world. Our recourse as consumers is personal communication since the media is paid by advertising to push Nutrasweet/Equal/Diet Coke, etc..

1987 Department of Defense admits that, despite a treaty banning research and development of biological agents, it continues to operate research facilities at 127 facilities and universities around the nation.

1989 During which time the number of French children at risk of growth-hormone-related CJD had practically doubled, the first French children fulfilled that tragic legacy. In 1993, those responsible for this travesty were threatened with manslaughter charges. By 1997, France had half of the world's 100-plus cases of pituitary hormone-related CJD.

1990 More than 1500 six-month old black and Hispanic babies in Los Angeles are given an "experimental" measles vaccine that had never been licensed for use in the United States. CDC later admits that parents were never informed that the vaccine being injected to their children was experimental.

1991 Although the general elitism of human-pituitary programs restricted this brand of medical madness to North America, Europe and Australasian, Third World children and women did not altogether escape the insanity of applying Frankenstein medicine to social conditions. A medical report in 1991 linked the CJD death of a young Brazilian man, like those of five youthful New Zealand men and women, with a childhood treatment involving pituitary growth hormone obtained from the US. Unfortunately, the fate of women in Mexico City whose breasts were injected with US pituitary hormones in an appalling experiment to increase the volume of milk in lactating mothers (some already pregnant again) will probably never be known.

1992 It was discovered the federal violence initiative--the federal government's agency-wide plan to go into America's inner cities to experiment on children in the hope of finding genetic and biological causes for violence. We opposed this program as racist and abusive of children. Our efforts led to the cancellation of this program. It also led the chief sponsor of the program, psychiatrist Frederick Goodwin, to resign from his post as director of NIMH and to leave a career in the government. The fenfluramine studies at Columbia and Queens College are part of the violence initiative. They were created under its umbrella before it was cancelled. They confirm our fears that while the public aspects of the violence initiative were withdrawn, the actual individual projects continue unabated.

1992 Boris Yeltsin confirmed that anthrax was being researched at Sverdlosk and vowed to stop all "Soviet" BW research. Unfortunately, defectors have contradicted Yeltsin and there are rumors that although the 'official government' statement and ideal may be an elimination of biological weapons, the military is still actively pursuing a BW program on its own.

1993 The FDA approved aspartame as an ingredient in numerous food items that would always be heated to above 86°degrees F (30°Degrees C). An act that can only be described as "unconscionable"

1994 One has only to learn what really happened to the Christians in Rwanda between April and July of 1994 to imagine what may lie in store for Christians here in America at some time in the not-too-distant future. After the Christian Tutsis had been disarmed by governmental decree in the early 1990s, Hutu-led military forces began to systematically massacre the defenseless Christians. The massacre began in April 1994 and continued until July 1994. Using machetes rather than bullets, the Hutu forces were able to create a state of abject fear and terror within the helpless Christian population as they systematically butchered hundreds of thousands of them. The United Nations immediately convened hearings on the genocide taking place in Rwanda, but Madeline Albright, the American Ambassador to the United Nations, argued strenuously that neighboring African nations should not be allowed to intervene until the "civil war had come to an end." In reality, of course, there was no civil war since those being slaughtered had no weapons with which to defend themselves; it was simply a matter of mass murder. In addition to blocking intervention by neighboring nations, Madeline Albright also insisted that the word "genocide" must not be used, and that the United Nations forces stationed in Rwanda were not to be allowed to intervene. In the three months that followed, between one-half and three-quarters of a million Christians were systematically dismembered, hacked to death, and slaughtered in the bloody carnage that ensued. Tens of thousands of Christians were murdered in their churches; tens of thousands more were murdered in their hospitals and in their schools. On several occasions, United Nations soldiers stationed in Rwanda actually handed over helpless Christians under their protection to members of the Hutu militia. They then stood by as their screaming charges were unceremoniously hacked to pieces. At the end of the carnage, in late July 1994, the American government rewarded the Hutu murderers with millions of dollars in foreign aid. Strangely, the American press has remained silent (Subversio n Of The Free Press By The CIA) about the fact that almost all of those who were slaughtered were Christians, and it was the policies of our government that were primarily responsible for blocking efforts by neighboring African countries to intervene. The Population Control Agenda

1994 With a technique called "gene tracking," Dr. Garth Nicolson at the MD Anderson Cancer Center in Houston, TX discovers that many returning Desert Storm veterans are infected with an altered strain of Mycoplasma incognitus, a microbe commonly used in the production of biological weapons. Incorporated into its molecular structure is 40 percent of the HIV protein coat, indicating that it had been man-made.

1995 Dr Phyllis Mullenix, former head of toxicology at Forsyth Dental Center in Boston and now a critic of fluoridation. Animal studies which Mullenix and co-workers conducted at Forsyth in the early 1990s indicated that fluoride was a powerful central nervous system (CNS) toxin and might adversely affect human brain functioning even at low doses. (New epidemiological evidence from China adds support, showing a correlation between low-dose fluoride exposure and diminished IQ in children.) Mullenix's results were published in 1995 in a reputable peer-reviewed scientific journal.

1995 The University of Rochester's classified fluoride studies, code-named "Program F", were started during the war and continued up until the early 1950s. They were conducted at its Atomic Energy Project (AEP), a top-secret facility funded by the AEC and housed at Strong Memorial Hospital. It was there that one of the most notorious human radiation experiments of the Cold War took place, in which unsuspecting hospital patients were injected with toxic doses of radioactive plutonium. Revelation of this experiment-in a Pulitzer Prize&endash;winning account by Eileen Welsome-led to a 1995 US presidential investigation and a multimillion-dollar cash settlement for victims.

1995 U.S. Government admits that it had offered Japanese war criminals and scientists who had performed human medical experiments salaries and immunity from prosecution in exchange for data on biological warfare research.

1995 Dr. Garth Nicolson, uncovers evidence that the biological agents used during the Gulf War had been manufactured in Houston, TX and

Boca Raton, Fl and tested on prisoners in the Texas Department of Corrections.

1996, 27 June without public notice, the FDA removed all restrictions from aspartame allowing it to be used in everything, including all heated and baked goods. The truth about aspartame's toxicity is far different than what the NutraSweet Company would have you readers believe.

1996 A new scientific paper dealing with a meta-analysis of 23 different scientific studies on the relationship between first-trimester abortions and breast cancer was published in a British medical journal. That study clearly demonstrated a higher incidence of breast cancer in women who had hadfirst-trimester abortions. In response to that publication, the American Medical Association (AMA), the American Cancer Society (ACS), and pro-abortion/population-control advocates joined together in an unholy alliance to attack the conclusions of the authors, and to block all efforts to disseminate that information to American physicians.
The Population Control Agenda

1997 October. Speaking from Washington, DC, Nobel Prize winner for discovering the role of molecules known as "prions" in the invariably fatal brain illnesses such as "mad cow disease" or bovine spongiform encephalopathy (BSE) in cattle, and Creutzfeldt-Jakob disease (CJD) in humans, Dr Stanley Prusiner from the University of California predicted that the first drug therapy, which would not necessarily be a cure for BSE or CJD, was at least five years away. At the same time, on the opposite side of the Atlantic, the post-mortem of Chris Warne, a 36-year-old fitness fanatic from Derbyshire, England, revealed that he was the 21st victim of the new variant of CJD which had spread from BSE-infected cattle to humans via the food chain. Only 18 months earlier, a British House of Commons admission that BSE-infected meat had probably caused the CJD deaths of 10 youthful Britons left the British meat industry in tatters. Since then, the history of BSE has gradually unfolded to reveal a brain-dead imperialism, one which, while blinded by its own arrogant greed to inflate market profits, has treated public and, indeed, world health with gay abandon. Formerly a rare disease which affected less than one per million in most countries, one worst-case scenario predicts that BSE-infected meat will push the incidence of CJD in humans to claim 10,000 British lives by the year 2000, and a further 10 million by the year 2010. Another predicts that half the British people, some 30 million, will be left brain-dead by CJD. As Chris Warne's mother commented, her son was a health-conscious sportsman, but "after

winning medals in March, by July he couldn't stand on his feet, and by October he was gone".
Volume 5, #1

Researchers at the US Army Medical Research Institute of Infectious Diseases (or USAMRIID) at Fort Detrick in Frederick MD have reconstructed and modified the H1N1 Spanish Flu virus, making it far more deadly than it ever was back when it was responsible for the 1918-1919 flu pandemic that killed over 20 million worldwide and over 500,000 here in the US.

FRANCE is facing a new health scandal following allegations that the prestigious Pasteur Institute willfully ignored warnings that up to 600 children were being injected with cancerous hormones.

The disclosures that children may have been put at risk emerged during a new investigation into the link between the growth hormones and Creutzfeldt-Jakob disease (CJD), which caused a major scandal when acknowledged in the Nineties . So far, 74 children have died of CJD after being treated with growth hormones extracted from the bodies of victims of neurological illnesses in the Eighties.

That scandal and the contaminated blood affair in which 4,000 people were infected with HIV through unscreened blood transfusions - despite the availability of an American test forthe virus - have contributed to France's acute sensitivity on health issues. When the contaminated blood affair came to trial in 1998 , it was alleged that authorization for the American test was withheld to give the institute time to develop a rival French test.

The latest claims suggest that in 1985 the institute sold a batch of growth hormone to French hospitals without waiting for safety checks which showed the batch to have cancer marker cells at five times the permitted limit for use. The institute is further alleged to have made no efforts to withdraw the batch once it was aware of the risk.

References

Cole, Leonard A. Clouds of secrecy:
the army's germ warfare tests over populated areas,
Rowman & Littlefield, Totowa, N.J. , 1988

Hersh, Seymour M. Chemical and biological warfare:
America's hidden arsenal,
Bobbs-Merrill,
Indianapolis, 1968

Murphy, Sean.
No fire, no thunder: the threat of chemical and biological weapons,
Monthly Review Press,
New York , 1984

Piller, Charles.
Gene wars: military control over the new genetic technologies,
Beech Tree Books,
New York, 1988

Spiers, Edward M. Chemical and Biological Weapons:
A Study in Proliferation,
St. Martin's Press,
New York, 1994

A Higher Form of Killing:
The Secret Story of Chemical and Biological Warfare
by R. Harris and J. Paxman,
p 266, Hill and Wang, pubs.

Covert Action Information Bulletin #28 ($5),
Box 50272,
Washington, D.C. 20004;

Bio-Attack Alert ($20), Dr. Robert Strecker,
1501 Colorado Blvd.,
Los Angeles, CA 90041;

Radio Free America #16 by Dave Emery and Nip Tuck
(3 tapes, $10),
Davkore Co.,
1300-D Space Park Way,
Mountain View, CA 94043.

Critique - Exposing Consensus Reality,
P.O. Box 11368, Santa Rosa, CA 95406.
$15.00 for three issues (one year).

Project Paperclip by Clarence Lasby,
Atheneum 214, NY, and Gehlen:

Spy of the Century by E.H. Cookridge,
Random House.

DESIGNER DISEASES: AIDS As Biological & Psychological Warfare
by Waves Forrest

Contaminated Early Polio Vaccinations Linked To Cancer Epidemic
By Robert Matthews & Adrian Humphreys
The Sunday Telegraph and National Post Ontario,
Canada 5-18-99

On Line References

History of Biological Warfare

Eugenics

http://www.holisticmed.com/aspartame/

http://www.nexusmagazine.com/

The Population Control Agenda

Get links to over 200 sites on aspartame

US Government Experiments On Children During The Cold War

Chemically Induced Compliance: The Drugging of Kids and Garbage
Science in America

http://user.mc.net/dougp/ahm/cor1.htmEugenics

The Illuminati Wants to Reduce the Population with 90%

http://www.healthnewsnet.com/humanexperiments.html

Silent Weapons For A Quiet War

Another Dark Chemtrail Hypothesis

Subversion of the free Press by the CIA

Comment

From Alan Cantwell
11-15-00

1976 Nobel Prize went to American scientist Carleton Gajdusek for his experiments demonstrating that injections of kuru brain (1967) and CJD brain (1969) reproduced similar illnesses in chimpanzees.

A striking feature of AIDS is that it's ethno-selective. The rate of infection is twice as high among Blacks, Latinos and Native Americans as among whites, with death coming two to three times as swiftly. And over 80% of the children with AIDS and 90% of infants born with it are among these minorities. "Ethnic weapons" that would strike certain racial groups more heavily than others have been a long-standing U.S. Army BW objective. (Harris and Paxman, p 265)

The "discovery" of the AIDS virus (HTLV3) was announced by Dr. Robert Gallo at the National Cancer Institute, which is on the grounds of Fort Detrick, Maryland, a primary U.S. Army biological warfare research facility.

I would quibble about substantiating evidence for the last paragraph (Gallo, HIV 1976 timeline).

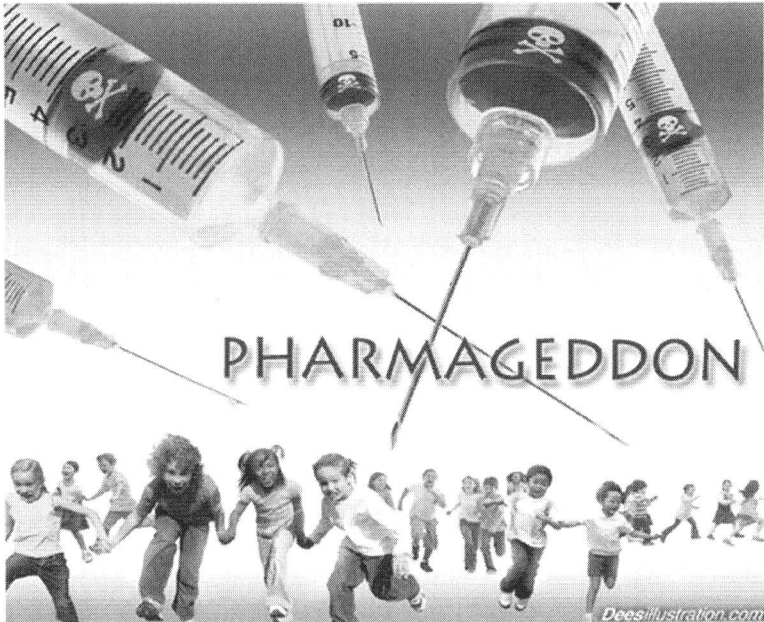

PHARMAGEDDON

Deesillustration.com

809 VACCINES

"Your failure to be informed does not make me a wacko." -- John Loeffler

I have no medical training, but I can read.

I find this topic sorely distressing. Aggravating that distress is that I am not sure if it is simply a case of human madness and insanity initiated by callous greed, or if in fact there is something far more sinister than mere corporate greed implementing and sustaining this assault on humanity.

There is little doubt when the facts and case histories are laid open and bared that untold death, debilitation, and injury are a direct result of the vaccination "industry".

Regardless of what I think, it is imperative that you, the reader, put yourself in a position where you really can make an informed decision about the entire subject rather than just blindly accept and submit yourself and family to this practice. Death and permanent injury are not denied by the "industry", rather they play down the unfortunates numbers and statistics as just bad luck, or a result of "complications" that are unfortunate. Put it this way: would you join a queue knowing at every so often one of you would randomly be taken out and summararily executed? Would you put your children in that line? Would you allow yourself or family to play with a loaded revolver?

As this is indeed such a painful issue (and I have had family issues relating to "bad reaction" to vaccines that resulted in our sane family doctor advising "no more vaccinations" for the child") I must personally be brief in my comments. However the matter requires your most urgent attention and investigations.   Hereunder are some pointers and information that are merely a start.   The resources available for your consideration are larger than you can imagine.

In short, we the people are being wilfully and knowingly killed off. No one is being held accountable for a genocide.

****

1963. The mass **vaccination** campaigns of the 1950s and '60s may be causing hundreds of deaths a year because of a cancer-causing virus that contaminated the first polio vaccine, according to scientists. Known as SV40, the virus came from dead monkeys whose kidney cells were used to culture the first Salk vaccines. Doctors estimate that the virus was injected into tens of millions during the vaccination campaigns, including several million in Canada, before being detected and screened out in 1963. Those born between 1941 and 1961 are thought to be most at risk of having been infected.

Mid-1970's. The incidence of AIDS infections in Africa coincides exactly with the locations of the W.H.O. smallpox vaccination program in the mid-1970's (London Times, May 11, 1987). Some 14,000 Haitians then on UN secondment to Central Africa were also vaccinated in this campaign. Personnel actually conducting the vaccinations may have been completely unaware that the vaccine was anything other than what they were told.

1978. The Hepatitis B vaccine study appears to have been the initial means of planting the infection in New York City. The test protocol specified non-monogamous males only, and homosexuals received a different vaccine from heterosexuals. At least 25-50% of the first reported New York AIDS cases in 1981 had received the Hepatitis B test vaccine in 1978. By 1984, 64% of the vaccine recipients had AIDS, and the figures on the current infection rate for the participants of that study are held by the U.S. Department of Justice, and "unavailable."

****

"As a legislator, I believe mandated smallpox vaccines are very bad policy. The point is not that smallpox vaccines are necessarily a bad idea, but rather that intimately personal medical decisions should not be made by government. The real issue is individual medical choice. No single person, including the President of the United States, should ever be given the power to make a medical decision for potentially millions of Americans. Freedom over one's physical person is the most basic freedom of all, and people in a free society should be sovereign over their own bodies. When we give government the power to make medical decisions for us, we in essence accept that the state owns our bodies." (Ron Paul MD, LewRockwell.com)

Vaccinations - good or bad? updated April 2008

The idea of vaccination is that if you give the immune system a small "taste" of a bug (such as polio, whooping cough etc) it will make antibodies which will protect one against future exposures to the real thing. Good idea, but in practice it is not as simple.

My medical training tells me that all these issues should be resolved by logical argument. But in the modern world, all these arguments are tainted by vested interest (primarily from drug companies) and it is difficult to trust the data with which one is presented. Therefore one ends up working from either limited data, or untrustworthy data, or common sense and experience and ends up with a belief. So what you are getting below are my individual conclusions, but it is up to every parent to find what information they can and make up their own minds.

The evidence that vaccinations reduce incidence of disease is pretty thin. Most infectious diseases have declined as a result of improved hygiene and nutrition. Doctors believe that vaccinations work and are reluctant to diagnose a disease in a vaccinated child. So for example since polio vaccine, polio is rarely diagnosed, but there has been an increase in aseptic meningitis.

The medical profession, backed up by the pharmaceutical and chemical industry, are experts in cover ups. When doctors find themselves in trouble they close ranks. Most people have seen cover ups for themselves with drug side effects (which kill huge numbers of people every year but are hushed up). I see cover ups in patients with pesticide poisoning, with problems from silicone breast implants and in Gulf War syndrome. Doubtless there are others and I know vaccine damage is covered up and/or denied. I have seen too many children with serious health problems dating from vaccination for which there is no other explanation for their illness. I have to believe the evidence of my own eyes.

Vaccines can cause harm

There is now strong evidence that part of Gulf War Syndrome was caused by multiple vaccinations. MMR has been linked with autism and there is still a case to be answered here. There are many cases of brain damaged children following triple vaccine (diptheria, pertussis, tetanus).

Vaccines may be causing harm in unseen ways

Polio vaccination may be the cause of the huge increase in post viral fatigue syndrome. Before polio vaccination, post viral syndrome was rare. This is because people caught polio (which occasionally results in paralysis) which is an enterovirus. They mounted a vigorous immune reaction against polio virus which gave them cross-immunity against all other enteroviruses including Epstein Barr (glandular fever), coxsackie B, ECHO etc. This protected them against post viral fatigue since this most commonly follows an enteroviral infection.

We now know that many cancers are caused by viral infection. Obvious examples include hepatitis B (primary liver cancer), cervical wart virus (cervical cancer) and AIDS (Kaposi's sarcoma). Chronic myeloid leukaemia is probably virally induced. How many other cancers could there be from which we are protected by proper exposure to a virus, but not protected by vaccination? Nobody knows the answer to this question. And certainly no studies are being done.

What is in a vaccine?

Not just bits of bacteria and viruses. No immune system is going to react vigorously against a few dead or half alive (attenuated) cells. To turn the immune system on a vaccine needs an immune adjuvant added. These include aluminium and mercury which are toxic in their own right. It may well be that autism following MMR is actually a mercury problem.

Vaccines are made from bugs which are grown in animal tissues including beef. There is evidence to suggest that the cases of new variant CJD in young people may be due to direct injection of prion from these tissue cultures.

So what is the alternative?

We should be tackling infectious disease by good hygiene and boosting the immune system.

Good hygiene

By good hygiene definitely I do not mean obsessively wiping down working surfaces with antiseptic wipes. Indeed this is counter productive because we need daily exposure to bacteria to train and programme the immune system. What I recommend is proper public health measures such as:

* Not pumping raw sewage into the seas for people to swim in.

* Not making animals travel hundreds of miles to slaughter houses so they crap themselves on the way and get covered with shit, contaminating meat subsequently. Please try to buy local produce, or organic produce which has animal care standards.

* Not keeping chickens so intensively that they need constant antibiotics to survive chronic salmonella.

* Moving towards more organic farming practices i.e. away from intensive farming, use of properly composted animal waste, using local suppliers etc.

* Sexually transmitted diseases are presently all too common. Take proper precautions.

* We should not be concentrating sick and ill people in large general hospitals. This means that antibiotic resistant organisms can develop and spread quickly from one patient to the next.

* There are many other ideas for good hygiene. It is important to think carefully for yourselves. Please do not assume that "hygienic" chemical solutions are the answer.

Boosting the immune system

Human beings live on a knife edge with their immune systems. The immune system has a delicate balancing act because it needs to be able to recognise bugs and attack them, it must recognise cancer cells and attack them, but it must recognise "self" i.e. human bacteria/bugs and human cells and and ignore them. It is already confused by chemicals.

We should not be thinking about getting rid of the bug. This will always be impossible simply because "nature abhors a vacuum" and if you get rid of one bug, another will take its place.

Therefore we should be thinking about individual resistance to disease i.e. making people so healthy through good diet, good micronutrient status (vitamins and minerals) and freedom from toxins (i.e. red herrings and obstacles) that the immune system can easily resist any bugs that do gain entry. For example, measles can cause eye damage, but not if there is good vitamin A status.

The trouble is that against all these arguments is the combined weight of the medical profession and pharmaceutical companies who financially drive government and control the Press telling us that vaccination is safe and desirable. Nowadays logical argument no longer prevails and policy is dictated by big business and cash.

So what vaccinations would I give my child today?

No DPT in the first few months of life (I would look for protection from breast feeding).

I would give polio because I do not want to risk paralysis and I believe good nutrition will protect my child from other severe enteroviral infections.

No MMR (I want my child to get these infections young when the immune system, with good nutrition, can deal efficiently with these infections). See MMR vaccination - should my child have it?

Good HealthKeeping is a website with information on obtaining single vaccines.

Once my child started running around outside I would give tetanus vaccination.

No BCG.

With a daughter, I would check rubella status as a teenager and use vaccination if she was negative: I do not want her to get rubella during pregnancy.

In conclusion

These, as I say, are my beliefs. They may well change in the future as I learn new things.

For a list of vaccine ingredients refer to RENSE.COM

Rense.com

Vaccine Ingredients -
Formaldehyde, Aspartame,
Mercury, Etc
11-11-4

This following list of common vaccines and their ingredients should shock anyone.

The numbers of microbes, antibiotics, chemicals, heavy metals and animal byproducts is staggering. Would you knowingly inject these materials into your children?

Acel-Immune DTaP - **Diphtheria-Tetanus-Pertussis** Wyeth-Ayerst 800.934.5556
* diphtheria and tetanus toxoids and acellular pertussis adsorbed, formaldehyde, aluminum hydroxide, aluminum phosphate, thimerosal, and polysorbate 80 (Tween-80) gelatin Act HIB

Haemophilus - **Influenza B** Connaught Laboratories 800.822.2463
* Haemophilus influenza Type B, polyribosylribitol phosphate ammonium sulfate, formalin, and sucrose

Attenuvax - **Measles** Merck & Co., Inc. 800-672-6372
* measles live virus neomycin sorbitol hydrolized gelatin, chick embryo

Biavax - **Rubella** Merck & Co., Inc. 800-672-6372
* rubella live virus neomycin sorbitol hydrolized gelatin, human diploid cells from aborted fetal tissue

BioThrax - Anthrax Adsorbed BioPort Corporation 517.327.1500
* nonencapsulated strain of Bacillus anthracis aluminum hydroxide, benzethonium chloride, and formaldehyde

DPT - **Diphtheria-Tetanus-Pertussis** GlaxoSmithKline 800.366.8900 x5231
* diphtheria and tetanus toxoids and acellular pertussis adsorbed, formaldehyde, aluminum phosphate, ammonium sulfate, and thimerosal, washed sheep RBCs

Dryvax - **Smallpox** (not licensed d/t expiration) Wyeth-Ayerst 800.934.5556
* live vaccinia virus, with "some microbial contaminants," according to the Working Group on Civilian Biodefense polymyxcin B sulfate, streptomycin sulfate, chlortetracycline hydrochloride, and neomycin sulfate glycerin, and phenol -a compound obtained by distillation of coal tar vesicle fluid from calf skins Engerix-B

Recombinant **Hepatitis B** GlaxoSmithKline 800.366.8900 x5231
* genetic sequence of the hepatitis B virus that codes for the surface antigen (HbSAg), cloned into GMO yeast, aluminum hydroxide, and thimerosal

Fluvirin Medeva Pharmaceuticals 888.MEDEVA 716.274.5300
* influenza virus, neomycin, polymyxin, beta-propiolactone, chick embryonic fluid

FluShield Wyeth-Ayerst 800.934.5556
* trivalent influenza virus, types A&B gentamicin sulphate formadehyde, thimerosal, and polysorbate 80 (Tween-80) chick embryonic fluid

Havrix - **Hepatitis A** GlaxoSmithKline 800.366.8900 x5231
* hepatitis A virus, formalin, aluminum hydroxide, 2-phenoxyethanol, and polysorbate 20 residual MRC5 proteins -human diploid cells from aborted fetal tissue

HiB Titer - Haemophilus **Influenza B** Wyeth-Ayerst 800.934.5556
* haemophilus influenza B, polyribosylribitol phosphate, yeast, ammonium sulfate, thimerosal, and chemically defined yeast-based medium

Imovax Connaught Laboratories 800.822.2463
* rabies virus adsorbed, neomycin sulfate, phenol, red indicator human albumin, human diploid cells from aborted fetal tissue

IPOL Connaught Laboratories 800.822.2463
* 3 types of **polio** viruses neomycin, streptomycin, and polymyxin B formaldehyde, and 2-phenoxyethenol continuous line of monkey kidney cells

JE-VAX - Japanese Ancephalitis Aventis Pasteur USA 800.VACCINE
* Nakayama-NIH strain of Japanese encephalitis virus, inactivated formaldehyde, polysorbate 80 (Tween-80), and thimerosal mouse serum proteins, and gelatin

LYMErix - Lyme GlaxoSmithKline 888-825-5249
* recombinant protein (OspA) from the outer surface of the spirochete Borrelia burgdorferi kanamycin aluminum hydroxide, 2-phenoxyethenol, phosphate buffered saline

MMR - **Measles-Mumps-Rubella** Merck & Co., Inc. 800.672.6372

* measles, mumps, rubella live virus, neomycin sorbitol, hydrolized gelatin, chick embryonic fluid, and human diploid cells from aborted fetal tissue

M-R-Vax - **Measles-Rubella** Merck & Co., Inc. 800.672.6372
* measles, rubella live virus neomycin sorbitol hydrolized gelatin, chick embryonic fluid, and human diploid cells from aborted fetal tissue

Menomune - **Meningococcal** Connaught Laboratories 800.822.2463
* freeze-dried polysaccharide antigens from Neisseria meningitidis bacteria, thimerosal, and lactose

Meruvax I - **Mumps** Merck & Co., Inc. 800.672.6372
* mumps live virus neomycin sorbitol hydrolized gelatin

NYVAC - (new **smallpox** batch, not licensed) Aventis Pasteur USA 800.VACCINE
* highly-attenuated vaccinia virus, polymyxcin B, sulfate, streptomycin sulfate, chlortetracycline hydrochloride, and neomycin sulfate glycerin, and phenol -a compound obtained by distillation of coal tar vesicle fluid from calf skins

Orimune - **Oral Polio** Wyeth-Ayerst 800.934.5556
* 3 types of polio viruses, attenuated neomycin, streptomycin sorbitol monkey kidney cells and calf serum

Pneumovax - **Streptococcus** Pneumoniae Merck & Co., Inc. 800.672.6372
* capsular polysaccharides from polyvalent (23 types), pneumococcal bacteria, phenol,

Prevnar **Pneumococcal** - 7-Valent Conjugate Vaccine Wyeth Lederle 800.934.5556
* saccharides from capsular Streptococcus pneumoniae antigens (7 serotypes) individually conjugated to diphtheria CRM 197 protein aluminum phosphate, ammonium sulfate, soy protein, yeast

RabAvert - **Rabies** Chiron Behring GmbH & Company 510.655.8729
* fixed-virus strain, Flury LEP neomycin, chlortetracycline, and amphotericin B, potassium glutamate, and sucrose human albumin, bovine gelatin and serum "from source countries known to be free of bovine spongioform encephalopathy," and chicken protein

Rabies Vaccine Adsorbed GlaxoSmithKline 800.366.8900 x5231
*rabies virus adsorbed, beta-propiolactone, aluminum phosphate, thimerosal, and phenol, red rhesus monkey fetal lung cells

Recombivax - Recombinant **Hepatitis B** Merck & Co., Inc. 800.672.6372
* genetic sequence of the hepatitis B virus that codes for the surface antigen (HbSAg), cloned into GMO yeast, aluminum hydroxide, and thimerosal

RotaShield - Oral Tetravalent Rotavirus (recalled) Wyeth-Ayerst 800.934.5556
* 1 rhesus monkey rotavirus, 3 rhesus-human reassortant live viruses neomycin sulfate, amphotericin B potassium monophosphate, potassium diphosphate, sucrose, and monosodium glutamate (MSG) rhesus monkey fetal diploid cells, and bovine fetal serum smallpox (not licensed due to expiration)

40-yr old stuff "found" in Swiftwater, PA freezer Aventis Pasteur USA 800.VACCINE
* live vaccinia virus, with "some microbial contaminants," according to the Working Group on Civilian Biodefense polymyxcin B sulfate, streptomycin sulfate, chlortetracycline hydrochloride, and neomycin sulfate glycerin, and phenol -a compound obtained by distillation of coal tar vesicle fluid from calf skins

Smallpox (new, not licensed) Acambis, Inc. 617.494.1339 in partnership with Baxter BioScience
* highly-attenuated vaccinia virus, polymyxcin B sulfate, streptomycin sulfate, chlortetracycline hydrochloride, and neomycin sulfate glycerin, and phenol -a compound obtained by distillation of coal tar vesicle fluid from calf skins

TheraCys **BCG** (intravesicle -not licensed in US for tuberculosis) Aventis Pasteur USA 800.VACCINE
* live attenuated strain of Mycobacterium bovis monosodium glutamate (MSG), and polysorbate 80 (Tween-80)

Tripedia - **Diphtheria-Tetanus-Pertussis** Aventis Pasteur USA 800.VACCINE
*Corynebacterium diphtheriae and Clostridium tetani toxoids and acellular Bordetella pertussis adsorbed aluminum potassium sulfate, formaldehyde, thimerosal, and polysorbate 80 (Tween-80) gelatin, bovine extract

US-sourced Typhim Vi - **Typhoid** Aventis Pasteur USA SA 800.VACCINE
* cell surface Vi polysaccharide from Salmonella typhi Ty2 strain, aspartame, phenol, and polydimethylsiloxane (silicone)

Varivax - **Chickenpox** Merck & Co., Inc. 800.672.6372
* varicella live virus neomycin phosphate, sucrose, and monosodium glutamate (MSG) processed gelatin, fetal bovine serum, guinea pig embryo cells, albumin from human blood, and human diploid cells from aborted fetal tissue

YF-VAX - **Yellow Fever** Aventis Pasteur USA 800.VACCINE
* 17D strain of yellow fever virus sorbitol chick embryo, and gelatin

http://www.informedchoice.info/cocktail.html
Vaccine Liberation Information
NOTE: THIMEROSAL = MERCURY
http://www.vaclib.org/pdf/exemption.htm

Vaccinations: Good, Bad or Just Plain Ugly

The FDA and other "watchdog" government agencies seldom are called to account for erroneous or irresponsible decisions. In the Dow Chemical silicone breast implant suit, the government was recently awarded $9.8 million for medical expenses paid out through Medicare and Medicaid. It didn't seem to matter that another agency, the FDA, of the same government had previously approved the use and sale of these implants and is currently considering whether to allow them to be sold again.

Further, these same agencies show definite bias when it comes to evaluating the risks associated with drugs. A good example is the fact that the agencies are constantly pushing for vaccinations and flu shots. For some reason, however, they neglect to tell the public that **the preservative in these flu shots and vaccines is mercury.**

IS THERE SUCH A THING AS HEALTHY MERCURY?

When it comes to other sources of mercury, though, they are extremely vigilant. They have issued repeated warnings on the consumption of various fish, including tuna, shark, swordfish, and mahi-mahi, because of possible mercury contamination. And since mercury is particularly harmful to nerve cells, government health authorities have stressed that infants and small children shouldn't be fed these foods, and pregnant and nursing mothers should avoid eating tuna also.

However the facts state that most canned tuna contains less mercury contamination than tuna steaks, which come from larger tuna. It's hard to tell how much, if any, mercury these products contain. Smaller fish are safer, and so are fish like sole, sardines, herring, bass, catfish, salmon and shellfish.

Although the EPA (Environmental Protection Agency) has determined that the maximum allowable daily exposure to mercury is 0.1 microgram per kilogram of body weight, the new flu vaccine for babies, called Fluzone, contains 25 micrograms of mercury per 0.5 ml dose.

Practically all vaccines contain mercury and aluminum. And vaccines are not "safer" sources of these toxic minerals. It doesn't matter if the mercury comes from fish or from a vaccine. The potential for neurological damage remains the same. But for some reason, even though we're warned about fish consumption, vaccines and flu shots are strongly encouraged and, in many instances, even required by law. It shouldn't come as any surprise that more babies seem to be developing autism problems, and the risk of developing Alzheimer's disease is steadily increasing.

ALZHEIMER'S LINKED TO FLU SHOTS

In the year 2000, there were approximately 5 million people in the U.S. with Alzheimer's, and it has become the fourth leading cause of death in individuals over the age of 75. By the year 2010, it is estimated that over 7 million individuals will have the disease, and by 2025, 22 million will develop Alzheimer's.

As the general population continues to consume more contaminated food, water, and medicines, these predictions may very well prove accurate. One expert at the 1997 National Vaccine Information Center (NVIC) International Vaccine Conference stated that anyone who had five consecutive flu vaccine shots increased their risk of developing Alzheimer's disease by a factor of 10 over someone who received only two or fewer shots.

A powerful herb to prevent alzheimer's

It's worth mentioning, while we're on the Alzheimer's topic, that the elderly in India have the lowest incidence of Alzheimer's disease in the world. Only 1 percent of the elderly in India suffer from Alzheimer's. In contrast, the Alzheimer's Association in this country says that 10% of our population over 65 years old has the disease, and half of those over 85 have Alzheimer's. Researchers have theorized that the low incidence of Alzheimer's among the Indian population could be due to their increased consumption of the spice turmeric, a component of curry. Animal studies have supported this theory.

Studies have shown that when either turmeric or curcumin, (a major component of turmeric) was added to the diets of animals bred to develop Alzheimer's, the brain damage was significantly lessened. [Neurobiol Aging 01;22(6):993-1005] [J Neurosci 01:21(21):8370-8377]

Turmeric has been shown to have very strong antioxidant properties that can be very effective at normal dietary doses. This spice may be one of the easiest and least expensive methods of combating the growing epidemic of Alzheimer's disease.

Better than a flu shot

When it comes to beating the flu, **selenium** can increase your odds. Selenium is a necessary mineral for the production of antioxidants within the body. New animal research from the University of North Carolina has found that a dietary deficiency of selenium may cause a harmless strain of the flu virus to mutate into a virulent pathogen.

When selenium-deficient mice were given a known flu virus and compared to mice with normal selenium levels, researchers found that the selenium-deficient animals experienced far more serious symptoms, such as lung damage. Based on this new research, other researchers are wondering if the more potent viruses, such as HIV, also mutated in environments where there were selenium deficiencies. It makes sense when you consider the well-known fact that most of the worldwide flu outbreaks originate in China, where large segments of the population are selenium-deficient.

Whether you decide to get flu shots or other vaccinations is a personal choice but as you weigh the pros and cons of such a decision, **don't be naive enough to think any of our government agencies have your best interests as their top priority. It could be a fatal mistake.**

THE VACCINATION
By Patricia Crutchfield

His trusting eyes looked up at me
He smiled his sweetest smile
What a precious gift from God he was
My son my first born child,

The nurse came in and weighed him
Put a thermometer briefly in his ear
Then she told me to take off his diaper
And expose his plump little rear.

I did as I was instructed
For I knew the procedure by now
It's time for his next vaccination
This time I won't flinch, I vow.

The syringes and vial of the serums
Lay benignly on her sterile steel tray
And though I try to watch her,
I find myself turning away.

His scream at the prick of the needle
Sends a bolt of pure terror through me
It's animal like pitch was not normal
And I turned around quickly to see.

His beautiful body went rigid
Then spasmed again and again
What's happening to my poor baby?
And what can I do to help him?

I could sense the nurse's pure panic
As she called out to the doctor to come
The seconds that passed seems like hours
And where is that screaming coming from?

I open my eyes in a room filled with light
The silence a deafening roar
My husband is standing beside me
He says everything fine, but his tears tell me more

I try to sit up, but I'm weary
Another needle pierces my arm
I drift off once again into darkness
But my mind beats a steady alarm.

Two days and two nights I am sedated
Until now no one tells me why
Then the doctor appears with my husband
And immediately I start to cry

My most precious gift has been taken
He'll never again be mine to hold
His body once so warm and loving
Now lays on a slab icy cold

I'm sorry says the good doctor
A reaction we couldn't foresee
Please accept my sincerest condolence
I guess it was just meant to be

Our son now plays with the angels
And my heart breaks anew everyday
Its the angels who tickle his tummy
And it's in their arms not mine, he will lay

A statistic, one in seventeen hundred
That's what they say of my son
But I say one child is too many
To die from a vaccination

So mothers do not be so trusting
Hear me before it's to late
Don't lose your child to the "program"
Investigate before you vaccinate

Families Raise Concern Over Mercury In Vaccines
Debate Continues Over Past Use Of Thimerosal
POSTED: 1:37 p.m. EST November 4, 2002
11:08 p.m. EST November 4, 2002 DURHAM COUNTY, N.C.

A growing contingent of parents believes a mercury-based preservative in those vaccines may have done more harm than good. In 1999, at the request of the Food and Drug Administration, drug companies agreed to begin removing a controversial preservative called thimerosal from vaccines. Some families believe the removal comes too late. Jackson Bono is a happy, curious 13-year-old challenged by a myriad of medical and developmental problems. Jackson has trouble speaking and focusing and works with a tutor.

"The toll it takes on a family is remarkable," said Scott Bono, Jackson's father. Like most parents, Scott and Laura Bono had their son vaccinated when he was a baby. They now blame his problems on thimerosal and its main ingredient, mercury.
"Little did we ever suspect that the very immunizations that were to protect him from childhood diseases were poisoning him with mercury," Scott Bono said. Thimerosal kills harmful bacteria and has been in vaccines for decades. In the early 1990s, the number of recommended childhood vaccines increased. Over the last decade the national autism rate has risen drastically. In North Carolina, the rate has more than quadrupled, according to the state Department of Public Instruction.

Some people see a connection. If you add up the amount of mercury in baby vaccines with thimerosal, the levels exceed those considered safe for adults by the FDA. The Bonos said Jackson was a normal, healthy baby until he received a bundle of vaccines when he was 16 months old. They said, soon after, he stopped talking and making eye contact. Jackson developed autistic tendencies, like spinning uncontrollably. He also suffered severe allergies, seizures and stomach trouble.

"It was a cruel tragedy that happened with our son," Laura Bono said. Dr. Samuel Katz, chairman emeritus of paediatrics at Duke, is considered one of the foremost authorities on vaccines in the country. He raises doubts that thimerosal ever hurt children. "Whenever we have a problem, we like to know whose fault is it. Unfortunately, vaccines have become an easy target," he said. Katz said, "The evidence to support these claims is lacking." However, in 1999, he recommended drug companies take thimerosal out of vaccines. A 2001 report from the National Institute of Medicine also concluded the evidence does not support the claims. Researchers conceded, "the hypothesis is biologically plausible."

"Given that its mercury and we know that mercury has no beneficial effects, my statement to the FDA was that there's really no reason to use something like thimerosal," said Michael Aschner, a Wake Forest University neurobiologist. Aschner has studied mercury for 20 years. Research from the University of Calgary backs up his work and found mercury can destroy brain cells. Aschner points out that the ethylmercury in thimerosal is different from the damaging methylmercury found in some fish. He feels the issue clearly deserves much more study.

"If you do it in a dish, ethylmercury does cause significant effects, toxic effects. There's no question about it," Ascher said. "But, again, what you have to be careful of is how you translate what you see in a dish into a human being." The biggest obstacle parents of special needs children face in making the thimerosal argument is the fact that millions of children, a vast majority, got the same vaccine and never got sick.

"Why is it that all people who smoke don't get cancer? The body reacts differently to different antagonists," Salisbury attorney Bill Graham said. Graham represents 40 families who believe thimerosal hurt their children. He believes evidence is mounting that federal regulators knew that thimerosal could be harmful long before drug companies felt pressure to remove it from vaccines. A study sanctioned by the Centers for Disease Control and Prevention shows infants immunized with thimerosal vaccines were 2.5 times more likely to develop neurological disorders, but it was never released. Instead, the study continued and the results changed. Graham questions why vaccines were never recalled.

"Do you think that thimerosal vaccines that are potentially harmful could still be out there? They could be. They could be on the shelf right now," Graham said. "I really think the thimerosal issue has become a feeding frenzy. It's like the sharks with blood in the water," Katz said. The Bonos said they do not want blood. They want families like theirs to be heard for Jackson's sake, and others like him. "He's lost his childhood and he may not ever be what he should have been," Laura Bono said. Parents like the Bonos can file claims with the National Vaccine Injury Compensation Program. Because of the debate over thimerosal, the federal government has put all the claims on hold until further studies are completed. There was no recall of thimerosal vaccines, so it is possible some could still be on shelves. Anyone with concerns should talk to their child's pediatrician and ask for thimerosal-free vaccines. Both sides of the debate stress the importance of immunizing children.
Reporter: Cullen Browder
Photographer: Gil Hollingsworth
OnLine Producer: Michelle Singer

FOR VAST AMOUNTS OF INFORMATION CHECK:
http://www.vaccinetruth.org/

Be Bold...Be Brave
Died of SIDS
Died of SIDS
Died of SIDS
Died of SIDS
Died of SIDS
Died of SIDS
Died of SIDS
Died of SIDS
Avoid the Grave
VACCINES ARE LETHAL POISONS YOU CAN'T TRUST
You are better off not going to the A.Z. Dept. of Health Services
Don't call the
National Immunization Hotline
800.232.2522 (english) 800.232.0233 (spanish)
www.whyimmunize.org

All truth goes through three stages. First it is ridiculed. Then it is violently opposed. Finally, it is accepted as self-evident."

(Schopenhauer)

****

"Condemnation without investigation is the height of ignorance." Albert Einstein

"In the field of vaccination, medical training is simple indoctrination."

****

Inoculations are the true weapons of mass destruction causing an epidemic of GENOCIDE
Rebecca Carley, MD
Court Qualified Expert in VIDS (Vaccine Induced Diseases)
http://www.drcarley.com

..discussing vaccination with a doctor is like discussing vegetarianism with a butcher...........(George Bernard Shaw)

What good fortune for those in power that the people do not think."
~Adolf Hitler

"When you once see something as false which you have accepted as true, as natural, as human, then you can never go back to it" - J. Krishnamurti

It also gives us a very special, secret pleasure to see how unaware the people around us are of what is really happening to them."   ~Adolf Hitler

" Fear of disease, fear of microorganisms, fear of the unknown, is the tool of the clever that keeps the weak in line"   ~
Tim O'Shea, DC

What a strange religion medicine makes. It's the only religion that is federally backed, and even amid scientific controversy, cannot be questioned openly without persecution or ridicule."

Why Doctors do not understand the evils of vaccinations....
"It is difficult to get a man to understand something when his salary depends upon his not understanding it!"
Upton Sinclair

No one has ever successfully proven that any child has ever benefited from an injection of rotting matter combined with nerve and brain destroying poisons, the actual ingredients of vaccines. – Dewey

What is the name of the test that can be given to determine if a child can safely receive a vaccine?
It's called a breath test. You hold a mirror in front of the child and if condensation appears, they are still alive and cannot "safely" receive a vaccine. - steve

"Uneducated people believe what they are told...Educated people question what they are told"

"People do not like to think. If one thinks, one must reach conclusions. Conclusions are not always pleasant."
-Helen Keller

You can't wake a person who is pretending to be asleep. ~ Navajo Proverb
The art of medicine consists of amusing the patient while nature cures the disease—Voltaire

"A truth's initial commotion is directly proportional to how deeply the lie was believed...When a well-packaged web of lies has been sold gradually to the masses over generations, the truth will seem utterly preposterous and its speaker, a raving lunatic." --Dresden James

"He's the best physician that knows the worthlessness of most medicines."
"God heals and the Doctor takes the fee." - Benjamin Franklin, (1706-1790)

For us to bombard a newborn baby with a whole battery of vaccines as, in effect, their very first immunologic experience I think is reckless beyond measure. I would say it borders on the criminal.   Dr. Moscowitz

If you think that something is right just because everyone believes it, then you are not thinking" - Vievienne Westwood

Knowledge makes a man unfit to be a slave."
Frederick Douglass

Men occasionally stumble on the truth, but most of them pick themselves up and hurry off as if nothing had happened.
 Winston Churchill

"First they ignore you, then they laugh at you, then they fight you, then you win." ~Ghandi

"Your failure to be informed does not make me a wacko." -- John Loeffler

I have no medical training, but I can read.

"The great tragedy of science - a beautiful hypothesis slain by an ugly fact." - Thomas Huxley

"If you think you're too small to be effective, you've never been in bed with a mosquito." - Betty Reese

"I know that most men, including those at ease with the problems of the greatest complexity, can seldom accept even the simplest and most obvious truth if it be such as would oblige them to admit the falsity of conclusions which they have delighted in explaining to colleagues, which they have proudly taught to others, and which they have woven, thread by thread, into the fabric of their lives."- Leo Tolstoy—

Right is right, even if everyone is against it; and wrong is wrong, even if everyone is for it --William Penn

APPENDIX

THOUGHTS AFTER

WRITING THE MAIN

WORK,

900 – LETS ASK A FEW QUESTIONS.

"There is no opinion, however absurd, which men will not readily
embrace as soon as they can be brought to the conviction that it is
generally adopted." - Schopenhauer

Before I seriously get into this writing I want you to know and understand
that for untold thousands of years the matters covered in this work have
been endlessly considered and discussed, and been the subject of endless
books, theories, treatises and opinions. Know also that throughout human
history probably billions of people have been killed or died for holding
one point of view rather than another. There are many viewpoints, many
opinions, but most lack any logic or sound reasoning. As, or if you read
this work you will need to constantly ask the questions: "Is this really
worthwhile pursuing? Does any of it matter or have any real meaning in
my life? Can it be of any value or importance at all?" I believe it to be
important. It is about our life and any possible meaning for and of it.

I am going to presume the reader has a working knowledge and
understanding of the Old Testament of the Christian Bible, and in
particular the first 2 books of Genesis and Exodus. This is a fair
assumption I think in a Western or Christian society as they are "the
beginning" and introduce us to the god/God/GOD, even Lord GOD, that
are the foundation of quite a few religions. They tell us of the "creation",
the origin of man, and of the history that leads us supposedly from the
very beginning creation until as recently as a mere 2000 or so years ago.
Surely a most awesome claim and one that is worthy of investigation. If I
do not use such a presumption then this writing shall become intolerably
cumbersome by way of asides and explanations. Should you not be
conversant with those writings in the bible then I recommend you make
yourself familiar with them no matter how odious that may initially seem,
for it will prove most rewarding as we analyse what exactly has been and
is even now going on. Really it will take only a few well-invested hours
in reading. Call me strange if you will, but it seems to me that any
information or records purporting to reveal to us the very details of the
origin of our species, and of our true place in the cosmos should be of
great importance. It must also fulfill certain criteria to be accepted and
taken as "for real".

Now the order of the creation as presented has been dealt with in my 2nd
and 3rd books. At this time I propose to record the materials again for this
book in an appendix. Likewise I have dealt with the entity referred to as

Jehovah (By whatever spelling or pronunciation – you know to whom I refer.) Who is the alleged creator of mankind, the human species, I have also covered, and also I have dealt with the "adversary" the one known among Christians as the devil, the serpent, as Satan. Whereas the bible gives and leaves an uneasy feeling that there is an unspoken and unrevealed relationship between this "adversary" and the "Father" (ultimate god to Christians etc.) and that "Father's" son, Jesus, my writings clearly reveal what is literally a family relationship, together with the "family" feuds and disagreements, rivalry etc. I have also dealt with that uncomfortable use of the plural personages words in Genesis, the "us", "our", etc. as well as the seemingly inescapable description of physical entities walking and audibly talking in the "garden". These are or were the imponderables of Genesis until one has learned to "see clearly", and to understand exactly what the story or record is all about, and who "they" are, and who "we" are.

What is significant about Genesis and Exodus it not what is recorded, but rather what is omitted, or not recorded. I refer to what are obvious gaps, omissions, lack of explanations, lack of information, and thus in many cases, a lack of reason and/or logic. The omissions only become glaring and obvious shortcomings when one asserts the right to question that which has for millennia been deemed so sacred and "holy" that one dare not, nor has the right to even think to question what is written.

In short millennia of tradition and upbringing, not to mention the almost immediate persecution or death of any who dared to question or doubt what is (obviously selectively) presented have imbued us with a passive acceptance of the records of Genesis and Exodus, and of the standard authorized "priesthood" (etc.) interpretation and significance thereof.

But as in the words of the famous song, "it ain't necessarily so." (The words that you're liable to read in the bible.)

So here we go again. And it is not "bible bashing", it is asking reasonable questions that are logically allowable.

MOSES, WHY KILL AND NOT EVEN ATTEMPT TO CONVERT?

As a result of movies such as "the 10 Commandments" with Charlton Heston et al, most western civilization people will be familiar with Moses and his discovery of his racial heritage, and his subsequent calling to lead his "people" out of "captivity" and into the "promised land". (This whole "promised land" thing is still the cause of so much death and misery between the current state of Israel and other Arab people in the area, about the right to live or possess the land in that area. This is yet another reason why the study and full understanding of those initial books of the "Old Testament" is so important. People are still being killed after the year 2000 AD because of what was recorded, and which people believe, in the books of Genesis and Exodus. If you do not think that is important, then talk with some people from all sides in that area.) This all led to serious confrontation between Moses and the head honchos of Egypt who it seems either did not know about (that's seriously doubtful indeed) the god who held power in an obscure corner of Asia minor, or simply did not consider such a claimed god of any real importance.

It begs a question. If the god who was revealed to Moses in a most obscure manner is really the god of *all* creation, of all that is, was, and will be, the true omniscient, omnipresent, omnific etc one, the creator of EVERYTHING, then why, please tell us all why, was it all so secret? And please don't give me apologist tripe about public revelation would remove any doubt and that state would not allow development of "faith" and such. As though too much knowledge would somehow be dangerous.

Do we read an account of Moses preaching and teaching to the leaders and people of Egypt? Does he come to Egypt as a standard version of a prophet, calling the people to return to god and "repent …. Blah blah blah"? Not at all. No, we get a record of demands, plagues, death, and horrors visited upon the (innocent) people of Egypt. Did this god actually hate Egypt and it's people? Well, yes, we are forced to believe this was the case, as later these people liberated by Moses were charged with the total genocide of all the people, men, women, and children, living in the land of Canaan. Seems this god of Moses was indeed a respecter of persons and played favourites. All else were to be killed. No wonder that the heirs of Judaism, the Christians carry on with the murderous tradition is it? They imagine *their* god glories in and requires the death of all people not of the *chosen* favourites. And of course it's easy for them to explain that with the killing of Jesus, the Israelites were no longer the favoured and chosen people, but that the former gentiles now were called to become "spiritual Israel". Oh yes, I've heard it all.

The Bible gives no information why this god of Moses demanded the death of all the people of Canaan apart from alleging they were evil. (A loving and forgiving god?) Records from other sources reveal quite clearly why this god of Moses, "Jehovah" demanded their total slaughter, and they reveal why this Jehovah said he was a "jealous god". Interesting. Not the only god, but a "jealous god". Of what would a sole creator have to be jealous? But if many "gods", none of who is the real omnific creator? Yes. (Gen 9:25, Exo 15:15, Num ch 14, 15 wherein god decides to let all then living of Israel die before they will take Canaan.) The following is one apologist's writing about it all:

*"Were the Canaanites **really** that evil? The Bible gives so few details it leaves the reader wondering. Unfortunately, most people have no idea how God views evil. They do not understand it and underestimate the danger. The Bible does not go into details because it does not want to perpetuate evil. God doesn't want anyone copying the Canaanites.*

Israel was a new nation just out of Egypt. God was teaching them to be a holy people (Deuteronomy 7:6, 28:9, Leviticus 19:2). They were entering Canaan, a land with religion and culture over 400 years old. Since the Canaanites were not about to change their ways, they would have to be removed.¹"

*"God issued two specific commands concerning the Canaanites east of the Jordan River (Deuteronomy 2:26-36, 3:1-11) and six commands concerning Canaanites in general (Exodus 23:31-33, 34:11-16, Numbers 33:50-56, Deuteronomy 7:1-5, 12:2-3, 20:10-18). The two specific commands were for the conquest of the kingdoms east of the Jordan. Of the six general commands, only Deuteronomy 7:1-5 demands the total destruction of the Canaanites. Deuteronomy 20:10-18 qualifies this by specifically mentioning the destruction of Canaanite cities. The other four concern **driving** them out, destroying their idols and not making any treaties with them."*

"As will be seen later, Israel followed God's instructions. The two Canaanite kingdoms east of the Jordan were completely destroyed, but the Canaanites on the west were not."

This is the writing of a truly presumptuous apologist indeed. We unwashed and unlettered common people have no concept of how this god views evil, nor do "we" understand evil. However that writer does, and obviously therefore sees why the mass extermination order is quite acceptable, along with the total destruction of an older civilization, as they were "not about to change their ways". What blatant rubbish and absurd apologist drivel. However such is the conventional thinking of the blind followers of Jehovah and his priesthoods.

Circumcision: Now what is and was that all about really? This god requested and demanded the mutilation of all males as a "sign" of a covenant. Today in 2010AD if any religious leader made a similar demand, that would be considered as a dangerous sign of a "cult", and rightly so. Yet all Christians, circumcised or not, read this, gloss over it and at best vaguely think, "Well it was his rules and requirement". Today we universally condemn the genital mutilation of some African females and their "circumcision".

Come on people. Let's really think about all of this and not just blindly accept it.

But above all, Moses is not recorded as making any attempts at all to teach the people of Egypt about the god revealed to him, the god who is subsequently assumed to be the top of the food chain as far as gods go. Does it occur to you that this is somewhat incompatible with the image of the same god that today is pushed and preached as being a loving caring and forgiving god, a god that is supposedly intimately familiar with each mortal?

STRANGE EVENTS IN GENESIS

There are many strange events recorded in the Old Testament book of Genesis. Several have been in my mental filing cabinet of imponderables since I was a very young man, and two of these events have only recently found some degree of satisfactory explanation and resolution.

THE WRESTLING INCIDENT.

This is an absolutely strange one if one holds to the traditional form of orthodox Christianity. It really finds no crystal clear purpose or explanation within the tenets of Christian doctrine. Let me quote from the King James Version, Genesis 32 starting at verse 24. Jacob is on the way to see his brother Esau.

"And Jacob was left alone; and there wrestled a man with him until the breaking of the day.

And when he saw that he prevailed not against him; he touched the hollow of his thigh; and the hollow of Jacob's thigh was out of joint, as he wrestled with him.

And he said, Let me go, for the day breaketh. And he said, I will not let thee go, except thou bless me.

And he said unto him, What is thy name? And he said, Jacob.

And he said, Thy name shall be called no more Jacob, but Israel; for as a prince hast thou power with God and with men, and hast prevailed.

And Jacob asked him, and said, Tell me, I pray thee, thy name. And he said, Wherefore is it that thou dost ask after my name? And he blessed him there.

And Jacob called the name of the place Peniel for I have seen God face to face, and my life is preserved.

*And as he passed over Penuel (*spelling is different on 2nd name*) the sun rose upon him, and he halted on his thigh.*

Therefore the children of Israel eat not of the sinew which shrank, which is upon the hollow of the thigh, unto this day; because he touched the hollow of Jacob's thigh in the sinew that shrank."

Well, I certainly found the story of interest and asked my local religious leaders of the day what it was all about and meant. With what I now call dumb "typical ignorance" after the hums and haws, most invariably opined it was an angel with whom Jacob wrestled, and some said it was all "wrestling in his mind". In his mind, leg out of joint?

Was it? Decades ago I thought not and I still am not sure as to with whom he wrestled or what it was all about. I figured it had to be a being of great power and authority, but who was in effect "slumming" on earth with mere mortals.

Certainly I put this being in the same category as the ones who Abraham met at his tent door, shared a meal with them, and who then saw to it that Sara would have a child. It would seem those same beings turned up and wiped out Sodom and Gomorrah after evacuating Lot and his family. Most assuredly they were not your normal human beings, and almost certainly not of our species. They are "not us". And that means "aliens" even if you prefer to call them "angels". Yet it was obvious from the writings that they were not so different from our average mortal "earther" or Adamite as to be recognizable as "not us".

But the one with whom Jacob wrestled? Jacob asked of him for a blessing, and he actually gave it, plus gave him a new name. Who presumes to be able to confer blessings and to give new names? A name ending with "el". There is huge significance in the word "el". Jacob then claimed, "I have seen god face to face, and my life is preserved." Who would that indicate Jacob thought of him as being? After careful analysis of the words I always figured that Jacob believed he was wrestling with god, a physical entity capable of physical combat. (This was to me one of hundreds of biblical texts that led me to believe that "god" simply had to be a physical entity, one who is manifest somewhat like us. I am speaking here about the god of Israel, this Jehovah as revealed to Moses, the chap who walked and talked in the Garden of Eden. There is just so much in Genesis etc that indicate a physical being as "god".) But if so then the god is certainly not omnipotent, or was just "playing" with Jacob. But if just "playing", why then did this being find the need to "play dirty", invoke his non-human powers, and dislocate Jacob's leg at the thigh? The scripture says it was because he saw he did not prevail over Jacob. That would make Jacob one hell of a mean dude with which to wrestle, or it would make the god (of Genesis, but not the "fabric of the universe" GOD.) not too much above man as far as physical ability goes.

But why even wrestle? What is that all about?

Needless to say the matter was never satisfactorily explained and remained in my "unresolved issues" mental cabinet for decades. Very recently a penny dropped and I correlated this story with another story that involved other gods' (of another culture) seeming propensity for wrestling.

The full context of the following is found in this book in supplementary reading, 801 – **Anunnaki History**.

It is said the Anunnaki are they who created our current species of earth humanoid by genetic manipulation and were thus in effect our "gods". They were not omnipotent, but very powerful nonetheless.

"The gods clasped hands together, then cast lots and divided: Anu to heaven went up; To Enlil the Earth was made subject; That which the sea as a loop encloses [South Africa?], They gave to the prince Enki.

To the Abzu Enki went down, assumed the rulership of the Abzu."

Unfortunately, for Anu, the drama was not yet over. Kumarbi had been left by Anu on the space platform orbiting the Earth. When Anu returned "up to heaven" (or at least, enroute), the two "gave battle" to one another. As Kumarbi momentarily bested Anu in the wrestling (the Anunnaki's preferred method for settling differences), "Anu struggled *free from the hands of Kumarbi". But then Kumarbi managed to grab Anu by his feet, and "bit between his knees", hurting Anu in his "manhood". Ouch, that must have hurt. **(This, if you can believe it, was a typical "hold" in Anunnaki wrestling.)** Anu then took off for Nibiru, disgraced and in pain, leaving Kumarbi behind with the IGIGI manning the space platform. Thus was delivered in the classic fashion of the Anunnaki the first blow that would ultimately pave the way for the "War of the Olden Gods." In the interim...*

I would point out that Jacob was en route to meet Esau, his brother from whom he had taken the "birthright" and now **settle differences.** Esau was as influential a person as Jacob and both of the same "patriarchal line"; Esau was effectively the first-born of the twins. My thoughts are that both would have been well acquainted with the Anunnaki or with god by whatever name or definition. (Assuming any of this has any reality at all, and it appears more probable than the disjointed "story" pushed upon us by the Christian orthodoxy. It would follow then that probably Jacob met one of Esau's Anunnaki confederates face to face in combat, in wrestling, which is the Anunnaki's *"preferred method of settling differences"*. Again "settling differences" was the precise mission of Jacob. After the combat, the mission was a total success. Probably success was assured because Jacob was capable of prevailing against Esau's champion. (Is it from this Anunnaki source that our human history records millennia of "trial by combat" decisions?)

What does it all mean or infer?

If this incident was a stand alone and unique story, then as it stands in Genesis, it is meaningless, and currently it is to most of orthodox Christianity. All it would do is add confusion to a host of sectarian groups who are groping blindly for meaning of the "whole thing". But when this unexplainable little piece of puzzle it put into the bigger picture, then it fits in very nicely. I submit it is another nail from a "sacred record" that fits (perfectly in fact) the data and description of the way of the Anunnaki. It gives more confidence that when we read the Old Testament, we are in reality reading a condensed account of our species' origin at the hands of a "not us" species. (Don't flinch. God by any definition must be an "alien" for he cannot have originated on this planet, as he supposedly created it. Nor can he be one of us, for he supposedly created us.) But wait, there is more. God, Jehovah, by whatever spelling simply becomes one of the Anunnaki, probably Enlil. Also of course it totally resolves the "Father and son" issue and the whole "3 gods in 1" unintelligible rubbish of Christianity.

The Anunnaki narative also resolves a statement by a major sectarian Christian religion that "Satan" in fact is a brother of the "god" who became Jesus the Christ. (Its Enki and Enlis exactly.)

Once we get past the mental indigestion caused by religions and the current paradigm, then we can begin to discover exactly who and what we are. Unfetted from the blinkers and blindness induced by millennia of indoctrination, we become capable of true self-actualisation.

It becomes convenient to add something I wrote several years ago here.

THAT GOLD "THING", AND MOSES

If you check the listings in the index under "gold" you will readily find that very early in the book of Genesis it was announced that gold was present on the earth. (Genesis 2:11) If it's mention when it was shows any order of importance, then we are compelled to conclude gold was VERY important.

In the "story" of the Anunnaki, gold is the single most important reason, in fact the only reason, for their even setting up camp on planet earth. With the acquisition of gold as the prime purpose for settlement, it became a "mere" matter of convenience for them with their technology to "engineer" a local species capable of doing all the real manual and menial work. This need for cheap local labour (so nothing has changed since the beginning has it?) led to the organizing of the human family, culminating with the earthers of Adam. All of this is covered is considerable detail in the supplementary readings section herein. It makes infinitely more sense than the total confusion of an unmotivated creation as taught by orthodox Christianity. If you have not read the "supplementary reading" then you must do so without loss of any more time.

Now the reason for the Anunnaki's need, yes need, for gold is barely touched upon in the supplementary reading, but it does provide information. Simply stated, it is widely claimed that after refining and treatment in specific ways it was ingested, used as a "food". This is the ambrosia, the food of the gods. This is the philosopher's stone that gives eternal life. This is the fountain of youth. This is the "what is it?" of Egypt. This is the golden shewbread. This is the cone shaped golden "bread" on ancient Egyptian walls. This is that which accounts for the Anunnaki's purported lifespan of thousands or even hundreds of thousands of years. (Hence our mere mortal's belief that the gods live eternally.) For more information, some of which is probably quite spurious or even "dodgy", but do the research on the Internet under "starfire" and "ORME". Story goes that the early ones of the human family were given and allowed access to this specially treated and refined gold and made it part of the diet that gave a very long life span. (As recorded in "Genesis" in the case of the early patriarchs.) I have made reference to those of the humans who lived in the compound of the gods, the Anunnaki. They lived in "paradise" (E.DIN), with the "gods", shared the food, the ambrosia or whatever name is used, and lived longer lives than those of the human species who lived in "hell" outside of the compound. (Yes it was from such a compound, Eden, from which it is recorded Adam and Eve were expelled.)

Those unbelievable life spans recorded in Genesis.

One of several things happened. (If any of this is true.) But to cut it short, whatever it was that did happen, humans became excluded and/or denied access to the specially treated gold, the fruit of life. (Moses possibly tried to re-create it.)

In consequence, the relatively speaking long lives of the earlier recorded patriarchs of Genesis began to decrease from near 1,000 years progressively till we get to Abraham who lived for just over 200 years. Did the "gods" just get mean or mingy or was it a case of a human hating Enlil withholding? I often wondered about this aging and dating in my younger days. Yes there was another one into the "unresolved/unexplained cabinet".

By the time of Moses, human life spans were relatively abysmally short. Yet it would appear that Moses was well acquainted with the "secret" (I hate the use of that word.) knowledge and supposed wisdom of Egypt. This was the domain of Enki (brother of Enlil) and his successors. Whereas Moses had knowledge of "god" and of the Egyptian theology, he professed ignorance and asked of the name of "god" once he crossed borders and ventured into Asia Minor. Now that is a similar situation to that of Jacob above.

This smells like a lot of local "gods". And it probably is, and that is just what is indicated in the Old Testament. (So henceforth ignore the claim that those of Egypt, or Canaan, or Persia etc. are "pagans". Their local honcho was simply another "person" of the same superior species and of course, had a different name and way of doing and dealing with things.

And this lets us know exactly why "Jehovah"/Enlil was a jealous god and of who and what he had to be jealous. We can also now severely disrespect commands from one local god to kill off all the followers of another "god" in that "god's" home territory. They are using and manipulating humans in their own wars and rivalry. This is where humans learned warfare. Sadly we find from Asian sources similar stories of the gods at war and using humans in their warfare.

There is the well-known account (as in Genesis) of Moses going up onto the mountain in Sinai and meeting with "god" (who's name some time earlier he did not know.) The identity of this mountain is of more importance than any religion pusher of Christianity will ever admit or perhaps even be aware.

I did the research and it goes like this: Orthodoxy has it that Moses went up upon Mt Sinai and met "god" there. However lesser known is a relatively close mountain in Sinai, Serabit El Khadim, where there existed at the time a vast complex (conveniently referred to today as a temple complex) where gold was refined and the "what is it" was allegedly produced. The "what is it" is that substance of Anunnaki origin as above. Now the interesting part goes like this, and I'll quote from the King James Bible. Immediately when he came down from that mountain.... he finds them with a golden calf fashioned from collected jewelry etc. whereupon…

"he took the calf which they had made, and burnt it in the fire, and ground it to powder, and strawed it upon the water, and made the children of Israel drink of it."

Now I don't know what that verse conveys to you, but to me that is unusual behavior. Anger and grinding it up I can understand. But the rest sounds ritualistic to say the least.

He made or caused the people to ingest the powdered gold.

And that is precisely what the "Star fire", "ORME", the alleged "philosopher's stone" is all about. But here is recorded that Moses did it. As we mentioned, Moses was no rank and file ex-slave. He was well learned in the ways of Egypt and it's "gods". Seems the gods of old Egypt had more, much more, clout than today's Christian god.

A very interesting extension of this thought is that once Moses had met the ruling god of his future country and later went to plead "his people's" cause before Pharaoh (name of whom is of no consequence) is that to a certain level, every "sign" or "miracle" he performed, the local "priests" of the local god (presumably really Enki by whatever name) were able to duplicate or exceed. But Exodus records the new god of Moses did prevail, but not vanquish the god in Egypt. (Rather like the "wrestler" above did prevail over Jacob, but did not totally crush or destroy him.) Recall Enlil of "Asia" was appointed supreme on earth and thus even though a brother, he was superior to Enki, of "Africa". (In case it has not occurred to you, Moses changed camp, and went from Enki and his domain, to that of Enlil, who was a strange entity who among other things wanted circumcision and a massacre of all Canaanites etc….) The biblical history from Moses onwards shows a sad tale of war and genocide under the control of this "god", commonly known among Christians as Jehovah. Even the wife of Moses is recorded as saying that this god is somewhat "nasty" in wanting blood. (Circumcision, or mutilation of the males.)

He was not a loving god as Christian churches today proclaim, and his "priests" though superficially benevolent, are still "nasty" and would eliminate (by death) all unbelievers and heretics were such possible. Recall the "apologist" recorded above who still thinks it was OK to slaughter an entire people of Canaan because of "evil"; the Jehovahite passion to destroy people is still with us. His priests killed and tortured. His church sponsored genocide. His church cannot deny this history. I have had problems with the history of "the church" since I was able to reason things, or early childhood. I still find persecution and wars intolerable.

I always hated this part of history. Now I understand it. It is not "my" history, and about now I am a little confused as to where I was going with all of this.

Yes. Gold. Importance. Its all gods' gold. Humans are created labour. It is ingestible after "treatment" and confers long life etc. They control it, they have it. Once they shared it but now they don't, and this is why we no longer live to be 1000 years old. It's all about these "aliens" you see… ("Aliens" meaning simply not of our species, outsiders to us.)

No, I am not mad, but who will believe me? There is a lot more.
I read in a magazine that since about 2004 this millennia, the gold deposits in Fort Knox etc have been confirmed as going missing and replaced with spurious bars of bogus gold. Bars that are largely tungsten with an overlay of about an eighth of an inch of real gold, and outwardly

undetectable as bogus.   This became proven with a shipment of such gold to China recently, and their subsequent analysis of the bars. (Drilling into them to confirm consistency throughout the bars)   Although no one seems to know or at least reveal where the real gold has gone, and some people are "no longer around", I have my firm suspicions as to where the gold has gone. One word: Anunnaki. After all, it is recorded that the acquisition of gold was the sole purpose for their migration to our planet earth, setting up camp, and "creating" us mortal ordinary humans.

Now how about that device Moses fashioned according to the instructions of "god", it was made of gold, (what a surprise.) and if the stories in the bible are remotely correct, it wielded some rather fantastic and at times lethal power.   The Ark of the Covenant, could that just possibly be a small sample of Anunnaki technology and power?

WHAT IS "EL" ABOUT?

The following article off the Internet covers the signifance of "EL" in fairly great detail and seems to be quite well researched and fundamentally correct. I see in it the (as I long thought and suspected) fact that indeed "EL" is one and the same as "ANU", and that we are indeed dealing with the same "family" of beings we loosely call "gods". Anu is the father of both Enlil and Enki, so here we have in reality, god the father, and god the son, and god the other son, who is an adversary to the first son. FASCINATING.

EL and Elohim

EL is the supreme creator god of the Canaanites who lives with the other gods on Mount Zaphon (similar to Mount Olympus of the Greeks but located at the mouth of the Orontes river near the border between Turkey and Syria). He is the father of all the gods and men and is often addressed as such by the Canaanite gods. He is the god of the earth and the air who is represented by a bull. He is derived from the Sumerian god AN. In the Bible EL is translated as God. Elohim is the plural form of EL yet in most places in the Bible it is used in the singular sense so it is also translated as God instead of gods. Strict monotheism was not fully developed in Israelite thought until their exile to Babylon. Before then Yahweh (translated as Lord in the Bible) was the god of Israel and Judah (officially their only god) whose principle power and characteristic was that of justice and righteousness. **Because he judged other peoples and gods he soon came to be seen as the supreme God** (the equivalent of EL), and finally as the only God for all people. Echoes of Israel's earlier stages of understanding are found in some old psalms as follows:.

- ○ Psalm 82:1: *Elohim has taken his place in the assembly of EL, in the midst of the elohim He holds judgment.*

- ○ Psalm 29:1: *Ascribe to Yahweh, O sons of EL, ascribe to Yahweh glory and strength.*

- ○ Psalm 89:6: *For who in the skies can be compared to Yahweh, who among the sons of EL is like Yahweh,*

The Semitic concept of sonship meaning "belonging to" or "having the characteristics of" as in the phrase "son of Judah" or "son of man" **means that the "sons of EL" could be viewed either as individual gods** or as differing characteristics of the god EL. The differing characteristics view is reflected in the following passages.

1 - One characteristic is that of location or tribe identification as exemplified by the passage where Jacob erects an alter to EL - the God (elohe) of Israel at Shechem:

- ○ Genesis 33:20: *There he erected an alter and called it EL-Elohe-Israel.*

2 - Another characteristic is the one of the covenant (*berith* in Hebrew) as exemplified by EL-Berith

- ○ Judges 9:46: *they entered the stronghold of the temple of EL-berith*

- ○ Judges 8:33: *As soon as Gideon died, the Israelites relapsed and prostituted themselves with the BAALs, making BAAL-berith their god.*

- ○ Judges 9:4: *They gave him seventy pieces of silver out of the temple of BAAL-berith . . .*

3 - Elyon is the divine characteristic of the heavenly location and is thus translated as "Most High" in the following passages.

- ○ Genesis 14:18-20: *And King Melchizedek of Salam brought out bread and wine; he was priest of El-Elyon. He blessed him and said, "Blessed by Abram by El-Elyon, maker of heaven and earth; and blessed be El-elyon who has delivered your enemies into your hand!"* (Salam is Zion according to Psalm 76:2)

- ○ Psalm 73:11: *And they say, "How can EL know? Is there*

knowledge in Elyon?" Such are the wicked;

- Psalm 107:11: *for they had rebelled against the words of EL, and spurned the counsel of Elyon.*

- Deuteronomy 32:8-9: *When Elyon apportioned the nations, when he divided humankind, he fixed the boundaries of the peoples according to the number of the sons of EL* (LXX and Qumran texts)*; Yahweh's own portion was his people, Jacob his allotted share.*

- Psalm 18:13: *Yahweh also thundered in the heavens, and Elyon uttered his voice.* (same as 2 Samuel 22:14)

- Psalm 21:7: *For the king trusts in Yahweh, and through the steadfast love of Elyon he shall not be moved.*

- Psalm 47:2: *For Yahweh, the Elyon, is awesome, a great king over all the earth.*

4 - Shaddai is the divine characteristic of unconquerable power and is thus translated as "Almighty".

- The oracle of Balaam in Numbers 24:16: *the oracle of one who hears the words of Elohim, and knows the knowledge of Elyon, who sees the vision of Shaddai, who falls down, but with his eyes uncovered:*

- Psalm 91:1: *You who live in the shelter of Elyon, who abide in the shadow of Shaddai,* The blessing of Jacob in Genesis 49:25: *by the hands of the Mighty One* (Abir) *of Jacob, by the name of the Shepherd, the Rock of Israel, by EL, your father, who will help you, by Shaddai who will bless you*

5 - Olam is the divine characteristic of immortality thus EL-Olam is translated as God Everlasting.

- Genesis 21:33: *Abraham planted a tamarisk tree in Berr-sheba, and called there on the name of Yahweh, El-Olam.*

- Psalm 75:9: *I will praise olem* (forever)*: I will sing praises to the Elohim of Jacob.*

- 1 Kings 1:31: *May my lord King David live olam* (forever)*.*

6 - Finally EL is part of several important names in the Bible such as IsraEL - meaning "may EL persevere", and BethEL - meaning "house of

EL", a city located 10 miles north of Jerusalem.

The plural form EL, "Elohim", originated when the sons of EL were considered separate beings yet it was still used after the functions of the various gods were seen to be simply differing characteristics of the same one God. This development is similar to the transition in usage of the phrase "United States" . Today we say the United States "is" (singular) instead of "are" (plural) despite its plural form and its original meaning as a combination of states.

Well then, it would certainly seem that what we are taught and asked to believe and accept by and in the Christian churches and sects of today has very little similarity to that which was known, understood, or prevailed among millennia or our ancestors who followed the supposed same god of today's churches.

I cannot know how all of this sits with you, or how you feel about it, but I am somewhat indignant about the entire orchestra of errors foisted upon us.

At some levels I see fraud, at all levels I see manipulation and control. And certainly there is population control, culling of species, genocide etc. involved. I see rather than the hand of a loving god, the hand of tyranny.

Yes there is something very wrong with what we are being asked to blindly accept and follow, and that dogma "ain't necessarily so".

901 EARLY DAYS OF QUESTIONING (2003-7)

For me it came as somewhat of a gut-wrenching shock to find that the Jehovah based Christian religion of my entire upbringing was as shallow and realistic as Santa Claus etc. Even though I was aware there were serious issues and flaws in the whole paradigm, I had no idea in my earlier (pre 2003) days that the **entire** Jehovahite edifice was as hollow as most sugar Easter Eggs. I suspected even before then that the Christian based edifice was quite like the oft-quoted whited sepulcher, namely nice on the outside, but hiding a lot of corruption. (etc.) I had been asked in the mid 1970's to give a discourse/lesson to a church priesthood group on the subject of "power of priesthood", based on the assumption that only the works (or miracles) of that sectarian group used the power and authority of god, and that all else therefore had to be "of the devil" and were thus using what was considered ultimately "evil" power, certainly not acceptable to or by "god". (I had somewhat of a reputation as not only a "scriptorian", but as a powerful and convincing public speaker.)

I did a lot of bible study; I did a lot of thinking, and asked a lot of questions. (I asked no man, but framed and posed the questions to myself.) With a modicum of surprise I discovered that all works for good (or indeed otherwise) and all "miracles" are and were equally valid and acceptable, but only if one was "neutral" or non-prejudiced. I "discovered" that when one thinks one is tapping into the power of god, or anything else, that in fact that is **largely** not the case at all, but rather they are tapping into what I judged must be innate human qualities and power.

Think very long and very hard about that assertion.

No man or scripture revealed this to me. It was truly a self-revealing truth. Perhaps before reaching this conclusion one must have some of what I call basic understandings of the ability of mankind. The lesson/discourse was given, and perhaps surprised a few people, as, like Enki's human creations, it was not exactly that which was ordered or asked.

Later I found that not only did I no longer have a valid religion based god and Jesus, but I also had no creator god as allegedly revealed in Genesis.

I had to ask many more questions. If the god of Genesis was not our creator, then who or what was? Was the obviously flawed and deficient "theory of evolution" the answer? I just knew that it could not be so.

As "facts" I had mankind on earth, with powers over his environment that many deny or fail to understand. For instance I found that the weather could become subject to personal direction. I found people could be healed of all sorts of ailments and disability. I found levitation could be reality. I found that one can influence others to a remarkable degree. These are but a few illustrations, and it is now obvious that at the time I failed to more fully understand it and what it all means. This is still the case but to a slightly lesser degree. What I knew for certain was that mankind was able to be an effective channel for this power, energy, or "authority". I had learned a specific formula to focus and use such "power", but as I had gone renegade, this was supposedly refuted, denied, and I should be wearing horns, changed colour etc. etc. (None of which happened.) Surprise, I found the "formula" was mere ritual, and without it the power and supposed authority still existed in tact.

Confused I retired to the "normal world" and hid myself there for a few decades. I practiced nothing. I performed nothing. I did nothing. I integrated into the underbelly of humanity.

Then one day I had cardiac arrests. Effectively I died twice that day. Effectively I returned to mortal life twice that day. Damn, the "power", the "force" was still acting upon and with me. My life in mortality had to continue. I hurt badly (physically and emotionally) and had to ask: "WHY?" Survival really hurts physically. I have recorded elsewhere my experiences with these arrests and "a little bit dead". Harking back to what this section is all about: If my paradigm was wrong, then what is the ultimate reality and source?

Gradually it unfolded, as a self-revealing chain of information. I asked endless questions, seemingly in a logical sequence, such as built one upon the other. Although I have numerous notes and writings, I shall endeavor to post them below now in chronological sequence. I intend to reproduce them exactly as written at the time. These are the writings recording some of my progressive discarding of error and realization of things that could well be very factual. Some will seem naive, some silly.

RELATIONSHIP – *AXIOMS & POSTULATIONS…*

'AXIOM': self-evident truth. universally received principle.

'POSTULATION': a claim. Taking for granted..assume..to assume as a possibility or legitimate operation without preliminary construction.

"Work with me on this one", and be patient as a chain of logic unfolds.

1. *"Matter" is spread throughout the universe.*
2. *"Matter" is all essentially the same, it is 'dust', elements and particles that are scattered universally, and of like construction and substance. (An atom of Hydrogen is the same here on earth, or in our body as it is a trillion miles across space.)*
3. *We, our earthly bodies are 'matter', the universal 'dust'.*
4. *We, 'mortal humans' (and other species) have intelligence. We have the ability to reason, to manipulate thoughts, to make decisions, to communicate, recognize and store data/information. We exist and live on this planet of 'dust', we are born of it, eat, drink, and breathe of it, we live, love, procreate and die on it, and recycle into it. But we are still at basic level, 'matter' with intelligence.*
5. *All matter is a form of, and interchangeable with energy...Ultimately therefore our very mortal bodies are a form of energy.*
6. *As matter is universally spread and the same, then the universe itself is in reality energy. Energy with pockets, spheres or bubbles of concentrated massed energy called matter. There is no space or place where there is 'nothing', or 'no energy'. Thus energy or force, call it by any name, it is the same concept and comprises everything that exists. (Call it 'prana', 'spirit', 'energy', 'the force', give it any name, but know that any such name is equally valid, just as we all drink H2O, but call it 'water' or by the words of another language, the name is irrelevant.)*
7. *If we as mortal humans are 'matter' which is 'energy' and also 'intelligent' as above, then it follows any or all energy must have similar properties, just as all 'dust' or particles are of the same constitution and properties. It follows that all energy has, or has the ability to manifest and possess intelligence.*
8. *Likewise, if this earth is 'evolving' or progressing or developing then it follows that the same should apply universally. As below, so it is above; as above, so it is below.*
9. *If these postulations are not so, (7 & 8 above particularly) then man must be recognized as the highest form (of energy and everything that can exist)- as the ultimate object in the entire universe.*
10. *This would seem totally absurd, as man is really relatively insignificant and very low in the 'pecking order' of bubbles or spheres of influence. Not only that, but consider his very nature, and ask, "Can we allow or postulate that such a one is the supreme form that does or can exist?" A savage beast that is generically, totally self absorbed and selfish. A ruthless being of low ethic and morals, who will exploit, dominate, and much worse, separate his fellow from life*

itself. We are 'part' of the energy, and 'part' of the matter. We are therefore mere partakers (part takers) of the experience. We are just another form or manifestation of the matter and energy. And we know we go into a recycle 'bin'.

11. *Matter and/or energy is not created or destroyed, it only changes in form. They are 'eternal' in nature.*

12. *It follows that 'we' are eternally locked into the universal energy/matter, which in itself is logically possessed of intelligence, for we are of it.*

That should be sufficient at this time and give enough to work with and attempt to mentally digest without getting severe mental indigestion. Let's hope you do not get mental constipation, a condition where the mental processes are blocked, and nothing can get past the blockage. Heck, I'm tempted to end this writing here and let the reader figure out the entire nature of the universe just from the above 12 issues. But for my own benefit I will continue a bit, just to direct my own thinking, conclusions, and set myself on a path that leads to issues of importance.

What IS important? Is the type of car we own or drive important? Is our status or prestige important? How about our homes or furnishings? Do we fret about having the latest gizmo cell phone or designer label clothes? Time to get priorities in order, and if they are not in order, then its time to consider carefully your tenure relative to life.

Matter is also used or manipulated by us to record or store information or data. In various forms and media, by art, by constructs using shape and form (consider what is alleged to be revealed by 'the' famous pyramid in Egypt in its shape and dimensions etc) in books and magnetic media etc we store information. All of these forms are of 'matter' and suffer the same fate as the human body. They will dissolve and recycle. What is left of records created, say, over 2000 years ago? Vast libraries lost, records of entire races (Maya, Inca etc) destroyed or lost. The forms have a use in utility as well as to pass on information and instruction. Consider the 'higher' forms from which we have gleaned information in times past and will yet in future gain information. Our solar system has given us much advanced information, information that has taken a long time to discover. A whole universe of form, function, purpose and meaning is before us for our education and information. Yet science as we have it does not understand fully how a human mind functions, nor credit reason and intelligence generally to what are considered lower species.

Yet all the information is before us. Hopefully then it will find meaning when it is understood and correlated into our own knowledge, recognized by our fragment of intelligence. The universal intelligence contains and reveals all things for it is the sum total of all things. In many cases pure mental indigestion and conceit prevent man from seeing the revealed information, which is 'reality' or 'truth'.

It was said by Jesus and doubtlessly countless others that 'the truth shall make you free'. Let's consider that a moment. How or in what way will it make you free?

Consideration of the 12 points at the beginning of this writing should set the mind off on a cycle of questions and discoveries until the full nature of the universe, man, and that which we call GOD is revealed clearly. Further not only the nature of all things, but also the purpose of all things, the relationship of all things, and our place within the entire scheme of things. Once understood one will not subject oneself to those of mortality who demand others follow them and their dictates, claiming the superiority of 'revelations', 'inspiration', 'faith', of 'obedience' to 'laws'. These are the blind leading and demanding the following of other blind. And the blind can be dangerous creatures. History has proven it. I believe it was Voltaire who warned to beware of the person who says, "believe as I do, or be damned", for soon he will say (and means) "believe as I do, or I will kill you". We have his warning and we have historical accuracy of the observation. Such is the nature of blind man, who is so blind as to suppose he is the highest form in the universe. No revelations, dreams, visions, nor faith nor laws are superior to truth. I know of one sect of Christianity that proclaims with temerity that once their leaders have spoken as a result of unrecorded revelations, then it is not up to people to think, but to follow without question. Sounds dangerous to me. Blind obedience to blind leaders. Is that your religion? Do you have the temerity to question the dogma of religion, or of science? Do you have a desire to fully understand all things, to know all things, rather than just believe or accept that which you are told to accept or believe?

Sadly most of mankind is in a pit dug by others - others who control people and "wealth" – who greedily accumulate for themselves and assume power and authority. That is why there is poverty and misery on earth on such a grand scale. **Religions** *invariably demand obedience at the risk of displeasure, anathema, excommunication, being cast out as untouchable. I have been there. Even death may result in some cases.* **Political institutions & Governments** *equally demand obedience and* *submission. You will obey and conform at the risk of confinement, fines, or other punishments including total social disgrace, making one a fugitive, or even death public or otherwise. **Socially** we are confined and forced to conformity. You must have certain values and beliefs or face ridicule and/or be ostracized. You must obey and respect, even revere, those deemed superior to you. You must toe the line, pay you dues and humbly accept the crumbs with which you are 'rewarded'. You must follow an orthodox religion, have a formal education, believe as do all others, act as all others, and be the compliant accepting little component that is desired of you.*

There are 'thought police' operated by employers, community, religions and sects, governments, educators, and science. Virtually at every level and component part of society and life on earth. We are subject to them. Truth will make you free. Conventional accepted thinking, thoughts, and systems of belief, knowledge, and activities are not necessarily true or correct, nor best.

Nations exist and we 'must' give allegiance. If war is warranted by the powers that control, we are expected from loyalty and in recognition of the crumbs we get to race to the blood festival. We must love whom we are told and hate and kill whom we are told. Sounds primitive to me. Barbaric?

I have read words of Ramakrishna who died in 1886. "I have practised Hinduism, Islam, Christianity, and in Hinduism the different sects. I have found that it is the same God toward whom all are directing steps, though along different paths." "The tank has several ghats. At one the Hindus draw water and call it jal; at another Muhammadans draw the same liquid and call it water. The substance is one though the name differs....But do not say your religion is better than that of another." A self-evident truth I would think, as it certainly fosters freedom.

*Be absolutely assured **all mankind** shares everything in common on this earth – the same air, the same water, foods, everything of the very dust of the earth, including the dust of recycled past life. This body is universally the same and of the same substance. Of what has one to boast over another then?*

Do not we all share a common origin at birth, and a same end at death? Do not our very elements return to dust to endlessly recycle? Are you not yet aware that you will dissolve to dust, or that your life is as the blink of an eye? Was it not just yesterday that you were a carefree child?

Not only are we of the same 'matter' but of the same energy source, for there is only one universal energy source. We share a common universal substance.

Really our differences can simply be put down to only two things, one is gender, and the other will be 'form' used on earth, and perhaps elsewhere. The latter is subjective. An illusion. 'Form' is the physical form including racial features (stature, color etc) physical features according to a genetic inheritance of the flesh.

Not only then are we 'all the same', but also 'partake of the same', have the same origins, end, and yes, GOD. We are all part of it. This is equality that is very real, hence in reality "there is neither Jew nor gentile, bond nor free." There is none above the other. How then should we act on earth?

Now then, what is important?

(That is hard to date right now. Between 2005 and 2007. Like as though that matters apart from perspective.)

SPHERES, bubbles, and us...

I have been puzzling for a long time over Einstein's relativity, and also over the so-called 'big bang' theory, which is not treated as theory but as fact, and dogmatically taught, rammed down our necks. I have read much on the creationist theory and of ongoing creation, plus interventionalism. For over 20 years now, nearing 30 years I have been a silent student of cosmogony and its related studies. I have sought information on cosmology etc as far as within my reach. I am also a keen student of mathematics to a 'certain' level. It was while assessing a book on mathematics recently that I came up with conclusions that I felt compelled to post and publish.... because NO ONE has ever published or printed it – or so it seems.

Now In years past I have many times awoken at night at whatever hour with a sweeping and majestic "aha!!!!" a realization or a discovery...and hastily scribbled it down...and been most amazed at a discovery, or realization... Maybe you also are like this, if it happens to me, in fact I know it has or will happen to you also. We do keep a pen and paper always with us – don't we?

Then later you discover that this information/data/whatever, is already known, and previously published to mankind nnn years ago. I often felt discouraged by these events that happen with alarming frequency.

Then wisdom cuts in and you know that anything you can ever know has been known to someone, sometime, somewhere. But what is IMPORTANT is that you have discovered it for yourself. You literally have found a truth. You have an elation, a zealous 'gotta tell everyone'…then find 'what the….this has been revealed…it is known" - disappointing?? Yes, BUT DO NOT LET IT BE THAT.

     1: Know you discovered it independently…it is your discovery. As such, it is far more vital and significant than information learned extraneously.
     2.It is a guarantee of deeper understanding and of more to come.
     3:It is an indication of your ability for independent thinking.
     4:You are as individual a thinker as anyone you can conceive of. You organize knowledge and develop further from it.

Perhaps 1 reason why you later "find" it somewhere is that after the discovery one is searching for validation of the findings in all other available relevant known sources.

There are lots more things involved but my time is short as is yours, and you can now think about it and gain more from your own mind than I could give you.

Here we go….

Yet again I was looking at an illustration or representation of curved space, followed by 'curved space applied to the cosmos'. You may be familiar with such illustrations. Also shown was a coloured illustration of a solar system as though laid out on a pool table, all the planets neatly pocketed in 'dents' and the sun in a deeper and larger dent. It would be obvious that any object approaching any of the objects would slide into or be diverted by the dents, which would show the effect of gravity on the object. Yet again as I looked at the pictures I felt extremely frustrated because I was certain they were WRONG, and did not show a correct picture. But what was wrong?

Why were such illustrations curving in only one direction or dimension on essentially one plane. OK, an object on that flat surface would be effected as could well be so illustrated, but what of an object not on that essentially flat plane. And surely 'space' is NOT a flat plane conveniently laid out in this manner. What of an object above or below that plane, or a set of objects. We could imagine a myriad of objects on a myriad of planes, indeed each object with a myriad of planes until untold billions of places exist to intersect each with every other object denting and curving it's space, shown only as a plane.

The illustrations did not do 'reality' justice – nor portray it any more than an illustration of an atom as a marble like ball did justice to the structure of an atom. Then I had it. A perfected mental image of the universe, structured along the lines of the atom.

In effect every object must 'behave' or be as individual atoms or particles and influence a complete sphere. Gone and must be is a mental image of flat space trying to be curved space. Now we have spherical or 'bubble' space, with billions of spheres or bubbles. Space must be a composition of infinite 'shells' created by individual particles. How can one illustrate that? I cannot begin to imagine how that may be represented on flat paper in a 2 dimensional format. But in the mind it can be done. A crude analogy would be to liken it to a formless mass of soap bubbles.

In this bubble space every such sphere influencing space must and does curve that space so much as to bend or curve back around itself and will describe a perfect sphere, a 'closed' sphere of influence, extending a certain distance in any and every 'direction' until its mass no longer is high enough to exert any influence. Rather like a magnet, its influence is felt or experienced in all directions, but gradually diminishing with distance until it no longer exists. If you can mentally construct an image of the influence of a magnet you have it. Bring many magnets together and see the interaction and you have it.

Big issue: Can you even see the 'lines of influence' of the magnets, or of the mass that creates the sphere or bubble of influence? No? But space is completely filled with such bubbles of influence. Billions of bubbles existing and interacting, influencing one the other in varying degrees. And our personally created bubble in their midst. Some spheres/bubbles will be within others, others only partially within and overlapping others.

Imagine an object orbiting our planet. It endlessly circles in various paths until and unless it either succumbs to gravity and falls, or accelerates to escape velocity and frees itself from orbit. We know under some conditions either event can happen. If it frees itself from the bubble of influence, the gravity, it will go off and find itself subjected to the 'next in line' bubble or sphere of influence, it will orbit the sun. If it accelerates free of that sphere, it will become primarily influenced by the next sphere, perhaps a cluster or group of stars, then 'upwards' in magnitude to the galaxy, then to a cluster of galaxies, and so on. Yet all these spheres co-exist and operate simultaneously and are 'balls within balls', and further, overlapping balls within balls.

In 1987 I was in Honolulu at a market, and saw a set of the famous 'balls within balls' of the type we generally see as carved from a single piece of ivory, and the ball is held on the upraised trunk of 3 elephants. (Mine is plastic material, but a beautiful representation) I had to have one, and bought one for about $10. It has fascinated me endlessly. Now I know why. It is an excellent representation of reality, not the elephants supporting the balls, perhaps, but of the balls represent the spheres or bubbles of influence each enclosed by the next 'order' of magnitude. What is at the centre or is the smallest particle? I guess (reasonably) each particle is entitled to believe that IT is the centre of all things. How large is the largest sphere? Not for us to imagine is it?

HERE IS THE 'RUB'....

All such bubbles or spheres are created by and contain mass or matter in amounts relative to the extent or size of the resultant sphere of influence. For instance the size of a black hole is determined by the mass it has absorbed. Mass or matter is a form of energy. We are seeing, indeed experiencing ourselves as concentrated masses of energy contained within not only our own sphere or bubble of influence, but equally contained within endless bubbles of influence.

We are tremendously insignificant indeed in the order of magnitudes that exist. But we each exist in the order of things.

007 – interlude, points to ponder...

(All of the following, except such as is within brackets, is copied from an interesting book: *The Secret Life of Plants, by Peter Tompkins and Christopher Bird.* Hopefully I will remember to put the page numbers as they apply to the copy. Published by Harper Colophon Books, Harper & Row, Publishers.

(My thoughts after reading it was: It is horrific what is being done to people in the name of "medicine", "nutrition", "science" etc. Hitler was an amateur and unskilled in the art of human misery and death – but maybe the teacher of how to set up a "government" and beauracy that can effectively do it, hide the secret agenda from the people and get away with it. That is so long as "they" control the power and the dissemination of news and information, and can credibly broadcast and spread mis- or dis-information. There is an absolutely *unbelievable* bitterness and resistance, even mocking hatred, of those who would teach "natural" health, healing, wholeness, diet, living, nutrition etc. It may seem unbelievable, but it is true, people are being imprisoned for using and or dealing in natural remedies etc.

(I heard a politician on TV scornfully saying that "natural remedies" were being controlled or made illegal because, and I quote, *"who wants to take (one of these products) and find that it contains handfuls of grass".* Wake up people of the world, better to take a handful of grass if so be the case, than an injection of formaldehyde, heavy metals, known noxious, toxic, and debilitating, even crippling or lethal compounds pushed by legalized drug cartels. Enough of that for now. On with the quotes)

No plant, says France, is without movement: all growth is a series of movements: plants are constantly preoccupied with bending, turning and quivering. He describes a summer day with thousands of polyp like arms reaching from a peaceful arbor, trembling, quivering in their eagerness for new support for the heavy stalk that grows behind them. When the tendril, which sweeps a full circle in 67 minutes, finds a perch, within 20 seconds it starts to curve around the object, and within the hour has wound itself so firmly it is hard to tear it away. The tendril then curls itself like a corkscrew and in so doing raises the vine to itself.

A climbing plant which needs a prop will creep toward the nearest support. Should this be shifted, the vine, within a few hours, will change its course into the new direction. Can the plant see the pole? Does it sense it in some unfathomed way? If a plant is growing between obstructions and cannot see a potential support it will unerringly grow toward a hidden support, avoiding the area where none exists.

Plants says France, are capable of intent: they can stretch toward, or seek out, what they want in ways as mysterious as the most fantastic creations of romance. ....

Plants seem to know which ants will steal their nectar, closing when these ants are about, opening only when there is enough dew on their stems to keep the ants from climbing. The more sophisticated acacia actually enlists the protective services of certain ants, which it rewards with nectar in return for the ants' protection against other insects and herbivorous mammals.

Is it chance that plants grow into special shapes to adapt to the idiosyncrasies of insects which will pollinate them, luring these insects with special colour and fragrance, rewarding them with their favourite nectar, devising extraordinary canals and floral machinery with which to ensnare a bee so as to release it through a trap door only when the pollination process is completed?

Is it really nothing but a reflex or coincidence that a plant such as the orchid Trichoceros parviflorus will grow its petals to imitate the female of a species of fly so exactly that the male attempts to mate with it and in so doing pollinates the orchid? Is it pure chance that night-blossoming flowers grow white the better to attract night moths and night flying butterflies, emitting a stronger fragrance at dusk, or that the carrion lily develops the smell of rotting meat in areas where only flies abound, whereas flowers which rely on the wind to cross-pollinate the species do not waste energy on making themselves beautiful, fragrant or appealing to insects, but remain relatively unattractive? ......

Some plants, unable to find nitrogen in swampy land, obtain it by devouring living creatures. There are more than 500 varieties of carnivorous plants, eating any kind of meat from insects to beef, using endlessly cunning methods to capture their prey, from tentacles to sticky hairs to funnel-like traps. ....

Whereas plants have been almost universally looked upon as senseless automata, they have now been found to be able to distinguish between sounds inaudible to the human ear and color wavelengths such as infrared and ultraviolet invisible to the human eye; they are specially sensitive to x-rays and to the high frequency of television. ....

...plants may at last be the bridesmaids at a marriage of physics and metaphysics.

Evidence now supports the vision of the poet and the philosopher that plants are living, breathing, communicating creatures, endowed with personality and the attributes of soul. It is only we, in our blindness, who have insisted on considering them automata. –(from "introduction")

(from pages 122 on, concerning Gustav Theodor Fechner,) ....In the Little Book Fechner put forward the idea that human life was lived in three *stages: one of continuous sleep from conception to birth; one of half wakefulness, which humans called terrestrial life; and one of fuller alertness, which began only after death. In Comparative Anatomy he traced the evolution from monocellular organisms through man to an angelic higher beings spherical in form and capable of seeing universal gravitation as ordinary humans perceive light, of communicating not acoustically but through luminous symbols.*

Fechner introduced Nanna with **the concept that believing whether plants have a soul or not changes one's whole insight into nature. If man admitted to an omnipresent, all-knowing, and almighty god who bestowed animation on all things, then nothing in the world could be excluded from this munificence, neither plant nor stone nor crystal nor wave. Why would universal spirit, he asked, sit less firmly in nature that in human beings, and not be as much in command of nature's power as it is in human bodies?** *(Nanna, the Soul Life of Plants published 1848)*

Anticipating Bose's work, Fechner further reasoned that if plants have life and soul, they must have some sort of nervous system, hidden perhaps in their strange spiral fibers. Going beyond the limitation of today's mechanistic physiology, Fechner referred to "spiritual nerves" in the universe, one expression of which was the interconnection of celestial bodies, not with "long ropes", but with a unified web of light and gravity, and forces as yet unknown. ....

According to Fechner, the psyche of plants is no more linked to their nervous system than is the soul of man to the human body. Both are diffused throughout, yet separated from all of the organs which they direct. "None of my limbs anticipates anything for itself," wrote Fechner, "only I, the spirit of my whole, sense everything that happens to me."

Fechner created a new branch of learning, called psychophysics which abolished the artificial separation between mind and body and held the two entities to be only different sides of the one reality, the mind appearing subjectively, the body objectively, as a circle is either concave or convex depending on whether the observer stands inside it or outside. The confusion resulted, said Fechner, because it was difficult to hold both points of view simultaneously. To Fechner all things express in different ways the same anima mundi, or cosmic soul, which came into existence with the universe, is its conscience, and will die when and if the universe dies. Basic to his animate philosophy was the axiom that all life is one and simply takes up different shapes in order to divert itself. The highest good and supreme end of all action is the maximum pleasure not of the individual but of all, said Fechner, and on this he based all his rules for morals.

Since spirit to Fechner was a deistic universal, it was useless to refer to souls as wholly individual, whether vegetal or human. Nonetheless souls provided the only criteria for forming a conception of other souls and making themselves known to them by outward physical signs.....Fechner also maintained that in its soul alone was the true freedom of any creature.

.... Fechner asked, "Why should we believe that a plant is not any less aware of hunger and thirst than an animal? The animal searches for food with its whole body, the plant with portions of it, guided not with nose, eyes or ears, but with other senses." It seemed to Fechner that "plant people" calmly living their lives in spots of their rooting, might well wonder why human bipeds keep rushing about.

...In the end, posited this German sage, was it not one of the ultimate purposes of human bodies to serve vegetal life, surrounding it by emitting carbon dioxide for the plants to breathe, and manuring them with human bodies after death? Did not flowers and trees finally consume man and, by combining his remains together with raw earth, water, air, and sunlight, transform and transmute human bodies into the most glorious forms and colors?

008 -PAST, PRESENT, FUTURE, OR NOW???

What I consider as 'now', is neither universal nor absolute. If an event were to happen on the sun for instance, I would see it as 'now' some 9 minutes after it happened. Space and the speed of light make our 'now' an uncertain concept or point of reference from there. I see an axe fall in the distance but hear the sound later, a flash of lightening and the resultant thunder seconds later. Even the fall of the axe or flash of lightening took some time to reach me.

A star may be hundreds of light years away, what happens here 'now' will not be apparent to any there till those 100s of years have passed. Another galaxy may be millions or billions of light years away.

I am told our radio/TV (electromagnetic emissions) go into space at the speed of light. I do not doubt this. Our space probes at say Jupiter or

Saturn send back signals that take hours to reach earth. 'Now' on that space probe is not perceived as such here. Yet there is no doubt it happened correctly, its just that two 'now' states have become involved. What about say, at Alpha Centuri? Some 4 years before our 'now' can catch up with their 'now'. Further out is simply longer, and the more 'lookers' that are involved, the more 'now' states exist. Kind of a simple thing to understand so far.

Lets understand this. On a planet of Alpha Centuri one turns on a TV and may see earth scenes from years ago presented as current events. Further out one may hear news that the Titanic has just been sunk, or that earth is now involved in its first world war. Their concept of 'now' on planet earth is quite different from that on planet earth. Their interaction, reactions etc, with and of events on earth occur much 'later'. Now that 'later' may be to us a distant 'futre', which to them is the 'present'.

Could it be that if we went out say 2000 light years and looked back with focus on earth, we may see a Roman emperor? After all, I read that we see stars as they were hundreds, thousands, or millions of years ago. Reminds me of what I once read decades ago, that there is a record of every event that ever happened in the entire cosmos, the Akashic (spelling not sure) record, recorded in electromagnetic energy (light, sound) that could be available to access.

Time and space are difficult to tie down to a 'now', a 'past', a 'present', or a 'future'. Yet I read that a "NOW" does exist at a universal level, and is the same and instantaneous across the cosmos. I read that sub-atomic particles react simultaneously regardless of the space/time that separates the particles. Makes me think of thoughts I had decades ago, that the speed of thought is independent of the speed of light or known physics, and the ultimate speed in any science or field. This is time travel speed. Sure this introduces all those feared 'psycho..." And 'para...' areas.

We may now define a "Universal NOW". It is manifest when an action/reaction seemingly occurs in one place, and is experienced across and in the universe simultaneously with no regard for distance or time separating any two places. It has been observed and recorded in physics. This sounds kind of like some of those vague definitions people use to define some of the attributes of 'god'. Omniscient, all knowing, knowing an event when the cause may be billions of light years away, nothing hidden from the perceiver. It has a related "Universal Presence" manifest by the ability of a particle being located in two or more places at the same time. Omnipresent, existing everywhere at the same time, there is no place where such a one does not exist or occupy. This well defines the universal energy field, everywhere at the same time and within the same "NOW" – aware of all events instantly, regardless of 'where' and the "when" is meaningless. To such a one or such a field, time and space are meaningless concepts. It is all ONE, self-contained and also CONTAINING ALL within itself. Hmmm, sounds like god again.

If our entire cosmos is such and if we are indeed contained within such, then it would be true that all that we can see, feel, etc is an illusion. Some philosophies have been teaching this for centuries and more. Much more on this "illusion" later.

Here is the marvel. We are indeed made of substance of the universe, elements of the materials, and within the time/space of the universe. Even if you do not for whatever reason accept a god, nor a spirit, it is UNDENIABLE that we are of the same substance of the universe. Made of star stuff as some authors have said it. This leads us to pursue certain trains of thought, and consider some inescapable alternatives. Question is: Do we want to ask the questions? Do we want to define the alternatives? Do we want to know?

010 -LOOKING AT ALTERNATIVES.

Let's attempt to define the alternatives to consider the issue of 'life as we have it'. You read this, I wrote this, it is safe to say therefore that we both exist. An undeniable conclusion surely. That's what is sought here, to put on the table all alternatives and issues to consider. Nothing will be presented as 'the path' or whatever. I think it fair to comment here however, that whatever our personal decisions, it would and should apply not only to humans on earth, but to every species everywhere or anywhere. As a wise man once noted, our earth is nothing special nor is our sun or solar system-or our galaxy for that matter. Most likely true. Everything is 'star stuff'. How impudent for us to think a Universal intelligence/God would grant unto mortal humans the supremely highest position that exists, then annihilate him in a blink. I do not present the following as exclusive of other alternatives, it just means that either I have not thought of them, or it was not critical in the alternatives. Or perchance they are/were ludicrous.

I will introduce 2 major alternatives or absolutes. 'A' for no universal 'Energy/God/Force' etc accepted nor acknowledged, for the so-called pure materialist. 'B' for those who do accept or could consider such a possibility. IN other words this is intended to include all readers...You either say NO (A) or Yes (B) or Maybe (B) otherwise just sit there and get older.

'A'

Life exist on earth & new life must be either created at conception or at birth,

Male or female determined by absolute chance at conception. Offspring will manifest (mostly) one gender only of choice of two.

Gender is unimportant, and new individuals are born male or female by chance, with no personality, they are 'blanks' essentially.

Born into the world and takes the 'star stuff' elements from the parents and is part of the earth.. It lives eats drinks and breathes the very elements of the material universe. It is flesh, dust, elemental matter, body taken from it and will return to it.. It will live and die.

Death. End in dissolution of the entire entity. The body dissolves back to elements, and no personality is likely to survive, as this view accepts no existence of spirit, force or whatever.

Existence seems pointless, and no explanation can deal with the issue of what causes one bunch of elements to form a live thing and another to simply be 'rocks'. There is no permanent change of status, no development, just existence and total, absolute annihilation.

'B' offers several alternatives..

All assume that a continuous life/force/energy/intelligence exists in the universe and that everything is part of that. In all the following variations, One is born into this world and takes a body of 'star stuff', elements of the earth – compliments of mortal parents. It lives, eats, drinks and breathes elemental matter of the material universe. A MORTAL BODY IS ANIMATED BY THE force/energy/god etc and TWO bodies thus coincide in space/time for the duration or mortality. The mortal body dies, dissolves, returns to dust. However:

'B-1'

Assumes GENDER is unimportant as the life/force/energy/god, whatever, has NO GENDER. Male or female is a chance event, accident of birth, and the new life created on earth assumes or becomes whatever is provided. It thus has no personality and is a 'blank'. After death, the 'life force' leaves the mortal elements on earth and re-joins the universal genderless force etc. Leaves one eternally genderless and therefore non-individual, no individual development. Is this pointless??

'B-2'

Here gender does 'pre-exist' as either M/F ying/yang whatever, but individual personalities do not exist as such. Conditions of 'B-1' apply with a difference following death. Post-mortal one continues as Male or Female but there are 2 alternatives now, either to re-join the collective gender group and lose individuality had on earth, OR continue as an individual M/F which would be development and make the mortal life a progressive stage. Perhaps not as pointless as 'B-1' type of life scenerio.

'B-3'

Here not only does gender pre-exist, but so do individuals, Such individuals by whatever criteria take up an appropriate M/F body on earth. As such, the newborn mortal is not totally a 'blank' as in all the above alternatives, life on earth has the additional role of providing a flesh body and experience to a pre-existing individual. THE DREAM BODY AND THE MORTAL BODY REFLECT THIS DUAL EXISTENCE OF INTELLIGENCES.

This seems a likely alternative, as it provides genuine logic and development. After mortality the individual continues as an individual with memory of the learning experience in mortality. Further options: remain thereafter without 'flesh' body, or 'restore' such a body later. There is an assured status change of some sort. A big question is: is a body of flesh, star stuff elements needed at all? The dream body seems to function perfectly well without such.

Well that's the end of that little exercise and it is not exclusive. What's the point of this? Well if you don't know it goes like this: One day maybe you will be like me, knowing death is just a knock away. For some it comes with a date attached to a question mark. For others its more like a huge probability – we have passed the figures acceptable to the actuary. You cannot even get term insurance. There will come a time when every mortal would question the options, want to know the 'odds'…with out the jiving.

The above table lets you determine the options. 4 columns, 4 sets of circumstances on a 'YOU FIGURE IT YOURSELF' basis. So…you figure. Which one are you? Know just one thing: matters not the choice, you will pass. Enjoy life and let's later think of some things that made it all worthwhile.

(This article has had to be presented a second time without the 4 columns as when posted to the www, the columns vanished and the result was shambles.)

012 -TOGETHER, IN SICKNESS AND HEALTH.

For a long time the other night I lie awake thinking about various aspects of life and I caught a vision of our nature in this world. It came about after contemplating the generally ignorant and fallen state in which our species finds itself.

Now Western Science seemingly is sadly and totally lacking in understanding and ignorant, or at least unaccepting, of the full true nature of mankind. Yet it has expressed some fantastic truths that must surely lead to a true understanding of our nature. Perhaps therein is the problem with science, it leads only to knowledge rather than 'understanding'. It is known that the entire cosmos, all that there is, is a form of 'energy'. It is known that 'energy' can be converted into 'matter' and visa versa. It is known that the bulk of 'matter' is 'vacant space' and that solid matter is as rare as -and even then, undefinable. It is as a grain of sand within a house. (Nucleus of atom to 'size' of entire atom) It follows that what is known as solid matter as we generally accept and speak of it is really, as solids go, an illusion. An illusion that is nonetheless solid and impenetrable to other matter, including ourselves. It is known that any sub-atomic particles are 'interchangeable' in all chemical elements. One electron is as any other, likewise a proton, neutron etc. It can measure the energy binding an atom to itself, and even devise ways to release that energy. It can modify atoms by forcing an atom to take on new particles to create ions etc. All very marvelous really. This gives a most magnificent base to launch thousands of contemplative sessions to discover for oneself that which science will not accept, or worse, scoffs at, ridicules etc.

I think the reason for that attitude is that such discovery and contemplation is not the scientific method, and may be used and embarked upon by anyone who cares or dares. This means they cannot control what is and what is not accepted, and thus cannot be the gods of the dogma any longer. I will mean the loss of their perceived power, authority, and control. Once that may have been important to the world, when man was largely ignorant and superstitious. Such men needed gods of dogma to guide them and save them from deeper ignorance and superstition. A lot of intelligent free thinkers exist now, and a lot say 'to hell with the dogma, the authority, we do not need a professor or doctor to guide us in our thinking.' Well these days a lot of 'others, outsiders' or whatever have a lot of contributions to make that are perhaps just as valid as data established by scientific method.

So then, we know that man is a compilation of energy and matter by virtue of his physical body alone. We know that the physical body of matter is largely illusion, and is energy 'masquerading' as matter at best, and a lot of the physical factors are powered by energy also. (Brain functions, nerves, heartbeat etc) It exists in time/space here in this weird and wonderful combination for a short time only. We have established that the so called physical part is composed of the very elements of it's earth, which in turn are composed of remnants of stars, this knowledge compliments of the dogma of science. All mankind shares this construction along with absolutely everything on earth, yes, even the earth itself. It is also composed of star dust, is electrically charged, an 'illusion' that is really energy or 'force', and it also so manifests itself for what is in reality for a short time only, then it too will be recycled in the great cosmos. Strikes me as rather a grand system of things. All pervading energy that is all things and powers all things, and manifests as matter, yet the guru's of scientific dogma scoff at the ancient principle and belief in 'prana' and such, that seems to me an accurate enough (non-scientific) description of what its 'all about'. Likewise they make a mock of such things as –dare I say these words- astral worlds, spirits, higher planes, and hundreds of other such things, ideas or thoughts, working models, and 'non-scientific' explanations or beliefs which are at times more valid than so called science itself.

For example: Does faith healing work? Seemingly it does without doubt at times. (Now this is not to say they are 'scam free', but hey, I have read accounts of scientists falsifying results and scamming.) Has 'ESP' been verified as reality at times? Sure. Is levitation reality? I have seen it. Do people die from voodoo, black magic, or curses? Absolutely they do, no doubt about that one. Has man the ability to have an experience of being 'outside the body", the OBE? Been there a few times myself also. Near death experiences and return to 'this world'? I accept it and have returned after two cardiac arrests involving about an hour's absence. No doubt there are many 'phenomena' you may have experience with that I did not mention, but are equally valid.

You get the idea, all of these are valid, working things that science will have nothing to do with, BECAUSE I suspect, they have no control of the scientific method and dogma. They cannot preside as the high priests of science over things in the public domain, over which they can have no control nor discipline those who do not 'toe the line'. They say a thing is "not proven" and demand "proof", claiming no "proof" exists of this or that as yet. Do those healed by the faith healer not constitute living proof, or do those healed ask for "proof", certification of their healing? Credential waving "authorities" demand proof, but will only accept proof supplied and forthcoming from their own ranks, and even they bury that which is contrary to existing dogma or challenge the rulings or opinions of "authority". Very like church leaders who deny revelation if it is contrary to what they already accept. Thus science does only reject, but mocks, ridicules and would make out as simple fools those who do not unquestioningly accept their claimed, assumed, and presumed superior knowledge or wisdom. More like superior ignorance. It's the old kill the messenger thing.

Religion generally fares little better in my books. Now I don't ever want to be called one who is prejudiced unless it is prejudiced towards truth or logic and against ignorance, stupidity, superstition, or arrogance. (Yes I do believe in equality, we are all star dust and more of that soon) Let me give a simple illustration. Yesterday, 1/8/2004 I picked up a newsletter from a local 'Christian' church. The topic, 'Does God still give revelation' etc. Basically it said 'NO' that finished (conveniently) when the 'Bible' was compiled and that was the final word of and from 'god'. Tough for God or us, if he has any legitimate instructions etc, for a LARGE body of His 'loyal church' are not about to hear it nor receive it. Picture this: God on throne, sees comet coming to earth, considers it and the wisdom of giving a warning and instructions to a new generation for an 'ark' (they have the technology, and I will help) He makes the call...no answer. He thinks maybe call Jerusalem next call, or Tokyo. He knows where not to call. But is that attitude bad? It gets WORSE. If God is claimed to have given revelation, so the article continues, and it goes contrary to what the church ALREADY accepts, then the church leaders being obviously infallible, declare that the revelation is false. This leaves no room or way for god to get a hearing to correct any wrong ideas, interpretations, or understandings of his previous communications, not to mention to change his mind, or alter, add etc to previous words. In other words, the leaders are infallible, understand perfectly, need no more, need no "divine" counsel or help, and will neither hear nor accept any more. 3 monkeys come to mind. Such are they who once declared the world not only flat, but also the centre of all that can exist, and man as the culmination of god's 7 day work-a-thon. Now all this flies in the face of reason does it not? This from a church that taught the world IS flat, and IS the centre of the universe, and God is a white caucasian obviously. Oh yes and male of course. It follows then, said the doctors of divinity dogma, that, being supreme, we can rape the world; do as we will, for god is with us. Hmmm. Voltaire warns along the lines of beware the man (church etc obviously included) that says, "believe as I do or god will damn you....he means and will turn to "believe as I do or I will kill you..". How open minded is the 'traditional Christian church? They will stuff down your neck a one sided "sharing" of ideas. No thanks; and yes, many dissenters have perished, killed by their 'holy' hands. They would do it again if only it would be undiscovered. You doubt me? Read about "ethnic cleansing". Individuals who do not comply on ethnic, moral, religious, or god knows what grounds, are disposed of. Killed. Welcome to planet earth and its life forms.

Generally, science fails us, as does religion generally. The State is worse, for it is a vehicle solely for the preservation of the status quo, to lose no more for those in power or authority, the landed, the wealthy, the 'nobility', and now, the corporations. But maybe the corporations and the state shall be dealt with in another writing. The state DOES NOT serve mankind. It makes/creates/uses war to increase power, wealth, and authority of those privileged ones who write the song sheets from which the politicians and parliamentarians sing and quote. It serves man's rulers and keeps "us" in our place. It will suppress and imprison its citizens; it will remove and kill with a veneer of legality those who would raise a voice to object. You do not think that history can repeat "holocaust"?

What is the nature and source of the animating force? Its fine to say that man has a body of elements of the earth, that those elements are recycled residue of stars. It's a bag of chemicals of (now) known and understood componentry. Its mostly space, its illusionary, it is in reality energy. But whence comes the 'force' /whatever name you want to use, to ORGANISE this bag of magical tricks? No way can a bag of protons, neutrons and particles organize themselves. There is more than energy afoot here for sure. Electricity has been around since year dot, (Lightning etc.) yet has not evolved or organized. Our brain waves and heartbeats are 'energy'/electrical etc, yet break down and cease. Science calls it entropy or whatever. Matter or energy cannot organize itself. Yet something obviously does this trick. For we exist. Do we not?

So here we are - US. United in time and space – UNITED IN SICKNESS AND IN HEALTH, UNTIL DEATH US DO PART. A lump of star dust matter formed from a planet, inhabited by an already existing live 'entity' who has the ability to use the dust and convert it into living tissues to becomes a new earther person, who after pain and travails, separates from it's previous 'universal origins' to become a new and separate life...one that will also eat star dust, now planetary dust, and turn that into living tissue that will not only replicate itself, but think, eat, love, laugh, cry, mourn, celebrate, hope, think, reason, read, write, believe, hate, get sick, and one day die. A lump of star dust cannot of or by itself do these things. No more than a monkey with a typewriter and a zillion years can punch out the complete works of Shakespeare. It is not in the realms of reason, belief, nor mathematics. No more likely than throwing together a BMW from a rock pile, or a space shuttle from a car wrecking yard.

Excuse me; I have just taken a break for a magnificent meal I was making. Now I can appreciate that corny line in the movies where everything 'tastes like chicken' – the universal recycled star dust forming the chicken is going into and ingested by other recycled star dust. Given time science will maybe call me generation 9 and the chicken generation 23a, being the 5th manifestation of the recycled same dust - that is if ever it accepts anything. Back to the 'matters'.

Nothing herein is presented as anything except my 'musings' shared with you to maybe stimulate your thoughts or amuse you, or to express myself.

The vision alluded to earlier in this writing. I see an individual entity, not a man, nor anything I can define. Kind of like the introduction to the being in the Jeff Bridges movie "Starman'. It is a glowing glimmering point of light and vibrating energy of unknown dimension. It is part of the entire cosmos yet also individual. It is an individual of equal status to all else. If god/God/GOD is the entire cosmos, then this is a component part of GOD along with every form that exists. It is of particles and elements as yet unknown, not of the star dust stuff, for it is energy and intelligence. It is independent and not subject to space/time as we know it. It is an intelligent cosmic 'energy' force, individual in nature, and equal to all things, part of all things, aware of and knowing all things. It is literally part of GOD. I give this entity no name, but I perceived it. It is the Individual, and in my language perhaps that is enough of a name.

The Individual drifts into this life and becomes part of this world. It is not a journey in space or maybe even time. It is an event in the cosmic "now". It submerges itself into a human form and 'forgets' its identity etc. More on this later in another essay. It adopts a form that maybe Plato referred to. The form is perfect, but the adaptation may not be so perfect, for it is the 'n'th generation or implementation of that same star dust pattern, the 'n'th- generation of the genetic materials. "Near enough" is good enough for this 'trip', "not near enough" results in termination. (Death to the embryo, fetus, infant etc) The Individual has no imperfections of 'form' but the physical form used in this 'incarnation' may have many imperfections. Birth to mortality has just happened, and the Individual now literally lives with the consequences, no longer manifest as the bright radiant Individual. The Mortal Individual has begun its incarnation and life on earth.

I do not intend to paint a long picture here, but just to give the bones. The Individual is now a Mortal Individual but still the original self. (Whatever that is) The difference is that it is now a DUAL ENTITY OF COSMIC 'ORIGINAL' ENERGY, JOINED WITH A RECYCLED 'STAR DUST' BODY OF THE 'EARTH', UNITED IN SICKNESS AND IN HEALTH TILL DEATH DO THEM PART. It is literally a part of what we call GOD, come to the earth, and coupled with flesh which is elements of the earth, united till the dissolution of the flesh in 'mortal death' - and what GOD has joined together (we are warned) let no man put asunder. To terminate such a one is WRONG. It is contrary to the workings of GOD. The flesh is united with the Individual; it has become a union, a 'marriage' in mortality till death of the flesh. I do not pretend to understand any accountability for violations etc.

Here in mortality any genetic or other defects are worn by the Individual in the 'near enough' cases. This may lead to a mortal experience of deformity, sickness, misery, or early death. We will not even consider any factors such as geography, race, country, society, gender, status etc at this time. Now it seems to me on reflection that the 'form', the body, regenerates and replaces itself by the taking in of elements of the earth. We eat, breathe, drink etc, and cycle the elements into a gradually growing and self-replacing body. The body regenerates, but any defect given at birth also duplicates and continues. This is according to that body's blueprint. (Now it gets weird. All this is of illusionary matter which is mostly space and ultimately 100% energy) It seems it runs on a parallel and separate 'programme' to the Individual, the Individual running a 'perfect' cosmic/GOD stuff programme, while the mortal runs a lower grade recycle 'n'th generation programme which accepts defects and perpetuates them. Don't know about you, but I find the whole concept strangely logical…and somehow familiar.

This is the world's record for a preamble to 'why the hell do I have to have heart surgery?'

I answer myself. The form or genetic pattern given by this world dictates that I have heart disease at this time. God/GOD did not give it to me. It is the result of what science would call 'natural causes and effects which may include genetics, diet, blah blah'. May be it just could be remedied by resort to some of the practices referred to above, to faith healing etc.

But in my case at this time and in like manner for thousands of mortals, this is either not contemplated, or for various reasons not effective. (One day we may deal with the 'mere' effects of disbelief for whatever reasons it exists – many) So being denied the opportunity to provide the world with evidence of a miraculous 'remission', there are fewer opportunities left to me. One is to reach in and change that pattern, that form, which the mortal flesh uses to regenerate itself. The offending 'piece' may be removed, modified, or killed off. Then the laws of replication shall ensure the offending part is not replicated. (If thine eye offend thee, pluck it out…shades of medical science) So if my offending mitral valve is cut out and replaced with whatever, the removed bit is no longer part of my 'form' or pattern, then it can and will no longer duplicate that defect. So by surgery this matter of a mortal body defect will be remedied. Yet it is all chemicals, elements, particles, lots of vacant space, those recycled, and universal energy/'force'. It may appear a difficult or complicated concept, but with a little mental exercise is quite simple.

Intervention can correct a fault in 'forms', by whatever means of intervention that work. The incoming new (and recycled) particles in the mortal Individual conform to the now modified 'form'.

Then that mortal body dies to this world, is a burden to the Individual, and the Individual must shed it as one does a set of worn out clothing. The individual drifts out of this world, and out of this space/time as we know and experience it at this moment. We will cover more on that later also.

It returns to universal/cosmic 'now'. I seriously doubt and sorry folks, I do not believe for one moment it will haunt familiar places, bother about nor attend to any funerals of the flesh any more than we attend to or mourn our laundry. That just defies logic, or reason. I doubt any Osiris, Enki, or Jehovah still frequents or returns to once familiar earthly habitats.

It returns as the poet said, to the god from whence it came…to its home. Sounds good and right to me. But hey folks, I'm on a holiday at the moment, and even though I may know my GOD and FATHER on a first name basis, I am enjoying the holiday, and would love to stay just a little bit longer. I'm not quite ready to go (back) home yet.

We are all the same in every essence before, during, and After Mortality. We are all part of the same Cosmic Force, The same GOD.

We are also all of the same earth matter, all share the same recycled natures of the body, and all eat, drink and breathe of the same star dust called earth. We are all dual Individuals, God and man, married one to the other in sickness or in health till death do part, with a warning for no one to put asunder, for no one to divide the flesh. It is all just to good, logical, familiar, and correct to doubt.

Yet science refuses to either understand or more correctly accept and endorse. Many scientists have favoured a religion. But the momentum of the whole thing shall proceed with or without the approval of doctors of science. They will fail and be forgotten just as my ancestors of 5000 years ago are largely forgotten. They are oblivion to come - just as are our current mortal bodies. But it is sad that just because the men of science cannot pull (things mentioned above) apart, reconstruct, duplicate, wind up, write untold papers about, and above all, build individual (not Individual) reputations about, then it will be anathema. I am scientific anathema. Welcome to my world.

So do we understand why things NEVER get better? Why the previously foreseen and dreamed of Utopia did not eventuate? Why the history of man is monotonously full of 'repeats'? Why god does not intervene and slay this lot or that lot? Or why god does not identify with a pope or rabbi or me, or you? And why we are (shudder) allowed to get sick or die? Or why children die? Can we now imagine what is the fate of children or infants who die? If you understand the above, you will no longer be subject to ignorance or crafts. (Why the Individual is released to its former state - that mortality is merely ended—not an eternal damned soul, nor an eternal baby, etc.) Why do men perpetuate these horror alternatives? Easy answer, to gain power and authority by rule of fear over the ignorant and superstitious. Understand that we all as Individuals need the same EXPERIENCES AND GROWTH. This world gives us that. And we all need it and get it in the same environment of greed etc.

This is why Utopia has never been created and realized, and will forever be only a vision. But beyond…

014 -SUPERIOR INTELLIGENCE/DREAM BODY..

This writing is totally "extempore." As have been several other writings. But it raises yet another complicating issue and answers a question I had or raised in *a previous* writing…. does that dream body ever have an awareness of the "waking body"? In other words, when we are asleep and dreaming do we ever get to know we are asleep and dreaming – and additionally, get to know 'WE' have another body at another level, operating independently of the body within which we are then functioning???

Further to that—and fascinating beyond words, can one such body communicate to the other level of the same basic individual intelligence?? I doubted it when I wrote t*hat* posting.

But then my memory kicked in. I recalled an incident from personal experience, recorded at the time. I think I could be forgiven for overlooking or forgetting this personal experience. I do have some personal journals. My life has had such momentous events as to motivate me early to keep some records. I refer to an entry recorded as "DREAM. 17.5.1972. Reconstruction of 24(?)11-71. NITE OF 23/14-11-71" (sic) here follows the record as it exists word for word – a comment will follow:
Some of the words bracketed are "today's" comments.

"I saw an old ruined cathedral. At the altar monks were at prayer. I saw beneath the altar and into a crypt. Beyond the crypt and church was an old cemetery. A funeral was about to be held. No grave was dug and no coffin was there. A bucket of sand was the "body and coffin". (Punctuation is as recorded) I had a spade & started to spread it around, but I put it in the wrong place. I gathered it up and correctly placed it. Some was left over & this I placed in a hole were a rose was to be planted. Kathy (my estranged and departed first wife) was watching & seemed angry she drove off & didn't hear or heed my calls after her.

"Frank (her father) had done some work for some people and they weren't (I did punctuate that..this is exactly as the record is) happy. We were there & I jumped the back fence. (seems I was escaping?) ((the last bracketed note appears in the written record))

"Fences were on all sides of me & I was going uphill. Someone was waiting for me at the top near the fence. But I jumped a fence on my RHS and made good my escape.

"I meet a woman, married and young, I piggy back her down to the beach, Somewhere at Redcliffe. But I ran away from her.

"A woman shot me in the hand with a dart. I saw it hit me and the wound it made. It immediately began to paralyse me. I could not talk only make noises. I was a slave to the woman my movements were like a zombie. Somehow I got a gun and shot her. I watched as the dart hit her chest and fell off – ineffective. My mum gave me a silver pistol & I shot her with this. Immediately I was e from the paralysis.

" I tied a scarf around my leg (right?) & left a lot hanging to assure a safe trip. I flew south but was pursued. My pursuers were destroyed (in a car.) As I landed the people were duck shooting. I landed amid the shooters in a trench (sort of) and buried my webbed feet in the ground.

"AT ONE STAGE OF THIS DREAM I REALIZED THAT I WAS DREAMING – I THINK IT WAS AFTER THE 'KATHY DROVE OFF BIT." REALIZING THIS I CEASED THE DREAM, GOT UP AND WROTE DOWN THE DREAM.

"WHEN I HAD DONE THIS I SETTLED DOWN AND THOUGHT TO REMEMBER WHAT FOLLOWED AS IT WOULD BE IMPORTANT. UPON AWAKING I LOOKED FOR THE NOTES BUT THEY DID NOT EXIST – I HAD DREAMED EVEN THIS, OR MORE LIKELY CONSCIOUSNESS INTERVENED & I PROJECTED TO DO IT ASTRALLY. IT COULD BE HOWEVER THAT THE ENTIRE DREAM WAS IN THE PROJECTED STATE. Most assuredly upon physically awaking I recorded it in full detail – these notes having been destroyed by another party later.)

There is the record I have. Exactly as it is..spelling, ampersands, etc ---as is. Here are a few mind blowers:

I had totally forgotten this 'experience'.

Now I can totally recall it clearly, as if it happened last night.

Here is the follow up note, and it blows my understanding, but here it is and is REAL:

"(At one stage in this dream I realized that I was dreaming – I think it was after the 'Kathy drove off bit." Realizing this I ceased the dream, got up & wrote down the dream. When I had done this I settled down & thought to remember what followed as it would be important. Upon awaking I looked for the notes but they did not exist – I had dreamed even this, or more likely consciousness intervened & I projected to do it astrally. It could be however that the entire dram was in the projected state. MOST ASSUREDLY UPON PHYSICALLY AWAKING I RECORDED IT IN

FULL DETAIL – THOSE NOTES HAVING BEEN DESTROYED BY ANOTHER PARTY LATER.)

The above is a reproduction of my notes dated as shown from 1971. They are as the notes show, case sensitive, ampersands and all, but they do not encapsulate all my memory....I slowly recalled this as one of MANY memories....see, I challenged for memories of the dream body knowing it was that, and that it knew another body existed...alongside itself........(what is the next level??)

Yes the dream body does know...and it can know more than we care to know.

Maybe, just maybe, we on this *dream* level are in 'cruise control' and *generally* don't *need to know or make decisions that need to be carried over into "normal waking state"*.
I sure as hell have experiences that are (fortunately) recorded, but we forget....now about that memory of the dream, once it is triggered, it comes back fully.....for instance there was a "voice" that instructed me to write everything thing that had been and would be revealed... It was that 'voice' that commanded me to 'wake up' to record everything that had happened (or been revealed) and to record everything that would be yet revealed. I did all that – but as yet offer no interpretations.

017 – THE FINAL WORD?

There has been quite a lot of questions asked, and a fair amount of information thrown in so far, but let me just add a few correlated matters. Now, no "proof"is offered up with these matters and no references will be provided. It will be squarely up to the reader to do the research, as only in doing that will the veracity of the statements be established. In any case, has any reader ever gone to the alleged source materials of writings that meticuously list the sources, origins, authorities etc of any claims? I have not. Also, as I propose this to be the end of the writings for some time, if not "for ever" some seemingly unrelated matters may appear to be just casually thrown in. If that seems the case, let it be known that I see vitally important implications with such matters, but do not propose to deal with them in depth here, or perhaps, at all. There will be abundant other books and materials dealing with every matter or issue raised or to which I refer. Accept such issues as deemed supportive of a "grand interpretation", and not as red herrings or unsupportable fringe lunacy. I repeat, do the research and find the writings. Here goes with some short statements.

"Change" only happens because of the involvement of people, us or others. It must be observed. Again the falling tree, unobserved in the forest. Its related to the famous postualation: "for every action there is…reaction".

Mathematics is more important and makes grander statements than most people could barely begin to understand. Mathematics is a very precise language that expresses things that would otherwise take volumes to explain, and even then would be misunderstood. The progression from 1 upwards, and interpretations thereof is worthy of serious consderation. It is quite amazing that if there exist say 2 people, a 3rd entity, a modification of each's awareness, is created by their action/reaction to and with each other.

There is a virtual mountain of data evidencing that plants actually and have been recorded as reacting to the presence of people. Equally it is evidenced that by a person's mere thinking about a specific plant, that a reaction to that thought is expressed and recordable from that plant. Folk lore reports "green fingers".   Equally others cannot grow anything successfully and their plants always die and wither.
These facts alone should conclusively evidence the power and force of the energy nature of thought, of "mind".   There is more that just circumstantial evidence for the reality of what some call "psyhic energy". (loads of scams abound sure, but that is the case in every field that involves human endeavour.   Politicians, medical fields, lawyers, manufacturers of every conceivable type. Everything is corruptible by humans if it can be used to gain influence, power, wealth, whatever.)

A reminder that sub-atomic particles react with others across "space"as though no time or space existed. Quite contrary to physics as we understand them of course. It is well noted that the very attempt to locate or identify the location of a sub-atomic particle will, by virtue of the attempt to involve mere observation, directly effect location itself of the thing that one is attempting to observe and locate.   This just screams that there is more about the nature of the cosmos than we could begin to even grasp. Frankly, our science of physics is sadly too basic and crude

On the subject of science etc. let it be remembered that "science"only asks and seeks to identify "how", not "why". Newton is quoted as saying, "it is enough that gravity really does exist, and act according to the laws which we have explained….." And Galileo, on the subject of accelleration of falling bodies; "the cause of the accelleration of the

motion of falling bodies is not a necessary part of the investigation".
Science only addresses the objective "how", and this is why it always
seeks "proof", whereas to ask "why" one crosses the boundary from
objective and provable (as either right or wrong) into the realm of
subjective.   No proofs can exist in that realm.   Subjective, is
interpretation, it is realm of "mind", and science will have nothing of that
for it cannot regulate and "dogmatise"it. "mind" is free from any but the
Individual's own control, if even then.

What can be disturbing is the realisation that what we accept as a genuine
conclusively provable long established reality is not necessarily that at
all.   It can be painful to contemplate too long at this for it is "our"
universe itself. Consider thus: The light from the planets takes time to
reach us, from minutes to hours of it. Thus we "see"them as they
"really"were minutes or hours ago. They are not really where we "see"
them at all. Likewise light from observable stars takes years to centuries,
even thousands of years to reach us. They are not as or where we "see"
them "now" at all.   Stars, clusters, galactic clouds can be tens of
thousands of ligh years from us, and galaxies millions to billions of light
years (light speed) from us. Our perceivable universe is not really as
"we" see it at all. It is as a collage pieced together and called "now" for
convenience. Worse, because of this time lapse caused by distance and
light speed, it can be demonstrated that no one will "exactly" share or
agree with what we "see". Dare I use the words, but its all to to with:
Time and Relative Distance in Space.   Yes that gives the acronom
TARDIS. Co-incidence? Maybe. Reality, or one's perception of it, is
quite unique to that Individual.

"Mind", and I am sure you agree we all seem to experience if not actually
individually possess one,   does not seem to be a manifestation of
"matter". Matter being that star stuff that gets buried, burned, or however
recycled when one "dies". It appears that thought is a form of energy, not
bound by matter, time, or space, As energy it is detectable to and by
other energy forms, witness the plants etc. (do your own research and
don't scream for "proof") Yes, I am sure so-called "psychics" can and do
exist and function well. Some may call them "sensitives", but its only a
name isn't it?   I submit that billions of such "minds" functioning
simultaneously on this world alone must represent and present a fantastic
energy force. So what one asks? Well if one mind can rule, control this
star stuff mortal body, what of billions of such? Yes the mind of one,
controls the matter making up the body of that one, and more also. When
that Individual "mind" leaves or departs from that star stuff body, then

the body will recycle, it is not viable. Mind over matter. How to clearly get to my point?

If one mind controls the mass of matter, then it is establishable that matter is organised, controllable etc by mind. It is evidenced in science that it is the very existence of matter, also known as mass, that causes, is the source of, the very fabric of time and space. It is also a "known" that matter is only another representation or state of "energy". (the e=mc2 thing) Therefore, ultimately there is only energy, whatever is may be perceived as by "mind", which itself is pure energy.

Dang. Oh yes, whatever the mind can conceive and believe it can achieve.

Let me share a personal experience. It "proves" nothing of course, but it is an interesting Individual example of what, why, and how we accept, and can even change our perception of reality. This is a copy of notes I made in hospital September 2004, after days of the most disturbing events and perceptions.

Now as I'm about to go to bed everything is as though covered by a few feet of swirling clear water. Goodnite at 10.26pm. Its now extremely grotesque – gone 12.30 (night time) and EVERYWHERE I focus or look there are zillions of fluorescent tube like worms, only smaller than cotton, all writhing in a mist, like little thread worms – all waving into the air. They are not there of course, and this I can demonstrate (and do so) by careful close study of a surface. But it gets scary what this effect can do to one's face, or clothes, in a mirror. Everything is alive with colourful waving, flowing worms.

SUNDAY (12th) 7.46am. Now I have it all figured out – we are all gonna die here. See people only check in and never check out. Well I've been here since 30/8/04 and I have never seen people, anyone, go home. (yet earlier I note someone gone home!!) They come in and those left sane, disappear in the night. Now I gotta be careful who sees this, and I gotta get out this morning. I waked finally only to find a cold and bleak day with the laws of physics no longer working. I'm dead or in hell, so are the others obviously. Last nite I spoke with an Indian Doctor, one of the surgeons. He knows that some of us see the walls, floors, etc as moving. Last nite an older lady in the ward "cracked up" and was wheeled off to an isolated room. We go insane in here some of us.

SUNDAY (12ᵗʰ) 7.11pm I have learned that some times it is necessary to not only ignore things but to "not see them" at all. It is beyond any powers of denial – it is for survival.

Thus today I determined not to see nor dwell on floors, walls, clothes or sundry other things as have in the past been 'alive'. In consequence my sanity is preserved, but the poor lady patient wheeled out last nite may have had experience none would enjoy – not the vilest horror movie sadist even. That lady did look calmer today, and is wearing an oxygen mask.

The point in the above is that I made a conscious decision as to what I would "see" and what I would "not" see. By that decision I changed "reality"as I was, or had been "seeing" it. The change is perceived reality was almost instant. I became a "convert". I think we create our own reality more than we can imagine in our wildest dreams.

How many and how often I wonder do some feel literally like prisoners contained and held within the body they "walk around in"? How many know or suspect that something is just not quite right with the "setup"? We know and feel we are really and literally looking out throught these little windows called "eyes". We, the real us, the Individual is within, contained, a prisoner, and not of this earth, We *know* that "we" are NOT the material framework we see that people perceive of as "us". For this reason and thus some of us make every attempt to *dumb down* ourselves to rebel against the imprisoning body and releive the pain of obvious confinement. Yes it is sabotage born of frustration, misinformation, vague and ill defined resentment caused by our ignorance of our very real nature. The perception of "me" as being within looking out is there, but not fully *realised.*

Why are kids "kids"? Probably only because they are so new at experiencing their new "now" state that they have not adapted or adopted enough presentations of various realities/experiences of others as their own. When they "join" us by accepting all as we do, then we will see them as "one of us" - yes "they have become as one of us", in the words of Genesis.

We believe what we want to believe. If we can conceive it we can believe it. In the words of the New Testament, we can be allowed to believe a lie. And in believing the lie we are not free. Man are we so "not free". Yet we believe we are, and we perceive that we are so free. It is written: "there is none so enslaved as those that think they are free."

Later I just have to write about the life on earth experience from a social and political point of view. Fascinating.

So we can, and doubtless a lot of Individuals do, develop "false memories" already referred to earlier. We accept such false memories as total as "actual experienced
reality".

So where does all this lead us?

My ever wise oldest daughter wisely drew my attention back to "real reality". But let me say that if everyone "knew" and acted upon things herein presented, then I doubt there would or could be any real Individual development, overcoming, or self discovered self realisation, that elusive "self actualisation" often crowed about. Would there be any Individual progress? Self-realisation seems to me to be a key issue in ultimate satisfaction with oneself, regardless of mortal stature or status.

It all leads me with my daughters guidance to the final words.

I now believe we can ask questions that will lead to gaining understanding and the correlation of things. We can develop and progress – but I fear we will always come to a stage where we realise and thus know that WE LACK THE INTELLECTUAL CAPACITY OR ABILITY to say we really can understand "it all" or the deepest principles behind the complexity and seeming harmony of man, nature, or the universe.

Whereas science asks and addresses the "how" reasonably well, for questions framed thus seek objective answers and are thus mostly "provable", individually and independently varifiable without variations; the fuller understanding it seems can only be gained with an understanding of the "why".

When we ask "why" we will invariably have no provable data. Any answers no matter how intelligently, logically, or otherwise determined or decided, are at best subjective. Subjective = non provable, ultimately subject to acceptance by means of belief, faith, imposition, logic, reason or whatever. "Why" answers generally cannot be written in the precise objective language of mathematics. I submit we can never validly claim we "know" such things. For this reason the creeds of religion recite "I/we believe in….." With rare exceptions of some that claim "I know that….." Yeah, right.

Thus at the end of this presentation of our contemplations, ponderings, or "meditations", we must conclude that all our inspirations, conclusions, or however we may name them, are really "subjective" and thus it is our Individual mind alone that has determinded what is, or what is not, OUR reality. (remember the decision in hospital) It, OUR mind, then accepting what we decide as real, implements it's programmed functions and acts out, creates, or does whatever is necessary to make the reality. (need a false memory to back it up? No problem. Need not to see something? Simple.) Our mind will then create what is needed to sustain our conclusions to make them (to us) real, actual, factual objective undeniable reality. In this state martyrs applaud their fate, and in this state (hopefully not as martyrs) we shall inevidibly leave this earth.

But who else cares about any of these things about which I have written.

As Julie pointed out to me, Most people are just too involved with things that have successfully kept them busy and occupied literally all their "lives". They have no interest in such things. After all, don't almost all of us turn away those who try to bring us "good news"to our doors. What can it possibly matter what conclusions we accept as "our reality" to anyone except ourselves? After all, a man convinced against his will is of the same opinion still.

All of this is written therefore knowing that there's a fair chance you will never have any real interest in such things. It is prepared and presented as a signpost, a pointer, perhaps a gentle nudge in another direction, perhaps a course of questioning to pursue, should you ever start the questions, or wonder, "what next?"

Probably the final words are: There is no reality.

902-THE ULTIMATE DREAM OR THOUGHT.

"If you think you're too small to be effective, you've never been in bed with a mosquito." - Betty Reese

Years ago I wrote that there exists a thought that all of this mortal world and all within it is not only an illusion, but in fact merely a "thought" within the mind of "GOD". That is somewhere within the preceding 3 books, but I cannot find the quotation easily, and I am somewhat impatient to pursue the matter.

When I made reference to that thought or philosophy, I said I would address the question at some **future** time. At the time I lacked the depth of understanding, or whatever, to really address the issue. My question was, "if it is a thought in the mind of god, then what is that about and who's thought could it be."

I am now going to seriously address that question and that issue on 30 March 2010. (Not that there is remotely any significance about the date except for my reference.)(finished 18/5/10)

It has been said and suggested that all that is, even our individual life experiences, are not only illusion, but (perchance, possibly, probably) mere thoughts in the mind of "GOD".

Several issues emerged for me originally: 1: "god" was not defined or identified. 2: the whole concept or idea is not "orthodox" and therefore "anathema". It was not within my accepted paradigm at the time. (Not that I understood the meaning of the word "paradigm" at the time.) 3: It originated from a source not countenanced by orthodox Western thinking.

I first encountered that thought, paradigm, philosophy, decades ago and it troubled me immediately, and for many reasons. It was just too absurd in relation to conventional Christian orthodoxy, yet it rang a bell of reason and truth in my deep subconscious mind. I sensed it involved a crucial issue to which I would have to face up one day.

I have written (in non-scientific terms) about the "Fabric of the Universe". It is re-produced within this book.

What is needed at this time is to understand that we do not and cannot exist except **within** as "part of" that "FOU". (Hereafter short for "Fabric of the Universe".) This is the omnific force and energy field that is the origin by any meaning to "the force". It is the basic and fundamental energy that IS, (not "fills") the entire cosmos. It is the source of all energy and consequently of all matter. This IS the "fabric of the universe" that has finally been perceived by mortal human physicists. It is so basic that it alone is all that there is, for **all things** are in reality merely a part if it. At its most basic level of being understood, this is omnific power and essence sometimes called "GOD". Yes it is somewhat awesome, hard to understand, or come to grips with, but this does not mean we must hold it as unspeakably sacred and worthy of worship etc. It is not a mystical, spiritual, or religious thing, but an underlying fact now uncovered by physics and it is capable of being understood.

By "omnific FOU" I mean, there is nothing that can exist outside of its sphere, or "whatever" name we can give to a "sphere of operation" that incorporates all that can be, and that includes all intangibles **including our thoughts and emotions.** It is the field of information and energy that is identified at the most minute and sub-atomic level. It vibrates with information, and exists even within what was once considered to be a vacuum, or "empty" space, even within the space within nucleus of an atom. This is the power behind all, even "strings".

It carries any information that can exist. Period.

It permeates all. It has no "past", "present", and "future".

It self exists, there is no point in questioning its origin. Being the omnific source of all, it incorporates all intelligence. Of course it preceded anything we may consider as "matter", for it "creates" these.

Existing at "Its" level, it writes/creates all that is and can be. Being the underlying fabric of the universe there is nothing that is not contained within it. (If any of this thinking is correct.) There is nothing "outside" of it, and by deduction and logic, named.)

Now what gets interesting and difficult to correlate is that we, each and every mortal human, are a component part of this fabric of the universe. Perhaps "component part" conveys a wrong concept. We are really merely a "part of" rather than a component part. I hope you can understand the difference.

This does not mean it sustains, agrees, disapproves or even judges what we mortals by the action of our very though, may impose or deem as reality. It "merely" carries the information. Any "Information" may be intercepted, read and interpreted by a suitable means and subsequently seen as a "reality" to that which intercepted the information. (The receiver is "tuned in" to a specific array of information.)

The Fabric of the Universe in incorporating all things, contains all of our thoughts and actions because in reality we really operate from that level. We erroneously *think* we operate in a mortal body, dwelling on "earth", and here and now in some time/space. It IS "us" and we are perhaps unfortunately not aware (generally) that we are only this world's physical manifestation of IT.

Please bear with me on this one and take it one step at a time:

Consider the "fabric of the universe" as I have described it so often in my many writings. It is my "quantum soup"; it is the "prana" of legend. It matters not one bit what you think or accept or otherwise, it IS the underlying reality, (more basic than even "gravity", for gravity is merely an effect of it's qualities and associated mathematics.) the fabric upon which every thing that is, was, or can be, is founded. It is a quantum physical fact. It permeates all that is and can be. It exists within every known and knowable particle – and thought. For it *is* all of those things.

As (not "if") it is the underlying source and energy while also carrying or possessing all "information", it's attributes have been identified and claimed as the confusing basic "god" of western theology. This is unfortunate.

There is therefore a source of "energy" that is ultimately demonstrably the source of the entire cosmos, and more.

This same source of energy is the source of all intelligence, within the entire cosmos, and in no way restricted to our mortal dimension. We exist as a mere facet of this ultimate source.

Now ask: W H Y ?

Why should any omnipotent, (all powerful, seeing it is the only power) omniscient (all knowing, seeing there is nothing that can be known that is not already and immediately within itself and its awareness) omnific (source of all that can be, a creative force) if it really existed, why would it frankly muck around with "creating" us?

Are we to be as tadpoles in a bottle? Forget Christianity and its limited views or convoluted interpretations and ignorance. No, assuredly we are part, one small part, of its conscious awareness, intelligence, and existence. This is the "god-stuff" part of us, to which I refer in my writings, that defies definition. This is the source of intelligence, awareness, thought, and life itself. This is why we have powers, and for what we determine as "good" or "evil". (Also because of this, it is indeed fact that "god" knows each and every one of us, our thoughts, desires, etc. and nothing is "hidden" from "him". But understand that this FOU "god" is not as an individual person, and frankly would not care in any manner whatsoever about what we do, think, or whatever. The FOU only operates in an eternal NOW state and a neutral state.)

Yet Christians believe "God" created us. How many ask "why". Seriously, ask the question: "Why?" Was he bored? As a self-existent one, was he lonely?

Alas perhaps that line of questioning is where the whole paradigm is wrong. It is anthropomorphic, and seeks to place the FOU in a position of similar status and subjectivity as us. (In understanding or mental ability)

It would seem that Genesis presents us as created and present before "God", and the conversations and decisions recorded are all later man made constructs. It may be seen that Genesis is not about God of any stature claiming domain, demanding worship, explaining "himself" and/or us etc. but is about man becoming as an "outcast" separated from "god" and trying to explain the "what happened so we accept it". Is it man trying to appease "god", get into the good books so to speak? Or is it all really the degenerated and severely condensed account of the Anunnaki playing as gods consequent to our construction?

Regardless of those interesting aside questions, and their implications, they reveal there are many viable alternative interpretations to information in Genesis etc. We do know from diverse religions that the same "facts" can be used to sustain numerous alternative explanations.

But these thoughts and paths are deviations from the quest for an answer to the thought:

Whose thought or dream is it?

First, we should look to and understand our own life and our ability to have a dream "life" and a "dream world". There are realities here that have been dealt with in my previous books.

In this mortal life we have our body of flesh and blood that functions well in this 3 or 4D world. So well indeed because it was "purpose built" for this world and dimension. That's the fact, but it's the "who, what, when, where and why" questions that cause the disputes and misunderstandings. Understand that regardless of origin, whether god created, alien intervention, evolution or found growing in a cabbage patch, this body is designed and functional for this earth world. It really serves no other purpose or world. No use for it in (most) dreams, or "astral".

Also a fact is that this mortal human with, or who is, the flesh/bone body, has thoughts, dreams etc. that are not a physical component part of that marvelous body. He lies down, goes to sleep and at times remembers his dreams.

Those dreams are as realistic (most often) to the individual while remaining in that dream state, as are conscious awake experiences to the same individual when in the usual awake state. **Now that presents two states of realistic and memorable experiences enjoyed by any one individual.** Note that while in either state that neither usually has any awareness that another state of existence or experience even exists. (Obviously one may vaguely remember dreams sometimes.) Interesting?

Question is this: Is there perhaps another (third) state of our existence of which we are generally and presently totally unaware that is within (the) hyperspace? If we are indeed multidimensional entities as described earlier in this book, regardless of earthbound body of flesh and blood, then there is a distinct and definite probability that this mortal life in its entirety is no more than the equivalent of that higher dimensional self's rambling and perhaps ultimately meaningless dream. Just as meaningless as are the events and experiences of our mortal body's dream world and life meaningless to the mortal self.

Looking beyond that distinct possibility, then ultimately the thoughts, feelings, dreams, experiences, indeed the sum total of all of each individual's total existence is firmly fixed in the fabric of the universe. As each individual has his place within the fabric of all that can be, wherein there is no "past, present or future" but only NOW, then it is simple to see and say that yes, we are all thoughts in the mind of "god". (All existing as one within the Fabric of the Universe. We then are the "creations', "expressions", of the ultimate source. Call that a dream?

Why not? For it will end just as surely as any dream ends.

**(First published in "It Ain't Necessarily So" July 2010.
Revised with minor edits April 2013.)**

The following article is extracted from my written notes from the Wellington Hospital while having heart surgery. This is somewhat relative to this essay. The full contents of those writings in this book as an "appendix".)

Saturday 4 September 2004 7.29am:
I have just woken up alive (to this earth) this time. That may sound strange – but previously I have "woken up" twice and been dead to this world I will go clean teeth and get my head around this thing.

The "other world" incorporates this world, totally entwines it – but from this side of it (mortality) one cannot full access/express or explain the full relationship or its reality.
At 1.29am I woke up in severe pain – like a cramp on my left side chest and arm – severe and nasty. I rang for a nurse and found my nitro spray – used it and pain subsided totally in a few minutes. I dozed and dreamed often. Got up at 2.30 for toast and honey.
In dream to waking state I was having difficulty as in 'dream' I was aware of 'levels' up to at least 10, but as I got closer to and more fully awake, these levels evaporated, no longer available, and in waking I could only access or know to 4 levels. Somehow I knew – in waking – I was not "right", so submerged into sleep, and sure enough – awareness/knowledge of 10-11 levels again. Faded into waking, same evaporation or non-access even full awareness of these levels.
It was exhaustingly frustrating and I did realize that in 'waking' those levels were simply not available, but names and things of the lowest 4 levels only could be had.
Then I woke up or was fully aware – with full awareness of all the levels referred to. It was SO QUIET. SO peaceful. Then I knew "this is dead" – but I was fully awake/aware/alive; but I knew I was dead. Hastily I 'submerged' back into the previous level so as to re-emerge to mortality – DEAD AGAIN. A third time lucky, if you call access to only 3 – 4 levels lucky. But if association with fellow mortals is lucky, then I am lucky.
I have memory of things that are going to be near impossible to share or explain. I am at peace, a little physically uncomfortable, but at peace.

903-OBSERVERS AND OBSERVATION

Men occasionally stumble on the truth, but most of them pick themselves up and hurry off as if nothing had happened.
Winston Churchill

The basic information in this section is reasonably well known, but unfortunately I doubt that it is well known outside of scientific circles. In those rare cases where it is known, I think that the full importance and extent of its application may not be really understood or appreciated.

It is as important in understanding the nature of all levels of reality, as is the understanding that hyperspace is an essential reality. It is as important to understanding all things as is the fact that we, as mortals, are multi-dimensional beings, and this life is but one manifestation of our existence is to understanding the nature of humans. Without it's understanding, the causal effects of a vast amount of phenomena and "observations" are misunderstood, misinterpreted, or simply unknown.

For example, most people will be aware of experiments and research carried out mid last century into the observed reactions of plants to humans and other things. However regardless of what the other things may be, (Brine shrimp dumped into boiling water, cooking eggs etc.) in all cases humans and human observations and expectations were involved. The fact that humans were directly involved in all of those researches and experiments is of the utmost importance, but totally overlooked as a vital causal factor. A lot of conclusions were made based upon limited understanding of exactly what was happening and what forces were in operation. However a lot of tremendously interesting associated research was subsequently motivated by the observed results. All this research points to a common causal factor, human involvement, observation, expectations etc. Note I use the word "factor" not sole cause.

Decades ago I began to suspect that there probably was a very important and powerful PK effect in operation that was caused by either the subject of investigation, the observers, or both. This would almost certainly be unknown, unsuspected, and at an unconscious level of the participants. I saw this as the probable underlying cause of such diverse things as healings, hauntings, ouija phenomena, ESP, in fact with the application of thought, one could see its fingerprint signs associated with most phenomena. But as usual in such things so many decades ago, there was only a forest of subjective reports, lots of opinions, and a vast confusing array of claimants for such psychic, occultic, or visionary abilities as and of themselves.

Let us now turn to some more recent reports and writings associated with the role of observers and observation on results obtained and subsequently recorded. It becomes obvious there is still a lot of ignorance of causal effects of observation and observers themselves as people still unwittingly jump to what are probably wrong conclusions about so much.

"the new physics, by contrast, restores mind to a central position in nature. The quantum theory, as it is usually interpreted, is meaningless without introducing an observer of some sort. The act of observation in quantum physics is not just an incidental feature, a means of accessing information already existing in the external world; the observer enters the subatomic reality in a fundamental way and the equations of quantum physics explicitly encode the act of observation in their description. An observation brings about a distinct transformation in the physical situation. When someone looks at an atom, the atom jumps in a characteristic fashion that no ordinary physical interaction can mimic. Common sense may have collapsed in the face of new physics, but the universe that is being uncovered by these advances has found once more a place for man in the great scheme of things." ("The search for a Grand Unified Theory of Nature – Superforce" Paul Davies. Ch. 2 final para. 1984)

"....The German physicist Otto Frisch, the discoverer of nuclear fission, describes the classical picture as follows:

'It takes the line that there is definitely an outside world consisting of particles which have location, size, hardness and so on. It is a little more doubtful whether they have colour and smell; still, they are bona fide particles which exist there whether or not we observe them.'

We might call this classical philosophy 'naïve realism'.

In quantum physics this simplistic classical relationship between the whole and its parts is totally inadequate. The quantum factor forces us to perceive particles only in relation to the whole. In this respect it is wrong to regard the elementary particles of matter as things that collectively assemble to form bigger things. Instead, the world is more accurately described as a network of relations.

To the naïve realist the universe is a collection of objects. To the quantum physicist it is an inseparable web of vibrating energy patterns in which no one component has reality independent of the entirety; and included in the entirety is the observer.

The American physicist H. P. Stapp has expressed the quantum concept of particle in these words:

'An elementary particle is not an independently existing unanalysable entity. It is in essence, a set of relationships that reach outward to other things.'

"A further consequence of quantum physics concerns the role of the observer, the person who actually carries out the measurements. The fuzziness of quantum uncertainty does not carry through to the actual observations we make, and so at some stage in the chain between the quantum system of interest, up through the experimental equipment, the dials and meters, our own sense organs and brains, something must happen to dispel the fuzziness. The rules of quantum physics are quite definite on this point. In the absence of an observation a quantum system will evolve in a certain way. When an observation is made, an entirely different type of change occurs. Just what produces this different behaviour is not clear, but at least some physicists insist that it is explicitly caused by the mind itself." **(ibid. Ch 3, second last para.)**

Paul Davies is Professor of Theoretical Physics at the University of Newcastle on Tyne. He holds a doctorate from the University of London where he spent 8 years as a lecturer in mathematics.

Lyall Watson was involved with checking out the validity of psychic surgeons in the Philippines and makes specific mention of a situation that would seem to exactly verify and prove the above statement that "something" is happening when observation is made of some events with the use of scientific equipment with a view to recording and establishing the event. He experienced a puzzling continual failure of equipment and was unable to actually record what he experienced and witnessed.

"Since my experience, others have tried to identify the phenomena by using capacitor plates and other electronic apparatus, but without success. On occasion the apparatus fails to work, but more often the response fails to appear in the presence of instrumentation that would establish its reality beyond all reasonable doubt. After all my time in the Philippines, I am satisfied that the elusiveness of the phenomena has nothing to do with deliberate fraud or an unwillingness to perform in the presence of scientific equipment for fear of being found out. The fault seems to lie in the instruments themselves and in the experimental attitude they engender." **("The Romeo Error", Lyall Watson. Ch.9)**

Doesn't that comment of Watson's remind us of the frequently reported equipment failure, or failure of events to happen relative to such things as

Loch Ness, UFOs, bigfoot etc. Manifestations fail to occur or equipment fails for the observer.

Relative to the phenomena of recording "voices", (Raudive et al.) we find the following information in Lyall Watson's book "The Romeo Error". (Lyall Watson is a professional life scientist with PhD from London University in 1963.)

"....If several people listen to the same segment over and over again and write down their independent interpretation, these sometimes match, but very often they will be totally different and perhaps even in different languages. When words can be distinguished with any clarity, they seem to use the names of those present, or of close friends, or to refer to circumstances known to those involved. Raudive and others argue that this proves that the communications come from the disembodied dead, but the same facts support an alternative explanation.

....Analysis of the voice phenomenon shows that the best results are obtained by those who are emotionally involved in the proceedings.

....Nothing has ever been found impressed directly on to a stationary tape, and no recordings with voices have ever been made by a machine that ran quietly by itself in a screened enclosure or in an empty room. People must be present and, while they are, the possibility remains that they could be unconsciously responsible. ....but I cannot help thinking that the unconscious may still be involved

....The more I look into the phenomena that concern apparitions of all kinds, whether seen or heard or sensed in any other way, the more certain I become that none of these things occur in a vacuum. I believe that without the presence of a living body, and this may be strictly confined to the bodies of certain kinds of organism, it is impossible for an apparition to manifest itself in any way. It may even be impossible for it to survive at all.

Without the living, there may be no dead." ("The Romeo Error" pages 178/9)

Maybe then, just maybe, if no one is in the forest to hear the tree falling then it makes no noise.

"Both monsters and saucers have occasionally been photographed at a distance, both have sufficient reality to be picked up on the screens of

sonar and radar equipment and yet neither leaves behind any good material evidence that can be analysed and used to prove their reality beyond doubt. Monsters conveniently fade away at the crucial moment and saucers actually disappear like ghosts when observers get too close. Carl Jung correlated UFO reports with psychic manifestations and shrewdly suggested that both in some way be connected in our minds, perhaps by a collective consciousness. He said that "the psychic aspect plays so great a role that it cannot be left out of account". Jacques Valee drew a similar parallel between UFOs and early European supernatural lore and noted that many accounts of flying saucer landings include all the classic manifestations of religious apparitions and the fairy faith. He concluded that "the mechanisms that have generated these various beliefs are identical".

"....The merits of both physical and mental arguments are considerably diminished by the discovery that psychokinesis exists, that it is possible to produce physical effects at a distance by purely mental means....The fact that those who come closest to these phenomena, usually receive information structured to support their own beliefs or fears, suggests that these apparitions cannot be independent of the minds of those involved." (ibid, p174/5)

Perhaps more correctly he may have observed that the merits of an event being of either physical OR mental cause are diminished, for it seems most **observations may well be the result of a combination of both, which surely defines a PK event.**

GHOSTS

Here is an interesting observation from Lyall Watson that does give additional information that supports the concept that the observer and his attitude, beliefs, thoughts, expectations etc. have a most basic and direct effect upon what is being observed, or thought to be under observation.

*"...In England, one person in six believes in **ghosts** and one person in fourteen thinks that he has actually seen one. These are enormous numbers of people, and I have no intention of suggesting that they must all have been mistaken, but to me there is one strange and significant thing in all their sightings. All the ghosts of which I have ever heard, wore clothes...The fact that people see ghosts as they or someone else remembers them, fully dressed in period costume, seems to indicate that the visions are part of a mental rather than a supernatural process. In those cases in which several people see the same apparition, it could be*

broadcast telepathically by one of them. And where a similar ghost is seen by separate people on separate occasions, I assume that the mental picture is held by someone associated with the site." (**"Supernature" Ch 9, "ghosts"**)

"Broadcast telepathically" is not to be mocked or doubted. It is a very real phenomenon. In part 05 of this book is the section on "Mind". There I record events commonly encountered as a consequence of hypnosis in cases of regression to supposedly validation re-incarnation claims, or UFO/alien abduction cases. Also "therapists" etc. without actual formal hypnosis often unwittingly solicit exactly the testimony or statements that they seek but remain unspoken to the "therapee". The person undergoing hypnosis, regression, counselling or therapy as often as not becomes sensitive to exactly what the operator is seeking, even subconsciously willing to be manifest, and in consequence unwittingly oblige with the sought material. I made reference to how this type of activity can generate "false memory" in a subject. Note it is not confused memory, but the implanting of totally new and unreal thoughts as memory of things experienced. PK effect where one definitely causes an effect on the mind of another.

So there we have the basic details of the effect and result of observation and of observers.

If you give the whole thing some thought it becomes an inescapable fact that we humans, the observers, are not only an integral part of the whole system, but have the ability to actually influence or cause "things". Whereas initially or in isolation that may seem to be quite a strange and unrealistic situation or claim, when one understands that we are a component part of the Fabric of the Universe, and carry with us as our "god stuff" a share or part of the power, force, energy and intelligence of that fabric of the universe, then this can be acceptably understood.

There are undoubtedly infinitely more vast underlying factors associated with that human status. For instance, if in this world we are so able to influence results, effects etc. by mere observation, and are told we use maybe less than 10% of our potential, then what could ensue if a greater percentage of potential were accessible?

In another section we asked the question and looked at probable answers to "whose ultimate Dream or Thought?" is this experience of mortal life. If in mortal dreams we are able to create and manipulate our dream environment, fly and often manifest super powers, then why should we not be able to develop similar abilities in mortality if indeed mortality is a dream state for a higher multi-dimensional self? Perhaps the subject and information in this section indicates that this is precisely what we are unwittingly and continually doing. (We create the world we experience.)

Who knows then what the effect of us becoming fully alert, and turning this mortality into a totally and fully lucid dream may cause? After all, that can occur in our sleep and dream state in mortality with some astounding results.

(First published in "Now and Then" first edition December 2011. Edited and reviewed April 2013.)

904-ME – HERE AND NOW

"Then I woke up or was fully aware – with full awareness of all the levels referred to. It was SO QUIET. SO peaceful. Then I knew "this is dead" – but I was fully awake/aware/alive; but I knew I was dead. Hastily I 'submerged' back into the previous level so as to re-emerge to mortality – DEAD AGAIN."

"I know something – now I know nothing No memories except swirling embracing all devouring 'evil'. I was devoured. I was

hopelessly and forever trapped in a recycling evil dream of vast unpleasantness."
(Bob's Legacy – Book 1)

The trouble is that I know all of this and more. And I know that not only do people not know, but also don't care.

I become increasingly confused by the claims or allegations that the individual, as, or in the form that the individual experiences in this (temporal) mortality, will endure forever or eternally as presumably the same unchanged individual. Unchanged that is apart from the obviously necessary physical adjustments that would need to be made for the physical star stuff body to so endure forever. Whatever "forever" means. Frankly I think the word meaningless in this concept.

It would imply that the personality, the memories, all that makes us an individual "us" or in fact "me", is destined to survive "forever". I think it paradoxical that "commencing" from here and now we are alleged to have no end of existence, yet to have had a beginning, a childhood, an incremental development right up to this point in time, this current "now". What if we died at mortal age 5, or whatever age? Is that to be the "start"?

I analyze myself, my very being, and I conclude that in reality all I ever experience is always simply and just an ever-changing state of **"now"**. All else is in the mind. I have no memory or claimed memory of anything before my alleged birth into this star stuff world. I find the claim for everlasting existence for Bob Maddison as Bob Maddison one fraught with untold numbers of problems and lack of rationality or logic. On the other hand I find no difficulty with the concept of individual "me" intelligence existing "forever". That component is indeed part of the very quantum soup that is the fabric of the universe, whereas "Bob Maddison" is a mere transient identity that seemingly had a beginning, was given a name and a form (body) and will in the manner of a transient being, simply terminate its physical mortal existence. The star stuff will recycle, of that there is no doubt, and the energy that experiences "me, here and now" must likewise return to its source.

It has often been questioned as to how exactly an eternal "Bob Maddison" by any name would exist, and what such a one would do. The movie "Zardoz" postulates that after a few centuries boredom sets in and one deteriorates into an "apathetic" who thenceforth does nothing at all. I heard the question somewhere, "what does one do when one has bungy jumped all around the universe?" I tend to think the same. Indeed what would one do imprisoned in a "Bob Maddison" persona eternally?

Existing in a "here and now" state however ultimately is all that we can experience or know, and when one puts the mental operations into gear that becomes self-evident. All else is memory, hearsay from external sources, or conjecture. "Here and now" is perhaps the one ultimate reality.

So with this in mind, I imagine in the ever-changing flow of the "here and now" I experience and know as Bob Maddison, there will be a change at some stage. The "me", the eternal fabric of the universe stuff, that god stuff within this body, will experience a putting aside of the "Bob Maddison" identity and experience. Bob Maddison will die, and "me" will return for duty or reassignment to the life force that gave it.

After all, would one really want to live eternally, plagued with all the mental baggage one accumulates in even a brief experience such as mortality? Imagine after untold millions of years meeting someone, and recalling "old times". Does that even make sense? Do the Einstein thing and just use your imagination and mentally put yourself one million years into the future in that claimed eternal individual life of yourself as that Joe or Jane Doe. Would the concepts of "whatever happened to...." Or "how are your family/children" etc have any meaning? If one spends enough time thinking about this situation, it becomes obviously untenable. Or how about those who claim we will spend eternity at the feet of "god" singing his praises? Think hard about that one. Mentioned earlier in these writings were the questions about the future for those with wasted, lost, or shortened mortal lives. The more one thinks about it and broadens the thinking, the more problems with reason and logic one finds.

So here I find the problem. Yet the facts seem certain and beyond dispute that this "being" that is currently "us" will go in two separate directions when the "here and now" determines the time is right.

FORM AND IDENTITY.

Another reason for my confusion or bewilderment comes from contemplations as to our "true" form and nature. More so if it is indeed to endure for "all time". Then of course there is the matter of our true or real identity.

The person known in this world as "Bob Maddison" is a creation *of* this world. I had a beginning here and I will have and end of existence here. No doubt about that. My name was changed when my mother remarried in the 1950's, and no one left alive on this planet knows who my mortal father was. My beginnings on earth are now shrouded in mist, and lost because of well kept secrets and the death of all generations prior to mine. However working just with what I do know, it is established that "Bob Maddison" is a mortal and temporal earther life form. Memory indicates that once he had virtually **no personality** and **no memories** that precedes specific establishable memorised events in his ever-changing "now". He was once in effect a *"blank"*. He may well still be such.

Likewise his mortal body is purely a creation of this world, this planet. I have extensively dealt with mortal form elsewhere, and reiterate that this body seems *designed along specific lines and for specific identifiable limited purposes.* It is truly a limited utility vehicle, designed to work, learn, ingest, excrete, procreate and *do little else*. It serves adequately for this life, planet and conditions only. Its physical brain will cease practical functionality after a specific time, and at a given age will start to shrink.

It begs the question. What then is our true form? Further, what is the individual's true identity. In reality, do we as individuals even have a permanent or long term (eternal?) identity or "name"? I doubt it would be, as in my mortality, "Bob Maddison", as that name begs to be purely incidental, variable, and a mere quirk of fortune.

Surely the name as is manifest on this earth as "Bob Maddison", or by any other earth given name for an *earth given body* could not be an "eternal" name. No, they must surely be temporary in nature only. How rash to presume that "me" who only became "Bob Maddison" by reason of mortal birth as a blank programmable mortal, will now for all eternity, starting from planet earth "dot", will remain as that same identity. It defies reason to claim such, and would indicate the required amount of "brain work" has not been used to fully understand the claim and the deficiencies that will reveal themselves. The *god* stuff that animates this mortal earth flesh body must and does have "elsewhere its beginnings", as the verse so succinctly states. My point that must be *clearly* understood is that it was NOT known as "Bob" in any (or "if any") pre-mortal state. If you fail to understand that, then finish reading this now. Or re-read it from the beginning.

Likewise I totally doubt that its "form" was, and indeed is, probably much like that of mortal human life either. **I think it somewhat** arrogant to think or thoughtlessly assume that this mortal shape would thereby be the acme of physical development given the literally millions of diverse forms that currently exist on planet earth alone. Perhaps then, as a truly multidimensional being or entity, it may be more correct to assume or presume that there is no *absolute* form, but that such an entity may well be what is now known as a *"shape shifter or changer"*. (As in and from the "movies")(Note also that often in "dream state" we do not seem to actually be "embodied" at all, but function perfectly, apparently disembodied, as a "formless" intelligence, seeing everything.)

Such an *attribute* would accommodate and make acceptable (or understandable) claims by visionaries (etc.) that sightings, contact, and other events with various forms of beings/entities, (non-earther mortals) occur, exist or have been experienced. (This also has been covered in my writings.)

That at least would not be illogical, and at the same time would easily accommodate claims and reports of various forms of beings/entities by visionaries and such as claim sightings or contact with non-human mortal beings. We should give this serious thought, but most people will not.

It is clear to me then, that the whole matter of the nature, form, and identity of our true selves needs some very serious questioning, rather than blindly accepting the claims made by those obviously not qualified to make such claims or give such assurances.

EVER ONWARDS

So here we all are, on little old backwater planet earth not really knowing who or what we are as individuals, and no comprehension of the nature of man the species. (Meanwhile we watch the T.V., drink the tap water, use the toothpaste, eat the supermarket food, take vaccines, go to church and not think, and think we are "free". Etc.) We are mostly merely processed people, passing mortality with no "merit" badges.

Generally anything beyond that is just a worse and total confusion. The acceptable common paradigms of "god, man and the universe" and "destinies" areas are the almost exclusive domains of the ignorant and blind who vainly attempt to lead the unlearned blind.

Yet clues exist for us. For instance individually we fastidiously record absolutely every minutiae surrounding our personal existence. We can replay the most obscure of memories even from dreams, as well as mentally re-live, re-taste, and re-experience the most trivial and seemingly inconsequential of things. **We are unbelievable recording devices**. Yet we have no pre-mortal memories. (No, we will not re-visit reincarnation etc here again as its covered elsewhere.) One may ask if this is purely for our own individual requirements or benefits, **or is "something" feeding off or downloading these memory records**.

I have considerable respect for the whole "Anunnaki" story and clearly see therein the origins of the bible's Genesis. **It is entirely possible that the record of modern homo-sapiens-sapiens origin at the hands of an alien geneticist bent on creating a species of dumbded down, were procreating slave labour could be correct. Upon extensive analysis I find it answers more questions than it poses**. Even the historical timing is right. Where I had mental indigestion was figuring out the full story and consequences if that record is in fact correct. What are the implications for all the "Bob Maddisons" that make our species?

How did this "Anunnaki, Enki, Enlil" et al fit into the framework of any "real" issue of who we really and ultimately are? In other words, was there the ancient claim that "Enki" manufactured the current human race, engineering an intelligent species of mortals, irreconcilable with the acceptance (knowledge) of that species certainly having a body of star stuff earth, while being animated and driven by the "god stuff" energy?

A kind of mentally shattering concept to get one's head around. The god of Christendom certainly has no part in this model. Unless one comes to the logical conclusion that "he" or "they" (the gods) are certainly there, only not one but several, and they now have revealed individual names. Jehovah by whatever spelling (such matters not, regardless of claims otherwise) becomes unmasked as the human hating Enlil. Even that revelation sheds unbelievable light on biblical records of its god's dealing (frequently violently destructive) with human species. It also sheds light on "genesis god's" insecurity, incessant demands for loyalty, severe punishment, harsh laws, intolerance to all not obedient to the letter, and obvious lack of love for mankind. Also tells us why Moses had to ask this god who he was, because Moses had evidently not dealt with him before.

The impositions of such as Jehovah, Enlil etc has been dealt with in these writings, and my opinions have not changed since that was written on 16 October 2006.

Refer: -WHAT OF GOD? WHICH, WHO, AND WHERE?

So for whatever reason, by whatsoever means, perhaps we merely accepted to do a tour of duty on this earth, we have entered a mortal shell, driving it via the interface of the brain, and find ourselves on this earth, wiped clean and devoid of all knowledge of anything else. Yet we record all here, thus logically this is not a new talent. Even if it is an "Enki, Enlil" creation or manufacturing thing and we are serving as working brutes, then this does not mean, infer, or imply that the "me" within each of us is not sourced or have it's origin somewhere else. That is what was the source of my mental indigestion. It was solved with the realization that there was effectively "two creations". Somewhat like the 2 creation accounts that are clumsily revealed and recorded in the early chapters of Genesis. (As one religion states, "one account in Genesis was a physical creation, the other was a 'spiritual' creation of mankind *before coming to earth".)*

Perhaps also there are no untold zillions of years of eternal future, but always and only just a "me, here and now", and the "here and now" changes one's identity, form, and goodness knows what else. All the untold "here and now" states would indicate one's continuing to experience, observe, and record all things. As an old "Bob Maddison" identity drops off (subsequent to a mortal death) and is no longer current or important, it needs be put aside, forgotten. Assuming individual survival, I think it must be so, else one would remain forever limited, anchored eternally to whatever blind prejudices, ignorance or conceit possessed in this one brief mortal experience. That would also infer this life is the paramount cycle, and that seems wrong, conceited, and illogical.

The main issue to understand is simply that although the identity of Bob Maddison as I currently know and experience him may be lost, it does not matter. Understand that you and I have effortlessly and without trauma experienced the loss of our earlier mortal selves frequently. As we change we "put aside", outgrow the older perhaps less understanding and developed self. As we change that self becomes forgotten as it is no longer the then current "me, here and now" us, but more like a "former us". I became somewhat aware of our true changing nature some decades ago when I recognised that I was no longer the same Bob Maddison as I could recall from various past events or times. Entire attitudes, belief systems, even personality become so changed as to challenge the belief that it is in fact still the same person. People change, they really do. This is one reason why I am so set against state imposed death sentences etc.

We all exist only as "me, here and now" and can only at best recall what or who we once were earlier in our current incarnation. It is no loss at all, as it is still the real "me" that progresses along the "here and now" path. I shall always be "me, here and now" even if I forever forget the experience of a life as Bob Maddison for that brief mortal span. I shall forever be alert, intelligent, and experiencing. I doubt I would ever wish to eternally (whatever that means) remember and thus experience all the events of such a brief and ultimately shallow life experience as is afforded by mortality. How could one possibly start so-called "eternal life" with the base of such an insignificant and generally meaningless life as that of a Bob Maddison. No doubt as I pass in death and am forgotten to all, likewise I shall forget this life and experiences just as I wake up and soon forget the contents and experiences of the dream body accompanying me on this journey.

Of course none of this is claimed as correct, true, or real in part or in total, but serves as a statement of current thinking of the current Bob Maddison. Who knows, what is real or not, so complex is the mind even with its human limitations. Maybe the only real thing is the mental exercise one gets from all the contemplations and reasoning.

(First printed and published in "The Human Disaster" November 2010. Reviewed and edited April 2013.)

INDEX, important notes.

This index is that from the 2nd edition of this book. The text of that book was formatted in font size 16, and took 562 pages.

The current 3rd edition was reduced to size 14 font and reduced text to some 454 pages.

This has meant that all the contents of the index, which now has additions to it as the 2nd edition was reviewed and edited by me, now shows page numbers that are not correct for this edition. Those numbers relate to the text of the earlier edition.

I do not propose (at least at this time) to alter all the numbers shown with entries to correctly locate the page number to this edition. That would be too much to effectively do with my current state of mind and concentration. In any case, I think perhaps most people rarely dip into an 'index' to locate a specific reference in a book such as this. I do and did, but most don't and wont.

"ELEGANT SOLUTION"

Therefore I have added to the front of the 'index' the table of contents as it appears in that 2nd edition. Thus if you wish to locate an article from the index to the text, say "waking up", you will see page 141 revealed. This table of contents reveals that is in item 007 between the "old" pages 117 and 144. In other words about 3 pages from the end of that section. The amended table of contents of this edition (front of book) show it now as pages 93 – 114, so expect the reference to be near 3 pages from the end of that section. Sounds clear to me, hopefully for you also.

TABLE OF CONTENTS

PART ONE

what is in them – mercury etc. - Alzheimers

SOME INTERESTING THOUGHTS REVEALED.

Or at least I think so.

INDEX, important notes.

This index is that from the 2nd edition of this book. The text of that book was formatted in font size 16, and took 562 pages.

The current 3rd edition was reduced to size 14 font and reduced text to some 454 pages.

This has meant that all the contents of the index, which now has additions to it as the 2nd edition was reviewed and edited by me, now shows page numbers that are not correct for this edition. Those numbers relate to the text of the earlier edition.

I do not propose (at least at this time) to alter all the numbers shown with entries to correctly locate the page number to this edition. That would be too much to effectively do with my current state of mind and concentration. In any case, I think perhaps most people rarely dip into an 'index' to locate a specific reference in a book such as this. I do and did, but most don't and wont.

"ELEGANT SOLUTION"

Therefore I have added to the front of the 'index' the table of contents as it appears in that 2nd edition. Thus if you wish to locate an article from the index to the text, say "waking up", you will see page 141 revealed. This table of contents reveals that is in item 007 between the "old" pages 117 and 144. In other words about 3 pages from the end of that section.

The amended table of contents of this edition (front of book) show it now as pages 93 – 114, so expect the reference to be near 3 pages from the end of that section. Sounds clear to me, hopefully for you also.

TABLE OF CONTENTS

PART THREE

PART FOUR

SUPPLEMENTARY READING

SOME INTERESTING THOUGHTS REVEALED.